Critique of Everyday Life

VOLUME II

Critique of Everyday Life

VOLUME II

Foundations for a Sociology of the Everyday

◆

HENRI LEFEBVRE

Translated by John Moore

With a Preface by Michel Trebitsch

VERSO

London · New York

Liberté · Égalité · Fraternité
RÉPUBLIQUE FRANÇAISE

This book is supported by the French Ministry for Foreign Affairs as part
of the Burgess Programme, headed by the French Embassy in London
by the Institut Français du Royaume Uni

First published by Verso 2002
This edition published by Verso 2008
Copyright © Verso 2008
Translation © John Moore 2002
Preface © Michel Trebitsch 2002
Preface translation © Gregory Elliott 2002
First published as *Critique de la vie quotidienne II: Fondements d'une sociologie de la quotidienneté*
Copyright © L'Arche Editeur Paris 1961
All rights reserved

1 3 5 7 9 10 8 6 4 2

Verso
UK: 6 Meard Street, London W1F 0EG
USA: 20 Jay Street, Suite 1010, Brooklyn, NY 11220
www.versobooks.com

Verso is the imprint of New Left Books

ISBN-13: 978-1-84467-192-2

British Library Cataloguing in Publication Data
A catalogue record for this book is available from the British Library

Library of Congress Cataloging-in-Publication Data
A catalog record for this book is available from the Library of Congress

Contents

Translator's Note

This translation is for the people of Amara, who taught me how everyday life can be an art and a festival.

Itzuli dudan liburu hau Amaratarrei eskaintzen diet. Gora gu eta gutarrak.

Except when preceded by (*Trans.*), footnotes are from the original. When titles appear in French, the quoted material is my own translation.

Preface

The Moment of Radical Critique

Michel Trebitsch

How have the analysts, even master-thinkers, of the early twenty-first century managed to neglect a book as brilliant as the second volume of the *Critique of Everyday Life*? Assuming one has sufficient historical sense to discount the inevitable scoria of the vocabulary of the period – in other words, the ubiquitous Marxist terminology – it must in all honesty be acknowledged that we are dealing with one of the major works of the turn of the 1960s. Henri Lefebvre was then on top intellectual form – productive, creative, publishing some of his most accomplished works and dozens of articles in the space of a few years. The unqualified private college teacher of the inter-war period had, in the meantime, become a researcher and, soon afterwards, a recognized if unconventional academic. The Communist intellectual in search of legitimacy with those he always called the 'official Marxists' made a resounding break with 'the Party' at this point, making him one of the main figures of the contestation that prepared and prefigured the events of May 1968.[1]

The gap separating the first and second volumes of the *Critique of Everyday Life* – from 1947 to 1961 – is long enough, but not as long as that between the second and third (1961–81). However, it was marked by various extremely powerful, predominantly political upheavals against the backdrop of the *trente glorieuses*, which meant that everything changed at the beginning of the 1960s not only for Henri Lefebvre, but as regards the whole ideological and cultural climate. The 1947 book, it may be remembered, derived in large part from the pre-war period and could only have emerged in the short-lived context of the Liberation, just before the doors of the 'iron

curtain' closed shut and the Zhdanovite ice age set in.[2] Between that
date and 1961, nothing less than the trauma of 1956 occurred – the
invasion of Hungary, Khrushchev's report and, for Henri Lefebvre,
the start of a fairly slow process of detaching himself from Communism in the name of 'revising Marxism'.

The key book of a key moment, this volume is presented in a rather
remarkable form explaining precisely these basic changes and, in
addition, its author's lucid, even precocious, consciousness of them.
Nearly a third of its 350 pages are in fact devoted to 'Clearing the
ground', attempting, as Lefebvre indicates, a balance sheet of the
transformations in everyday life over the intervening fifteen years.
The first volume of *Critique of Everyday Life* already had 'Introduction'
as its sub-title. These prefatory texts, or inventories, are at one with
Henri Lefebvre's approach: the desire constantly to link the conceptual with the experiential; the autobiographical dimension of
theoretical reflection; a relationship to 'experience', in Hannah
Arendt's sense of the word. As Lefebvre formulates it with the utmost
clarity in his 'axiomatic' chapter, knowledge of society is impossible
without a critique of this society. This is the thread that will guide our
reading: the essential link, forged during the 1950s, between the political whirlwinds generated by the rift of 1956 and the overall
development of the field of the social sciences, especially sociology
and its ideological function. What is so interesting about this book is
that we have before us a mature work, firm and rigorous in its expression, resolute in its theoretical ambition, and with few equivalents in
the rest of Lefebvre's output. It can be read as a veritable 'discourse
on method' in sociology – in particular, because it aspires to restore a
properly philosophical rigour to the latter. And it determined a scholarly stance in Henri Lefebvre which, lifting him out of intellectual
marginality, gives all its force to the core of the project: the development of a *radical critique* of what exists that serves to clarify his
trajectory during subsequent years. For what is in play, beyond the
second volume of *Critique of Everyday Life* and the case of Henri Lefebvre, is a longer intellectual history, which could even be extended to
Pierre Bourdieu, whose first major works appeared in the very same
years. Here, however, we shall confine ourselves to the 1960s, taking
the 'critique of everyday life' as a central element in a history of the
'ideas of May' which, in as much as it remains dependent on the

effects of fashion and *a posteriori* reconstructions, remains to be written.

If posterity has retained any image of him from the 1960s, it is that of Lefebvre the political agitator; and here we shall indeed be examining the impact of his oeuvre, in particular its influence on the ideas of May '68, of which *Critique of Everyday Life* (the second as well as – retroactively – the first volume) forms a major component. But a condition of this is that we take the book as a highly theoretical endeavour, unlike the more polemical works of the period; that we recognize in it a surprising contemporaneity in its reading of the social, or what Lefebvre himself defined as the 'social text' – landscapes, cities, streets; that we carefully read his attempt to develop the formal implements and specific categories – his terms – of a critical sociology. One will retain, for example, the twenty or so pages on the 'idea of structure', where we find one of the best definitions of structuralism, and also one of the most virulent attacks on it at the very moment when the debate was at its height.[3] But in fact, much more broadly, the sociology that Lefebvre attempted to construct was defined with reference to the two currents dominant at the time: 'quantitative' sociology, which he criticized for sticking to enumerations and classifications that cannot exhaust reality; and, equally, 'participatory' sociology, the sociology of surveys and questionnaires postulating a spontaneity of the social rejected by Lefebvre. It is not within my remit to analyse the content and concepts at stake in this sociological controversy, which runs through the book – especially since they are presented to readers clearly enough. On the other hand, that controversy makes it possible to grasp what is essential if we are to understand the intellectual history of the 1960s: the fundamental link between sociology and politics, between the institution of contemporary French sociology and attempts to renew revolutionary thought in a rupture with Stalinism. This is the movement, which began well before May 1968 and continued for part of the 1970s, I refer to by the notion of 'radical critique' – a phrase to be found in Lefebvre and others. It is this closely linked relation that I would like to track through the dual trajectory, professional and political, of our philosopher of the everyday.

The Centre d'études sociologiques

In retrospect, we may start with a commonplace about 1968, according to which sociology and sociologists, students and teachers, were essential driving forces behind the May events. 'An immature discipline without any openings, sociology launched the movement of May '68,' wrote Georges Pompidou in *Le Nœud gordien*; and the idea that sociology was a site of revolutionary thinking because it was a dominated discipline pervades Bourdieu and Passeron's *The Inheritors*, one of the cult books of the period.[4] Underlying this commonplace are several deeper questions about the development of the discipline after the war, and its role as analyst and catalyst of a certain number of debates about society, as well as about the personal trajectory of Lefebvre who, even though he was now integrated into the university system, remained marginalized with respect both to the royal discipline of philosophy and a party that rejected this particular form of 'bourgeois science'.

In 1948, following a brief spell at Radio Toulouse where Tristan Tzara had introduced him at the Liberation, and then a return – briefer still – to secondary-school teaching, Lefebvre found himself among the six researchers appointed to the Centre d'études sociologiques, a laboratory of the Centre national de la recherche scientifique founded in 1946 by Georges Gurvitch, whom Georges Friedmann was to succeed in 1949. We must say a word about Gurvitch, an unusual character, 'the outcast from the horde' as he characterized himself in an article on his intellectual itinerary published in 1966, just after his death.[5] A socialist revolutionary, Gurvitch was exiled from Russia in 1921, first to Prague and then, in 1924, to Paris, where he took his doctorate in philosophy, before succeeding Maurice Halbwachs at Strasbourg in 1935. Exiled once again during the war – to New York, where he worked with the New School for Social Research – he returned to introduce American sociology for the first time and then challenge it. His international openness and personal charisma have often been stressed, but, remaining a philosopher in his references and categories, he was never himself fully integrated into French sociology. And yet, connected to a whole network – Lucien Febvre's sixth section of the École pratique des hautes études and the Conservatoire national des arts et métiers where Georges Friedmann was appointed the same year (1946) – Gurvitch represented both the link and the rupture with the Durkheimian legacy, with the sociology of social facts; and it was around him that what has been called the 'second foundation of French sociology' developed after 1945.[6] Hitherto hard to distinguish from social psychology and philosophy, of which it formed one of the diplomas, sociology had only been represented by a few posts at Paris, Bordeaux and Strasbourg. A generation later, in the 1970s, the main actors in the history of French sociology had passed through this small Centre d'études sociologiques.

With Henri Lévy-Bruhl and Gabriel Le Bras around him, and assisted in the secretariat by the marvellous Yvonne Halbwachs, widow of Maurice, Gurvitch founded the Centre d'études sociologiques with some singular, curious figures, who were rather non-academic and possessed little academic capital (few were *agrégés*). Their recruitment was a matter of chance, of relations forged in the Resistance and political activity (Edgar Morin), while two of them came from Uriage (Henri Chombart de Lauwe and Joffre Dumazedier); and of an interest in the working class, which explains the early specialization in the sociology of work (Georges Friedmann), but also in urban sociology and even the sociology of religion. This is the heroic context in which we must situate the arrival in 1948 of Henri Lefebvre, who had known Friedmann since the 1920s and who rapidly became Yvonne Halbwachs' god. Lefebvre was never a Gurvitchian, but Gurvitch, engaged with the problem of revolutionary change and defender of a fairly complex vision of a 'dialectical' sociology – a sociology of the totality – could not but be appreciative of his post-war publications, particularly *Critique of Everyday Life*. About his entry into the CES we possess the testimony of a second-rate novel by Françoise d'Eaubonne, *Le Temps d'apprendre à vivre*, where he is depicted in the form of the Marxist philosopher Hervé Lefort, and where she describes the highly politicized atmosphere of the Centre, several of whose members, like Lefebvre or Morin, were Communists.[7]

Initially Lefebvre put considerable effort into the area of rural sociology, creating a rural sociology group in 1950 to which he invited the best French rural scholars (Daniel Halévy, Michel Cépède, Louis Chevalier, René Dumont), and embarking on area surveys – in particular, in the Tuscan countryside in 1950–51.[8] During the war he had worked on the Pyrenean valleys, going through the archives of pastoral communities and discovering in them a kind of 'primitive communism' that had permeated his composition of *Critique of Everyday Life*. From this research he derived his doctoral thesis on *Les Communautés paysannes pyrénéennes*, defended in June 1954 (his first academic qualification since his *diplôme d'études supérieures*, obtained thirty years earlier in 1924!).[9] His work was marked by a militant dimension, by his links with Italian agricultural unions and even his influence on the Jeunesse agricole chrétienne in France, but also because his empirical research was systematically coupled with theoretical publications, on ground rent and agrarian communities, culminating in a *Traité de sociologie rurale*, the manuscript of which seems to have been stolen, and which put him out of tune with the PCF, then at the height of its Lysenkoist phase. This political investment was, moreover, to cost him an 'affaire Lefebvre' with the directorate of the CNRS. In 1953, during the 'Journées nationales d'études des intellectuels communistes', in his report on the Cercle des sociologues communistes he had attacked the 'police sociology' of the bourgeoisie, which indexed the working class, and had set about Gurvitch and Friedmann by name.[10] The reaction of the CNRS was immediate (the Cold War was then in full swing): he was demoted back down to secondary schools. Lefebvre defended himself in a statement, 'Protestation de M. Henri Lefebvre contre la fin de son détachment au CNRS';[11] and a campaign organized by the researchers' union, led by Alain Touraine and Edgar Morin, led to his reinstatement and his being granted tenure as *maître de recherche* in October 1954.[12]

Arguments and the 'Revision of Marxism'

At this point in time Lefebvre was already fighting on two fronts: while, vis-à-vis bourgeois sociology, he sought to develop the idea of a Marxist sociology, as regards the Communist Party he had to explain that sociology served a purpose and could not be reduced to bourgeois science. In truth, the misunderstanding went back much further. With the first volume of *Critique of Everyday Life*, we left Henri

Lefebvre verging on the status of official Communist Party philosopher, particularly with his participation in the anti-Sartre offensive
(*L'Existentialisme*, 1947) and the publication of his short 'Que-sais je?'
text *Le Marxisme* (1948), which remains the best-selling text in the collection at Presses Universitaires de France and which, like his 1939
book *Dialectical Materialism*, was to serve as a reference for generations
of Marxist intellectuals. The idyll, it may be remembered, lasted two
years at most. By 1949, Lefebvre found himself back in the position
of marginal Communist he had occupied for thirty years, from his
adhesion in 1928 to his exclusion in 1958. As early as 1948, the party
paralysed his projects, pulped a work he had already written,
Méthodologie des sciences, and delayed his *Contribution à l'esthétique* until
1953. And he was challenged on several occasions in *La Nouvelle Critique* for his 'neo-Hegelianism' and his intolerable claim to preserve
the relative autonomy of philosophy from political imperatives.[13]
What actually interested Lefebvre was not proletarian science as
defended by Zhdanov from 1947 onwards, still less the relative or
absolute immiseration of the proletariat that formed a great debate of
the 1950s, and even less Lysenko. What interested him was analysing
the debasement of everyday life in the modern world, marked by the
subject's separation from itself and the objectification of the object
reduced to reification, to the object losing any aesthetic value, to the
poverty of the modern world.

Nevertheless, the process of breaking with the Communist Party
was rather strange and poses the question, formulated by Edgar
Morin in the half-tone portrait he drew of Lefebvre in his 1958 *Autocritique*: 'Ah! Why did this butterfly crawl like a caterpillar for years?'
Why did Lefebvre remain in the PCF so long? asks Morin, while suggesting that he paid for 'his small margin of dialectical autonomy
with total political subservience'.[14] In fact, in contrast to the successive waves of intellectuals who were excluded from the party or
withdrew from it from 1948 onwards, Lefebvre did not make a mark
in any of the major crises – the Prague coup, the condemnation of
Titoism, the Kravtchenko affair, the Rajk trial, the Doctors' plot; or
even when faced with the earthquake of 1956 – the Twentieth Congress of the CPSU and then, in October, the Soviet intervention in
Hungary – when he had knowledge of Khrushchev's report very
early on, as early as February, during a trip to the GDR at the invita-

tion of the Berlin Academy of Sciences.[15] This was because his problem was more theoretical than directly political. In this sense, the first shock dates back to 1955, on the occasion of a lecture on Lukács to the Hungarian Institute of Paris when Lefebvre, while polemicizing with Raymond Aron (*The Opium of the Intellectuals*) and Merleau-Ponty (*Adventures of the Dialectic*), rejected the Zhdanovite thesis of 'proletarian science'. Attacked in the Communist press, he copped a warning from the party leadership, which prevented publication of his lecture.[16]

The key question for Lefebvre, as for a number of intellectuals at the time, was the crisis of orthodoxy and the revision of Marxism. The main anchorage point of this challenge was to be the journal *Arguments*, founded in 1956 and wound up by its editors in 1962, in which the prime movers were Edgar Morin, Jean Duvignaud and Kostas Axelos.[17] A 'research bulletin' rather than the organ of a group, this journal gathered together thinkers excluded from the PCF and a number of people from the socialist left who wanted to renovate socialism. Before and after the Twentieth Congress, the initiative of these revolutionary intellectuals was to seek to renew Marxism by all available means. Lefebvre himself only published two articles in it, and following his exclusion from the Communist Party – one in 1959, 'Justice et vérité', on Nietzsche (no. 15); the other in 1962, 'La signification de la Commune' (no. 27). A loose grouping round *Arguments* sought to rethink French society, particularly after de Gaulle's victory, which posed some new problems; to rethink modern civilization, the reign of bureaucracy, technique, the 'new working class' (Serge Mallet), 'fragmented work' (Georges Friedmann); to rethink international relations by posing the question of the Third World. In the name of a methodological position that consisted in trying to reason (the meaning of *Raggionamenti*, the title of the Italian journal that worked with them), to pose questions and not to try to offer an interpretative line on Marxism, they pondered a key word – 'alienation' – rediscovered via the young Marx and Lukács. Lucien Goldmann's *Hidden God*, Pierre Naville's thesis *De l'aliénation à la jouissance*, Roland Barthes's *Mythologies* – all these works from 1956–57, which coincided with the evolution of *Annales* towards the 'longue durée', shifted examination towards the everyday and modernity. Lefebvre's contribution to the question in this period was to be his long introduction to the second edition of *Critique of Everyday Life* (1958), in which he sought to examine what had changed between 1947 and 1958 in the modern world, and where he refocused on the question of alienation. In addition, *Arguments* opened itself to foreign currents (the Frankfurt School, Lukács, Marcuse, Kolakowski). Alongside the various movements attempting to revise Marxism in France, we should in fact introduce a series of international dimensions, whether the shock of Algeria, or Cuba, or Yugoslav self-management, and later that of the Chinese Cultural Revolution. However, the main point here is to clarify the parallel between debates on the 'revision of Marxism' and debates on the function of sociology. Just as *Arguments* served, in Rémy Rieffel's phrase, as a political 'decompression chamber' for the exit from Stalinism, so the Centre d'études sociologiques and the *Cahiers internationaux de sociologie*, founded by Gurvitch, served as a scientific and cultural 'decompression chamber'.[18] It was in part the same authors who confronted each other in both – Morin, Duvignaud, Balandier, Touraine, Naville – so that it is legitimate to define an axis extending from sociological research to the journals and magazines that relayed these questions to a wider public (*Esprit, Le Nouvel Observateur*), and the recurrent themes of surveys and colloquia clearly prefiguring many of the concerns of 1968: fashion, needs, social classes, urbanization, technical society and civilization, tradition and continuity, the sociology of change, prediction in sociology, the critique of modernity.

For this dual debate assumed a public character. Lefebvre's opposition to the party line had long been internal, notably within the oppositional cell of the Centre d'études sociologiques. But it soon extended to the 'fractional' groups *L'Étincelle* (Victor Leduc, Jean-Pierre Vernant, Hélène Parmelin, Maurice Caveing, Maxime Rodinson) in 1957 and, above all, *Voies nouvelles* in April 1958, where he published several articles – in particular, a set on 'Marxisme et théorie de l'information' in the first two issues that attracted a lot of attention.[19] This was the context in which Lefebvre published an article that was key in everything that happened thereafter, 'Le marxisme et la pensée française', which drew up a disastrous balance sheet of the theoretical regression of Stalinist dogmatism. Published in the Polish journal *Tworczosc* at the end of 1956, released in June 1957 in *France-Observateur* and in July-August in *Les Temps modernes*, the article earnt him exclusion from the editorial committee of *La Nouvelle Cri-tique* along with various others.[20] This analysis was resumed and extended at the beginning of 1958 in *Problèmes actuels du marxisme*, pub-lished by Presses Universitaires de France.[21] At the same time, he participated, together with the *Temps modernes* circle and the Mendésist left (Bourdet, Martinet) around the Club de la gauche, in a number of discussions on the 'new left' and the 'new working class' that led to the foundation of the PSA and then the PSU, which Lefebvre never joined. He was to be criticized for all this. But it was on political grounds that a procedure to exclude him was initiated in June 1958. He was criticized for his prolonged 'activity of breaking away' through publications in the 'bourgeois press' (*L'Express, France-Observateur*, the *NRF, Les Temps modernes*), his revisionist works (*Problèmes actuels du marx-isme*) and his 'blatant fractional activity' in participating in the Club de la gauche and oppositional publications (*Voies nouvelles*).[22] Pro-nounced for a year, the exclusion would in fact prove definitive: he would never return, despite the lines thrown him at the beginning of the 1980s by a party only too happy, in times of famine, to have a last intellectual to digest.

This exclusion calls for three observations. The first is the violence of the attacks the PCF unleashed against him, launching against the quarry its intellectuals – Gilbert Mury, Guy Besse, André Gissel-brecht, Lucien Sève, Jean Kanapa – and making him a privileged target at its Fifteenth Congress (1959). The virulence was commensu-rate with the 'extreme patience' of the PCF, to adopt a phrase of Lucien Sève from 1960.[23] This was because the loss of Henri Lefebvre was, as David Caute indicates in his classic *Communism and the French Intellectuals*, a heavy blow for the party.[24] But it was also the case – second observation – that, whatever the official grounds, the viru-lence and vulgarity of these attacks were directed at an intellectual, not a political figure. Henri Lefebvre is a unique example of an intel-lectual, a philosopher, excluded for his ideas: Althusser was not excluded and, as for Garaudy, it was the politburo member who was ousted.

If the political break was obviously fundamental in allowing Lefeb-vre to develop his thinking in total freedom, there was no real theoretical discontinuity in his desire to construct a living Marxism, freed from dogmatism and committed to the analysis of contemporary phenomena. Certainly, he responded to his exclusion by publishing an initial analysis, 'L'exclu s'inclut', in *Les Temps modernes* as early as July 1958. Above all, as if it represented a veritable liberation for him, he threw himself into the composition of *La Somme et le reste* – that strange narrative of a 'philosophical adventure' which remains for many his major work.[25]

From revolutionary Romanticism to the Situationists

'Having entered a Romantic, Lefebvre left a Romantic', wrote Maurice Blanchot in the fine portrait ('Slow Funeral') he drew of him in *L'Amitié*. If he stayed, it is because he believed it possible, thanks to the position he occupied, to maintain an opening, even if it sometimes meant playing a double game: 'a philosopher's head is a hard head, even unbreakable'.[26] In the interim, Lefebvre published another article in the *NRF*, drawing less fire from 'party intellectuals', which was different in scope and destined to have a different echo in the coming decade. This article, 'Vers un romantisme révolutionnaire', taken up and reworked on several occasions, notably in the *Introduction to Modernity* in 1962, ushered in his phase of 'radical critique', making it possible for him to quit the Communist Party 'from the left'.[27] In this text, Lefebvre revived the 1925 ideal of a revolution that could only succeed if it extended not merely to the economic infrastructure, but to mentalities and culture; that set out – hence the notion of revolutionary Romanticism – from the critique of modernity which was for him at the heart of nineteenth-century Romanticism, from a refusal of the modern world. This Romanticism must be oriented towards the production of oeuvres and the production of man himself – what Lefebvre, like many people in the Stalinist era, called 'the new man'. This text seems to me be essential for understanding the process of rupture and the various developments in which he was engaged from 1956 to 1958.

But first, in order to appreciate his sensational entry into radical critique properly, we must resituate Henri Lefebvre in the context of the scholarly legitimacy he acquired at the turn of the 1960s. Contrary to retrospective reconstructions, we may note that sociology was now no longer quite what it had been in 1945–46, when he joined the CES.[28] As early as 1946, Gurvitch had launched the *Cahiers internationaux de sociologie*, the first such journal since the disappearance of the *Annales de sociologie*. Under the direction of Friedmann, the CES, installed in 1951 with the Ecole pratique des hautes études on the rue de Varenne, had already been transformed into a genuine laboratory, conducting area surveys, forming research groups, while Gurvitch, appointed to the Sorbonne, launched the 'Bibliothèque de sociologie contemporaine' at Presses Universitaires de France, and directed the French version of a big *Traité de sociologie* long regarded as authoritative. The Gurvitch era was succeeded by the era of Stoetzel. Jean Stoetzel, a Sorbonne professor at the same time as Raymond Aron, became director of the CES in 1956; appointments to it now speeded up. In the academy, a key turning-point occurred with the creation in 1958 of a degree in sociology, which thus became an academic discipline in its own right. The same year, Gurvitch founded the Association internationale des sociologues de langue française. Relying on a system of publications, with Éditions Anthropos augmenting Presses Universitaires de France, and multiplying through the foundation of several journals alongside the *Cahiers*, particularly the *Revue française de sociologie* (1960), these were the years of major colloquia and public visibility for the discipline.[29] The turning-point represented by Stoetzel, who had staked out his position as early as 1946 in a kind of manifesto ('L'esprit de la sociologie contemporaine'), was still more profound on the methodological and ideological level. In demanding an empirical and even neo-positivist sociology, primarily preoccupied with quantitative techniques and indifferent to theory, Stoetzel consciously and explicitly established the discipline in the framework of the 'dominant ideology' and, more specifically, as a site of intellectual elaboration of major reforms implemented at the beginning of the Fifth Republic as regards technological modernization, planning, and national and regional development (DATAR). If this development cannot quite be reduced to a victory of 'American sociology', it did at least mark a crucial reorientation and explains the reaction of Henri Lefebvre and several other Marxist sociologists (Edgar Morin, Pierre Naville), who at just this moment were embarked upon the enterprise of revising Marxism and who proposed, in various forms, a much more militant vision of sociology.

For Lefebvre, this was expressed by the abandonment of rural sociology, an area in which he was replaced by Henri Mendras, who would direct his research towards the 'second French revolution': the end of the peasantry and France's entry into modernity. In the account of research in the CES in 1959, published in the first issue of the *Revue française de sociologie* (1960), Lefebvre's themes were as follows: 1) 'Research on needs in the framework of the family (How mothers see the needs of children. Sociology of everyday life. Theory of needs. Research into needs in the family framework). 2) The birth of a city (Lacq and Mourenx). 3) Monographs on villages'. We are at the pivotal point of an evolution that was going to lead towards urban sociology and, more broadly, a sociology of daily life. Thus, in 1960 Lefebvre created a 'Research group on everyday life' at the CES. It was at this point – the production of Volume II of *Critique of Everyday Life* – that he was to quit research for university teaching. Elected as a professor, in October 1961 he was appointed by the liberal philosopher Georges Gusdorf to the sociology chair in the faculty at Strasbourg, formerly held by Gurvitch, where he would remain until his election to Nanterre in 1965. Developing an academic practice that was self-directed in character, particularly with the creation of an autonomous department of applied sociology, his reputation with the bourgeoisie of Strasbourg rapidly became inflammatory and his courses would mainly attract those students most disposed to protest.

This is the manifold context in which the passing but striking encounter between Henri Lefebvre and the Situationist group must be placed.[30] The influence was to be fertile and mutual – for Lefebvre, who revived the strategy of rupture of the 1920s avant-gardes; and for the Situationists who, prior to heaping abuse on him, drew much of their theoretical inspiration from his work. Founded in 1957 around Guy Debord, Raoul Vaneigem, Asger Jorn and Constant, the Situationist International was itself the inheritor of several movements like the Lettrist International of Isidore Isou and above all COBRA (Copenhagen, Brussels, Amsterdam), created in 1948 and dissolved in 1951, with which Lefebvre maintained relations, as is indicated by his correspondence with the Belgian poet Dotremont, or his influence on Constant (Neuwenhuys), who was to draw upon the *Critique of Everyday Life* for his initial urban projects in the *New Babylon*. But it was indeed the article 'Vers un romantisme révolutionnaire' that prompted Lefebvre's encounter with Debord. As early as the first issue of *Internationale Situationniste*, the 'Thèses sur la révolution culturelle' were explicitly constructed with reference to that article: 'Lefebvre offers us a track for critique of the contemporary world, but he does not propose a political project for making the revolution.' From the outset, as we can see, the relations between Lefebvre and the Situationists were complicated and critical; they were not of the order of filiation or affiliation and, as the Situationist International made clear during their rupture, he was never a member of the movement. But it was with the thought of Henri Lefebvre that the Situationists were fundamentally in dialogue; and there was even a phase of shared existence, trips, stays in Lefebvre's house in the Pyrenees, genuine collaboration, since Lefebvre involved Debord in the work of his research group on everyday life within the CES.[31]

For a start, both parties had in common the idea that everyday life is governed in the modern world by the reign of scarcity, not by the wealth of the consumer society; that everyday life has become disconnected from historicity amidst industrialization and accumulation; that it has been debased into uniform, repetitive everydayness by its separation from the great cosmic, natural and vital cycles; that the individual is herself divided (this is Deleuze's 'capitalism and schizophrenia'), separated from herself and the world in the modern world. Such alienation can be expressed in terms of poverty. Guy Debord came to give a talk to the research group on everyday life in 1961, in which he launched the saying 'everyday life is literally "colonized"'.[32] This was a saying with a prosperous future ahead of it: expressly quoted by Lefebvre in the second volume of *Critique of Everyday Life*, it was to be met with again in 1967 in the manifesto *On the Poverty of Student Life*, and would even reach as far as Habermas in 1981, in his *Theory of Communicative Action*, which contains a whole chapter on the colonization of the everyday.

It was in response to this poverty and alienation that the Situationists developed a theory of revolution, even 'cultural revolution', in terms of 'revolutions in individual everyday life', which is at the root of the theory of situations. In their most theoretical text, 'Théorie des moments et construction des situations', they in fact defined themselves with reference to the 'theory of moments' developed by

Lefebvre in *La Somme et le reste* and then in *Critique of Everyday Life*.[33] Spatio-temporal, 'constructed situations' are said to supersede moments as so many procedures for rupture, acceleration, subversion with respect to daily life – particularly the Situationist *dérive*, close to the Surrealist *promenade*, which consists in passing so rapidly from one district to another that an effect of acceleration and fluidity, breaking with the everyday, is created. The main site of experimentation is the city, but also as an object of experimental town planning, an anti-Le Corbusier city, constructed to counter uniformity, based on an architecture of the labyrinth, of complexity, which makes it possible not to take reality for such. But there is a divergence between Lefebvre and the Situationists over what utopia consists in: abstract utopia or concrete utopia. Is experimenting with a different kind of city a concrete utopia that already forms part of the revolution? Or does it remain at the level of architectural designs?[34]

It was here that the tensions were to crystallize. The Situationists were to be stymied by the eternal problem of avant-gardes since the Surrealists: the difficulty, even impossibility, of articulating cultural revolution and political revolution. As early as the first issue of *Internationale situationniste*, and again in no. 3 ('Sur le dépérissement de l'art', December 1959), the Situationists had criticized Lefebvre, and indeed Goldmann, both defined as 'representatives of independent revolutionary thinking', for having nothing to offer on the organization of a political force. But it was Lefebvre's relations with the 'new left', particularly with what they dubbed 'Argumentist dung', that led to the rupture. The Situationists could not accept the revision of the 1957 text 'Vers un nouveau romantisme?', taken up again by Lefebvre in 1962 in *Introduction to Modernity*, where he related Situationism to this new Romanticism and reduced the group to a youth movement.[35] Above all, at the same time Lefebvre published an article on 'La signification de la Commune' in the last issue of *Arguments*, foreshadowing his 1965 book *La Proclamation de la Commune*.[36] These few pages had been requested by him from Debord and Vaneigem, who defined the Commune as 'the greatest festival of the nineteenth century'. This was the key theme of the revolution as festival, which would dominate the whole of May '68. But in 1962 it was the occasion for the violent break with Lefebvre, consigned to 'the dustbin of history' and accused of being a plagiarist, a renegade, a 'Versaillais of culture'.[37]

Starting from there, we could, notwithstanding the sensational rupture, expatiate on the basically fairly direct influence of Henri Lefebvre, appointed in the interim to Nanterre in 1965, on Situationist texts that would serve as a theoretical reference-point for May '68 – especially Guy Debord's *The Society of the Spectacle* and Raoul Vaneigem's *The Revolution of Everyday Life*, both of which were published in 1967. Did the *radical critique* characteristic of Henri Lefebvre's position at the time, and which aligns him with the current of *critical theory* in unorthodox Marxism, have an immediate impact on a movement that accorded more importance to 'cultural revolution', the seizure of symbolic power and 'seizing speech', than reversing economic and social 'infrastructures' and capturing state power? Rather than responding to that question, by way of conclusion I should like to take a different tack, starting from recent works on Michel de Certeau and the comparison that might be sketched between the author of *Critique of Everyday Life* and the author of *The Practice of Everyday Life*.[38] The works of Henri Lefebvre on everyday life were 'a fundamental source' for de Certeau, as he signalled in the general introduction to his book.[39] Unquestionably, the two part company on numerous points – notably, the historical apprehension of daily life, which is relocated by the philosopher in a history of modernity, whereas the historian confines himself to a 'phenomenology of social micro-behaviour pitched at the level of the *longue durée*'. But they coincide, particularly with respect to Marcuse and his pessimistic definition of the 'consumer society', in a reading of consumption not as sheer passivity within mechanisms of domination, but as a form of production, production of a different kind that comes to disrupt the established order – the 'anti-discipline' that is at the heart of de Certeau's thinking, as of Michel Foucault's. In *On the Edge of the Cliff*, Roger Chartier has provided a fine analysis of this central hypothesis of *The Practice of Everyday Life*: 'To a rationalized, expansionist and at the same time centralized, clamorous, and spectacular production corresponds *another* production, called "consumption." The latter is devious, it is dispersed, but it insinuates itself everywhere, silently and almost invisibly, because it does not manifest itself through its own products, but rather through its *ways of using* the products imposed by a dominant economic order.'[40] And it is above all here that we detect a proximity, even a direct influence of Lefebvre on de Certeau, on the basis of some fundamental ideas in de Certeau about 'tactics and strategies'. The terms, which are quite explicit and analysed at length, are to be found in Lefebvre, as a development of the Marxist concept of *praxis*, in Volume II of *Critique of Everyday Life*, which de Certeau read very closely. In it Lefebvre precisely defines the critique of everyday life as a 'theory of tactics and strategies', tactics referring to the everyday, to stagnant and trivial reality, and strategy to the domain of action and decision-making.[41] We can even go somewhat further: if *invention* in de Certeau is not that far removed from *critique* in Lefebvre, here is to be found the genealogy of the very idea of a science of daily life, which has been so essential in the recent renewal of the social sciences. 'Insofar as the science of man exists, it finds its material in the "trivial", the everyday', Lefebvre asserted as early as 1947, with reference to Marc Bloch.[42] This attention in Lefebvre to familiar gestures, to what he elsewhere calls 'the minor magic in everyday life', even treated in terms of survivals, certainly does not make him the grandfather of 'micro-storia', but definitely does open up the path to a contemporary reflection on the complexity of the 'forms of experience' and the role of an anthropological approach to the critique of modernity.

CNRS, Paris, June 2002
Translated by Gregory Elliott

Preface

Notes

1. The text of this preface draws on a talk on 'Henri Lefebvre et la critique radicale' presented to the working group on 'Les années 68', Institut d'histoire du temps présent, Centre national de la recherche scientifique, 17 March 1997 (see the group's *Lettre d'information*, no. 23, July 1997). This talk served as the basis of my contribution, 'Voyages autour de la révolution. Les circulations de la pensée critique de 1956 à 1968', in G. Dreyfus-Armand, R. Frank, M.-F. Lévy and M. Zancarini-Fournel, eds, *Les Années 68. Le temps de la contestation*, Complexe, Brussels 2000, pp. 69–87.

2. I take the liberty of referring readers to my introduction to the translation of the first volume, *Critique of Everyday Life*, trans. John Moore, Verso, London and New York 1991, pp. ix–xxviii.

3. See, for example, p. 176 below: '*Structuralism* proceeds by privileging structure absolutely, and by absorbing within it the other terms we are considering, along with the relations they designate. Without admitting to do so, it substantifies it, presenting it as an essence and as something intelligible, thus acting as a belated marriage broker between Aristotelian ontology and a Platonism which dares not speak its name. Stability becomes both active and formal, the prototype and model for the real.'

4. Georges Pompidou, *Le Nœud gordien*, Plon, Paris 1974. Very few works have tracked the relation between the development of sociology and the great ideological debates of the post-war period. See Michael Pollak and François Bédarida, eds, 'Mai 68 et les sciences sociales', *Cahier de l'IHTP*, no. 11, April 1989.

5. Georges Gurvitch, 'L'exclu de la horde', *L'Homme et la société*, no. 1, July/September 1966. Cf. especially Georges Balandier, *Georges Gurvitch, sa vie, son oeuvre*, Presses Universitaires de France, Paris 1972; Phillip Bosserman, 'Georges Gurvitch et les Durkheimiens en France, avant et après la Seconde Guerre mondiale', *Cahiers internationaux de sociologie*, vol. LXX, January/June 1981.

6. Terry Clark, *Prophets and Patrons: The French University and the Emergence of the Social Sciences*, Harvard University Press, Cambridge, Mass. 1973; 'Reconstructions de la sociologie française (1945–1960)', *Revue française de sociologie*, vol. XXXII, no. 3, July/September 1991. See also Alain Drouard, 'Réflexions sur une chronologie: le développement des sciences sociales en France de 1945 à la fin des années soixante', *Revue française de sociologie*, vol. XXXIII, no. 1, January/March 1982; 'Les commencements des *Cahiers*. Une anthologie', *Cahiers internationaux de sociologie*, vol. 101, July–December 1966.

7. Françoise d'Eaubonne, *Le Temps d'apprendre à vivre*, Albin Michel, Paris 1960.

8. Henri Lefebvre, 'Les classes sociales dans la campagne. La Toscane et la Mezzadria classica', *Cahiers internationaux de sociologie*, no. 10, 1951. On what follows, see Rémi Hess, *Henri Lefebvre et l'aventure du siècle*, A. M. Métailié, Paris 1988, pp. 165–72.

9. His secondary thesis, *La Vallée de Campan*, was published in 1958 by Presses Universitaires de France in Gurvitch's collection.

10. See 'Rapport du cercle des sociologues', in 'Journées d'études des intellectuels communistes', *La Nouvelle Critique*, no. 45, April/May 1953, pp. 247–50.

11. BN Fol Ln 27 72054.

12. Hess, *Henri Lefebvre et l'aventure du siècle*, pp. 152–4.

13. See, in particular, Henri Lefebvre, 'Autocritique. Contribution à l'effort d'éclaircissement idéologique', *La Nouvelle Critique*, no. 4, March 1949, and 'Lettre sur Hegel', *La Nouvelle Critique*, no. 22, January 1951.

14. Edgar Morin, *Autocritique* (1958), coll. 'Politique', Seuil, Paris 1975, pp. 113–14.

15. Cf. Henri Lefebvre, *Le Temps des méprises*, Stock, Paris 1975, pp. 94–6.

16. Henri Lefebvre, *Lukács 1955*/Patrick Tort, *Être marxiste aujourd'hui*, Aubier, Paris 1986; see my contribution, pp. 21–4.

17. *Arguments* (1956–62), reprinted in 2 volumes, Privat, Toulouse 1983 (with prefaces by Edgar Morin, Kostas Axelos and Jean Duvignaud and presentations by Olivier Corpet and Mariateresa Padova).

18. See Rémy Rieffel, *Le Tribu des clercs. Les intellectuels sous la Ve République*, Calmann-Lévy/CNRS Éditions, Paris 1993.

19. See Dominique Desanti, *Les Staliniens*, Fayard, Paris 1975, p. 324; Victor Leduc, *Les Tribulations d'un idéologue*, Syros, Paris 1985, pp. 203–4.

20. Henri Lefebvre, 'Le marxisme et la pensée française', *Les Temps modernes*, nos 137–8, July/August 1957.

21. Henri Lefebvre, *Problèmes actuels du marxisme*, Presses Universitaires de France, Paris 1958 (fourth edn, coll. 'Initiation philosophique', 1970).

22. See *France Nouvelle*, 19 June 1958; *Le Monde*, 20 June 1958.

23. Lucien Sève, *La Différence*, Éditions sociales, Paris 1960. Attacks on Lefebvre, including those of an *ad hominem* variety, were kept up from 1955 onwards, particularly in *Cahiers du communisme*.

24. See David Caute, *Communism and the French Intellectuals*, André Deutsch, London 1964.

25. Henri Lefebvre, 'L'exclu s'inclut', *Les Temps modernes*, no. 149, July 1958, pp. 226–37; *La Somme et le reste*, 2 vols, Le Nef de Paris, Paris 1959 (reprinted Méridiens-Klincksieck, Paris 1989).

26. Maurice Blanchot, *L'Amitié*, Éditions de Minuit, Paris 1962, chapter 8, pp. 98–108.

27. Henri Lefebvre, 'Vers un romantisme révolutionnaire', *NRF*, no. 59, October 1957; *Introduction to Modernity*, trans. John Moore, Verso, London and New York 1995.

28. See above n. 6, particularly 'Reconstructions de la sociologie française (1945–1960)', *Revue française de sociologie*, vol. XXXII, no. 3, July/September 1991.

29. Cf. 'Les cadres sociaux de sociologie', 1959; 'Signification et fonction des mythes dans la vie politique', 1962; 'Les classes sociales dans le monde d'aujourd'hui', 2 vols, 1965.

30. See *Internationale situationniste, 1958–1969*, facsimile reprint, Champ Libre, Paris 1975. For a bibliography, readers are referred to the numerous studies, of variable quality, which have appeared in the last two or three years.

31. See *Le Temps des méprises*, pp. 109–10.

32. *Internationale situationniste*, no. 6, August 1961.

33. *Internationale situationniste*, no. 4, June 1960.

34. This is the theme of 'a different city for a different existence' defended by Constant (*Internationale situationiste*, no. 3, December 1959), as of Lefebvre's analyses of the new town planning as 'experimental utopia' (*Revue française de sociologie*, July/September 1961), which were criticized by *Internationale situationniste* for reformism (no. 6, August 1961).

35. See Lefebvre, *Introduction to Modernity*; and cf. *Internationale situationniste*, no. 8, January 1963.

36. Henri Lefebvre, 'La signification de la Commune', *Arguments*, nos 27–8, 1962; *La Proclamation de la Commune*, Gallimard, Paris 1965.

37. Lefebvre was the target of a Situationist tract published in Februrary 1963, 'Aux poubelles de l'histoire'. *Internationale situationniste* was to return to this affair at length in its three last issues, even after May 1968 (no. 10, March 1966, no. 11, October 1967, and no. 12, September 1969), thus marking its pique at the rupture. Lefebvre himself would respond one last time in 1967, in *Positions contre les technocrates*, accusing the Situationists in their turn of having been unable to propose anything other than an abstract utopia.

38. I refer readers to my text 'Henri Lefebvre en regard de Michel de Certeau: Critique de la vie quotidienne', in Christian Delacroix, François Dosse, Patrick Garcia and Michel Trebitsch, eds, *Michel de Certeau. Chemins d'histoire*, Complexe, Brussels 2002.

39. Michel de Certeau, *The Practice of Everyday Life*, trans. Steven Rendall, University of California Press, Berkeley 1988, p. 205 n. 5.

40. Ibid., pp. xii–xiii. And cf. Roger Chartier, *On the Edge of the Cliff: History, Language, and Practices*, trans. Lydia G. Cochrane, Johns Hopkins University Press, Baltimore and London 1997.

41. See below, pp. 132–9.
42. Lefebvre, *Critique of Everyday Life*, vol. 1, p. 133.

Clearing the Ground

1

Is it enough to launch ideas and to hazard hypotheses, when some may be fruitful, and others sterile? No. If we are to advance knowledge, it is essential that we deploy a set of concepts which has inner coherence. For the scientist and philosopher alike, coherence is a basic requirement. However, should this requirement go beyond certain limits, which in fact are hard to define, it becomes system for system's sake, and restricts intellectual scope and theoretical inventiveness. There may also be the danger that changes which may be occurring in the field of study itself will be overlooked. For this reason, research in all scientific fields, and particularly in the social sciences, is governed by a twofold imperative: first to guarantee that the thought and concepts employed be coherent, and second to take into account whatever new and probably unforeseen insights may be emerging in the area being studied and in the conceptual apparatus being used. This twofold imperative is not always easy to satisfy, and in an age such as ours when so many things are changing, but not all and not all in equal measure, it is difficult to steer a firm course between systematic thinking and essayism.[1]

This difficulty is apparent in a large number of contemporary works. In some, the reader is aware that coherence is given prominence. The author isolates a theme and examines it in depth, or tries to examine its implications and consequences without ever going beyond those specific limits. He theorizes in order to produce a lucid piece of work (or at least apparently lucid), thus seeking to impose a logical order on the enormous confusion of ideas and the immense disorder of facts. The success of certain ideas (that of 'structure' for example) and the influence which certain works have had may be attributed to this concern. Such strict thematization may guarantee unity and cohesion, but does it not also run the risk of overlooking some of the realities and innovations, in particular those elements which are not easily thematized and conceptualized using standard, accepted concepts, and are thus intractable to logical coherence?

On the other hand, there are other more essayistic works which try to capture the complexity and the rapid, multiple transformations of the modern world – and it is quite right that they should do so. However, their authors are facing different dangers: that of over-estimating change at the expense of what is stagnating or regressing, and that of composing a rhapsodic and discontinuous work with no inner connections between its various parts. Such works make no attempt to find either a thread to guide them through the laby-rinthine complexities of the modern world, or a precise definition or evaluation of what these complexities are.

2

The object of our study is everyday life, with the idea, or rather the project (the programme), of transforming it. So, what has happened so far? In the last fifteen years everyday life has undergone extensive transformations, and this has prompted us to ask whether in fact our aim has not been achieved, in remarkable and unexpected ways, by social practice itself. We have also had to ask ourselves whether the everyday as we had previously defined it[2] has not been absorbed by technology, historicity or the modalities of history, or finally, by poli-tics and the vicissitudes of political life. These are questions which have also troubled many of those who originally supported the idea, the aim and the author himself. We still need to find an answer to them, since our previous answer has been overtaken by circum-stances. It would be pointless to pretend that these obstacles strewn in our path have not obstructed the way forward.

However, it will not require lengthy thought or extensive docu-mentation to observe that although the everyday has indeed been modified, and in a contradictory way, it has not disappeared. It has not been absorbed by culture, by history, by politics, or by technology. The situation of the everyday per se has become increasingly serious. It is true that technology is penetrating it much more than it did twenty years ago, and it is impossible to ignore the importance of domestic science, for example; but we also know that technology and domestic science have not eliminated the most trivial aspects of everyday life; by reducing the time spent doing tedious chores technology raises very clearly the problem of available free time. Rather than transforming the everyday into a higher creative activity, it has created a vacuum. Another example is the way very few people's lives have been changed by air travel, and even then only in minor ways. Will interplanetary travel prove to be the same? Probably. At some time in the future – although it is difficult to say when – such journeys will be the preserve of a technical, social and political 'elite'. It is easy to imagine that one day 'mankind' will have travelled beyond the sun, while on earth actual men, peasants for example, will still be hoeing the land, transporting things on donkeys and mules, and perhaps living in hunger. *Uneven development* remains the prime law of the modern world, and there is much to learn and to be said about it. The distance – the gulf – between the everyday and technology is mirrored by the gulf between investment in the arms industry or interplanetary exploration and investment in the construction of new housing estates.

Only days of revolution, those days 'which are equivalent to twenty ordinary years' (Lenin), allow everyday life to pursue history and perhaps briefly to catch up with it. Such days occur when people will not and cannot go on living as they did before: the everyday as it has been established is no longer enough, and it affords them no satisfaction. And so they shatter the boundaries of everyday life, bringing life as it is lived into the domain of history. The conjuncture is momentary. They separate once more, or at least in our experience of so-called 'modern' life and society they do. The major stirrings and creative drives of revolutionary events have a totalizing impact. For a brief moment they bring the elements of totality together, after which these elements separate out once more. The results of history differ from the goals pursued and the aims envisaged, which is something we will call 'historical drift'. Certain elements of totality assert themselves and become quasi-autonomous: arts, technology, politics, sciences. The everyday withdraws into itself. These complex relations can be understood either from a historical and political perspective, or from the perspective of the everyday. Here we have chosen the latter. This is not to say that the former is faulty or bad, merely that it can sometimes lead to a dead end. Sometimes the political theorist will recommend that situations mature slowly until such time as the lived and the historical coincide again; patience has revolutionary virtues. At other times, the very same theorist of political history will recommend quickening the pace, on the assumption that humanity only sets itself problems it is able to resolve, and as historical moments happen only briefly and infrequently, anyone who lets them pass by will pay dearly for his lack of impatience and imagination . . .

Finally, it is irrefutable that public (political) life has penetrated private life, and vice versa. Today private life is saturated with items of general, social and political information. Equally, public and political life has become 'personalized', as they say. As we shall demonstrate, this interaction has resulted in an indisputable 'reprivatization' of practical and social life and a withdrawal into a family existence, in other words into a 'private' everyday.[3]

Of course, we shall return to these themes, and this is only an initial reply to those sociologists, historians and politicians who have denied and who continue to deny the importance of the problems of the everyday in the modern world, some going so far as to deny that it even exists. When we look closely, we can see that this denial constitutes an astonishing paradox, and we need to discover what it means and what the reasons for it are. Meanwhile, let us emphasize yet again the efforts which literature, cinema and even some specialists in the social sciences have made to get closer to the 'lived', to eliminate the arbitrary transpositions of the everyday, to grasp 'what is extraordinary within the ordinary', and 'the significance of the insignificant'. Questions of the value of this or that novel or film[4] or aesthetic theory apart, all this proves the validity of a critical study of everyday life.

3

In the Introduction to Volume I of *Critique of Everyday Life* we presented a programme of empirical and theoretical research, beginning
with the elaboration of a *theory of needs*.

In the event, and for reasons we will explain forthwith, this programme has proved difficult to achieve. We will be quite open about
these reasons, since in our view they compromise neither the concept
of the everyday, nor the programme itself. Quite the reverse: they
consolidate them, since they foreground the real and complex problems to which they are linked.

Established and slightly shop-worn concepts are easy to work with.
Empirical study of social reality requires more patience. It is not
more difficult per se. The real difficulty begins when concepts which
are new and as yet not fully clarified come into confrontation with a
mass of empirical documentation, and our thinking is prepared
neither to give up those concepts in return for innumerable observations, nor to give up facts in return for a conceptual abstraction. As
its programme implies, analytic and critical study of everyday life is
particularly suited to the bringing together of facts and concepts.
This does not mean that it presents a preordained highway along
which to travel. On the contrary, it must blaze its own trail between
philosophical reflections and fragmented and specialized research.

Working with general concepts, we can define man as a 'being of
need' and construct a theory based on need and the world of need.

We can show how through need, want and the consciousness of
want, man and his consciousness leave nature, childhood and a
whole magical fairyland behind, though not without nostalgia and
regrets. It is through privation that consciousness realizes that it has
been hurled into life and the world, forced to create its own world in
a distance relative to the (natural) being it was initially given and
relative to itself, compelled forever both to recreate and to surmount
that distance. The god-like amazement of seeing the world for the
first time and the marvel of first smiles are not enough. If he is to
work and to create, man must experience want. Without the experience of need and want, without actual or potential privation and
destitution, there can be no being – consciousness, and freedom
will never spring forth. In the land of its birth – 'nature' and the

unconscious – being remains a prisoner. It is in and through need that freedom is born and finds ways of acting, and if it is to modify the real, there is a fissure in its hard surface which it must discover and penetrate. Finally, need defined as want is the starting point from which man begins to explore a world of possibilities, creating them, choosing between them and making them real. He enters the domain of history. His consciousness can never come to an end. The consciousness of individuals opens on to social consciousness and vice versa, and the multiplicity of human consciousnesses opens on to the world.

This set of propositions is based on classic texts, and notably on a large number of texts by Marx, some of which are very well known, others less so.[5] The result of a theoretical development of this kind (and it could be a lengthy one) would not be without interest; but it is philosophy in its accepted, classic sense: a philosophy of want and need, unilateral and abstract like all philosophy. It turns need into a 'world'.

While not forgetting it, we will leave this conceptual development behind us; let us look towards what is called the 'concrete' (wrongly so: the concrete is also present in philosophical abstraction). In the press, in (visual or written) advertising, in household budgets and accounts or just simply in language, it is easy to observe that an immense number of needs are being expressed. These needs are precise, as are the goods[6] (objects) which are proposed or imposed in order to satisfy them. We are no longer considering need in general, but rather the need for this or for that, and thus defined in relation to 'this' or to 'that' (the object, the product, the goods: its absence or the enjoyment of its possession). Let us note that the apparently clear concept of satisfaction and of the fulfilment of a need – the need for *this* or for *that* – is in reality very obscure. Being in its entirety feels the pressures of need, whether it be satisfied or not. Will we simply describe, classify and 'typecast' these needs, and nothing more? That is how economists who specialize in consumer studies, or purely empirical sociologists, approach the matter. For us, the real problem is how to transfer from *need in general* (as a form of existence, as a manifestation of being) to the *need for this or for that* (in other words to a desire which is both individual and social, and as it manifests itself in everyday life). This theoretical transfer may not be impossible, but it is prodigiously complex. We will have to bring together an analytic presentation of needs and a dialectical determination of desires. If we are to arrive at a theory of the situations (concrete, of course) of social man, we must not lose track of the generic or general concept of man as 'being of need' when confronting the mass of contemporary facts.

We may be anticipating and taking the bloom off the part of our book which will be explicitly devoted to this question, but this does not worry us. Here as much as elsewhere we do not intend to avoid repetitions, or to take up the same theme, or to cast different lights on the same subject, or to treat different subjects using the same concept. What does social experience provide? *Desires*, transient and many-faceted desires, together with their 'motivations'. In spite of the indecisive character of this last concept, or rather because of it, we are led to something diffuse, obscure and real. To overestimate the 'motivations' of desires and desires themselves is to fall into subjectivism, psychologism and classic idealism. To disregard them is to fall into simplified and vulgar materialism and determinism, in which we forget man's obscure depths and his development. There are innumerable desires, some with often strange motivations. There are few fundamental needs: hunger and thirst, sex, play perhaps,[7] maybe the simple need to expend accumulated energy. Theorists do not agree either on the quality or the quantity of 'elementary' needs, or on the possibility of reducing them to a single, initial, primordial fundamental need: libido, *Trieb*, drive, will for being or will for power, etc. How can we pass from need or needs to desires? In other words: *what happens between them* in the *transition* from the one to the other?

Need is determined biologically and physiologically. It is 'generic': it belongs to the human species. Desire is at the same time both individual and social; in other words it is recognized – or excluded – by a society. Need is determined quantitively: a human organism needs so many calories, so many hours of sleep, etc. An industry needs so much energy and so many raw materials, so many machines. Desire however is qualified or qualitative. But these observations are too simple. Need is also spontaneity and vitality, and also depth and relationship to depth. So sexual need seems generically linked to reproduction; in the individual it cannot be separated from an organ and the way it functions, from a certain determined quantity of organic material, sperm or ova. At the same time, it is not only the drama of the relations between one individual and another (or the other) individual which is sketched out and foreshadowed through this need, it is not only the drama of the link between individual and species, it is universality which is being offered or withdrawn. These are the problems (or as philosophers put it, the problematic) of love. The biological and organic fact now appears like an initial and unique nucleus of being, now like a group (family) specificity, now like a general principle relative to the problems of the species, now like a proposed universality. We cannot limit ourselves to the organic or biological fact; as such, it is as abstract as the absolute idea of Love per se . . .

On the other hand, it is still too simple to see desire as qualitative and need as quantitative – the one psychological and sociological (or psycho-social), the other biological and physiological. There are needs which are social, objective and quantifiable: needs for so many sources of energy, so many houses or schools, etc. Economists and sociologists know these needs well. On the sociological level (to use the still-unclarified term 'level'), need and desire are still separate one from the other. A single human reality appears with two faces, one brutally objective – social need (for this or for that), the other subtly subjective – desire (for this or for that or for something else by means of this or that, or even for nothing or for the infinite or for pure surprise), with motivations which give meaning to the desired object and to desire itself.

There are many mediations between need and desire. In fact, there is everything: society in its entirety (productive activities and the modes of consumption), culture, the past and history, language, norms, commands and prohibitions, the hierarchy of values and preferences. Desire only becomes desire when it is assumed by the individual via his conflicts in a conscious amd accepted way, and when it is consciously confronted with 'goods' (the object) and the enjoyment afforded by them. It only truly becomes desire when it becomes a vital and spiritual power, accepted and used by the individual, and when his life is metamorphosed into a creative consciousness, creating and created: by becoming need once more. Initially, need is nature; it becomes a creative activity and comes to an end in the works creativity produces.

Now this is an immense journey, fraught with obstacles and pitfalls, empty spaces and gaping holes. The definition we have given of desire seems to be necessary, in that it condenses experience. And yet, if we accept it, it points to a limit, a kind of horizon. One may ask oneself whether there has ever been a true desire or even a true desire truly fulfilled. Kant, that theorist of the virtuous action, used to ask himself whether there had ever been a virtuous action which could conform to his concept. At every step of the immense journey, how many potential failures, deviations, regressions, mistakes correctable or beyond repair! But self-regulatory systems, such as feedbacks, do exist, which may be fragile and yet are real in the context of determined contexts and structures; an overall balance is established between differing needs, between satisfactions and dissatisfactions, as between offers and demands. Conversely, self-regulation does not appear to exist psychically. Always relative and forever in question, the balance of desires must be fought for time and time again. In the fabric of the everyday, the pathological and the abnormal are a constant menace to us.

Dreams, with their discontinuities, their surprising 'suspenses' and their obvious absurdities, sum up the transition from need to desire. They re-enact the journey from the certainty of need to the uncertainty of desire. Dramatically, they condense an enormous dramatic, social and individual history, marked out by symbols. It is not only the failures and the possibility of failure which they display, but also the illusory solution to potential failure which makes a different, more serious failure inevitable: nostalgia for the cosy warmth of the lost homeland, the journey back to an original state without problems, repetitions, refuge in symbols, and escape into a past of natural being in order to evade the problems of the being which is as yet unattained. In a spontaneous 'digest' of the drama of desire, dreams signal gaps and deviations, and in doing so make them more serious. If dreams re-enact the tremulous birth of desire, then should not desire act like dreams, going beyond the critical surface which separates sleeping and waking, images and the everyday, and create itself in an external form?

We are beginning to perceive an infinitely complex dialectical movement, which for the time being we will sum up with several propositions:

a) Desire is profoundly different from need. It can even go so far as to struggle against it, until it frees itself.

b) Initially, however, there is no desire without a need as its nucleus, its point of departure, its 'base' or 'foundation'. A desire without need can only be purely artificial, an extreme case which even the most subtly refined moral or aesthetic values or artificial modes of behaviour find difficult to create.

c) Sooner or later desire turns back towards need in order to regain it and to regain itself. By reinvesting itself within it, it rediscovers spontaneity and vitality. It is a return journey which crosses through the objectivity, impersonality and indifference of social need, as it is conventionally understood.

This dialectical movement permeates the everyday. It gives it life. The everyday is the space in which dialectical movement advances or comes to a halt, in an unpredictable blend of opaqueness and transparency, of clear-sightedness and blindness, of determinability and transience.

Therefore there is a transfer from need to desire which crosses the social and society in its entirety. This transfer is sometimes continuous, sometimes interrupted. Between myself and me, or if you like, between 'I' and 'me', or rather between 'me' and 'I' caught up in everyday life, there is everything. First and foremost there is language, which allows a consciousness of desire to be achieved and then inserted into praxis.

But this vision is still too simple. The transition from need to desire and the vital return of desire back to need, in order to reabsorb itself within it, this transition which the complexities of the journey have already impeded, is also obstructed by extraneous interventions. We live in a determined society (bourgeois or capitalist rather than socialist society, since that is different and in any case too badly understood for us to undertake a study of its everyday life). In 'consumer society', which is allegedly based upon mass consumption and massive production for needs, the manufacturers of consumer goods do all they can to manufacture consumers. To a large extent they succeed.

The consumer does not desire. He submits. He has 'strangely' motivated 'behaviour patterns'. He obeys the suggestions and the orders given to him by advertising, sales agencies or the demands of social prestige (not to mention worries about solvency, which are far from negligible). The circuit from need to desire and from desire to need is constantly being interrupted or distorted. These 'orders' from outside become subtly abstract fragments or absurdly concrete 'motivations'. Desires no longer correspond to genuine needs; they are artificial. Need no longer metamorphoses into desire. The process becomes complicated, or disintegrates. And yet it does not disappear; it continues its journey from the vital to the social, from want to fullness, from privation to pleasure, even if its nature is misunderstood or unrecognized. However, the 'system of needs', which Hegel considered to be the cement of social life, no longer seems coherent. It has been dissociated or shattered. As Guy Debord[8] so energetically put it, everyday life has literally been 'colonized'. It has been brought to an extreme point of alienation, in other words profound dissatisfaction, in the name of the latest technology and of 'consumer society'. Now this technology could make a different everyday reality *possible*. However, these very same causes have uniform effects, equalizing social needs and bringing 'desires' in line with one another; they replace previous highly diversified 'lifestyles' by everyday ways of living which are analogous, if not identical.

Therefore there can be no knowledge of the everyday without knowledge of society in its entirety. There can be no knowledge of everyday life, or of society, or of the situation of the former within the latter, or of their interactions, without a radical critique of the one and of the other, of the one by the other, and vice versa. For this knowledge, negative concepts (distance and omission, dissatisfaction, frustration or, more generally, alienation) are as indispensable as the positive ideas in use in the fragmented sciences.

4

Volume I of *Critique of Everyday Life* also promised a schematic of the situation of women in modern society. Two types of consideration prompted this intention. First, 'women' in general bear all the weight of everyday life; they are subjected to it much more than 'men', in spite of very significant differences according to social classes and groups. Their situation sums up what the everyday is. Second, this situation is an indicator and a measurement of the degree to which the human is achieved (or not) in a determined social practice, at a certain level of economic and social development, and at a certain degree of culture and civilization.

Now over the last ten years, this theme ('the situation of women' or 'the feminine condition') has subsided into literary and journalistic banality. It has given rise to polemics which have been as vague as they have been violent, and to very specialized monographs on points of interest but of minimal importance.

The salient feature of these polemics is that they were directly linked to political questions and to some quite astonishing political positions.[9] Like all polemics, they have their share of bad faith. Obligatory options, in other words choices, bias, partisan attitudes, party attitudes – all these make for an inextricable confusion. Everyone excels when it comes to pointing out other people's weak points. So, with statistics and texts at their fingertips, their partisans have no difficulty in showing the extent to which our society persists in disadvantaging women. And, with statistics and texts at their fingertips, the opponents of this neofeminism have no difficulty in showing that we are being threatened by a kind of modern matriarchy or gynaecocracy.

When polemics start off on the wrong foot, it is difficult to intervene without taking sides. This debate was a confrontation between misogynists and gynaecomaniacs. What was the point in intervening? Critique of everyday life has time on its side; it requires patience; it would be rather more in favour of people who wait for situations to mature (but it avoids those who let these situations atrophy, and who are human beings of another sort).

First and foremost the study of feminine reality implies the intervention of concepts which are still underdeveloped, for example the concept of *ambiguity*. If we say it is underdeveloped, it is because confused intuitions about obscure situations are often mistaken for concepts. If the object of the concept of ambiguity appears to be confused and unclear, the concept itself needs to be all the more clear and explicit.[10] In this day and age, who would deny that in 'being' or 'existence' or in 'life' or in 'praxis' there is much that is unclear and obscure? If the concept of unclearness and of obscurity remains unclear and obscure, in other words if there is no concept, irrationalism triumphs. If the concept of unclearness and obscurity can be clarified, then a (relative) rationalism will impose itself.

Study of the women's press, and above all of the so-called 'romantic' press, reveals a feminine world of singular ambiguity. That it wishes to promote women socially is obvious, yet vague, and it does not go beyond certain characteristics (themselves ambiguous) of the vaguely defined social group they comprise. In the 'feminine world' the analyst notices innumerable times the resurgence of myths, of cosmological or anthropological symbolisms, which, from the perspective of modern science and technology, are all outdated. These resurgences are analogous to something taking place on an apparently higher level than that of the 'romantic' press. If we have seen the rebirth of myths in literature, art and culture, the criticism which attacked these myths needed to be subtler than before; we have seen the appearance of symbolisms, notably in cinema, at a time when old symbols were being discredited and antisymbolism was intensifying its campaign under the banner of realism or neoclassicism.

The analyst ponders these contradictory phenomena. He looks at these publications which sell in their millions and asks himself what link they establish between the everyday and the imaginary. On one hand he tries to isolate themes (good luck and bad luck, chance and destiny, happiness and fate) and their combinations, transferred to the context of cosmological reference: the stars and their conjunctures. On the other, he tries to capture the affective tonality maintained in these readings. He discovers an ambiguous mixture of very practical texts and of texts about the imaginary. His impression is that often the practical texts (such as recipes, menus, dress patterns) read like dreams, and that conversely the imaginary texts read in a practical fashion, in a perpetual toing and froing from one to the other, in a never-ending equivocation which reproduces itself indefinitely.

It is not easy to define what this ambiguity means. Is it a symptom of the weakness and childishness persisting in a large number of women? Is it a victory on the part of obscurantism and superstition? Is it proof that this social group, 'women', is badly integrated in the society in which we live? Is it a sign of resistance to the primacy of technology and the rationalist ideology in industrial society? Or on the contrary is it a confused protest against the shortcomings of technology or a confused but profound perception of the role randomness plays? These questions need to be addressed.

It could be maintained that these facts and symptoms would disappear within a truly rational society in which the integration of women had been perfectly achieved, and where they would work normally in conditions which would resolve their specific problems. One may also think that this 'feminine world', with its mythologies and cosmologies (horoscopes, systems of correspondences and interpretations) demonstrates the permanence of a need or a deep desire to deny the triviality of the everyday by opening it up to the marvellous and to a kind of poetry, sometimes clumsy, sometimes subtle, which art and literature rediscover in their way but without being able to invest it in the everyday. This desire for another dimension of the everyday and the social may address itself to old-fashioned representations, but this does not make it any the less legitimate. It is like a serious game, an aestheticism for people deprived of art.

More concretely, the analysis of texts specifically directed towards women and their preoccupations reveals the permanence of *cyclic time scales* of biological and cosmic origin at the heart of the (intermittent or continuous) linear time scales imposed by technology and industrial labour. Now the link between the everyday and cyclic patterns and time scales, the time of day and night, week and month, season and year, is obvious. Furthermore, women's physiological and social lives place them at the junction between the controlled sector and the uncontrolled sector, which explains the role ideas such as good luck, bad luck or destiny play in their consciousness. All this reveals the link between the 'feminine world' and everyday life in a much clearer light. This link will be seen to be more profound than the (indispensable) studies of budget-time, women's work within and outside the home, etc., would have us believe.

Once more we see ourselves directed away from specific facts towards society in its entirety, and the analysis of totality. The study in isolation of the 'feminine condition' conceals more than one trap. Although it starts from characteristics which are indisputable, such a study runs the risk of recreating a metaphysical entity and an occult quality – the feminine, femininity – or conversely of dissolving these characteristics by considering important everyday problems to be minor ones. In order to avoid both these risks, we will not study the 'feminine condition' as a discrete unit, but instead we will divide it up across the whole range of our critique of everyday life. Thus the initial programme is restructured. While we will maintain the project for a *theory of needs*, we will abandon the theme of the feminine condition as a discrete and separate entity.

5

The obstacles confronting critical research into everyday life would be of little more than anecdotal interest if they did not afford us a theoretical experience. Here we are in the domain of movement, a domain which is at the same time extremely 'structured'. As we have just seen, it has been necessary to reconsider the concept of everyday life, to intensify it, to modify it, and to situate it in society as a whole. Research was focused on a huge pile of empirical facts (such as the appearance of new needs) and on a huge pile of documents (such as the 'women's press' and its themes). At the same time, a difficult conceptualization – to use the jargon of the social sciences – had to be undertaken.

Research in the domain of scientifically necessary abstractions (*concepts*) has adopted a threefold aspect. We have had to challenge a certain number of ideas and methodological tools, which had already been accepted but which were not yet fully developed, by confronting them with facts. An example would be the idea of *level*, which we will examine in a special section in chapter 2 in order to demonstrate how everyday life is one *level* of social reality. We have also had to introduce concepts which are new, but which correspond to a certain stage of knowledge and which therefore tie up with preoccupations and areas of research other than those relating to everyday life. An example would be the concept of the (*whole or total*) *semantic field*, which we will examine in chapter 4. By extension, we have had to *make concepts dialectical*, whether or not they are already known and accepted. Finally, it has been necessary to try to introduce some order into the immense theoretical and practical confusion which seems to be an aspect of modernity in general and the social sciences in particular, and which cannot be overlooked. This confusion stems from the proliferation of hypotheses, the considerable number of studies carried out, and their extremely uneven quality. When attempting to introduce some order and clarity, we must avoid simplification and artificial coherence. We have already pointed out this danger. It will confront us again in relation to ideas which are indispensable, but which if used or misused in an oversimplified way will allow us to substitute seductive and superficial coherences for the complexity of the facts. Some examples of this would be the ideas of *structure* and of *totality*, to which we will also devote some methodological considerations.

6

Among all these obstacles, one in particular is worth attention, namely politico-ideological controversies which, though inevitable and indispensable, have vitiated the atmosphere for research.

The social science sector is too involved in certain important interests not to be damaged in this way. The ensuing debates can be extremely lively, and perhaps this is to be welcomed. All in all, it is preferable to stagnation and indifference. The worst thing is that the one does not always exclude the other, and sometimes stagnation and indifference go hand in hand with virulent polemics, which are irrelevant to the actual issue.

No knowledge in any domain can move forward without controversy (and this is particularly true for political economy, sociology and history). Behind ideas there are men, and these men have their interests and their passions. Behind men there are other, vaster interests, those of groups, classes and nations. Only someone naive – or an academic – would insist that there should be a climate of affability and cosy tranquillity in the social sciences. But beyond a certain limit, it becomes almost impossible to work.

So in the last few years, how have these controversies changed? In the following way. It used to be agreed as a fact of civilization and the acquisition of culture that discussions degenerated when their arguments were used *ad hominem*. Now for some time many discussions, if not all (when they are carried out in public rather than by way of gossip or whispers), have rushed headlong and shamelessly beyond the pale. They begin with what used to be the conclusion. They become personal. They try to discredit, to disqualify, to dishonour. They try to show that the person they are arguing with is not 'valid'. They belittle him. In doing so, and without being aware of it, they are belittling themselves; the discussion itself is belittled, and they pretend not to notice.

If bourgeois thought, and we include liberalism in this, is trying to occupy a kind of artificially serene high ground, where it would be exempted from those genuine discussions which go right down to the 'foundations', then current dogmatism, and above all Marxist dogmatism, is just as guilty of breaking with the rules of dialogue. As a result the atmosphere is unlikely to improve overnight. Under the influence of Stalinism, controversies have become political operations deploying the techniques of propaganda. If you wish merely to 'neutralize' your opponent, you are being nice to him. More often than not, you will try your hardest to 'eliminate' him. As is always the case, these procedures of ideological warfare have gone well beyond the limited circle in which they originated. Bad manners have spread like wildfire. The good manners of liberalism are rather out-of-date, and have offered a feeble and timorous resistance.

The result is a generalized terrorism which would merit a study all of its own and which is part of a fairly serious and virtually ubiquitous contradiction between the creation of a new democracy and the undermining of the very foundations of this democracy. If minds, ideas and concepts manage not to be 'neutralized', then they are 'eliminated'. In the ideological jungle, terrorism rules. Everyone uses the same arsenal: intimidation, threats, repression. Terrorism paralyses. Be they liberals or not, those who 'resist' will suffer; ideas become stale and lifeless; men become tired and grow old. All the better for dogmatism and tyranny, or whatever you want to call them. Force and power have won. The procedures of the intellectual mandarinate and the techniques of intellectual gangsterism complement each other, though it is not the same men who use them.[11]

7

Putting this to one side, let us recapitulate the objections and aims of those who reject the idea of 'everyday life', or who deny that it has any interest. The arguments have been presented sometimes verbally,[12] sometimes in written form. We will sum them up without quoting names or texts. We will begin with the least 'intimidating' ones (by which we mean those who least use the authoritarian method).

Common-sense objections (Common sense is the trivial reflection of a fragmented practice, and should not be confused with good sense, which is nearer to analytic understanding and Cartesian reason.)

'To begin with, everyday life does not exist as a generality. There are as many everyday lives as there are places, people and ways of life. Everyday life is not the same in Timbuktu, in Paris, in Teheran, in New York, in Buenos Aires, in Moscow, in 1900, in 1960. In fact, what do the words mean? Whatever is repeated on a daily basis? The action of opening or shutting doors, of eating and drinking? Only organic functions correspond to your definition. Utterly without interest.

Everyday life in art? In politics? That must mean the everyday life of the artist, of the politician, what they eat, what they drink, how good or bad their digestion is. As far as art or politics is concerned, utterly unimportant. You are just a vulgar materialist . . .'

Reply

'Do you really think you have understood what the words *critique of everyday life* actually mean? Is it a question of describing, comparing and discovering what might be identical or analogous in Teheran, in Paris, in Timbuktu or in Moscow? Such an aim would indeed be restricted to the basic and the physiological. The aim of a critique of everyday life is quite different. It is a question of discovering what must and can change and be transformed in people's lives, in Timbuktu, in Paris, in New York or in Moscow. It is a question of stating critically how people live or how badly they live, or how they do not live at all. Would you go so far as to say that everyday life cannot change? If so, you destroy your own argument, because you have already admitted that it can. Critique implies possibilities, and possibilities as yet unfulfilled. It is the task of critique to demonstrate what

18

these possibilities and this lack of fulfilment are. Do you think that basic physiological demands – organic functions, as you call them – are external to social life, to culture, to civilization, and are thus unchangeable, or relatively so? Such a postulate would be highly debatable and highly dangerous. Moreover, the term "everyday" has misled you. You take it literally rather than seeing its deeper meaning. Do you think that the repetitions which take place each week and each season are not part of everyday life? Frequently, and not for the last time, we have taken rhythms and cyclic time scales to be one of the contents of the everyday, with all that they organize and command, even when they are broken and fragmented by linear time scales. This is something which supersedes "the everyday" in its strictest sense. And another thing: do you think that art is external and superior to real life, and that what the artist creates is on a tran-scendental plane? Similarly, do you think that politics and the state are above everyday life and external to society? Critique of everyday life encompasses a critique of art by the everyday and a critique of the everyday by art. It encompasses a critique of the political realms by everyday social practice and vice versa. In a similar sense, it includes a critique of sleep and dreams by wakefulness (and vice versa), and a critique of the real by the imaginary and by what is possible, and vice versa. This is to say that it begins by establishing dialectical links, reci-procities and implications rather than an unrelated hierarchy, as you do. Finally, please note that what you say about the diversity of every-day lives is less and less true. Technological or industrial civilization tends to narrow the gaps between lifestyles (we are not talking about living standards) in the world as a whole. Having said that, your argu-ment has a point and raises a question. Would everyday life be merely the humble and sordid side of life in general, and of social practice? To repeat the answer we have already given: *yes* and *no*. Yes, it is the humble and sordid side, but not only that. Simultaneously it is also the time and the place where the human either fulfils itself or fails, since it is a place and a time which fragmented, specialized and divided activity cannot completely grasp, no matter how great and worthy that activity may be . . .'

Objections from historians

'Everyday life is an aspect of history, an interesting one, maybe, but minor. To study it in itself and for itself entails certain dangers. Like it or not, aren't you falling back on the anecdotal, on something external to events and their deep-seated reasons and causes? Over the last few years there have been volumes and even entire series dedicated to everyday life in such and such a society, at such and such an epoch. Sometimes these are the work of serious historians. But do you honestly believe that they do not bypass history, that they are not merely marginal or anecdotal? Except when they deal with archaic societies, and are written by ethnographers, they add nothing to what we already know . . .'

Reply

'Agreed on one major point: history is a fundamental science. The human being is historical and its historicity is inherent to it: it produces and is produced, it creates its world and creates itself. Having said that, let us not simplify the process of historical becoming, and let us avoid historicism. Everything is historical, agreed, but not equally so. History as a science does not exhaust the human. It neither eliminates nor absorbs political economy, sociology or psychology. Remember what we sometimes refer to as historical drift, in other words the gap between intentions, actions and results. There can be no history without a critique of history itself. Above all remember the issue of uneven development. In the links between mankind (human groups) and nature, is that not a significant factor? And there is not only history, but culture too, and civilization . . . The more we distance ourselves from our "Promethean" society, and the more we look back towards archaic societies, the less the everyday life we are able to reconstruct is distinguishable from culture and historicity (in so far as there was history and historicity in such societies). In archaic groups, difference seems to disappear. Could their everyday be defined as the secular as opposed to the sacred? But the former haunted the latter, since even the humblest functional object was not just a product, and even less a thing, but a work of culture and art. Whether it was perfect or only half-finished, it was the bearer of multiple symbols and meanings! Let us not idealize this past. Let us not lapse into ethnographical romanticism. For us, here, the question is the modern everyday. We observe that history has had the following result: the separation from what is historical per se of that other aspect of history and of the human which we call the everyday. Today, in our society, everyday life and culture, everyday life and historical event, are dissociated (but without losing their solidarity completely). Marx was the first to perceive this characteristic of the period. Read the *Critique of Hegel's Philosophy of the State* again, where Marx points out the modern rift between private and public life which did not exist in antiquity or in the Middle Ages.

> The abstraction of the *state as such* was not born until the modern world because the abstraction of private life was not created until modern times . . . The abstract reflected antithesis of this is to be found only in the modern world. The Middle Ages were an age of *real* dualism; the modern world is the age of *abstract* dualism.[13]

We could study literary history, and in particular the history of the novel, in this light. We would see how the narrative of the novel distances itself from the epic and the tragic, just as the everyday it describes becomes distant from historical action and cultural totality. In fact it is true that at certain moments institutions, culture, ideologies and the most important results of history are forcefully brought into the everyday life over which they formerly towered; there they find themselves accused, judged and condemned: grouped together, people declare that these institutions, these ideas, these forms of state and culture, these "representations" are no longer acceptable and no longer represent them. Then, united in groups, in classes, in peoples, men are no longer prepared to live as before, and are no longer able to do so. They reject whatever "represented", maintained and chained them to their previous everyday life. These are the great moments of history: the stirrings of revolution. At this point, the everyday and the historical come together and even coincide, but in the active and violently negative critique which history makes of the everyday. After which, the wave subsides and spreads out in a backward surge. What other moments are there when the distance between what history makes possible and what it has achieved becomes so great, like the distance between what men have wanted, what has resulted, and what they have lived? History is necessary, but by itself it is inadequate. According to Marx, this historicity is nothing more than a summary of the prehistory of mankind, and indeed the men it tries to define become aware of alternative forms of knowledge and critique.

To sum up, the historian wishes to challenge the critique of everyday life in the name of science: but critique of everyday life will in turn challenge and accuse history in so far as it is a mere series of faits accomplis, in so far as it is history which has reduced the everyday to the state in which we find it!'

Objections from philosophers

'Be careful! There are particular sciences and there is philosophy. Each social science has its own domain, its vocabulary, its specific concepts and operational techniques. As for philosophy, it has its own concepts, terminology and intentions. It seeks either to attain being, or to totalize knowledge, or to bring something or other which has hitherto eluded it into language, in other words into consciousness and knowledge, or finally, to construct a total and totally coherent discourse. Does your critique of everyday life fall within any particular social science? It would seem not, even though now and then one glimpses a taste for sociology, and even unilateral sociologism. Does it come under philosphy? No, you have said so yourself. Rather it would claim to supersede philosophy by dismantling it and filching some of its categories. In a word, if we admit and accept that these disciplines correspond to precise theoretical procedures and to a certain general structure of human knowledge and consciousness, then it does not fit into any one of them. Moreover, what you call everyday life is simply what has been lived, and inauthentically lived: Heidegger's "ontic", external to the ontological; this is precisely what the philosopher must avoid if he is to unveil the authentic and to reveal the truth of being. Instead of lifting them, you are going to make these veils more opaque, and without contributing to the accumulation of positive learning and knowledge of the real.'

Reply

'The general question of philosophy has been debated time and time again, and at this point we will return to it only briefly. Because of its failure to supersede itself by fulfilling itself – or by fulfilling the aims and aspirations of philosophers by superseding abstract philosophical thought – philosophy finds itself in a difficult situation. It goes on seesawing between system and experiment, between state ideology and anarchizing critique. Today, if we must provisionally redefine it, our definition would differ from yours: it is an attempt to bring the greatest possible quantity of present-day human experience, the experience of our so-called "modern" era, along with the practical experience of love, political action or knowledge, into a set of reflections and concepts. This will bring us out of systematic tradition and the generally accepted tautology which turns philosophical discourse into a philosophy of discourse. In this effort to experience a totality (and the limits of discourse itself) philosophy includes a critique of philosophy, and this involves critique of everyday life on more than one account. To begin with, it is a mode of the "lived" which we have no right to overlook or to parenthesize in the name of higher or supposedly higher experiences. On the other hand, after the great hopes fostered by revolution, is not the situation of the everyday a specific experience, even a political one? What did Marx mean when he maintained that it would soon be time to stop interpreting the world and to begin transforming it? Did he mean simply the outside world? Here and now, we say no. For Marx, to transform the world was also and above all to transform the human world: everyday life. When they interpreted the world, philosophies brought plans for its transformation. Were we to fulfil philosophy, were we to change the process of the philosophical becoming of the world into the process of the world-becoming of philosophy, would that not be to metamorphose everyday life? We will therefore go so far as to argue that critique of everyday life – radical critique aimed at attaining the radical metamorphosis of everyday life – is alone in taking up the authentic Marxist project again and in continuing it: to supersede philosophy and to fulfil it. As far as the problem you pose is concerned, namely that of "relevance" in relation to a specific fragmented science, we will return to it shortly, and more than once. You formulate the problem in a very narrow way, thus vetoing anything which fails to fit into your self-imposed framework. In any event that is merely a secondary problem. It is true that critique of everyday life raises the question of authenticity, but it does so in its own particular way. Everyday life per se is neither the authentic nor the inauthentic. Instead it could be seen to define the milieu and the moment in time where they come into conflict, where authenticity justifies itself and must show its credentials. To take some examples from everyday life, neither love nor the relations between parents and children, say, are stamped in advance with inauthenticity. Doesn't all love want to embody itself in the everyday? Isn't that its wish? If you judge otherwise, it is because you are defining the authentic as exceptional and in the end as solitude, failure and death. It is to counter this excessive and speculative hypothesis that critique of everyday life launches its challenge: "Either man will be in the everyday or he will not be at all. He will live his everyday life by superseding the everyday life he lives today, or else he will no longer be. As long as everyday life has not radically changed, the world will be the same as ever. It is up to radical critique to bring those changes to the world! . . ."

As for the "lived" and *Lebenswelt*, the entry of such terms into philosophical thought marks a date or rather a turning point. Henceforth, philosophy must choose. It can stay within its habitual context and preserve its traditional categories, i.e., pure research into being by means of meditation: ontology. In this case it lapses into dogmatism, into the pure and impotent description of what exists, or into irrationalism. Conversely it can metamorphose into a critique of everyday life which uses the old ideas, above all the idea of alienation, but in a new way (which is difficult and problematic, and as yet to be determined). The option is not apparent everywhere, and is not always clear. The paths cross. Although the idea of inauthenticity is confused, it is a critical idea which we can use when we need to, modifying it and giving it practical meaning and content.

When philosophy tries to use the term the "lived" in a way which encompasses a determinable experience it immediately gets closer to becoming critical analysis of everyday life. Where does the intersubjectivity Maurice Merleau-Ponty talks about in his latest book[14] express itself, and where can it be grasped? The reply leaves no grounds for doubt, in our mind at least. All that remains is to add the negative dimension, that of radical critique.

Perhaps we will dare to go even farther and to say:

The time has come to summon up that elusive and pregnant reality, the everyday, and to bring it forth into language. The content of so much discourse has been based upon the everyday, but without being explicit or overt. Let us bring it openly and coherently into language and discourse, while not forgetting that language and discourse have their limits. Is that not a specifically philosophical procedure, or what, according to you yourself, used to be an essential procedure of philosophy? This is how Freud proceeded with sexuality, Marx with praxis, labour and production relations, Hegel with dialectical movements, Aristotle with language, logos and logic, and others with political life, the state, history, etc. With an action such as this as starting point, other creations which supersede it will become possible . . . Would this be too ambitious?

Objections from the fragmented sciences

'The social sciences – economics, history, sociology, psychology – are at an empirical and positive stage, that of specialization. They have left empirical and philosophical generalities behind once and for all. The scholar must define as narrow a *field* as possible. Then he must explore it, get close to it, and as soon as he can quantify it, he must treat it in a precise way. Thus such a scholar will no longer accept the concept of "everyday life" any more than he will any other general, totalized concept. This is all the more reason for him to reject a "critique" which cannot distinguish the value of positive facts, since by essence it denies facts in the name of a value. The scholar wants to be purely empirical and purely positive.'

Reply

'Specialists have every right, except the right to condemn critical thought to silence in the name of a conception of the real which they rarely explain and which is not relevant to anything. The "positivity" of this realness derives from critical thought, which begins by establishing that the negative and the possible are just as "real" as the positive real. The conception of a reality which would be the personal property of the specialist dealing with it produces a curious attitude: a paternalism, not to say an imperialism. Nothing gives these specialists the right to observe everyday life from aloft and from afar simply because they do not deem it worthy of being a specialism.

In any case, it would be easy to demonstrate that their specialisms often overlap into everyday life: they cut into it technically. Too many specialists regard their "field" as private property. As far as their "realness" is concerned, they have a curious way of dealing with it, which consists in thickening it, giving it consistency, making it so stiff it stands up by itself. As housewives say when they whip cream or make mayonnaise: they thicken it. Once it has "thickened", this realness is no longer a small field; it is a domain, a region, and if it has been whipped up by an expert hand it even becomes a little "world". Next, once his right of ownership has been established and he holds the deeds in his hand, the specialist can relax completely, enjoying his field and thinking about who he will bequeath it to. He can also think about extending it by appropriating more land. He becomes a touch imperialistic. Once the specialist becomes an unwitting technocrat, this is how his alienating and alienated, reifying and reified attitude functions. However, the best possible reply would be to integrate a "conceptual development" with a coherent set of empirical research programmes. We think that study (critique) of everyday life lends itself particularly to such a confrontation between facts and concepts. It goes without saying that concepts which originated in philosophy but which are no longer part of any philosophical system (alienation, totality, cycle, repetition, the process of dialectical becoming, etc.) must be tested by facts. If they survive this test, they will take their place among those concepts which allow us to dominate the plethora of facts and to go beyond the scope of fragmented research; in other words, they will become scientific concepts. As we know, an orientation of this kind is not without its difficulties. How are we to demolish an edifice as sturdy as philosophy? If a construction is coherent, how are we to extract separate concepts from it? And then, how are we to confront these concepts with facts in order to make them concrete? According to what criteria are we to ascertain that they have become experimental and that they have graduated from speculative philosophy to scientific knowledge?

These difficulties are at the heart of our research. They are its specific problems. In any event, critique of everyday life (in so far as it is knowledge as well as critique) consists of a twofold rejection of fragmented specialization and of the elevation of any specific science into the sum total of the other fragmented sciences (and is thus a rejection of sociologism, historicism and psychologism). There is a precise point on which we can reassure the specialists. Critique of everyday life is not intended to be a new specialism, or a particular branch of sociology. What it is undertaking is a total critique of totality. The most specialized and most technical research programmes are legitimate only if they satisfy the following conditions: that they do not change into a technocratic dictatorship within the social sciences (and elsewhere) and that the specialists admit the "positivity" of several negative and critical concepts which do not introduce value judgements external to the facts but which are clearly necessary for those facts to be understood.

We find that once the specialist has "set" the real to a compact consistency, giving the illusion of concrete perfection, it is often more apparent than real. The world of appearances lends itself to such treatment. The dialectic of what is real and what is apparent is well known. There is no pure appearance, no phenomenon which could only be a phenomenon without something behind it. The "real" displays itself by means of phenomena, thus by means of appearances: what is essential is made manifest. Thus every appearance and every phenomenon contains a certain reality. They reveal and they conceal this reality. To reach the essential, knowledge must both grasp it and push it to one side. Let us add here and now that these concepts of dialectical logic and methodology must be made relative. Appearance from one point of view is reality from another point of view. Thus, for the sociologist, up to a certain point, the psychological is appearance, and vice versa.

In critical analysis of everyday life, today's "consumer society" represents such a world of appearances. It hides a deeper reality: the manufacture of consumers by those who hold the means of production and who produce for profit. Consequently their perception of what needs are is governed by the profits to be gained from them. At the same time, this appearance contains and reveals a certain reality: the elimination of traditional "lifestyles", the levelling of needs, and the narrowing of the gaps between needs and lifestyles (and as we have said before, this does not mean the equalizing of standards of living).'

Objections from culturalists and structuralists

'How right you are to criticize the fragmented knowledge provided by specialized techniques and to wish to integrate them into a corpus of knowledge! But come on, at least be coherent! Follow your thinking through to its logical conclusion. What is a corpus of knowledge without organization, without an inner structure, without systematization? So, if a coherent structure such as this is to correspond to reality, surely general concepts, forms and structures must already be inherent in that reality. All knowledge relates to a totality. The idea of totality belongs at the centre of the real and at the centre of knowledge. This idea alone can guarantee that the two correspond. Moreover, in this day and age this ancient philosophical idea is becoming more precise. The ideas of structure, form, signification, culture and world-view make it more concrete; when they separate it from specifically philosophical systematizations, they give it the capacity to explore the real. If these ideas are profound enough to permit inexhaustible explanations, they are exhaustible in terms of the historical, economic and sociological humanness they encompass. From the moment it ceases to refer to a totality, critique of everyday life has no object . . .'

Reply

'The present prestige of the concept of *structure* arises largely from a general confusion. How could a concept which brings order and classification to all this chaos not be welcome? However, this coherence should not obscure movement. If the logical application of the concept of structure disguises the "destructurings" and "restructurings" which are in operation – the changes and action of the negative – then that too must be submitted to radical critique. Once the theoreticians of a science have discovered a fruitful concept, after a relatively extended period of time they often lose their scientific circumspection. They too forget that, inevitably, every concept and every technique has its limits, and so they proceed like the philosophers of the past did, and like specialists and technicians are doing today. They extrapolate from a strictly determined investigation. They transform the fruitful concept into an absolute, an ontological principle. They too become dogmatic. Thus an implement for knowledge, which is valid in certain conditions and in a determined sphere, is turned into a fetish. Over the last few years we have seen how the importance of certain otherwise valid concepts, such as structure, signification and totality, has been exaggerated to the point of fetishism. This fact is all the more remarkable in that certain minds which have strayed along the path of fetishism and dogmatism have in the past been often brilliant and worthy opponents of other fetishisms and dogmatisms. In this way we pass from the methodologically legitimate use of "structure" to a dogmatic structuralism, from the valid use of "culture" to a culturalism. More particularly, as soon as the theoretician believes he has grasped the idea of *totality*, it lays itself open to dogmatic misuse. At that point, he will either integrate you into his totality, or he will reject you.

The excuse of these theoreticians is that only by employing concepts can their limits be determined. How can one tell in advance whether a certain use is legitimate or not? Experience shows us that use quickly becomes misuse. Ideas have boundaries. We must do everything in our power to find out where these boundaries lie, and if we are to map them out we must cross them. Extrapolations and exaggerations are inevitable. All in all, a dogmatism which presumes to mark boundaries, and to signal danger zones in advance, presents more dangers than speculative unilaterality. These are likely to lead to the same tempting deception: dogmatism and the ontological illusion.

Theoretically, every concept exhausts itself. Thus excesses, superfluities, extrapolation and fetishisms contain within themselves their own critique (which is not to say that dogmatisms are capable of autocritique!). In practical terms, "scientific milieux" are human groups, and behave like many other groups. They will only give up on an interest, a technique or an idea when it has become "*saturated*". This consideration leads us prematurely into the everyday life of science, into the sociology of the mandarinate and the sociology of boredom. Let us put it to one side. Conclusion: we must resign ourselves to seeing concepts used until they are exhausted, and consequently to witnessing the saturation of these milieux. Let us generalize with the following Hegelian aphorism: the moment a dogmatism triumphs is the moment its end is nigh.

Having said that, it is impossible to separate "life" (nature), everyday life and culture into a kind of theoretical triumvirate. Such a distinction would duplicate the old theory of the three elements of man: the body, the soul and the mind. But these are merely preliminary considerations, not really pertinent to our concerns and, when all's said and done, they are merely academic. Let us go to the heart of the matter. Yes, there are social structures which maintain and cement society "as it is" (by aligning it with things, which, as we know so well, are what they are) on different levels of existence and consciousness. The principal function of these social structures is to obscure the horizons of everyday life, making it appear as a mere series of real moments within the real, and nothing more.

Yes, there is a culture which plays its part in structures, and it is located alongside other superstructures with less dignified names. Its main function is to make everyday life (apparently) coherent, to establish its coherence with itself and with the so-called superior norms and models, to blend "existence", "the lived", "the everyday" together until they are indistinguishable, and until future possibilities are blocked off, and the metamorphosis of the everyday appears impossible.

To the age-old problem of philosophers: "How can what is *be*?", to Kant's problem: "How can we know what we know?", to the problem of more recent thinkers: "How can what is born be born", we add another, simpler but just as serious: "How can men live as they are living, and how can they accept it?" Put another way, why does not every one of us imitate the man (the bourgeois) Kierkegaard talks about, who without warning feels he is suffocating and begins shouting: "Give me something possible! Give me something possible!"? This is an incontestable cultural fact, and demonstrates the effect structures have.

Voluntarily or not, when structure and culture are fetishized there is a risk that, although they are provisional and questionable, they will be turned into absolutes.

Our avowed aim is on the contrary to dissolve these structures and to demonstrate their state of dissolution in the very procedures of their restrictive functions. It is also to demonstrate the advanced disintegration of a culture which is all the more "negative" because it wishes itself and calls itself "positive". Because it claims to create something real, it is all the more destructive of future possibilities.

However well-meaning their scientific intentions are, the purveyors of structuralism and culturalism have not thought their concepts through, and this is our bone of contention with them. We will employ these self-same concepts in our arguments against their apologists, and against others as well.

As for the idea of totality, the problem is even more complex, and we will need to consider it very closely.

The idea of everyday life is only meaningful within a totality, but we must perceive that totality dialectically. If totality (society as a whole, social structure, culture, etc.) is to correspond to anything at all, all it must do is admit and contain levels (or if you like, "degrees" or "stages"). Everyday life can be defined as a level of social practice within totality. Or, in less unattractive and more poetic words, as a somewhat neglected fragment of it.

This introduces an additional reason why it is essential to elucidate the constantly used but as yet unclarified concept of *level . . .*'

The 'class perspective' and its arguments

'The real life, the everyday life of the working class has nothing in common with that of the bourgeoisie. It is therefore impossible to conflate them in the same concept, or to study them under the same heading. That would be an idealist distortion: the point of view of a sociologist who ignores class contradictions. Moreover, if it is true that the world and life must be changed, why study the very thing which has to be changed, which has to be transformed? The hardships of proletarian life should only be considered in order to provoke shame and anger, in other words for propaganda reasons only . . .'

Reply

'The partisans of the "class perspective" often forget that the proletariat and the bourgeoisie make up the same society, which is much more complex than the representation of two conflicting forces, face to face and mutually exclusive. Even in the struggles and conflicts of class and their antagonisms, the wholeness of society does not disappear (which is what justifies terms such as "society", "world society", "society as a whole", etc., which otherwise would be meaningless). This is a truism which Stalin himself sometimes had to point out to those class-perspective dogmatists who were frequently guilty of class subjectivism. To round this point off, let us add that "society" is not only French society (or American, or Russian, in other words one specific national society), it is also capitalist (or socialist) society, modern industrial (or technological) society. While accepting that they designate units or types which are larger than a country or a nation, we have yet to determine the exact meaning of these terms, and exactly what the links between them are.

In a specific society (French and capitalist for example), at a certain state of development of the productive forces, at a certain level of civilization, do the *needs* of the working class differ absolutely from the needs of the bourgeoisie? This study demonstrates that they do not. Indeed, these needs are similar, and as we have already said, this is the reality of the otherwise mystifying idea of "consumer society". Needs are related to the productive forces and their level of development. Even more significant would be the question that, if the proletariat differs from the bourgeoisie from this perspective, would it not be because of the liveliness, complexity and abundance of its needs and desires? Certainly, while there is a quantitative and qualitative disparity (of "standards of living") between the extent to which these needs and desires are satisfied, needs tend to equalize. Privation and frustration (with their corollary: protest activity) imply and reveal the growth of needs, if only in their initial stages. This idea is important. It could be that an eventual and certainly *possible* social transformation might come from the pressure brought by needs more than by absolute poverty, want and pauperization.

When the unremitting partisans of the "class perspective" presented the car, the refrigerator, the washing machine and the television set as examples of superfluous and parasitic consumption by social strata which themselves were parasitic, they made several mistakes (objectively and scientifically speaking). They failed to understand the growth of needs and the way they have been used – and diverted – in bourgeois society. They confused differing facts: political propaganda via the television, for example, and the generalized need for information and communication. They replaced knowledge by ideology and real problems by the illusion of dogmatic certainty. In a word, they were perpetuating a rather old-fashioned, almost mythic image of the working class: a mass united by poverty, destitution, toil, absence of pleasures and profound want, including the want of basic needs.

In the general theory of needs, we will demonstrate how the proletariat as such contains the total human phenomenon – need, work, pleasure[15] – and how it remains close to the fundamental spontaneity which is revealed in these three dimensions. Dogmatism has no right to reduce the working-class social and human being to a single dimension, labour (on the pretext of saving the working class from reformism and of preserving an abstractly revolutionary project).

In this light, the bourgeoisie presents a mutilated reality, in that all it wants is pure pleasure. It is stricken by alienation, different from but more profound than the alienation which mutilates groups within the working class. Through dissatisfactions and privations, the working class maintains and asserts human totality. In other words, it bears what is most burdensome in the everyday. All it has is its everyday life. And if its life is to be transformed, then everyday life must be transformed, or to put it another way, sooner or later the working class will transform itself and will transform "the world" by transforming everyday life. That is the truth within "the class perspective", a truth which is not apparent in the discourse of those who support it . . .'

The political argument

'Political revolution transforms the world. It starts by transforming everyday life, since it happens precisely when the members of a society no longer wish to go on living as they have lived hitherto. It is true that this initial transformation is not absolute: it continues during the construction of socialism and the gradual transition to communism. Historical circumstances can facilitate this transition or hinder it. In any event, after the revolution, everyday life in socialist countries has nothing in common with everyday life in capitalist countries, which are controlled and developed by the bourgeoisie. It takes on a different meaning. Political consciousness, the consciousness of man living in the future and for the future, is enough to change it completely. Any comparison would be meaningless, and can never be anything other than absurd. So that in itself to compare means to betray, to deny, to reject what is essential in favour of what is contingent.

Reply

'In the political or "party" perspective it is not difficult to detect the extension of the "class perspective" pushed to the absolute. The Marxist officials who support it confuse the ideological with the lived, and this confusion makes up part of their ideology. The error is twofold: to exaggerate the role of ideology is to compromise it by wrongly muddling it up with the praxis it produces or "reflects". There is no longer any distinction between what knowledge, ideology, theory and praxis really are. A philosophical blanket has been thrown over everything.

It is certain that in the countries of the "socialist camp", ideologies and, more generally, superstructures have changed in the wake of a political revolution. Therefore everyday life has changed for people living on the plane of superstructures: the political and administrative apparatus, the militants, the ideologues, the men of politics. One can see that as ideologues, statesmen and members of an apparatus, they set themselves up on a plane exterior and superior to the everyday. Since Marx, this analysis has formed part of the theory of the state, of ideologies and of superstructures.

In the socialist countries, profound and irreversible historical changes have taken place in terms of society as a whole. All well and good. Politically, the state has transformed itself, although without moving towards the withering away contemplated by Marx and by Lenin. Economically, the process of accumulation is accelerating, above all in heavy industry (production of the means of production). As far as technical progress is concerned, these countries are in the lead. However, in so far as we know anything about it, the experience of the socialist countries demonstrates that their everyday life is changing very slowly. Everyday life may well be the slowest thing to change, and as soon as it experiences any difficulties, it may even adopt the old forms again, falling back into time-worn ruts. It can be backward, and very much so, in terms of the processes operating at the economic base (the productive forces) and at the apex (the ideological and political superstructures). Between the two, on the intermediary level of social relations, the everyday drags itself along in the wake of change. More than that: it resists change. Individuals and groups, including the working class, withdraw into the everyday,

34

or at least when comprehensive changes do not offer them a new, acceptable and desirable lifestyle. Can one blame them? The masses come together to make revolution because they are no longer willing to live as hitherto. If revolution fails to bring them the new life they hoped for (and which perhaps can be expressed in Utopian terms: revolution, communism), if the revolution only changes representations, these masses seek refuge in an everyday which is an extension of the previous one: private life, scant public or political life, family life, life based upon the close relations of neighbourhood and friendships. Could not these facts be responsible for one of the inner contradictions of the world socialist and communist movement? On one hand, an officialized ethic encourages this withdrawal, which makes it possible to distinguish between work and life beyond work, and thus to devote the maximum energy to productive labour. On the other hand, is it not sometimes necessary to shatter the stability of the everyday and the obscure resistance it puts up through the structures it re-establishes at times of important change?

Now let us go to the heart of the problem. Official Marxism is inspired by Marxist thought. In fact, it does retain a certain number of concepts and representations (in political economy, in general politics, in philosophy and in ideology). However, it has lost sight of the initial Marxist agenda. Moreover, the purpose of the general philosophy which has placed itself under the patronage of Marx is to conceal this oversight or omission. Its role is to entertain and to divert. In the name of philosophical materialism (historical and dialectical, the one hopelessly confused with the other), it makes no attempt to reinstate the initial Marxist project, improperly insisting instead upon the materiality of the outside world, on its exteriority and anteriority in relation to thought and consciousness. The test and criterion of this abuse is the theory of the withering away of the state, which was essential to Marx and Lenin, but was concealed during the Stalinist period.

What did Marx want? What did the initial Marxist project consist of? Let us reinstate it once again in all its authenticity. First and foremost Marx wanted to change everyday life. To change the world is above all to change the way everyday, real life is lived. In so far as the times he lived in allowed him to contemplate such hypotheses, Marx considered that the upheaval in external nature and the conquest of space as a result of technical development on a colossal scale would only happen after human life had been metamorphosed.

How did he imagine this would be? We know that he was careful not to construct the future along the lines of Utopian socialists such as Saint-Simon, Fourier or Owen (although their theories had inspired him). He was mindful of the role of the unforeseen and the new in historical development (and how right he was!). Nevertheless he suggested certain tendencies which must be prolonged or promoted if superior wholeness and totality is to be achieved, if divided man is to be superseded, and if "the world turned topsy-turvy" is to be set aright again.

In Marx there are two projects for the transformation of everyday life. They lie halfway between Utopia and practice, but they both imply a total revolutionary praxis.

The first project is of an *ethical* order. It stipulates that the reciprocity of the needs and desires of men (as individuals and groups) be recognized. It implies the knowledge and, even better, the transparency of the relations between the two. It implies the end of the "social mystery", in other words of everything which makes the relations between men opaque and elusive, and which conceals these relations from their consciousness and their actions.

It is clear that this project is an extension of Hegelian thought, but with one essential modification. It is no longer the state which embodies and fulfils the ethical idea. On the contrary it is private, everyday life which raises itself to the superior level of the ethical; it is as though one of the effects of the withering away of the state is that the state's very substance is assimilated by the domain which has been kept exterior to it, subordinated to it and reduced by it to an abstraction which is a reverse but symmetrical image of the state's own abstraction. Marx proved the state guilty of malpractice: by its very essence it perpetuates the social mystery, swathing "private" and "public" social relations in murky shadows, by the simple fact that it splits them, divides them and makes them abstract.

The second project is *aesthetic* in nature. It is committed to the notion of art as a higher creative activity, and a radical critique of art as an alienated activity (exceptional, allocated to exceptional individuals and producing exceptional works which are external and superior to everyday life). At one and the same time, art must fulfil itself, and then supersede itself. Ultimately it must disappear. The creative activity of art and the work of art foreshadow joy at its highest.[16] For Marx, enjoyment of the world is not limited to the consumption of material goods, no matter how refined, or to the consumption of cultural goods, no matter how subtle. It is much more than that. He does not imagine a world in which all men would be surrounded by works of art, not even a society where everyone would be painters, poets or musicians. Those would still only be transitional stages. He imagines a society in which everyone would rediscover the spontaneity of natural life and its initial creative drive, and perceive the world through the eyes of an artist, enjoy the sensuous through the eyes of a painter, the ears of a musician and the language of a poet. Once superseded, art would be reabsorbed into an everyday which has been metamorphosed by its fusion with what had hitherto been kept external to it.

All in all, according to the first model, in the realms of the state and of politics, and consequently in objective morality and the law, the social powers of men have been alienated. They must turn back to and reabsorb themselves in private life in order to metamorphose it. According to the second model, men's spiritual powers, which have been realized but alienated in art, must journey back to ordinary life and invest themselves in it by transforming it.

As it happens, the duality of these images of what is possible opens up a new problem, that of the supersession of this duality in an even more total metamorphosis of the everyday, which would be achieved by the intervention of a unifying praxis.

Utopia? Fantasy? Imagination? It's unimportant. If one is inspired by Marx, everything must be judged in relation to his project: reality, what is possible, what has been achieved, history, revolution.

In fact, Marx provided very practical bases for this "Utopian" project: the growth of the productive forces in a pleasure economy (geared towards the greatest satisfaction of the greatest number of social needs and individual desires, quantitatively increased and qualitatively refined), the withering away of the state, etc.

It is evident that world revolution has not exactly followed the path Marx predicted. Why should we not admit it? The power alien to human thoughts and intentions, which we must call "destiny" ("historical necessity" and at the same time "randomness", "chance", "historical drift" in terms of projects and actions) is alone responsible. There has been no revolution in the advanced industrialized countries. Capitalism has corralled it. Revolution has been forced to abandon everything which in the first few years still corresponded to the original project. It has been forced to devote itself to accumulation, to giving priority to heavy industry, to maintaining a powerful army with all the equipment this entails. Thus technological imperatives have moved to the foreground. In a remarkably uneven development, everyday life has lagged behind technology to an immense degree! Given all the random circumstances, this was inevitable and "necessary". We must recognize the work of historical necessity in so far as it has made reality deviate in relation to the project, and results in relation to intentions. Let us accept this discrepancy. We should evaluate it rather than deny that it exists. If knowledge does not gain from this, then ideology will.

Has Marx's programme lost its meaning and validity? No. It is still the only project which implies a true conception of what is humanly possible. Why? Because it is alone in not contemplating simply a transformation of ideas or representations – an ideology – but rather a total metamorphosis of everyday life, bringing to an end those divisions and contradictions which make "the real" and "the possible" lag behind in a period when *uneven development* has become the norm.

Up until now, one of the great paradoxes of the twentieth century has been that capitalist economy has apparently taken the form of a "pleasure economy". Like a caricature of itself, this economy sometimes goes so far as to become organized waste. Since it conceals the economy of power while organizing, controlling and pulverizing pleasure, it is a form of mystification. In fact, as regards quantity and quality, it is very restricted. In a contradictory way it arouses many needs and desires, some artificial, the rest unsatisfied. Satisfaction is characterized by accident and contingency. It is "a stroke of good fortune", a windfall, a happy piece of luck. In so far as the words mean anything, joy and happiness consist of a series of favourable encounters and chances. Freedom, so frequently exalted, is no more than the skill of making the most of luck and chance . . . This explains the importance of luck and chance both in the highest theoretical thinking and in the ideologies some extremely unsophisticated people adopt and "live" on a practical basis . . .

However, it is still true that the socialist countries have not even begun to develop the features of a genuine pleasure economy. Far from it! Supposing that the imperatives of accumulation become less urgent in the USSR, for how many more years will they predominate in China? This does not mean that everyday life in the USSR, or elsewhere, is not already taking on some new qualities. The satisfaction of needs has lost its accidental, contingent and risky character, at least in part. If this constitutes a new quality, it does not mean that other aspects are obscured. Only a concrete, on-the-spot analysis of everyday life, using all the possibilities open to investigation and eschewing all ideological preoccupations, would allow us to specify the differences on this level between socialist society and capitalist society.

Next we could compare the everyday lives and everyday-life relations with their ideological representations. In so far as we are able to make this comparison, on the bourgeois side money gives prestige and power, in other words every possible joy, while on the socialist side it is prestige and status, in other words power, which give a range of advantages, one of which is money or its equivalents. Does this reversal rectify the world turned topsy-turvy, the upside-down world Marx talks about? Hardly.

Meaning or signification can change while "reality" remains analogous and stable, or perhaps we should say, almost stable. This is doubtless true. But if radical critique denounces the snares of "significations", which change while real substance does not, if it rejects moralism and the operation which consists in mistaking moral appearance for concrete reality and reality for the manifeston of the moral, why should it spare the official ideology of socialism? The ideological presentation of the acceleration of the cumulative process and of the intensification of productive labour as the fulfilment of socialism or of communism is objectively inadmissable. Scientifically, socialism can only be defined as production subordinated to social needs (and not to political imperatives). That in the course of a strategic operation and at a decisive moment the politician should declare: "If you're not with us, you're against us", is inevitable. The logic of decision-making demands it. But while ideologues are forever imposing this implacable logic on concepts and thought, knowledge cannot accept it. It goes against its own laws. They say:

Give us a few more years breathing space. Socialism, in other words the colossal creative effort of the masses guided and directed by scientific ideology, will resolve all the problems simultaneously: the conquest of space, the development of the backward countries, the satisfaction of every need, genuine sexual equality in everyday life, the conditions for happiness and for the flowering of individuals, the unleashing of their creativity, of lifestyle and the art of living, and reasons for living.[17]

Very well, let them have this breathing space. We are patient. For a start. the fact that they are still asking us to be patient and to give them a breathing space means that they are asking for the possibility that "history" should continue without being interrupted by some gigantic catastrophe. Very good. How could we refuse to support such an idea? We live in hope, which is to say that we have returned to the Marxist project; we are reinstating it in all its authenticity; we are presenting it once again as the aim and meaning of history. And yet we feel anxious and we admit it. We already know that history does not always go the way we would wish. It creates; at one and the same time it brings the unforeseen (which knowledge discovers "after the event" to have been necessary, except when ideology disguises this necessity!) – and the irreversible. The past weighs heavy. Socialism will never be exactly what it would have been had history proceeded in another way. What does it need to put "history" right, to halt its drift? Who can we turn to? Who can we trust? In the willingness or the good intentions of leaders and of specialists in economics and politics? Marx warns us about falling into this naive trap, as old as the world itself. Only the growth of social needs, the subdued but constant pressure of the proletarian masses, can shift the process in this direction. Constant pressure, i.e., gradual effectiveness (to use careful and precise terminology). In short, we have no choice but to place our bets on democracy.

As for revolution in general, and on the conceptual plane on which we are operating here, we say of it what Rimbaud said of love: 'Revolution must be reinvented.' And we must not worry about tactics or political strategy, or even about being immediately effective. As in Marx's thought, revolution must be reinvented, starting from a conception of what is possible. In other words, it is a choice between the various possibilities, then returning once more to the present and to the real to grasp them and to judge them. First, and patiently, we

have reinstated the initial Marxist agenda, a project which is both
Utopian and practical, the idea of a total praxis which will resolve
the contradictions by eliminating all alienating divisions. Second, in
taking Marxism up again as radical critique of everyday life in this
way, we are shedding light on precisely what revolution would
change, if the real stopped lagging behind the possible. Third, we will
continue measuring the gaps between the following terms: revolution
and achievement, the real and the potential. Last, in so far as knowledge has strength, and gives more than just ethical patience and
aesthetic irony, we will bring pressure to bear on the situation in an
attempt to narrow these gaps. In Volume I of *Critique of Everyday Life*
our aim was simply to give the everyday access to history and to
political life. Today we must build a long-term policy on how to
answer the demands for a radical transformation of everyday life.'

8

How can everyday life be defined? It surrounds us, it besieges us, on
all sides and from all directions. We are inside it and outside it. No
so-called 'elevated' activity can be reduced to it, nor can it be separated from it. Its activities are born, they grow and emerge; once
they have left the nourishing earth of their native land, not one of
them can be formed and fulfilled on its own account. In this earth
they are born. If they emerge, it is because they have grown and
prospered. It is at the heart of the everyday that projects become
works of creativity.

Knowledge, science and scientific discovery sometimes consist of
brief instants of discovery. Yet science has its everyday life: training,
teaching, the climate in scientific circles, administrative questions,
the way institutions operate, etc.

The professional soldier dedicates himself to heroism. The army
prepares itself for war; that is its aim and its purpose. And yet
moments of combat and opportunities to be heroic are thin on the
ground. The army has its everyday life: life in barracks and more precisely life among the troops (otherwise known as the 'contingent';
lexical familiarity may veil what is ironic and dialectical about this,
but here, as elsewhere, the 'contingent' is the 'necessary'!). This

everyday life is not without its importance in relation to dreams of heroism and the fine moral ideal of the professional soldier. It is the springboard for sublime actions. Questions of rank, promotion and military honours are part of it. There is a saying that army life is made up of a lot of boredom and a couple of dangerous moments.

Let us consider the state and the practical operation of its managerial spheres. There is an everyday life of the state. It is not the same thing as the everyday (private) lives of public figures. It has a well-known name: bureaucracy. There is a political everyday, the everyday of parties, apparatus, relations between these bodies and the masses who elect them and whom they administer. To study the everyday life of the state would thus be to study *in vivo* and *in concreto* the functions and the functioning of bureaucratic apparatuses and their relation to social praxis. Emerging above this everyday life are important decisions and dramatic moments of decisive action.

Factories, trades unions, work and the relations between workers all have their own everyday life. And from that everyday life come strikes, or the introduction of new technologies, etc.

9

Should we define the everyday as the petty side of life, its humble and sordid element? As we have already said, yes and no. Yes, this small, humble and sordid side of all human existence has been part of the everyday since time began, and until there is a project and a policy to restore technical possibilities to the everyday in order to overturn it from top to bottom, it may well be so for a long time to come.

> Every day thousands upon thousands of women sweep up the dust which has gathered imperceptibly since the previous day. After every meal, too numerous to count, they wash the dishes and saucepans. For times too numerous to count, by hand or in the machine, they remove the dirt which has built up bit by bit on sheets and clothes; they stop up the holes the gentle rubbing of heels inevitably makes; they fill emptied cupboards and refrigerators with packets of pasta and kilos of fruit and vegetables . . . [*which explains the following definition of everyday life:*] The ensemble of activities which of necessity result from the general processes of development: evolution, growth and aging, of biological or

social protection or change, those processes which escape immediate notice and which are only perceptible in their consequences.[18]

This attempt at a definition, with the vivid description which accompanies it, sheds a remarkable light on one aspect of the everyday: the reverse side of all praxis. However, it prompts several reservations and criticisms. Like all definitions, it tends to immobilize what it is trying to define, presenting it as timeless and unchangeable. And as definitions frequently do, it takes one aspect or one part as the whole.

If things were like this, the study of everyday life would be easy and critique of it would be effortless. It would suffice to note down and emphasize trivial details from one day to the next, the daily gestures with their inevitable repetitions. And after that a simple project: work, family life, immediate relations (block of flats, neighbourhood or village, town), leisure. The impoverished eloquence of tape-recorded interviews would reveal the poverty and misfortunes of the everyday. Analysis of the content of these interviews, and in particular of their language, would quickly single out a certain number of themes: loneliness, monotony, insecurity, discussions on solutions and the absence of solutions, on the advantages and disadvantages of marriage, on professional occupations.[19] One could possibly examine these themes using the well-tried methods of sociology or combinative analysis. One might succeed in determining fairly precisely attitudes within or towards the everyday (attitudes of acceptance, but more often of rejection) in certain groups. As well as quantifying in this way, the inquiry would retain a certain number of privileged pieces of evidence. It could even go so far as to attempt some experiments (similar to the somewhat too successful experiment in which a study group simulated a serious car accident in order to observe the behaviour of the other drivers on the road!).

With the help of a little irony, this path could lead us a long way. One may conceive of a sociology of the reverse images of society and of its duplicates, sacred or cursed. A social group is characterized just as much by what it rejects as by what it consumes and assimilates. The more economically developed a country is, the more gets thrown away, and the faster it gets thrown away. People are wasteful. In New York, in the promised land of free enterprise, the dustbins are enormous, and the more visible they are the more inefficiently public services operate. In underdeveloped countries, nothing is thrown away. The smallest piece of paper or string, the smallest tin is of use, and even excrement is gathered. What we are outlining here is a sociology of the dustbin.

Cemeteries, for their part, present a splendid 'negative' of built-up areas, villages, towns large and small. In their mirror, they faithfully 'reflect' social structure, economic life, and ideologies. As such, they deserve to be studied sociologically as much as any other social phenomenon. Finally, the men society rejects are no less interesting than those whom society assimilates, and down-and-outs still have a lot to teach us.

The sociology of 'duplicates' would not limit itself to these tarnished mirrors. It would study more attractive reverse images, although not necesssarily less disappointing ones. For example, 'leisure clubs'[20] where in the effort to break with everyday life by escaping from it, a strange everyday life, equally alienating and alienated, is reconstructed in caricature.

If this were all there was, critique of everyday life would only bring the disappointing aspects of social praxis to the fore. It would emphasize the trivial and the repellant. It would paint a black picture of dissatisfaction. It would tend to concentrate on the sordid side of life, on suffering, on a rather old-fashioned populism. It would use the pseudo-realism of a Bernard Buffet or the stammering, desperate lyricism of a Samuel Beckett as a means of understanding social man. If this were the only path it followed, critique of everyday life would be barely distinguishable from a certain branch of existentialism which took it upon itself – and very skilfully – to underline the marginal elements of existence. To a philosophy like this, all analysis of everyday life would contribute would be scientific jargon and a stodgy sociological pretentiousness.

The hypothesis of our study is rather different. According to this hypothesis, which underpins the programme as a whole, it is in everyday life and starting from everyday life that genuine *creations* are achieved, those creations which produce the human and which men produce as part of the process of becoming human: works of creativity.

These superior activities are born from seeds contained in everyday practice. From the moment groups or individuals are able and obliged to plan ahead, to organize their time and to use whatever means they have at their disposal, reason is formed in social practice. As day follows trivial day, the eye learns how to see, the ear learns how to hear, the body learns how to keep to rhythms. But the essential lies elsewhere. What is most important is to note that feelings, ideas, lifestyles and pleasures are confirmed in the everyday. Even, and above all, when exceptional activities have created them, they have to turn back towards everyday life to verify and confirm the validity of that creation. Whatever is produced or constructed in the superior realms of social practice must demonstrate its reality in the everyday, whether it be art, philosophy or politics. At this level alone can it be authenticated. What does such and such an idea or creative work tell us? In what way and how far does it change our lives? It is everyday life which measures and embodies the changes which take place 'somewhere else', in the 'higher realms'. The human world is not defined simply by the historical, by culture, by totality or society as a whole, or by ideological and political super-structures. It is defined by this intermediate and mediating *level*: everyday life. In it, the most concrete of dialectical movements can be observed: need and desire, pleasure and absence of pleasure, satis-faction and privation (or frustration), fulfilments and empty spaces, work and non-work. The repetitive part, in the mechanical sense of the term, and the creative part of the everyday become embroiled in a permanently reactivated circuit in a way which only dialectical analysis can perceive.

In short, the everyday is not a synonym for *praxis*. If we look at it in its entirety, praxis is the equivalent of totality in action; it encom-passes the base and the superstructures, as well as the interactions between them. This view of praxis may be rather too sweeping, but if we substitute it with something more restricted and determined, it will disintegrate into fragmented practices: technology, politics, etc. We will have to look at the category of *praxis* again. For us, the every-day is a *level*.

Critique of unfulfilment and alienation should not be reduced to a bleak picture of pain and despair. It implies an endless appeal to *what is possible* in order to judge the present and what has been accomplished. It examines the dialectical movements intrinsic to what is concrete in the human, i.e., to the everyday: the possible and the impossible, the random and the certain, the achieved and the potential. The real can only be grasped and appreciated via potentiality, and what has been achieved via what has not been achieved. But it is also a question of *determining* the possible and the potential and of knowing which yardstick to use. Vague images of the future and man's prospects are inadequate. These images allow for too many more-or-less technocratic or humanist interpretations. If we are to know and to judge, we must start with a precise criterion and a centre of reference: the everyday.

It is in this sense that in Volume I of *Critique of Everyday Life* we defined everyday life initially as the region where man appropriates not so much external nature but *his own nature* – as a zone of demarcation and junction between the *uncontrolled sector* and the *controlled sector* of life – and as a region where *goods* come into confrontation with needs which have more or less been transformed into desires.

This definition is not exhaustive, and needs to be more thorough. Let us go back to the definition we suggested previously. It raises several questions concerning the general processes of growth, development, maturation and decline. To what extent do these general processes (not only individual ones, but social and historical as well) go beyond the boundaries of the everyday? Do they abandon it? To what extent do they return to it?

This is a question which will have to be addressed.

10

Let us look at things from another perspective. Let us use our thought and imagination to exclude specialized activities from praxis. If this abstraction is successful, it will rid practical experience of discreet occupations like the use of such and such a technique or implement (but not, of course, in physical terms of effort, time consumed, rhythm or absence of rhythm). What are we left with?

Nothing (or virtually nothing), say the positivists, scientists, technologues and technocrats, structuralists, culturalists, etc.

Everything, say the metaphysicians, who would consider that this abstraction or analytic operation scarcely attains the 'ontic' and is still far removed from the 'ontological', i.e., it fails to grasp the foundation, being (or nothingness).

Something, we will say, which is not easy to define, precisely since this 'something' is not a thing, nor a precise activity with determined outlines. So what is it? A mixture of nature and culture, the historical and the lived, the individual and the social, the real and the unreal, a place of transitions, of meetings, interactions and conflicts, in short a *level* of reality.

In one sense there is nothing more simple and more obvious than everyday life. How do people live? The question may be difficult to answer, but that does not make it any the less clear. In another sense nothing could be more superficial: it is banality, triviality, *repetitiveness*. And in yet another sense nothing could be more profound. It is existence and the 'lived', revealed as they are before speculative thought has transcribed them: what must be changed and what is the hardest of all to change.

This proves the general methodological principle of *double determination*. In our opinion, this principle is essential to dialectical thought, which is not restricted simply to discovering links (differences, oppositions, polarities and reciprocal implications, conflicts and contradictions, etc.) between determinations. It discovers differences, dualities, oppositions and conflicts *within each determination* (by conceptualizing it, i.e., thinking of it within a concept).

11

Let us look from yet another perspective. Cyclic time scales submerged themselves immediately and directly in the rhythms of nature, in cosmic time scales. For a long time they held sway over human life: social man had not yet controlled nature, that is, he had not separated himself from it. His life was made up of a set of cycles and rhythms, from birth to death. The regular return of the hours, days, weeks, months, seasons and years gave rhythm to an existence which was organically linked to nature. We can go as far as the supreme cycle, the temporal system of the world, the Great Year conceived of by so many thinkers since Classical and Eastern philosophy (up to Nietzsche and Engels). Villages and cities also lived in accordance with these rhythms which did not control individual life alone. The alternation and rhythm of the generations had a profound effect upon collectivities (age groups, the preponderance of those who resisted death: old people, etc.).

The study of these time scales reveals several more precise characteristics. First, cyclic time properly speaking has no beginning and no end. Every cycle is born from another cycle and becomes absorbed in other circular movements. Cyclic time does not exclude repetitive action. The cycle is itself a repetition. However, in cyclic time, repetition is subordinated to a more 'total' body rhythm which governs the movements of the legs and the arms, for example. Second, these rhythms do not exclude enumeration and measurement; one number in particular is extremely privileged: *twelve* (with the submultiples and multiples of twelve: minutes, hours, months; the division of a circle into degrees; the notes of the tempered musical scale, etc.). Third, no genuine cycle returns exactly to its point of departure or reproduces itself exactly. No return is absolutely exact (a remarkable example: the way an octave is divided up, scales and the cycle of fifths in music). If it were otherwise, cycles would be vicious circles and the geometry of the circle would exhaust all that is physically real. Finally, cyclic and cosmic time has always been and remains the subject of magic and religious representations. It is noticeable that rational and of course industrial techniques have shattered cyclic time. Modern man detaches himself from it. He controls it. This control is first expressed by interruptions in the cycles. Cyclic time is replaced by a linear time which can always be reckoned along a trajectory or distance. Linear time is both continuous and discontinuous. Continuous: its beginning is absolute, and it grows indefinitely from an initial zero. Discontinuous: it fragments into partial time scales assigned to one thing or another according to a programme which is abstract in relation to time. It dissects indefinitely.[21] Techniques which fragment time also produce repetitive gestures. These do not and often cannot become part of a rhythm: the gestures of fragmented labour, actions which begin at any time and cease at any time.

However, cyclic time scales have not disappeared. Subordinated to linear time, broken into pieces and scattered, they live on. A very large part of biological and physiological life and a very large part of social life remain involved in cyclic time scales. Even if in a few very large cities (but not in France) public transport runs for 24 hours a day, even if a few very limited groups free themselves from the times conventionally allotted to customs such as resting, sleeping and eating, these customs remain deeply rooted. No matter how highly developed an industrial civilization may be, hunger, sleep and sex are still bound up with customs and traditions linked to cyclic time. And it would appear that emancipation from cyclic time always follows a difficult path, by way of antinature and lived abstraction. It is unnatural not to sleep at night, not to eat at specific hours, etc. How would the complete control of nature, i.e., the complete metamorphosis of everyday life, be expressed? By an arhythmic individual and social time (and also athematic, as in the example of contemporary electronic and concrete music, which shatters rhythmic time scales and traditional cycles) which would render any specific action impossible at any specific moment? By a transitory or durable group freely inventing its own rhythm? By the invention of new rhythms (of which the working day without breaks would be the blueprint)? That is the problem.

Critique of everyday life studies the persistence of rhythmic time scales within the linear time of modern industrial society. It studies the interactions between cyclic time (natural, in a sense irrational, and still concrete) and linear time (acquired, rational, and in a sense abstract and antinatural). It examines the defects and disquiet this as yet unknown and poorly understood interaction produces. Finally, it considers what metamorphoses are possible in the everyday as a result of this interaction.

In this context and in relation to this definition, we can see the everyday life of social groups in a more determined and three-dimensional way. For example, let us take a young farmer. His life is still governed by cyclic, cosmic and social time scales, especially if he is the son of a small landowning farmer in a rather backward region: days, weeks, seasons; seed times, cereal or grape harvests; youth, marriage, maturity, old age; births and funerals. He is aware of this set of cycles and of his place within it, no different from his place within the village (which still contains several features of farming communities) or the house (where the generations live side by side, among latent or violent conflicts). He can still feel more insecure in his links with nature than with society, i.e., markets, technology, urban life (unless the two impressions of insecurity are not brought together in a feeling of profound disquiet or panic). For him, the everyday appears as an organic whole which is in the process of disintegrating, but whose nucleus remains stable. Nothing separates childhood from adulthood, the family from the local community, work from leisure; nothing separates nature from social life and culture. When he is at school, he helps his parents in so far as his strength and the time at his disposal allow. As a child he has a precise and solid status which his village environment confers, a restrictive awareness of his social being which defines and limits him: 'As the son of so-and-so, he will become this and not that.' In spite of the symptoms of dissociation and the already backward character of this 'state', this young farmer still experiences a certain integration of the everyday with the cosmic on the one hand and with the community on the other. Threatening, fascinating, terrifying, the outside world is the city, it is technology, it is today's society in its entirety. A multiplicity of prohibitions still protect this young man and the nucleus of the everyday as he lives it from the ever more numerous and effective attacks from outside.

As for the young worker, he is both integrated within (modern industrial) society on a world scale and thrown to the mercy of deeper conflicts. From childhood on, what he experiences is dissociation and creative but painful contradiction. He very soon comes to know insecurity; his life feels dependent and disorganized, because rational forward planning is difficult in a working-class family (fear of unemployment or of the need to move, lack of ready money, inconvenient daily working hours, etc.). The opposition between school life and family life already presents a striking contrast; then comes the brutal transition from the life of a schoolboy to that of a worker. Life at work and life with the family offer a painful contrast. The young worker tends to assert himself in and via work; at the same time he is well aware that work imposes new dependencies upon him. It is only through a greater social dependence than before that he achieves a certain personal independence. However, he does achieve it: he will 'earn his living' by working; but soon he must take on new responsibilities, staying in or returning to the social norm, building a family and taking on a twofold dependency, both personal and social.[22] In factory life, the young worker sees himself caught up in fragmented linear time, the time of production and technology. In family life, he will rediscover cyclic, biological, physiological and social time scales.

The one enables him to resist and to compensate for the other, but the balance will be a difficult one, and certainly problematic.

1 2

Once we have outlined the definition of everyday life as a *level* (of social reality) we can consider the situation of individuals and groups in relation to this level. Conversely, it allows us to clarify the idea of level and the idea of the everyday as a level of reality.

Thus it is clear that in terms of the everyday, the situation of a housewife and a 'society woman', of a tool-maker and a mathematician, is not the same. The housewife is immersed in everyday life, submerged, swallowed up; she never escapes from it, except on the plane of unreality (dreams: fortunetellers, horoscopes, the romantic press, anecdotes and ceremonies on television, etc.). The 'society woman' gets out of it by artificial means: society life, fashion shows, snobbery, aestheticism or the pursuit of 'pure' pleasure. The mathematician gets out of it by way of an extremely specialized activity in which, as it happens, moments of creativity are few and far between. If he 'is' a mathematician and nothing but a mathematician, how insipid and unbearably obsessive he will be! The more highly qualified and technical an activity becomes, the more remote from everyday life the time it takes up becomes; and the more urgent the need becomes for a return to the everyday. For the housewife, the question is whether she can come to the surface and stay there. For the mathematician, the question is whether he can rediscover an everyday life in order to fulfil himself not only as a scholar (even if he is a genius), but also as a human being. And the 'society woman'? No questions, Your Honour.

Take this tool-maker. He has a 'good trade' (relatively speaking). Up to a certain point he likes what he does. He 'earns a good living'. But this prompts the question: *what life does he earn with his work?* The life of a tool-maker? Yes and no. Looking carefully, we would observe that his work may leave an impression on him, so that traces of it can be seen in his life outside the factory. And yet, if this man thinks only of his work, if his work and his position as a worker determine him when he is outside the factory, he is nothing more than an obsessive who has been mentally 'alienated', that is, unless he is a production activist who freely and voluntarily assumes responsibility for the alienation of labour in its entirety (which in one sense would disalienate him, but in another would alienate him more completely than anyone else!). More often than not this worker will have needs, desires or 'cravings', determined in part by the amount of energy he expends, his skill as a craftsman, his qualifications and his love of his work, but which cannot be deduced from them. These needs and cravings will be influenced by his past and his memory, his origins (a certain country, a certain province, a certain town). Generally he has a family, he has a certain way of living out the link between his work and his family life, and between the latter and the hours he devotes to leisure. What does he want? What are his preferences? What is he looking for in the games he plays, in the films he watches (unless he cannot stand playing games and going to the cinema)? Work is not enough either to determine this man's life in its entirety or to define what the everyday is to him. Nor can this everyday reality be defined by an arithmetical calculation: work + family life + leisure. He is one human being, the same everyday being who divides himself between these three sectors and undergoes these phases. He is the same and not completely the same. He keeps going through rifts and separations, in the divided (alienated) wholeness of his proletarian condition. Generally, because he is a proletarian and solidly based in the everyday, a man like this will not allow himself to be carried away by dissociation. Even if he has a variety of attitudes (in the factory, with his friends, with his trades union colleagues or in the café, with his family, playing games or at the cinema, on holiday, etc.) he does not have a variety of personalities, several 'me's. He maintains a sturdy wholeness, an individual wholeness, both in his everyday life, in the group (the working class) and in society as a whole. If we could watch him at work, we would doubtless perceive in his mannerisms and attitudes (towards his superiors, his peers and his inferiors) an echo of what he 'is' when he is not at work – and vice versa. This is because in that 'substance' or 'matter' which is neither substance nor matter as the terms are usually understood, i.e., in the everyday, every sector cross-refers to another.

What this provides is the representation of a kind of range or spectrum of situations, located between two poles which are not absolutely conflicting or separated: at one end, or rather *underneath*, men and women immersed in the everyday and submerged by it; at the other end, or rather *above*, men and women who have no sense of the everyday, detached, external, devoted to exceptional or artificial activities, integrated into groupings set up above society, 'society' people, 'pure' intellectuals, statesmen, etc.

On the lowest level, we can describe an everyday life of the people, but in the knowledge that to overemphasize it would be to become too absorbed in the sordid aspects of life. In the everyday experience of the people (or as it is usually understood, in the 'lower depths') cyclic time scales and rhythms predominate, but broken up, fragmented, eviscerated so to speak (but to an uneven degree according to social group). In the 'upper sphere' (as it is usually understood) linear time scales predominate, pointing in a single direction, but disconnected from one another.

In the 'lower depths', time and space are limited, and these limits must be endured; and yet individuals and groups have an environment; they find something compact and (relatively) solid around them and under their feet. It is a zone of sweaty, suffocating heat, of intimacy, where the temperature maintains an organic warmth. For those who have managed to escape from it, this zone is painful, even unbearable. Those who go on living within it do not really understand it, and cannot imagine any alternative to it.

In the 'upper sphere', space and time grow larger and wider: they open out indefinitely in the icy air of higher realms. Like rockets going up in a shower of sparks, activities run the risk of disintegrating and disappearing.

In the 'lower depths', people and relationships gravitate around symbols, the general meaning of which they do not understand, perceiving them only as given realities: the father and the mother, the sun, the earth, the elements. Each symbol acts as an affective and organic nucleus. It is not an innate archetype from the depths of time or being, nor is it a myth or some obscure existentialist matrix. It is a perceptible and perceived reality, the centre of a cycle and a sociocosmic rhythm: the nucleus of family life, the centre of the activity of the group throughout the day, the week or the year.

In the 'upper sphere', people move and act amid formal and conventional abstractions, or more precisely, amid signs and signals.

They have become distanced from the vitality and spontaneity of symbols. In order to wield power over nature (for themselves, or more often than not for others) they live through antinature. Thus the quest for power contains its own weakness, and weakness contains a certain power.

In the 'lower depths', people are weak but tenacious, like life itself. In more empirical terms, i.e., in terms of a description of praxis, they live inside a narrow time scale, with no understanding of what time is, not because they are stupid, but because they are unaware and powerless. They do not understand time (because they are immersed in it). They have little or no family history or folklore. Their origins are lost in the fog; it is amazing when family memories go back even as far as to grandparents. Moreover, as regards the future, actual wages and the way they are paid restrict the rhythm of forward planning. With hire purchase, forward planning becomes essential, and in restricted circumstances such as these, most people find it overwhelmingly difficult to accustom themselves to the rational and abstract kind of time implied by money and credit. They lie awake thinking about it. All they want is to get it over with. This abstract and long-term linear time ends up disrupting their rhythms. As for work in the 'lower depths', everyone knows that it is both fragmented and not very specialized. In the margin of the 'lower depths' we find certain jobs which are generally reserved for women, not only 'in the house', but in businesses and offices: cleaning, basic non-technical repairs, an endless response to the permanent process of erosion, soiling, wearing out and aging which all that is used or has life must suffer. Like all work, it remains implicated in cycles (days, weeks, months). Although it is essential, it is not cumulative, and what links it has with accumulation are only indirect and by the back door, so to speak.

In the 'lower depths', cyclic time is taken up in satisfying basic needs and basic tasks which are themselves governed by cycles. Like time, relative social space ('effective scope', as the American sociologist Lazarsfeld puts it), namely housing and environment, is given over to basic concerns. Every day, every week, the same places, the same aims, the same itineraries. People have very few 'relationships' or 'know' few people outside this space. They are anonymous within their own lives (which explains the passionate interest in the trivial news item, that 'poor man's tragedy'[23] in which destiny is revealed, symbols are reconstituted and anonymity is overcome in an effort to reach the great light of social day). This suffocating state of affairs has its compensation: the vitality and direct, immediate character of the 'lived', a sort of irrefutable concreteness.

In the 'upper sphere', there is much more adventure, more openings, more play; but people are always in danger of losing themselves, some in abstraction, others in artificiality, and others in pointless subtlety and refinement.

Thus, and gradually, we are establishing the everyday to be a level (in the way we talk of sea level and ground level).

13

More observations and objections from philosophers

'Well then, why not attempt a phenomenology of what is lived socially in the *Lebenswelt*, a description of space and social time in human, intersubjective experience? However, it's still not clear. Take me for example, I'm a philosopher and a teacher, and I give my philosophy lectures on a regular basis. Where in your opinion does the everyday start and finish for me? Isn't my activity entirely determined by something else, history of thought, say, the history of our society, institutions, the university, teaching syllabuses, etc.?'

Reply

'Let me take your questions one at a time. In the first place, the description we are trying to make here implies an analysis which is not really compatible with descriptive and purely phenomenological method. We are removing from *praxis* those activities which are apparently its most concrete and positive: the so-called higher activities. We are proceeding via abstraction, using analysis on the plane of the imaginary, because the operation requires a kind of imagination if it is to delve into the hidden life of visible and tangible human beings. The result may therefore *appear* abstract, fictitious and negative. What we are arguing here is that such an abstraction is legitimate and well

55

founded, because it reaches something which psychological or sociological evidence does not reveal or make immediately apparent. Our
thesis is that the negative is also positive, and that it is not a bad thing
to overcome the separation between the positive and the negative,
between description and imagination, between understanding and
analysis. In this way thought becomes dialectical by the very act of
thinking. Phenomenology, do I hear you say? Yes and no. In the first
place, no, for the reasons I have just given. And for other reasons.
How can we describe and understand anything if we make no attempt
to explain it? And no, because if we are revalidating the concept
(which is as negative as it is positive) we do so with a certain historicity. And no, because it is also a matter of changing things, and we
are *proposing* change by demonstrating what is capable of being
changed. Critique is inherent to our "monstration": critique of what
is "above" by what is "underneath" and critique of what is underneath by what is above.

And yet, to a certain extent, *yes*, it is phenomenology, because it
certainly is a question of the "lived". Yes, since whatever is total,
whatever is "mediated" and *"reflected"* through the multiplicity of
mediations, through culture and through language, must also turn
back to the unmediated in order to demonstrate itself, to offer itself
and become apparent. Objects, gestures, day-to-day words – they all
embody totality, in a real but fragmented way: on their *respective
levels*. They are partially beyond it, and yet they are a part of it. If
this were not so, there would be no mediation, no non-mediation,
nothing but permanent totality devoid of any real inner diffferences,
and all the more importantly, devoid of contradictions. To sum up –
using your vocabulary, Mr Philosopher – the total becomes a phenomenon. It expresses itself in fragmented actions, in gestures, in
objects, which are inconceivable without it, but which are not
defined according to it, since they have their own, specific reality: on
the level of the everyday. And now, my dear philosopher, allow me
to inform you that your activity – teaching philosophy – is both
everyday and non-everyday. In so far as it is an exceptional activity,
a mediation, a journey into the purely abstract and conceptual, philosophy is constructed above the everyday, even when it meditates on
life and the concrete. In so far as it is a social activity, integrated
within structured groups, with their models, their norms and their

social roles, such as the philosophy lecture, the lycée, the town, the university, it enters into the everyday. All the more so because you too "earn your living" by teaching philosophy. But what life do you earn? It cannot be reduced simply to philosophy itself, simply to the right to meditate! At least, for your sake, I hope not! In any case I think that like all human activities, yours can be examined on several *levels*: on the *biological and physiological* level (what you eat, the amount of calories you need to recoup your strength), on the *psycho-logical* level (your personal relationships with the students you teach, for example), and on the *economic* level (your salary, your expenses, etc.). Taking the content of a single activity considered on various levels, and using a specific part of that content, thought can establish a virtually unlimited number of sets (of facts and concepts). If we abstract them out, what is left? The everyday "lived", doubly deter-mined as the *residual deposit* and as the *product* of all the sets considered (and thus, in its way, a *total* phenomenon, that is, a level in totality, and on its own level, a totality.

14

Let us pause a moment to consider this new determination. Is the everyday a residual deposit? We must be clear about this. There is in effect a residual aspect to the everyday, since it can be defined by abstraction or by a series of abstractions. It could always become reduced and disappear. Let me give you an example. Take dreary and repetitive activities such as cleaning and repairing. To do away with the need for cleaning (by using materials which do not produce dirt, thus eradicating dust and smoke) would be to reduce the everyday and to lift it up methodically to the level where techniques operate. This would indeed be an objective: the metamorphosis of the every-day, which in our opinion implies a plan and a policy. However, this residual deposit is irreducible. Were we to suppress it would we not annihilate "being"? The study of everyday life does not focus solely on "survivals" in the sociological meaning of the term. One might just as well consider biological and physiological needs and desires as sur-vivals from primitive man! Let us suppose that in the not-too-distant future human cells will be created artificially (which is perfectly

conceivable) and given consciousness. This man-made human being
will still have vital rhythms, needs which are satisfied only to become
needs once more, desires which may or may not be fulfilled, which
come to an end and are born again. This "being" will obey certain
laws of "being" which for a philosopher are related to the profound
link between the non-finite and the finite, to the finiteness of the
expressions of non-finite being. This created "being" will still contain
an uncontrolled sector and a controlled sector, and thus it will also
imply a problematic of everyday life, a perpetual confrontation
between empowerment and powerlessness. It will experience an inner
struggle to *appropriate* life, a struggle against whatever *disappropriates* it
(whatever distorts it, degrades it or kills it). Can we say these are survivals? Yes and no. There can be no "survivals" without a real "base".
To this vague idea of survival we would prefer the much more concrete idea of *uneven development*. In our history, the uneven development
of sectors is also a consequence of history. Indeed, in uneven development the everyday defines itself as what *lags behind* history, but not as
what *eludes* history, events, development and human power. In history,
in development, the everyday is also *a product*.

The concept of the everyday can therefore not be defined as a kind
of existential illusion: the illusion in which we (social man *hic et nunc*)
appear and believe we can grasp what we are, in which we see ourselves from a certain perspective without knowing the reasons and
the causes, without understanding history and ontological truth.
Trapped at the centre of a kind of false consciousness or permanent
bad faith, we try to evade them: in a word, it is inauthenticity. No.
My dear philosopher, the level of *the everyday* is not the illusion of a
false consciousness. "How do we live?" This question does not stem
from ignorance, and moreover the problem cannot be resolved by
knowledge and knowledge alone, nor by language or logos alone . . .'

15

This spectrum analysis, which places human reality between two
poles, is not merely sociological. It also involves the psychological. In
our opinion, the psychological is also a level. If it can be opened up
to knowledge, it will present itself as a totality which encompasses

historical and social determinations. Understood in the context of a wider field, it is as though the psychological were encompassed by the sociological.

The study of everyday life reaches layers deep inside the 'social individual', i.e., a non-isolated consciousness and a non-separated psyche.[24]

First layer: resistant, external, morphological, a kind of membrane through which the osmoses between 'the individual' and 'society' occur. The individual rejects uncomfortable questions. He evades problems. He confines himself to banalities, to the accepted norms of trivial communication and behaviour. He is at one and the same time shut inside himself and boringly social. The outside makes him feel extremely uncomfortable. It is the superficial context in which the individual 'adapts' to the different social 'circles' through which he travels in the successive phases of practical life. But this peripheral stratum is also where social (linear) time scales and the gestures of industrial and technological labour graft themselves, in so far as they have not been actively adopted by the individual and are not the consequence of a stronger interest, that is, in so far as they remain abstract. And yet, in one sense, this external sphere is also to a certain extent the most internal sphere of all. It makes decisions: it is here that decisions are made.

Second layer: a vague discomfort triggers violent reactions and revealing turns of phrase (often in an aggressive way): 'What a life! Why on earth do we put up with all this?'

Problems emerge, and questions, and the individual replies with fumbling and disjointed answers using the models, the norms, the values and the hierarchic attitudes and behaviour patterns of whatever groups he has chosen to identify with. And within these problems ready-formed choices emerge, more or less consciously (and which consequently, as will become clearer at a later stage, echo the opinions of these various groups, implying involvement in their activity and acceptance of their tactics and strategies).

Third layer: Finally a deeper sphere is revealed, an affective nucleus (with its own characteristic tonality). It is the sphere of non-adaption, of vague rejections and unrecognized voids, of hesitations and misunderstandings. When we reach this sphere, we discover the dramatic situation of the individual in society. Usually, however, all the drama is removed. Unbeknown to the individual himself, it is smothered by trivialities, emptied of all expressivity which might be compromising, and even more, of all lyricism and rhetoric. In this sphere of secrecy, the secret itself is smothered to the point of becoming unrecognizable, and it is generally a petty little secret, involving a deliberate or imposed choice and a mutilation. This is where the process of alienation and disalienation, of fulfilment and incompleteness, of (partial) satisfaction and (partial) dissatisfaction unfolds. This is the sphere from which spring the projects, the half-dreams, the little everyday miracles which horoscopes and predictions rework and embellish. It is also the sphere where what is possible and what is impossible for the individual confront each other. It is the most internal sphere, and yet, in one sense, it is the most external one, the sphere where the history of the individual reveals itself in the history of society.

It is essential to note that on every 'level', in every 'sphere' and in every 'layer' we discover social *representations* which are like representations of society: norms, models, values, collective and imperative forms of conduct, rules and forms of control, in short what is meant rather vaguely by the terms 'ideology', 'culture', 'knowledge', etc. A sharper analysis would require us to distinguish the different stages at which these external/internal elements are adopted, are assimilated and effectively function. The most profound and most effective stage is where *symbols* are active (perceived not as such, but rather as vital realities which consequently cannot be defined as 'representations').

What is the general function of these representational elements? For better or for worse, they guarantee the reciprocal adjustment of needs and desires, of desires and ideas, of cyclic time scales and linear time scales, in short, of the aspects and layers of the social individual. They are the equivalent of the regulations by which a (relative) stability is maintained within the social entity, but at the heart of the psyche. They normalize the individual and impose a minimum amount of cohesion and coherence in his everyday life. They compensate for privations, conceal frustrations, hinder demands and deviances. No spontaneous or mechanical self-regulation takes place in the consciousness. There is no feedback to guarantee balance. This role is played by *representations* at the heart of the conscious being, the social individual, and not by processes of stabilization. Thus, among the conflicts they conceal and to which they offer pseudo-solutions, critique of everyday life reveals the equivocal and ambiguous representations by which symbols are underpinned and encircled.

Rather optimistically, Hegel believed he had discovered *a system of needs* – a kind of substance of civil society – in the links between the individual and the social. What we have discovered are more like systems of *representations*. They are very relative and, despite their tenacity, rather fragile, but they guarantee the everyday an amount of stability even in its moments of disappointment and drama.

(These analytical considerations correspond to empirically observable facts, to 'cases' and 'situations' which can be classified, thus making space for a typology. As an example, we could take those people who assume tasks and responsibilities in order to disguise the emptiness and ennui of their everyday lives: who want a large family so as to give their lives a meaning; who 'have ambitions' far beyond their own existences and their immediate associates, etc.).

16

We are moving closer to a detailed and precise definition of everyday life. Now that we have situated it at its own level, and looking at it more closely, we can observe that it contains levels of its own, layers, degrees, stages. Reciprocity, interaction, the hierarchy of these levels and degrees, all depend in part (but only in part) on approach, point of view and perspective.

How can we talk about all this without resorting to verbal artifice, or to that indeterminism which destroys every structure, every regularity and every law? Because 'what is most external is also what is most internal' and vice versa. This statement formulates a law. 'Commonplaces' are to be found both in the peripheral layer of the individual and in his affective nucleus. He has a limited and subjective perception of the conditioned responses to stimuli by which society adapts him, willingly or by force, to external conditions – and a limited and subjective perception of the symbolisms which rise up from the depths within him. For him, conditioning and symbols, external or internal constraints, are all mixed up together. We, however, are drawing distinctions between the various layers and spheres.

First we perceive the struggle against time which takes place within time, as well as the conflict between the simultaneous 'temporalities' of the individual – social being *in our* (industrial) *society*. Lagging behind that society, the opposite of all that is magnificent and flourishing, everyday life consists of a set of basic 'functions' from which the so-called higher functions emerge. Thus it encompasses the *immediate and natural forms of necessity* (needs, cyclic time scales, affective and vital spontaneity) as well as the seeds of the activity by which those forms are controlled (abstraction, reason, linear time). Next it encompasses the region where objects and goods are continually *appropriated*, where desires are elaborated from needs, and where 'goods' and desires correspond. This is a zone of confrontation between the necessary and the random, the possible and the impossible, what has been appropriated and what has not, and empirical good luck and bad luck. In this zone, broadening what is possible is not an effortless task. With its regions of fulfilment and unfulfilment, of effective and possessed (appropriated) joys and lack of joys, it is the realm of the dialectic between 'alienation' and 'disalienation'.

Finally, we have discerned a third level or degree. On the one hand this third level can be considered to be unmediated and empirically given, and can be studied in terms of 'ideologies' and 'moral values'. On the other hand it can be considered as mediating between the individual and the social, and, within an individual consciousness, between the individual and his own self. It is a set of practices, representations, norms and techniques, established by society itself to regulate consciousness, to give it some 'order', to close the excessive gaps between the 'inside' and the 'outside', to guarantee an approximate synchronization between the elements of subjective life, and to organize and maintain compromises. This social control of individual possibilities is not absolutely imposed; it is accepted, half-imposed, half-voluntary, in a never-ending ambiguity; this same ambiguity allows the individual to play with the controls he imposes within himself, to make fun of them, to circumvent them, and to give himself rules and regulations in order to disobey them.

Here, on its chosen territory, critique finds its points of impact. It mounts an attack on gaps and imbalances (between temporalities, between the 'basic' and the 'superior', the historical and the private, the social and the individual). It points out the gaps, the vacuums and the distances yet to be covered and overcome. It criticizes the role of society and the roles society imposes, which bestow a pseudo-coherence, a simulated adaptation and an illusory balance to the whole. It attacks alienation in all its forms, in culture, ideology, the moral sphere, and in human life beyond culture, beyond ideology, beyond the moral sphere. Critique demands the dissolution and the revolutionary metamorphosis of the everyday, by reducing its disparities and time-lags. By demonstrating theoretically that the everyday is not an immutable substance, it has already begun to dissolve it. Finally, it demands a twofold movement within a unitary praxis: that the everyday catch up with what is possible and that the processes which have been distanced from it return and reinvest themselves within it.

This broadens the critical programme presented in the introductory Volume I of *Critique of Everyday Life* considerably. There we restricted ourselves to a generalized and as yet abstract critique of alienation in general. We also considered, but rather vaguely, a reciprocal critique of the 'positive' real by dreams (and vice versa), of the lived by the imaginary, by art and by the ethical (and vice versa), in short, critical analysis of the fictive (non-practical) transpositions and metamorphoses of the everyday, in particular by aestheticism, 'values', the cult of personality and personalities, and rituals and superstitions, etc.

Our plan is becoming broader in scope, and clearer.

17

Let us view our subject in another light. We will start with a 'classic' distinction in general philosophy and methodology, the distinction between *form* and *content*. A content can only manifest itself and be grasped within a form. What we perceive is always the unity of form and content, with the result that several doctrines have felt able to challenge the distinction between the two terms. The theories which reject this distinction also reject any kind of analytical method. In fact, analysis and analysis alone breaks this unity. It abstracts form and consequently determines it per se. Those who believe they can grasp forms per se, unmediated, are just as erroneous as those who challenge the concept of forms. As for content, the intellectual act of analysis determines and constructs it per se, by separating it from form.

In the context of this study, what do we mean by forms? We mean ideologies, institutions, culture, language, and constructed and structured activities (including art). Previously we used analysis to abstract these forms. What did we say was left? A sort of 'human matter', the everyday – a sort of 'human nature', but with the proviso that 'human matter' or 'human nature' can only exist dialectically, in the endless conflict between nature and man, between matter and the techniques which wield power over it. Thus we must define everyday life in two ways: as a residual deposit and as a product. If in one sense the everyday is residual, it also expresses itself as the product of forms: what has been acquired and won via these forms, their human investment.

Resuming this analysis, we will still see the everyday as doubly determined, but in another way: at one and the same time as *unformed*, and as *what forms contain*.

Bit by bit contemporary sociology has discovered the importance of the unformed and has reinstated spontaneity as a social phenomenon. The unformed spills over from forms. It evades them. It blurs the precision of their contours. By marking them with erasures and marginal areas, it makes them inexact. The everyday is 'that', a something which reveals the inability of forms (individually and as a whole) to grasp content, to integrate it and to exhaust it. It is also content, which can only be seized by analysis, whereas the unformed can only be seized immediately or intuitively by participating in spontaneous activity or by stimulating it.

To conform to an already established custom, and while stressing the incomplete character of any isolated illustration extrapolated from concepts, let us give an example. *Bureaucracy* tends to operate for and by itself. By establishing itself as a 'system', it becomes its own goal and its own end; at the same time, in a given society, it has real functions, which it executes more or less effectively. Thus it modifies the everyday, and this too is its goal and its aim. However, it never succeeds in 'organizing' the everyday completely; something always escapes it, as bureaucrats themselves ruefully admit. The everyday protests; it rebels in the name of innumerable particular cases and unforseen situations. Beyond the zone bureaucracy can reach, or, rather, in its margins, the unformed and the spontaneous live on. There is something tenaciously resistant within this organized or possibly overorganized sphere, which makes form adapt and modify. Form either fails or improves; and this is how it manages to go on living. The 'dysfunctions' studied by certain sociologists are remarkable in that they stimulate functions and functionaries alike. They set them a multiplicity of problems which prevent them from going round in circles, and from setting up a perfect form and a vicious circle. Thus, in so far as it is both unformed and a content, the everyday 'contains' an ongoing critique of bureaucratic form and its effectiveness. All that is required is to single this ongoing critique out . . .

In this way we can get a better grasp of the double dimension of the everyday: platitude and profoundness, banality and drama. In one respect everyday life is nothing but triviality or an accumulation of commonplaces. Only those 'lofty' activities which abstraction sets to one side possess breadth and elevation. In other words, they alone are profound. And yet it is in the everyday that human dramas ravel and unravel, or remain unravelled. It is 'there' that veritable profoundness shines through and the question of authenticity is posed, or, perhaps, the question of vulgarity and non-vulgarity. The everyday is neither the inauthentic per se, nor the authentically and positively 'real'. When a feeling or a passion avoids being tried and tested by the everyday, it demonstrates ipso facto its inauthenticity. Although the drama of love may well consist in it being 'smashed against everyday life', in the words of Maiakovsky, the boat must brave the current or stay at its moorings. This test obliges subjective feeling to transmute itself into willpower, in order to confront something for which it is not responsible. Taken in isolation, failure is just as lacking in authenticity. Sooner or later all feelings, passions and intentions come face to face with their own limits. They fail, making future endeavours impossible, but this in itself proves nothing. Only the history of feelings or willpower, only the events they incite or assume responsibility for, only their confrontation with what is 'real' within 'the real', demonstrate anything. In the narrative of every endeavour, what counts is the combination of failure and what has been won prior to failure, rather than failure per se. An event has unfolded; it has taken time; it has taken its time. Time occupied by the onward movement of an event – failure – on a winding path through the murky thickness of everyday life, that is what counts. Perhaps this is what creates the 'novelistic'. The quality of a failure is more significant than the fact of having failed. Therefore, if everything in the everyday ends in failure, since everything comes to an end, the meanings differ. Could not successes sometimes be the worst failures? And sometimes failure can give birth to its own meaning, to its investment in the everyday, to what can be learnt from the drama, and to what will survive it.

In the everyday, platitude and profundity do not coexist peacefully. They fight bitterly there. Sometimes profundity and beauty can be born from a poorly determined and unexpected combination: an encounter. Later on, this chance event seems deserved, perhaps even predetermined. Once profundity and beauty are lived (and not simply gazed at or seen as a spectacle) they become *moments*, combinations which marvellously overturn structures established in the everyday, replacing them by other structures, unforeseen ones, and fully authentic.

When we talk about 'society/individual', 'need/desire', 'appropriation/pleasure' as though they were units, we should take care never to be misled by the way the logic of coherent discourse uses these words. These units are always conflictual, and thus always dialectical and in movement. In the everyday, when the 'human being' confronts within itself the social and the individual through the test of problems and contradictions which have been more or less resolved, it becomes a 'person'. What does this mean? In our view, a cloud of possibilities, gradually vaporized by choices – by actions – until it is exhausted and comes to an end: until death finishes it off. It is not an untroubled scenario making its way towards a foreseen conclusion, but rather a drama, the drama of personalization in society, the drama of individualization. In this drama, death is the only conclusion we can foresee, because it is necessary, and it comes only in unforeseen circumstances which depend on the narrative in its entirety.

In the everyday, alienations, fetishisms and reifications (deriving from money and commodities) all have their various effects. At the same time, when (up to a certain point) everyday needs become desires, they come across goods and appropriate them. Therefore critical study of everyday life will reveal the following conflict: maximum alienation and relative disalienation. Not as goods and objects to appropriate, but as objects of property, things alienate and even reify human activities and living men.[25] But in the link between pleasure and objects as goods, the reification engendered by these very things tends to break up. It comes up against a hostile force. The theory of alienation and reification must take this dialectic into account if it is not to lapse into that speculative form of reification known as dogmatism. *There is a 'world' of objects,* but it is also a human world, an area of desires and goods, an area of possibilities, and not simply a 'world' of inert things.

In commonplace speech, the words 'good luck' and 'bad luck' make an arbitrary connection between the results of randomness in society and randomness in nature. They also confuse necessity which has been misunderstood or subjectively unrecognized with what is objectively random. Such-and-such an individual is unlucky because his health is poor or because there have been pitfalls in his career. Better hygiene, or a medical breakthrough, would have spared him his health problems, and improved social organization would give this individual a better chance, etc. However, we know only too well that the power social man wields over material nature and the power individual man wields over social reality are not the same thing. Far from it. Everyday life is also the realm of the confrontations and distances which the words 'good luck' and 'bad luck' summarize in a naive dialectic.

The realm of randomness and alienation can be reduced. But can it disappear? It would only disappear if technology were to gain complete power over material nature, and the random were eliminated from the social. Here, as ever, the 'residual deposit' cannot be deemed to be reducible. Its disappearance, which would give the non-finite a limit (as absolute learning gives a limit to the non-finiteness of relative knowledge), is not even desirable. In so far as we can conceive it, it would only come about through social overorganization and a terrifying intervention by information technology.

In the meantime, a social failure can signify positive qualities (independent thinking, critical intelligence, rebellion). A biological misfortune can have happy consequences: a child with defects in one area may compensate by possessing exceptional qualities in another.

In the psyche too, development is uneven. If we make a fetish of the total, it can be devastating for 'being', since we are underestimating the plurality of the sectors within the *configuration* which situates or rather constitutes everyday life. Now and again we will need to lay bare a certain nefarious pedagogic illusion, and in doing so we will be able to to highlight the part played by education and its importance in everyday life. This illusion is twofold: on the one hand, a fetishism of the partial, and thus of the fragmentary and the specialized, an acceptance of fragmentation and a dismissal of totality; on the other hand, a fetishism of the total, an equalizing of differences, a superficial encyclopedism, and a belief in the complete mastery of pedagogy and human knowledge over 'human nature'.

There is a middle way between the dismissal of totality and the fetishism of the total, and critique of everyday life can help to define it.

18

In years gone by, when cottage industry, trades and guilds were still very important, the social man *par excellence*, the worker, was formed in and by labour. In this sense, man as an individual being and man as a social being were formed along similar lines. It was a relatively simple situation. Essentially, attitudes and behaviour patterns 'outside work' derived more or less directly from work itself. The individual 'was' this or that: a miner, a carpenter, a stonemason, a teacher, etc. Everyday life was almost completely determined by profession. It created well-differentiated but more-or-less caricatured human types, such as Hegel's 'abstract animals' or the social species in Balzac's *Comédie humaine*.

We should note that this process has not entirely disappeared. Consequently there are many confusions. Uneven development intervenes here as well. What is no longer true in the 'modernized' sectors of industry remains true in a great many more-or-less backward sectors.

Nowadays, in the advanced industrial countries, this situation relative to work and 'outside work' tends to be reversed. There is a shift in the focus of interest. It is the attitude towards work which is formed in everyday life (including those leisure activities which have become a part of everyday life which do not involve getting away from it all – or apparently so – with breaks or holidays), and not vice versa.

To be more precise: in days gone by, work had a 'value' in the ethical as well as economic sense of the term. There were work 'values': the idea of work well done, and of the product as a personal creation and to a certain extent on a par with the object created by a craftsman or an artist, etc.

With the fragmentary division of labour (and with the mass influx of unskilled workers and machine operators in factories), this traditional ethic has crumbled away. Work has lost almost all its appeal, and all the more so because it is fairly easy to move from one job or company to another. What we are describing here is a certain period in 'industrial society', definable by certain characteristics and by certain types of machine, and very bleak it is too. So, for the worker, work and life outside work have sunk into the same lack of interest, a lack which is poorly disguised by entertainments which are as noisy as they are empty. In fact, our society has not completely emerged from this period (just as it has not completely emerged from the period which preceded it, given the way previous forms of techniques and organization persist at the very heart of the most modern forms . . .).

Recent techniques, such as automation, call for abilities and knowledge even in work which has become passive – almost absence of work (such as the control and supervision of machinery). Technicians, employees and operations coexist in an organization which wants to be *stable* because it is in its interest to be so. This produces new concerns, such as stable employment and therefore stable living conditions, or credit facilities giving workers access to durable consumer goods (housing, household equipment, cars, etc). Obviously, these economic and technical demands give rise to a deliberate policy and an ideology.

Therefore one can see stable employment becoming the predominant concern in the most advanced working class, at least for a period of time during which a (conscious or unconscious) option is taken and its results are forthcoming. For indeed there is a genuine option here, which, we may add, is not irreversible (or so it would seem). In any event, the focus of interest is displaced from work, which in this context we take to mean the use of a technique and a set of implements. It focuses on everyday life in general. It is in the everyday outside work that the attitude towards work is formed. Work is no longer considered as an end in itself, but as the means to an end. People 'earn their living'. And yet again we ask ourselves: 'What life do we earn when we earn our living?'

We shall see, or rather we shall emphasize once again, that the life earned is '*private life*', and nothing but '*private life*' . . .

19

In our initial project, we proposed that critique of everyday life would include an *autocritique* of the everyday. Its principal aim was to confront 'the real' and 'the lived' with their representations, interpretations and transpositions (in art, in the moral domain, and in ideology and politics). From this comparison would have come a reciprocal critique of 'the real' by the imaginary, of 'the lived' by its transpositions, and of what has been effectively acquired by abstraction. In a similar way, our agenda included the confrontation between *private life* (seeing the individual as distinct from the social, but without separating him from society) and *public life* (the life of the citizen, historical man, social groups and the political state), and reciprocal critique of these two fragments of totality.

We proposed a single solution: that private life should be granted access to collective, social and political life, and that it should be allowed to participate within it. In other words we proposed the bringing together of everyday man and historical man, and the participation of everyday man in the problematic of totality (society as a whole). In this way the political sphere of the state was raised to the rank of supreme authority. Essentially, our critique was directed towards 'private life' which we defined as an impoverished sector of praxis, a backward and underdeveloped region at the very heart of so-called 'modern', industrial and technological society, in the context of capitalism. We intended to devote several chapters to the scrutiny of the petty magic of everyday life (habitual gestures and rituals, proverbial expressions, horoscopes, witchcraft, diabolisms), intending to eradicate them by submitting them to practical reason. Certainly, we did not intend to merge the individual with the collective and the private with the sociopolitical, but rather to raise them to the level of the collective and the historical, and thus via political consciousness to the level of the political. A relatively simple theory of alienation and disalienation seemed to satisfy all these requirements. Before the great disalienation which political revolution would bring about, but preparing for it and proclaiming it, the opening up of everyday life to public life and its active participation in history and political action would disalienate everyday man and negate his 'privation'. Far from disappearing, the everyday would become enriched and organically linked to totality: to the total man.

These oversimplified hypotheses betrayed a certain naivety. And this is where certain modifications have transformed our initial project. Over the last few years important changes have become apparent within the configuration made up by private life, political life, history and technology. How could critique of everyday life leave them to one side? We have already alluded to these changes, indicating that while not destroying our agenda, they introduce new elements. We will now stress the importance of these elements, and devote some time to explaining what they are.

In the first place, the mid-twentieth-century man who belongs to an 'advanced' society and who is using Marxism as the theoretical means of understanding that society will find himself in the same position as Marx vis-à-vis *history*. He cannot accept or confirm the historical as a series of events and processes. If he is not a professional politician, and if he locates himself in the sphere of knowledge, he will refuse to award history its 'degree in philosophy'. The politician is involved in a strategy, and whatever he has to say he says in the context of this strategy. In terms of history and the historical past which weighs upon the present day, he must 'save face'. If not, he will put his strategy and, of course, his political career in jeopardy (because another and more effective politician would immediately be found to carry out the task). This divorce between knowledge and politics, and the inevitable renewal of a sociology of politics which defines politics as politics per se rather than as the supreme science, present some very disturbing features. Never mind. This is not the place to worry about them. In his time Marx submitted politics – events, processes. tactics and strategies – to a merciless critical analysis. Starting from an objective determination of the strengths and the possibilities, and assessing what had and had not been accomplished, in terms of these possibilities, he examined the decisions, the mistakes and the failures. He did not use simplified and schematized hypotheses to deal with the facts; he did not recognize a constant and coherent 'progress' in all domains, or a unilateral determinism, or an absolute necessity. Marx never considered the historical as a set of *faits accomplis* to be accepted and recorded globally. While disputing the absolute of history and politics (and notably Hegel's philosophy of history and of the state), he studied what we will call *drifts*. He drew many lessons from the discrepancy between intentions and results.

Today we must call history into question, even the history we have lived and to which we have contributed. This so-called history has not yet superseded the prehistory of mankind. From decisions and actions, *something else* suddenly appears, something other than what was intended and planned. Although we may accept that through the intervention of the revolutionary proletariat the gap between the plan and the result has been narrowed (although this is debatable), it has not yet disappeared. Far from it! Men make their own history, but not in the way they wish it to be. They do not do what they want to do: they do not want what they do. There is more to the 'world' than philosophy predicted.

So what can we suggest everyday life should do to bridge the gap between the lived and history? How can we persuade it that its model should be the political sphere, the sphere which intervenes in history in an attempt – in the best cases – to make it and to direct it consciously? The split between private life and political consciousness is self-perpetuating. The two forms of consciousness are juxtaposed when in fact they could coexist. But in many cases, private consciousness gains the upper hand over a political consciousness obscured and starved as a result of the rift between the two.

We have had to bring the theory of the *withering away of the state* back to centre stage. This essential Marxist theory has been obscured by contemporary history (and by the history of Marxism in particular). Is it a Utopia? Probably. In fact, nowhere in the modern world is there a state withering away to any convincing degree, and there is nothing in line with the process Marx considered the future of history would be.[26] If there is anything Utopian in the theory of the withering away of the state, it will make it even easier for us to demonstrate just how Utopian Marx's thought is, and to refute several erroneous assertions yet again, but with more effective arguments. Utopia, i.e., a theory of what is distantly possible, is not an 'eschatology', a theory that the process of becoming might be brought to an end. It is the very concrete and positive idea of a history which has at last been orientated, directed and mastered by knowledge and willpower. The day when the gap between aims and results is narrowed, and the end of destiny (in other words the end of prehistory) is nigh, the withering away of the state will be at hand.

The withering away of the state or the practical possibility of it is an objective precondition for the resolution and supersession of the rift between *private life* and *political life* (between consciousness and political consciousness). The *private* will only rise to the level of the *public* when the public ceases to place itself in inaccessible and mysterious realms, and goes back down to the private to merge itself in the everyday once more. This process of supersession also plays a part in determining concrete democracy. Democracy must move towards the withering away of the state and the supersession of the conflict between the 'private' and the 'public'. If it does not, it is moribund.

So how can we propose to the private consciousness of the everyday man of today that its practical aim should be to become recognized by political and historical man? In so far as this mutual recognition might possibly heal the rift between consciousness and praxis, it remains an abstract ideal: an idea, a 'Utopia'. In so far as this recognition can be reduced to a simple fact among other facts, it has already been accomplished. In propaganda, which epitomizes state action and reasons of state, ideology and political consciousness target private consciousness. The aim is not to fill in the chasm and to achieve fusion through supersession. Propaganda leaves everyday life, consciousness and private life intact. It takes them as objects and even as 'things'. It insinuates itself inside them in order to shape them. It does not lift them up to the level of the universal. It fights with other ideologies for their possession. Is this inevitable? Certainly. It is destiny we are dealing with, in other words historical necessity and chance which have been turned into strategic necessity and tactical calculation. Recognition has only been unilateral, and unity has been achieved by means of confusion. Hence a paradox which will require further examination: the intensification of ideologies at a time when they are being discredited, and the (more or less deep or momentary) depoliticization of an everyday life which is prodigiously 'well informed' politically, at a time when pressing political problems demonstrate an urgency which nobody denies.

There is something else which acts equally as an innovation and a deterioration: the technical element. It forces us to formulate the fundamental demand of the everyday differently from the way we did in our initial project. It is no longer a question simply of carrying the private to the social via language, knowledge and concept – of raising the everyday up to the historical and then to the political. *Critique of everyday life requires a plan, in other words a policy which will raise the everyday to the level made possible by technology.*

20

We have already talked about the above idea, but it deserves and even demands further explanation, so let us clarify it. Although technology has gone very far and high above the everyday, and continues to do so, it has not abandoned this neglected sector to its own devices. Up to a certain point the everyday has ceased to be underdeveloped. *A technical vacuum*, long the characteristic of the everyday, has been partially filled in. Technology has introduced a host of household objects and gadgets. Thus small technical objects have become familiar (although many housewives still have no access to this 'familiarity' and persist in regarding technical knowledge, including that of small objects, as a masculine attribute). Indisputably, the uncontrolled sector has somewhat declined. Could it be that everyday life has become integrated within a 'technological milieu' or, to use our own terminology, within the controlled sector organized in accordance with industrial technology? Could 'industrial society' have given it a coherent and specific structure, thus separating it from contact with uncontrolled nature, or conversely allowing it to rejoin nature via the 'world' of technical objects and making it part of a set of dynamic balances, similar to the feedbacks, homeostases and scannings studied by specialists in autoregulations? Nothing allows us to confirm this. In fact, everything proves the opposite.[27]

74

With the introduction of the technical object within everyday life, the contrast between the aesthetic object (which may or may not be useful) and the strictly functional and utilitarian technical object has been revealed in a harsher light. Hitherto confined to being part of the décor of social life, the 'aesthetic/technical' or 'artistic/functional' dichotomy has entered into familiarity. The industrial aesthetic and the commendable efforts which have been made in the field of industrial design have not succeeded in conferring an aesthetic status on the technical object, nor a technical status on the aesthetic object. The 'world of objects' is marked by this dichotomy, which classifies them in two major categories. We cannot avoid the fact that extreme or moderate functionalism has failed time and time again to extrapolate a plastic art from the functional. The fact that aesthetic creation or production has become saturated with technology and abstract functionalism make these failures all the more astonishing.

Only partially technicized, everyday life has not created its own specific style or rhythm. Unconnected objects (vacuum cleaners, washing machines, radio or television sets, refrigerators, cars, etc.) determine a series of disjointed actions. Small technical actions intervene in the old rhythms rather like fragmented labour in productive activity in general. The equipment of everyday life finds itself more or less in the same situation as industrial mechanization in its early stages, in the period when specific tools had unique and exclusive functions. If these gestures increase effectiveness – productivity – they also split things up; they truncate, they make mincemeat of everyday life; they leave margins and empty spaces. They increase the proportion of passivity. Dialectically, progress consists of gaps and partial regressions. What is more, a reduction in the time devoted to productive actions and gestures which are now carried out by technical objects has raised the question of time itself, and already this is a very urgent problem. If we examine time as it is experienced by many of today's men and women, we will see that it is chock-a-block full and completely empty. On the horizon of the modern world dawns the black sun of boredom, and critique of everyday life has a sociology of boredom as part of its agenda.

Incorporation of the everyday within a concrete totality (the total or world man) via modern means of information and communication can be interpreted in a variety of ways. Is it correct to say that television gives the everyday a world-wide dimension? Yes it is. Television allows every household to look at the spectacle of the world, but it is precisely this mode of looking at the world as a spectacle which introduces non-participation and receptive passivity. The idea that the audiovisual as it was lived in archaic communities (in scenes of magic) could be reconstituted is laughable and frivolous. The mass media strip the magic of presence from what was the presence of magic: participation – real, active or potential. Sitting in his armchair, surrounded by his wife and children, the television viewer witnesses the universe. At the same time, day in and day out, news, signs and significations roll over him like a succession of waves, churned out and repeated and already indistinguishable by the simple fact that they are pure spectacle: they are overpowering, they are hypnotic. The 'news' submerges viewers in a monotonous sea of newness and topicality which blunts sensitivity and wears down the desire to know.[28] Certainly, people are becoming more cultivated. Vulgar encyclopedism is all the rage. The observer may well suspect that when communication becomes incorporated in private life to this degree it becomes non-communication.

Radio and television do not penetrate the everyday solely in terms of the viewer. They go looking for it at its source: personalized (but superficial) anecdotes, trivial incidents, familiar little family events. They set out from an implicit principle: 'Everything, in other words, anything at all, can become interesting and even enthralling, provided that it is *presented*, i.e., *present*.' The art of presenting the everyday by taking it from its context, emphasizing it, making it appear unusual or picturesque and overloading it with meaning, has become highly skilful. But even if the lives of the great and the good are 'presentified' in this way through the mediation of presenters, editors and producers, it is still never anything else but the everyday. And so communication passes from unmediated event (captured the instant it happens and where it happens) to unmediated reception, within the familiar context of the everyday. Concrete mediations – language, culture in the traditional sense, values and symbols – become blurred. They do not disappear. They are too useful. They are worn down, they deteriorate, and yet at the same time they hypertrophy. It is their mediating function which is worn away.

At the extreme, signs and significations which are nothing more than significations lose all meaning. At the extreme looms the shadow of what we will call 'the great pleonasm': the unmediated passing immediately into the unmediated and the everyday recorded just as it is in the everyday – the event grasped, pulverized and transmitted as rapidly as light and consciousness – the repetition of the identical in a wild whirling dance devoid of Dionysian rapture, since the 'news' never contains anything really new. If this extreme were reached, the closed circuit of communication and information would jeopardize the unmediated and the mediated alike. It would merge them in a monotonous and Babel-like confusion. The reign of the global would also be the reign of a gigantic tautology, which would kill all dramas after having exploited them shamelessly.

Of course, this extreme situation is still a long way away. It would be a closed circuit, a circuit from hell, a perfect circle in which the absence of communication and communication pushed to the point of paroxysm would meet and their identities would merge. But it will never come full circle. There will always be something new and unforeseen, if only in terms of sheer horror. There will be 'creations' which will stimulate informative energy and allow for a massive injection of new information. This extreme exists only in the mind's eye as a distant possibility, in the same way as the debasement of informational energy and the triumph of entropy are. And yet, this extreme allows us to imagine and determine certain aspects of 'the real'. The very least we can be sure of is that the mass media have not yet incorporated the everyday into a vaster, richer whole, such as spontaneity or culture. They have left it to its 'privation' while moving into this privation and taking it over. It is the generalization of *private life*. At one and the same time the mass media have unified and broadcast the everyday; they have disintegrated it by integrating it with 'world' current events in a way which is both too real and utterly superficial. What is more or less certain is that they are dissociating an acquired, traditional culture, the culture of books, from written discourse and Logos. We cannot say what the outcome of this destructuring process will be.

To conclude this point, let us say that we have many reservations about the terms we are employing: technological society, industrial society. Primacy of technology? Certainly, but technology does leave several essential sectors behind civilization, and outside it. Industrial society? Yes, but it is within this society that for the foreseeable future *uneven development* will go on producing all its effects.

21

Modified in this way by modern technology, the everyday has not disappeared. Although its problems may have changed, in a great many respects they have become worse. A prime example: new towns.

Here, the everyday reigns in what we might call the chemically pure state. The extreme example can be seen in practice. Here, everyday life is shrinking into private life. Every object has been calculated and technically realized to carry out a daily function at the lowest possible cost; it implies a series of actions, and brings them into being; these are actions which guarantee the bare essentials of existence, foreseeable and foreseen functional gestures which obey the peremptory suggestions of the Thing. When used, every thing must satisfy a need (not a desire, but a need: isolated, analysed, dissociated, and intended as such). And this integral functionalism could with some justification be seen as the best hypothesis: it is the best thing that could happen to people living in new towns and recent housing schemes; individual and social needs are too often overlooked, treated with contempt, repressed or frustrated.

Infinitely superior to the slums and workers' housing estates of the past, the flats and apartment buildings of today seem to offer the New Life in the Golden City. Propaganda shrieks it from the rooftops. And so we pass from exaggerated praise to exaggerated disparagement, from exaltation to despondency. Sociologically, the truth is that new towns reduce the everyday to its simplest terms while at the same time 'structuring' it heavily: the everyday in them is perfect and stripped bare in its privation, basic and deprived of basic spontaneity. It wanders around stagnantly and loses hope in the midst of its own emptiness, which nothing technical can ever fill, not even a television set or a car. Everyday life has lost a dimension: depth. Only triviality remains. Apartment buildings are often well-constructed 'machines for living in', and the housing estate is a machine for the upkeep of life outside work. Every object is determined by its function and is reduced to being a signal; it orders one thing and forbids another; it demonstrates behaviour patterns; it conditions. Let us describe a new town and analyse it dialectically.[29] Every town planning scheme conceals a programme for everyday life. Explicitly or not, it refers to an overall conception of man, of life and of the world. In our new towns, the project or programme is all too apparent. Everyday life sees itself treated like packaging: a vast machine seizes the worker's time outside work and folds it in a wrapping as sterile as the protective cellophane round a commodity. People are separated from group to group (workers, craftsmen, technicians) and from each other, each in his box for living in, and this modernity organizes their repeated gestures. The same machinery whittles down the number of essential gestures. That most of these housing estates depend upon technically outstanding firms – automated – where work is almost entirely reduced to the control and upkeep of equipment makes the emptiness all the more blatant. Of course equipment does not function by itself; technical objects make up an ensemble which requires occasional attention. However, this can only come when the technical object issues a message, a *signal*. The town and the factory complement one another by both conforming to the technical object. An identical process makes work easy and passive, and life outside work fairly comfortable and boring. Thus everyday life at work and outside work become indistinguishable, governed as they are by systems of *signals*.

Controlled by signals, paradoxically dissociated, everyday time becomes both homogeneous and dispersed. Work time falls into line with family-life time and leisure time, if not vice versa. In the new housing estates, objects with aesthetic pretensions appear ridiculous, and indeed they are, because they have been added on in an intentional and clumsy manner; there is nothing surprising about them, except perhaps the surprise of uneasiness they afford. As for 'entertainment', that too belongs in this sorry scheme, unless it is rescued by the vigorous initiative of those concerned. Men come home from a day's work which has been almost as far removed from consciously creative activity as the spectacle of the world which they now view on the television screen from the passivity of their armchairs. Women (who work less frequently in the new estates than in the old towns, where there are more 'tertiary' jobs available for women) get their household chores out of the way, put the nagging task of minding the children to one side, and immerse themselves as soon as possible in the 'romantic press'. Yet all it needs is to visit the perfectly automated factory at Lacq, or to gaze at the hills above it, and then to go into the new town which shelters its workers, to observe a striking contrast. On one side, dazzling wonders, on the other the poverty of 'pure' everyday life. Let us take a flight of Utopian fancy. Let us suppose that just as much care and money had been devoted to Mourenx-Ville-Nouvelle as was to Lacq, and that these funds had been used wisely. What would the result have been for its inhabitants? How would the chasm have been filled? By means of what marvels of town planning, of variety, of games connected to culture and all that is serious in life? . . .

22

Admirably made by women for women (which does not mean it has no male readers), the women's press demonstrates by its quantity and quality an obvious wish to 'promote' women. At the same time it reveals the uncertainties and ambiguities of such a promotion. If women are still trying to assert themselves, it means that they have not yet achieved their goal. But what is that goal?

The women's press and specifically the 'romantic press' provide a sort of feminine ideology. Now every ideology is an implement for effective action. Therefore – consciously or unconsciously – this press is part of a strategy. What are its aims? Who makes use of this ideology? A women's lobby or the vast 'unformed' group of women in general? The critical reader is unable to understand. At first it seems that the aim is to sell feelings and dreams, or rather to help women 'assert' themselves. But the plethora of means for self-assertion or compensation exceeds so limited an objective. Could the aim be (political or non-political) power in general, or rather, and more vaguely, the will for power? Could it be ethical? Could these vast means be targeting 'ethical' recognition of the 'feminine being', as yet equally unachieved for women as for men and their ever-hazy consciousness? Could it be aesthetic? Or, in an immense confusion, could it be both at the same time? Finally, could it be some sort of grand game without any precise objective?

What is certain is that individually and collectively the 'modern woman' is involved in a long, bitter struggle for 'being', without really understanding and without even asking herself whether 'being' means social role, importance, power, pathos, mastery of the self, beauty, fecundity, mysticity, conformity or non-conformity. No thing, no possibility is excluded. So could it be all these things simultaneously, in a marvellous muddle which no philosophy, no option, no mutilating reasoning could clarify? Perhaps!

There is an opposite point of view. Whoever wants 'being' without knowing how to define it, without being able to define it and without even wanting to define it is just as incapable of defining 'non-being', and runs the risk of confusing the two. Without scruple and without measure, the women's press mixes the everyday up with the imaginary (so that the project of a mutual critique of the everyday by the fictitious and of the fictitious by the everyday has been both achieved and superseded – as a theoretical project – in the women's press).

What the so-called women's press creates and offers is a 'world', a feminine world. Temporary or lasting, the specific and complementary traits of a 'femininity' are literally made into a world in the women's press. It is a world where triviality does not exclude the extraordinary, where the physiological does not exclude high culture, where the practical does not exclude the ideal, and where these aspects never become disconnected. It is not a logical world, coherently abstract or abstractly coherent. It is not a full, concrete universe analogous to a great work of art. Coherent in its own way, incoherent in an original way (which is not apparent as such to the men and women who accept it), rich in surprises, inhabitable and densely inhabited, this feminine world has no closure. It opens itself up to be looked at and touched, even to males: it tempts them and it can captivate them, since it is not their world and there is no longer a virile world (supposing that virile virtues, together with masculine shortcomings, ever made up a 'world' or were able to assert themselves and to live according to this mode).

The feminine world is ambiguous and muddled. It does not even reflect a given feminine 'essence', an eternal feminine whose homologues would be found in the ephemeral and the instantaneous. This world is a mishmash of the aesthetic, the ethical and the practical. It does not define an art or a moral domain, not even an art of living, but rather a moralism and an aestheticism, lipstick and powder for practical everyday reality which manage to conceal it or at least to make it look prettier from time to time. Nothing in this world or of this world is true, and everything is true, nothing is false and everything is false. Nothing is possible and everything is possible. Nothing is permitted and everything is permitted.

As far as men are concerned, this is a myth or a set of myths. In the eyes of society, it would be more of an ideology. In terms of women themselves, is it not a sort of Utopia? Everything happens as though the *image* (myth, ideology, Utopia, or what you will) of the *total woman* had replaced the image or the idea of the total man after the latter had collapsed. According to this interpretation, and we have no intention of glossing over its twofold irony, the feminine strategy – the strategy of 'women' as a vast, amorphous group or the strategy of their leaders – would have either a conscious or an unconscious goal: to form and impose the image of the total woman, a modern and practical version of the defunct 'total man'. After the demise of the latter, men themselves would accept the relay and the transfer, through powerlessness.

The illusion has changed. The image of the total man was political and revolutionary. It received its inheritance from a long and glorious past. It did not wish to separate virility from masculinity, virtue from skill and manual strength from mental strength; it did not claim to unite them easily. The state, history, wars and philosophy had influenced it, leaving traces and operating a hard process of selection. The image of the total woman is distinctly reformist and apolitical, confused and syncretic. It has the backing of this great force: newness, the effect of surprise, plus confusion and syncretism.

The total woman becomes everything because she does everything. She produces and directs consumption. She has children, she brings them up and educates them. She governs the family. She allows men to devote themselves to sterile games: politics, war, feelings, intellect. And yet artists create for her, woman, and about her.

The 'feminine world' the women's press offers us wishes to be total, so as to correspond to the total woman and to impose her image. It attains totality through confusion. And what a world it is!

Everything is found or reflected there, everything is recognizable, although not with the transparency desirable for a 'world'. Techniques and technology happily set up home with art and morality. Aestheticism and moralism bless these marriages, no better and no worse than any others. By using techniques, the feminine world has gathered together all 'worlds' past, present or future. It excludes nothing. In this it differs extraordinarily from that virile image which merely asserted its reality and inspirational values: work, courage, knowledge. Today philosophy is being distanced, and so, with all its demands, is the philosopher's lifestyle.

Recent and 'modern', still almost pristine, the feminine world has emerged from a series of tests which up until now it has avoided facing. It has even avoided the test of philosophy, for its birth co-incides with the moment when the withering away of philosophy is at its height, and indeed philosophical discussion has become one of its most charming and interesting subjects. And so it takes in the most ancient myths and the most apparently worn-out symbolisms. In a mode of assertive triumphalism, images of the time when 'woman' was a slave reappear – the queen, the beast-divinity, the servant-mis-tress, the doubly martyred and oppressed mother-wife. Figures of fatal beauty, of Predestination, of absolute Good Luck and marvel-lous Damnation cohabit with the representation of free initiative and practical effectiveness. Courageous and virile heroes, moths and mayflies consumed by passion's ardent flame, seducers who fall victim to their own magic powers, Princes, Kings, Knights equal to their own destiny, all make up the retinue of the total woman. The femi-nine world is woven of indecisive correspondences and uncertain analogies. Its life is nourished and maintained by confusion. It gener-alizes the individual and personalizes impersonal techniques, and cheaply too; all it needs is a perfume, a colour, or not even that: an intention, a signification. Cycles intertwine in a tepid and murky harmony, from the hours and the days to the seasons and to entire lives. In the distance hard, linear time passes by, the time of masculine efforts. Colours, perfumes, numbers reply to and correspond with the stars and their conjunctures. It truly is a world, a romantic cosmos stripped of risk and violence, where lyricism has become familiarity. Benign or malignant impulses shoot through it, and we can believe in them, and we can disbelieve in them while still believing in them.

Neither the most insignificant of magical gestures conjuring up misfortune, nor the most minuscule of superstitions fabricating the illusion of good luck, stand in the way of grandiose representations of human dramas, madness, passion and death, theatre and religion. On the plane of fiction, anecdotes and trivial events take on gigantic meanings. Conversely, tragic Images and Figures are reduced to the dimensions of everyday crimes, which above all are crimes against common sense.

This ambiguous world – this world of ambiguity – is also the world of universal muddle, where people talk colloquially about the sublime and use the same tone of voice when talking about the familiar. (And actually this is quite correct, since tone of voice metamorphoses whatever one is talking about, and in any case the familiar really does contain elements of the sublime, and vice versa). This world is neither true nor false. It is a microcosm: small, but for those who inhabit it immense and perhaps infinite. Ambiguity allows people to pass indiscriminately from anything to anything else. Cookery becomes a fairyland and fantastic stories are like recipes in a magic cookery book, flanked by articles on fashion and stories about the romantic agonies of a famous star or an oriental princess. Mystification? Mythification? No. It is less than that, and more, better and worse: it is the ambiguity of the everyday, exploited by an ambiguous consciousness which above all is not consciousness of ambiguity.

Hence 'something' irritating and captivating, slightly inane and very intelligent (sometimes). What? The everyday wrapped up and hidden away, metamorphosed and revealed. This 'something' which wishes to be total and in a sense *is* total appears in all its ludicrous weakness and poverty through its veil of transparent images. This pseudo-everyday is lived and perceived in the manner of an ambiguous consciousness (neither false nor true, half-false, half-true, thus contradictory, but without consciousness of the contradictions, so that these contradictions become blunted and weakened, and this could serve as a definition of *ambiguity* as a category of everyday life). It can easily be linked to the ever-changing important issues of current affairs, fashion, art, politics and history. At the same time it offers an escape from the genuine problems of art, politics, history, and, in the end, of modern life. It is a perpetual alibi, always accessible and welcoming. The doors of this world are open wide; you can walk right in. The seats are cheaper than at the cinema or the theatre. What matter if the quality of illusion and participation (or rather of non-participation) is not as high? What is important is that eventually these cosmetics make everyday life bearable, that boredom is diminished and worries are forgotten, that private life becomes open to wonder (in part knowingly simulated, like a kind of semi-astonishment). This confused world restores a sort of wholeness to disjointed gestures and interrupted rhythms. The 'lived' will be lived in the manner of the 'non-lived'; the possible and the impossible are mixed up together. By transposing it, fiction and half-sleeping, half-waking dreams will make an intolerable life livable by offering it meanings which will support it and deceive it without being deceitful. In this pseudo-world nothing is, and everything signifies. Like wan haloes, significations exploit without exploiting, mislead without misleading. The virile mind was never satisfied with significations. The impalpable coefficients of spirituality connected to things could never satisfy the philosopher. Man, the virile mind, wanted to be; he wanted being. Feminine in essence, and by its very 'presence' (if we can use that word, since it 'is' the opposite of presence and a parody of it: a substitute for being, in a state of collapse), signification bears witness to the downgrading of philosophy. Nevertheless, a vague question remains, amorphous and unanswered. Who are these multiple significations of things and actions intended for? Why are they never able to attain more consistency? Why are they incapable of being anything more than a moralistic or aesthetic intention?

These phenomena – and it is difficult to state with any certainty whether they are temporary or long-lasting – have some disconcerting aspects. Before the Second World War the women's press and 'romantic press' were scarcely out of the cradle, but in only a few years they became very powerful. They quickly gave a certain pitch to the press in general, to news journalism and even to the male-orientated press (which was henceforth isolated and quasi-specialized). The content of these publications altered very rapidly in accordance with general circumstances: it shifted from a relative immoralism after the Liberation to a concern with moral order, and from a humanism discreetly tinted with femininity to a religiosity openly tinged with mythology. The same topics reappear, but in different guises, so that their repetition soaks into the public only gradually. Quasi-permanent, symbolisms appeared in some surprising lights. In effect, ambiguity allows for almost inexhaustible variations on the same themes, each variation containing a few fresh details and, most importantly, a new tone. The same love story can suggest erotic emancipation or the need for a strict moral discipline, according to its 'tone'.[30] By studying this press historically we can measure out a variety of ingredients contained in this volatile mixture: the 'promotion of women' and its uncertainties, 'techniques for finding happiness', moral order, the vicissitudes and anguishes of modernity, etc.

The crowning achievement of the operation, if we can call it that, is to suggest and insinuate a moral order by means of anecdotes which pander to cynicism, immoralism, eroticism and a tasteless romantic sentimentality. A press with a vast circulation sells moral order wrapped up as immoralism, just like a government policy in apolitical wrappings, and ideology disguised as ideological detachment.

As we have already stressed, our study of the reality in question, namely the situation of women in 'modern' life, raises other problems, problems of society as a whole. Where does moral order originate? What does it correspond to in history, to what necessity, or lack of necessity? Does it correspond to something more general than the requirements of particular groups, and more humble than the requirements of ethics or philosophy? How does it come about that today, for the first time as far as we know, a 'moral order' is not being imposed by force, but seems accepted and even called for by the wishes of most, if not of everyone? As for 'techniques for finding happiness', what exactly do they consist of, and what are they aimed at? Is it the satisfaction of those basic, fragmented needs, comfort and wellbeing? Is it security, tranquillity, peace of mind through order and a new modality of clear conscience? And by what means – cooking, fashion, do-it-yourself, relaxation, sexual and emotional harmony, general or mental health, catharsis or relief of tensions, an end to the romanticism of passion and the sense of the tragic? How do those who promote and employ these techniques hope to avoid boredom? What link do these minor, everyday techniques have with technology, with art, with aesthetics and above all with aestheticism as a social phenomenon?

These questions lead us to the connection of modernized everyday life to modernity in general. Therefore they go beyond the confines of the 'promotion of women' taken in isolation. The more we consider the 'promotion of women' the more vague it appears, like the ambiguous base or 'foundation' of ambiguity itself. The elimination of age-old sufferings, such as pain in childbirth, has not suppressed the specific links between femininity and nature and its rhythms. The great hope that work would 'emancipate' women brought them many setbacks and disillusions. They soon discovered that work in factories or offices was scarcely less monotonous than housework, which in fact was being facilitated by new technology, and that they were in danger of being landed with both. Meanwhile, industry had introduced fragmented labour. The number of successful women writers is more an indication of the crisis and decline of certain genres (the novel, for example) than of the triumph of vital intuitions or of strongly original ideas. The violent feminine onslaughts in the domain of ideology are as much an expression of their lack of self-confidence as of their robustness. The press contains as many compensations, justifications and consolations as it does 'positive values'. The tactics and strategies it employs are surprising not so much for their brilliance, but rather for their powers of innuendo . . .

Beneath personal narratives and beyond their symptoms and expressions, we sense the strange and painful zone of the 'private Eros', a zone where failures and illusions, superstitions and false powers, the images and myths of powerlessness all converge.

23

Seen in this light, could we not say that of all new phenomena the 'reprivatization' of life is the strangest, and that to a certain extent it encompasses all the previous ones? To use a certain philosophical language which explains nothing and which would demonstrate the need for a deeper theoretical development of these concepts as well as of the facts themselves, the point of view of totality bears witness to a 'detotalization'.

Let us look at these facts more closely. They are paradoxical. The 'reprivatization' of everyday life, which both modified and confirmed the everyday in the modern world, started from 1950 onwards. It consisted of an escape from the nuclear threat and from the setbacks of history. It evaded civic tasks while at the same time suffering the mystifications of official public-mindedness. However, we cannot explain reprivatization by these historical conditions alone, nor as a simple reaction to certain setbacks. At the same time needs were being aroused, some new, some existing potentially as mass phenomena and only crystallized by advertising, by the mediation of which they were connected to their objects. What was most striking, and still is, was the isolated nature of these needs and of the way they were stimulated. Each one of them has its objects and its slogans. Therefore each has its own distinct satisfaction which does not become part of a coherent totality. The satisfaction of contingent needs by objects which are themselves external and contingent defines one of the characteristics of the new 'private life', where general economic and social necessity is expressed by a series of chances (needs experienced, needs satisfied). Once need becomes need for *this* or for *that* it loses its fundamental spontaneity, while failing to individualize desire. This does not make the process any the less irreversible. Options have been taken (for example, as regards the role and importance of the motor car!). *Growth of needs, alienation of desire* is how we expressed it previously. We can now formulate it more precisely: *the external necessity of needs and the randomness of satisfactions*, with private life continuing to be the arena of these disjointed needs and satisfactions, and the link which joins them together.

Sociologists have noted how the contemporary family has been reduced to its simplest expression: to its nucleus. They speak commonly and without irony of the (isolated) 'nuclear family'. Well, this nucleus is being consolidated.[31] This 'residual deposit' has not yet broken up. It manifests itself simultaneously as a residual deposit and as a product (which is something we have said about the everyday in general). The family has not splintered as was expected a few decades ago. 'Reprivatization' is none the less surprising for not deriving from a precise, foreseeable function. It demonstrates that maybe the social cannot be reduced to the functional, and that the 'residual' not only is able to persist, but can also grow stronger. In any case, specialists can argue endlessly about the functional and its links with the real and the structural. Could the private life and the family of today be 'suprafunctional'? In certain circumstances, would not shelter from external dangers and pressures define a 'function'? In fact, the emergence of needs and the consumption of goods in this day and age can be seen as being 'functional' in the 'institutionalized' framework of the family and of private life.

In any event, everyday, private or 'reprivatized' life and family life are these days intimately linked together. Although the everyday does not restrict itself to the internal life of the family group and to 'private life', it encompasses the things which affect them. Therefore it includes whatever escapes from other groups as such, something which should not make us forget that in its way private family life penetrates, emphasizes and colours everything which spills over into it – work, leisure activities, sociability, culture.

The difficulty here is that if we are to grasp all the contradictions of reality, we must not overlook a single one of its aspects. Let us recall Marx's very illuminating observation: 'The abstraction of the *state as such* was not born until the modern world because the abstraction of private life was not created until modern times.'[32] This formula allows us to place the everyday within modernity, and we will have cause to remind ourselves of it more than once. Indeed, the paradox of the situation is not the consolidation of family life reduced to the 'nuclear', nor the process of 'reprivatization'. What is surprising is the set of contradictions which accompany this process and which constitute it. 'Reprivatization' takes place while history is speeding up. It is not only linked to the setbacks, trials and dangers concealed within this headlong acceleration; it is also linked to technology. Well, beginning with radio and television, technology should have given private life access to social and political life, to history and to knowledge. But while life and consciousness are becoming 'globalized', consciousness and private life are withdrawing into themselves, and this produces some unexpected results. Predictable and expected, 'globalization' is being achieved in the mode of withdrawal. In his armchair, the private man – who has even stopped seeing himself as a citizen – witnesses the universe without having a hold over it and without really wanting to. He looks at the world. He becomes globalized, but as an eye, purely and simply. He 'learns' something. But what exactly does this learning consist of? It does not consist of genuine knowledge, nor of power over the things seen, nor of real participation in events. It is a new modality of looking: a social gaze which rests on the image of things but which is reduced to powerlessness, the possession of a false consciousness, quasi-knowledge and non-participation. Without seeing that it is doing so, this gaze banishes real knowledge, real power and real participation. It really is a *private* gaze, the gaze of the private man who has become social, and despite the fact that it harbours the potential for interests, for enjoyments, and for a kind of 'mosaic' of culture.[33]

'Reprivatization' has its pleasant advantages; it creates a certain taste and a certain skill in the use of everyday objects. At the same time, its end product is submission to an impersonal, encyclopedic and vulgarized culture; like the feminine press, it introduces moral order through innuendo; it facilitates all the rigging and fixing that goes on in mass information. It is the world as an entity passively perceived, and without effective participation, and processes unfold within it which are visible but inaccessible: technology, space exploration, political strategies. Under the socialized gaze which substitutes for the active consciousness of social practice, these processes vanish into the distance at breakneck speed.

So the word 'private' has not lost its main meaning: privation. Private life remains privation. The 'world' is there to plug up the holes, fill in the cracks, paper over the gaps, camouflage the frustrations. Time is crammed full and life seems fit to burst. Or else it is empty. 'Chock-a-block full and completely empty.'

At the same time as life was being 'reprivatized', power and wealth were being personalized, and by the same means. Public and political life became laden with images borrowed from private life. For a long time, perhaps from the start, 'public' men and women – in other words, powerful or famous people – were commonplaces. They belonged (apparently) to everyone. This illusion was part of the way politics operated. It was part of the essence of the state and of the culture which had been established above society while appearing to remain part of it. It was not incompatible with democracy as a political system. It was one of the more honourable and relatively profound contradictions of a democracy which had been relatively successfully established.

Using modern means, this illusion deploys itself in a vast representation of real and practical social life. We are spared no detail of the everyday lives of princes and queens, of stars and millionaires, since 'great men' and 'bosses' and even 'heroes' have an everyday life on a par with our own. We 'know' their bathrooms almost as well as we know our own, we 'know' their mansions almost as well as we know our own flat, we 'know' their bodies almost as well as we know our own. This 'knowledge', if we can call it that, is spread throughout the world by means of images, and helps to create the attraction or powerful influence these celebrities exert. They are slaves to this knowledge. They cannot do without it. They know this, and submit to the demands of the public and of publicity, even if it means that they too must find refuge elsewhere. In short, seen from this angle, grandeur and the sublime are restored to the everyday. The public becomes private and the private becomes public, but in appearance only, since power retains its properties and wealth its possibilities. The humblest citizen knows his prince. He has been able to see him close up, almost as if he could touch him; but once he accepts this illusion, he has stopped being a citizen. The humblest farm-hand 'knows' queens, princesses and filmstars. But if he really believes he has attained a 'knowledge' of something, he is being trapped by one of modernity's strangest and most disturbing alienations. The rift between the private and the public has been overcome in appearance only. The supersession of these two aspects of social practice is nothing more than an illusion.

The social appears more open and more transparent than ever before. The *socialization of society* has adopted new forms, more extensive than previous ones, and on a truly 'world' scale, but mystification, alienation and privation have also adopted a world dimension. However, it is curiously 'worldly minded', and turns the world into a caricature of itself.

The world carries on its business beneath a gaze which has become social. But what happens in people's homes, in the enclosure of their private lives and behind the wall that is their forehead? Viewed from outside, private life appears opaque. From the warm and damp intimacy within, it is what is outside which appears threatening, storm-tossed and opaque. Inside, we do not know what is happening outside, where events come from or what causes tensions.

The most petty side of the everyday becomes reassuring. There, in private life, we think we are sure of being loved or hated (or both at once), of being protected and smothered, of being taken care of and pushed towards morbid states of mind. We are given the assurance that however insignificant we may be, at least we exist. This is one nucleus of the everyday, and one of its polarities.

It is the place where significations rise and then fall away into insignificance. (Let us take a photo album. Every face and every scene contains an episode or sums up a period in someone's life; each image is loaded with significations. Very quickly, these faces and scenes fade away; they become forgotten, dying their own social death, and are dead for ever; dramas lose their cutting edge and things lose their halo of meaning . . .)

Thus 'reprivatization' is prolonging and replacing the individualism of the earlier period, by substituting the small family group in place of the individual. Our society harbours profound contradictions, which mark the necessary and inevitable 'socialization of society'. While not making it completely problematic, these contradictions do raise many problems. Groups are getting larger (cities, businesses, classes) while at the same time the differentiations at the heart of these groups are becoming more strongly asserted. Information is increasing while direct contacts are in decline. Relations are becoming more numerous while their intensity and authenticity are diminishing. Along with segregations come diversities, and with possibilities of initiative and freedom come stricter conditionings.

Withdrawal into the self is passive in relation to an overcomplex social reality which oscillates between innuendo and brutal explicitness, but it appears to be a solution of sorts. It is as difficult to assess as it is to understand. It cannot be said that 'reprivatization' has not been *actively chosen*. There has been an *option*, and a general one (social options, group choices, socially accepted and adopted proposals for choice). Nor can it be said that it has been chosen freely. However, the choice itself is imposed and the solution is indicated or countermanded. This constraint operates within a fairly narrow margin of freedom; the weight from outside and from the 'world' becomes increasingly oppressive for an intimacy which has been metamorphosed into a mass phenomenon.

Is this a lifestyle, or is it life unequivocally stripped of all style?

Although we would tend towards the second of these hypotheses, it is still too early to reach a decision; scrutiny of these hypotheses and this problem is part of the *sociology of boredom* . . .

Very oddly, 'reprivatization' threw critical study of the everyday off course. 'Reprivatization' confirmed the everyday, but in an unexpected way; it modified and reconstituted it more forcefully than before as 'privation' and as the domain of appearances. This unexpected consolidation threw the study of it off track, because it altered the subject and the way of seeing it, as well as the methods being employed.

We have left several of the most surprising historical conditions of 'reprivatization' to one side, for example the temporary or permanent loss of prestige of the collective. Seen as a historical phenomenon, this loss of prestige was itself motivated in many psychological and sociological ways: experience of the restrictive nature of the collective; an end to the illusion of a 'catharsis' for the individual and his troubles by means of the social; an end to the illusion of a happy equilibrium for the individual within the social; and the realization that economic and political organization and overorganization were absorbing private life without creating a lifestyle free of 'privation', etc. What is most astonishing in all of this is not that the collective had been resorted to, nor the fact that this failed. For a long period of time, people were hoping and waiting for a radical transformation of everyday life: a new life. Only the collective (or rather a certain representation of the collective) seemed capable of delivering this transformation. This was the meaning of the 'Utopian socialism' which was so closely linked to 'scientific socialism'. The history of socialism offers a twofold lesson: the fall of the collective as a transforming agent of everyday life, and the rise of technology and its problems. Given this twofold experience, and given that the idea of a revolutionary transformation of the everyday has almost vanished, the withdrawal into an everyday which has not been transformed but which has benefited from a small proportion of technical progress becomes perfectly understandable. No, what is most astonishing is perhaps the fact that this withdrawal has in no way stopped collective organization and overorganization continuing to operate on its own level: the state, important decisions, bureaucracy. 'Reprivatized' life has its own level, and the large institutions have theirs. These levels are juxtaposed or superimposed.

Consolidated around this nucleus, private life and the everyday provide an alibi for escaping from history, from failures, from risks and from threats, and this creates a gulf between 'the lived' and the domain of history,[34] which is a consequence of its setbacks and backward surges. But let us not be misled. To be reticent about history, to run away from the historical and from the problems of society as a whole (in other words, to run away from politics), is nevertheless one of the ways history is lived. The extra-historicity of modern everyday life is itself a modality of history and a demonstration of its inner conflicts. When the everyday consolidates itself as 'private life' it does not eliminate history, no more than what is determined eliminates the randomness it contains. 'No throw of the dice can eliminate chance.'[35] Hesitations, hiding places, escape routes, they all disguise many things and prevent nothing. Never did history pursue people to the extent it has since people have entrenched themselves against it and attempt to take part in events as spectators of images.

Nevertheless it remains true that not everything is equally historical, or equally 'cultural'.

Although in fact men do not escape history, or culture, or knowledge, and are fascinated by them precisely because of the growing gap between such external forces and their own lives, they nevertheless consolidate a level of reality which offers a kind of passive resistance to history and knowledge. In certain cases this resistance becomes active; and so, withdrawn within their own everyday reality, the members of a social group can oppose an enemy, an occupying power, a 'creator' of events or a political leader.

In our view, there is a sense to 'reprivatization'. It cannot be defined simply as the search for an alibi or a means of escape from history. In its reactions to the setbacks of revolution or the danger of planetary extermination, it is not simply burying its head in the sand. Clumsily but insistently, it is seeking an acceptable way forward: not an absolute barrier between the private and the public, between the individual and the social and the historical – nor a completely free passage which would abolish the characteristics of the former in favour of the latter, and which would be nothing more than a gaping void. Radical critique of 'reprivatization' does not stop us from understanding it; on the contrary, understanding it is just as important as explaining it.

Along with 'reprivatization' are various phenomena deriving from social links and relations: the reinstatement of certain affective tonalities (such as friendship and comradeship) and ill-defined values associated with groups linked by affinity or affiliation – a hesitant return to social spontaneity. Moreover, the 'world of objects' has assumed new importance, while at the same time it has become more diversified: familiar or unfamiliar technical items, useful or useless items, luxury items, aesthetic items, objects which impose certain behaviour patterns or which allow for initiative by appealing to the imagination, to emotions, to memory. To study this world of objects and how it is divided and classified would require a *logistics of everyday life*.

24

Is this a matter for philosophy or philosophical analysis? Yet again: *yes and no*. Yes, since critical analysis and presentation of the everyday use categories which originate in philosophy: appropriation, alienation, privation, power (of man over nature and over his own nature), need, desire, critical negativity, etc.

And yet, no. Before they can be used in the pursuit of concrete knowledge, these categories must be extricated from the systematizations within which philosophical thought has imprisoned them, and made to stand apart from any specifically philosophical system.

So what is the core issue? In our view, critical study of the everyday contributes towards a *dialectical anthropology* which is itself dependent upon (or coincidental with) a *dialectical humanism*.

The real core issue is to define mankind. Marxist dogmatism defined it by labour and for labour, as a producer. But active man creates the human world and, through the act of production, produces himself. He does not simply produce things, implements or goods; he also produces history and situations. He creates 'human nature': nature in himself and for himself, nature appropriated to man by means of his many conflicts. Marxist dogmatism determines man unilaterally, and foregrounds the outside world and the thing, and power over matter and material production. It has parenthesized man's nature and the inner appropriation of nature by the human. In its pedagogy, in its philosophy and in its propaganda, in its art and in its system of education, its conception of them is purely cursory.

All dogmatisms mutilate the human by determining it as something unilateral. They take away one or several of its dimensions. Our starting point is a totality, but differentiated according to dimension and level. Our starting point is a total human phenomenon: 'need–work–pleasure', 'speak–make–live'. The term 'phenomenon' shows the will to supersede philosophical ontology and not to presume to exhaust the human and the 'world' by defining them as essences.

Could the human be essentially cultural? Could it be defined by tools and technology, reason, Logos or language, by knowledge, by culture, by an analytic intellect which calculates and organizes? These definitions are just as acceptable and just as limited as definitions which use historicity, or practical reason which projects and realizes objectives by taking risks and options, and less rational definitions which use dreams, laughter, play, love or awareness of death.

'Man' is this, but other things (or other 'non-things') as well. He is a plurality of dimensions, a multiplicity of forms and structures. He is a shifting hierarchy of levels (which means that the usual concept of 'structure' must be modified and dynamized). Thus he is also the everyday, in so far as the everyday introduces an unevenly developed level into totality, which nevertheless transforms itself, and which above all *must* transform itself. In the words of Nietzsche, 'Man is the animal which is not yet defined.' We would add the everyday to the dimensions we have previously defined, and that everyday is something which urgently needs to be transformed, so that its theory cannot be separated from a revolutionary praxis which has been restored to all its former breadth, and from a vision of what is possible (and impossible).

Dialectical anthropology does not exclude culture but neither does it parenthesize nature in the name of culture (which would be a 'culturalism'). It studies the conflictual 'nature/culture' relation, particularly on the level where it manifests itself: in the everyday. It does not exclude the historical and does not place 'the lived' outside history. It studies the conflictual 'historicity/lived' relation, particularly on the level where it manifests itself: in everyday life. By concentrating on this humble territory, which forms and structures both inhabit, it hopes to avoid unilateralities and neofetishisms (of signification, of non-signification or of the thing without signification – of structure and of the spontaneous – of culture and anticulture, of totality and non-totality, for example).

This anthropology takes history into account but excludes 'historicism', which sees everything as being equally historical. It encompasses the study of political economy, but combines with a critique of political economy which rejects and refutes economism (the doctrine of economic determinism). Finally, it includes a *sociology*, in other words a conception of the social ensemble; but equally it includes a critique of *sociologism*, in other words of the attitude which privileges one set of facts and concepts in totality since it eliminates history and historicity, nature, and the problems raised by the links between them. In short, it eliminates a whole range of dialectical movements. Therefore, and not without paradox, we will offer both a dialectical sociology (or an attempt at one) and a critique of the foundations of sociology.

To put it another way, our guideline will be a critical study of what can and ought to change in human reality. By emphasizing one part (one level) of reality, and above all by referring to critique of this level of reality – to creative negation – we will attempt to grasp reality, but not to exhaust it.

25

As we continue in this direction towards our goal, we will soon come up against some run-of-the-mill methodological concerns. There are a certain number of formal and general concepts which we need to review in order to see precisely how we can use them: the concept of *level*, of *structure*, of *totality*, of *tactic* and *strategy*, and finally, of *model*. The latter is particularly important in that we will be proposing a model (or several models) of social reality: nothing more, nothing less.

26

Once we have clarified this conceptual equipment, we will introduce several specific concepts.

From the outset we will divide these specific concepts into two groups: categories of ambiguity and categories of non-ambiguity. The following concepts belong in the first of these groups: *ambiguity, misunderstanding, compromise, misjudgement* and *misuse, denial, agreement* and *contestation, connivance* and *complicity, disquiet, alibi*, etc.

We will rank the following concepts in the second group: *decision* and *opposition, dilemma* and *action logic, challenge* and *mistrust, refusal, choice, wager, risk, repetition* and *recognition, the possible* and *the impossible*, etc.

27

Finally, we will present a certain number of theoretical ideas and theories with the intention of interpreting the everyday within the context of society as a whole: the theory of the semantic field and of the social text; the theory of (cumulative and non-cumulative) processes; the theory of moments; the theory of the world of objects and of the logistics of things; the theory of doubles, of reverse images and of breaks, etc. We have already presented or outlined several of these theories in previous publications. Finally, we will need to return to the theory of alienation and the theory of praxis in order to clarify them dialectically.

28

In no respects is this lengthy conceptual development an end in itself, and nor is the knowledge it may produce. Concepts and knowledge are not ends, but means. Means for what?

To reply, and to bring this methodological summing up to an end, we would like to reiterate our principles as strongly as possible. *There can be no knowledge of society (as a whole) without critical knowledge of everyday life in its position – in its organization and its privation, in the organization of its privation – at the heart of this society and its history. There can be no knowledge of the everyday without critical knowledge of society (as a whole). Inseparable from practice or praxis, knowledge encompasses an agenda for transformation. To know the everyday is to want to transform it. Thought can only grasp it and define it by applying itself to a project or programme of radical transformation. To study*

everyday life and to use that study as the guideline for gaining knowledge of moder-
nity is to search for whatever has the potential to be metamorphosed and to follow
the decisive stages or moments of this potential metamorphosis through: it is to
understand the real by seeing it in terms of what is possible, as an implication of
what is possible. For 'man will be an everyday being or he will not be at all'.

This lengthy conceptual development will allow us to tackle a
determined and precise problematic: the theory of needs; the links
between everyday life, the modern city and housing developments;
the place and the future of art in the so-called modern world, etc.
Then we will be able to look at some of the questions which have been
treated in a methodologically flimsy way by certain recent authors.
Thus in *The Affluent Society*[36] Galbraith points out the drawbacks of the
'consumer society' in America, where the most important social needs
are left to badly managed public services; and then, starting from the
opposite political postulate, we have Moravia, whose *A Month in the*
USSR shows that whereas the public domain in the USSR is generally
remarkably well managed, most private needs are overlooked or
scorned. How can we explain this symmetrical breakdown in the two
conflicting modes of production in the world today? And what does it
mean?

One day we might even try to deal with questions such as: 'In conditions which in other respects are well defined, what is the social
cost of an ordinary individual life? And in equally well-defined conditions, what would be the social cost of a fulfilled individual life, if
such fulfilment had become the norm?'[37]

2

The Formal Implements

1 Axioms and axiomatization

We will not make a systematic attempt to construct a table of axioms, in other words a group of propositions which have formal properties: consistency (rigorous coherence without contradiction); independence (relatively methodical) of the statements proposed; sufficiency (completeness of the system); saturation; categoricity.

In our opinion it is possible to formulate axioms in the social sciences and especially in sociology, but impossible to build any particular science using deductive theories (in other words, to establish a closed system by 'saturating' that set of axioms). It goes without saying that it is imperative to make ample room for forms and formal systems, both as regards the methodology of the sciences and as regards the object of study itself. In social reality, forms have their own existence and effectiveness. This does not make systematizing and formalizing them an any the less erroneous and impossible enterprise. Research, conceptual development and theories are a matter for dialectical method, not deductive logic. For example, *counting*, which is used in mathematics with the utmost rigour, can be found in every discipline; however, rather than demonstrating the inexhaustible character of a continuum, the act of counting, of classifying and of exhausting a set of distinct units (an act which gives rise to operations and operators) does not constitute absolute intelligibility. Only mathematicians have been able to imagine that it does. The human mind and knowledge begin with small whole numbers; nevertheless we very soon imagine the infinitely large and the infinitely small, the continuous, the inexhaustible. For century after century the mathematician has made every effort to extend counting into large numbers (something done by machines nowadays); today his concern is continuousness, inexhaustible units, and order for its own sake within these units. The social sciences and the study of human data use counting, but already they are subordinating it to a more complex set of implements. All formal implements are subject to the conditions under which they are applied; all formal systems have their limits.

In the course of this study we have already come across some axioms – but without recognizing them as such. One in particular scarcely needs formulating: 'There can be no knowledge of society without critique of that society, of its representations (ideologies) and its accepted concepts.' Let us proceed by drawing up a provisional, non-restrictive list of the axioms it is appropriate to formulate as such.

Axiom of language: The sociologist speaks the same language as the men (individuals; members of a group) he is seeking to reach and whose way of life he wishes to understand.

Comments. This axiom lends itself to a trivial interpretation. It has been pointed out a thousand times that it is difficult to gain access to a group which speaks a different language than the scientist studying it. It is not only dialects, vocabularies, jargon and languages specific to determined groups (such as small farmers from a specific region of France, or workers in a specific trade and from a specific city) which set traps for the investigator.

Let us get beyond these banalities. The very way this axiom is formulated underlines a danger and a risk which we must confront empirically: its value as a regulator derives from its falseness on the immediately empirical level. No matter how simple the facts of the everyday may be, the investigator and the group he is investigating will *never* use exactly the same words in exactly the same way. Every dialogue is made up of two unequal participants: one wants to know, and speaks the language of someone who wants to know; the other remains hidden, even when he is perfectly willing to answer the questions. When the 'subject' of an inquiry, the interviewee, coincides with the 'object' of study and opens himself up unreservedly, we have someone abnormal on our hands, an exhibitionist, and there is all the more reason to mistrust what he tells us.

In sociology, most interviews (and the in-depth, undirected interview in particular) begin with a period of awkwardness, as investigators well know. Beginners would like to avoid or shorten this period; they do not realize how fruitful it is. That such awkwardness cannot be avoided, that uneasiness arises almost of necessity when a living contact is established, is something which techniques of group dynamics and psychotherapeutic interviews would confirm, were confirmation needed. In all cases, the dramatic content of the lived is concealed beneath evasive behaviour patterns. The interview starts with a sort of tacit challenge to the interviewee by the interviewer (to reach him, to grasp him, to know him) and to the interviewer by the interviewee (to put him off track, to elude him). The higher the stakes the greater the challenge and the deeper the uneasiness. While this uneasiness lasts, the investigator, unable to fight back a kind of mental vertigo, tries to clarify his representations and to refine his language. During this same period, the person being interviewed slowly agrees to receive or to release a portion of the 'real': an aspect of the hidden drama, the situation of his everyday reality. Any common language becomes apparent at the end of these dialogues, once the 'dialogue of the deaf' has been avoided. It is at the end, and not at the beginning, that the common language is to be found.

Sadly, the police interrogation, the psychological investigation, the dialogue between someone who wants to know and someone who resists being known, and the psychoanalytic interview, all have more than one point in common. The big difference is in the way the initial awkwardness is dealt with and modified, and in the degree of caution – which is simply a form of respect – with which it is made use of. Some interviewers try to influence their 'subject', who is also an 'object'. Others, more attentive and more circumspect, seek to know their subject while modifying him as little as possible. Such investigators will rank patience among the virtues which are a precondition of knowledge.

Subsidiary axiom: Signs and significations are not things. Expressions, symptoms and manifestations are not beings.

To achieve a common language in dialogue, the investigator (who, no matter how cautious and respectful, will always be an inquisitor) must avoid imposing his own language on this 'subject' who is also the 'object' of knowledge and the 'theme' of the investigation. When the 'subject' bends over backwards to accept the sociologist's terminology, his statements become unreliable. Evasion and defiance are more revealing and more valuable than the accommodating attitude beginners find so beguiling.

But there is a lesson to be learned from experiencing this awkwardness. We could call it: 'the sociologist's catharsis', or a major aspect of 'sociological culture'. A profound culture and a difficult 'catharsis' are essential for grasping the sheaf of givens which, though objective, in no way share the objectivity of things, and which represent nothing more than an approach by 'being' caught up in the drama of its everyday life. The significations of these givens are formulated in the very *act* of *dialogue*. What words other than action and dialogue could define this subtle, delicate and finely honed mixture of sympathetic friendliness and harshness, perhaps even cruelty, which alone is capable of bringing what is concealed by evasiveness and yet revealed by it out into the open? When crudely conducted, a sociological interview modifies the semeiology[1] it is trying to grasp and interpret, as radically as any police interrogation would. Knowledge and understanding between human beings, individuals and groups can only be reciprocal, in and via an exchange. The relation between the 'subject' and the 'object', between the investigator and the investigation as a common language is sought (i.e., a semeiology which will reveal the secret drama of the group and of the everyday individual in the everyday life of the group), is one which is learned and cultivated. The wish to learn and to understand should reveal 'being' rather than fixing it in its inevitable evasiveness, and that is the aim of this culture. The more finely honed it is, the less it will suppress, and the more it will be capable of overcoming the distances and obstacles set up by defiance and misunderstandings. It alone allows us to be genuinely concerned with human beings, in a way which justifies the wish for knowledge.

A culture such as this is conditional on certain qualities and talents, such as tact and speed. It requires training. And even more: that the investigator involve and compromise himself within the dialogue. Only via a return to his own everyday reality will he reach the everyday reality of the people he is interviewing. It is a detour he must take, and a disturbing one. He must purge himself not only of his ideological and theoretical prejudices, and of his limited vocabulary, but also of his value judgements, which perhaps constitute the biggest barrier of all.[2]

Inspired by qualitative or ordinal mathematics (groups theory, information theory) certain theoreticians in the social sciences would surely formulate another axiom: *All research consists of questions which can be answered by yes or by no.* For them, a question for which there is not a yes-or-no answer is simply badly expressed; it is a question which cannot be answered.

While taking care to make room for these theories, and for information theory in particular, we would challenge this axiom (which precisely would lead towards an integral axiomatization and to a purely logical cohesion of science). To exhaust reality, the number of questions which must be answered by yes or by no would be infinite. What is more, there are questions which demand replies other than 'yes' or 'no' and yet which bring knowledge. And perhaps this is the moment to stress the difference between *information* and *knowledge*. Those questions to which the interviewee replies and can only reply by yes or no provide information. The questions to which he cannot reply by yes or no bring knowledge. 'Are you happy?' After a moment's thought, nobody could answer with an absolute yes or no. Everyone will reply: 'Yes and no. In this respect, yes, in that respect, no. And in any case, what do you mean by happiness?' The person who does answer yes or no is informing us of a fact, that he is going through a phase of satisfaction or dissatisfaction, that he is being optimistic, that he is simplifying his opinion in order to communicate it, etc.

There is nothing worse than a questionnaire which is so well constructed that it believes it can exhaust its 'object'. It imposes clarity and the vocabulary of science upon the people it is seeking to reveal. Much more valuable in a dialogue are chance and game-playing, when the participants talk about this and that. In this case, meaning may spring from a chance encounter, similar to a reward or, to use the register of psychiatry, a 'gratification', although knowledge cannot consist of such fortuitous 'gratifications' alone.

A vocabulary which is clumsily and disrespectfully imposed leads us easily to a certain scepticism. Since the chosen terminology is unusable, would it not suffice to talk to people in any way we like, and to make contact through any subject at all, by skilfully using their own language? This is not valid either. Although game-playing may be worth more than inflexibility, and chance just as valuable as excessive rigour, cunning linguistic manoeuvres are just as ineffective as the use of crude and destructive terminological implements. The goal of research, which challenges the 'sociologist' per se, is to enable a dialogue to produce knowledge by means of mutual understanding.

Obliged to take the language of the individuals and the groups he seeks to understand into account, should the 'sociologist' eschew the language of his own group and of science? No. The language of science must be as precise as possible, and act as the common denominator between the symbolisms and modes of expression which research will discover across a range of different groups. What is more, there can be no science without terminology.

But where does terminology end? Where does jargon begin? Must the sociologist force himself to use nothing but familiar words, giving them a conceptualized meaning which differs slightly from their usual meaning? Would this be a way of establishing a common ground between the relatively incoherent or systematized semeiologies he is seeking to reveal and interpret?

The physicist and the mathematician do not have this problem. As specialists, they divorce themselves from everyday men. They are no longer concerned with the link between the terms and signs they employ and day-to-day vocabulary, or between their concepts and common sense (their everyday reality). The correspondence is apparent throughout the history of knowledge and science for whoever wishes to find it – the philosopher, for example. For the sciences of mankind, it is quite a different story. It must be possible to transfer from the day-to-day language of social praxis to scientific terminology at any time. If not, the terminology will lose contact with the first and final object of knowledge – praxis – and science will no longer come together with praxis to change itself into action. Jargon begins with the hiatus between practical language and scientific language. From that point on, well-integrated sets of facts and meanings may be constructed, but they will have one drawback: arbitrariness, linkage by jargon terms. Hence *the axiom of discourse* which we will formulate for use as follows: *In his memory and in his thinking, the sociologist of everyday life must maintain the linkage between day-to-day language and his own terminology, and the transition from one to the other. At every moment he must be able to translate the one into the other and to carry out all the necessary intermediary operations.*

In this way the sociology of the everyday is reinvesting specific knowledge with a philosophical requirement philosophers have too often neglected. Its science never becomes separated from *poetics*, in the sense given to the term by Diderot in the *Encyclopédie*: a set of rules which one applies to create a work in a given genre. *Poetics* here is the transformation of everyday life in and by praxis. It extends philosophy, it satisfies the requirements of philosophy, and it supersedes philosophy . . .

Axiom of strategies: Whether they are aware of it or not, social groups and individuals within groups have tactics and strategies (i.e., series of connected long-term or short-term decisions). Conversely and reciprocally, a set of individuals without a tactic and a strategy cannot be a social group.

Comments. We are giving a definition axiomatically. Tactics and strategies correspond to what in often vague and philosophical language are called projects, decisions, plans for action and for the future, or agendas.

In its particular manner, the immobility of groups (always more apparent than real, like the principle of rest and inertia in nature) provides a tactic and a strategy for survival. Survival in itself is a form of action.

Tactics and strategies do not exhaust the reality of social groups within themselves and in their conflictual relations with other groups. To formulate the theory in a way which would eliminate other aspects of reality (alienation, for example, or symbolisms) would be unjustifiable. Nevertheless, this axiom is extremely important. It eliminates the illusion of inertia and rest, and this is a point we would like to emphasize. The existence of a social group (with the individuals it encompasses) is permanently called into question, both in the short term and in the long term. It either knows this, is reluctant to know it, or does not know it. If it does not know it, the group (and the individuals) will sink into mindless stagnation. To put it another way, individuals can be differentiated by their degree of participation in the consciousness and action of the group; leaders are people who think up the tactic and, most importantly, the strategy, and who devote themselves to putting it into action. It is clear that everyday life within the group depends upon these constellations (the consciousness and participation of individuals, and the presence and activeness of leaders).

The axiom of strategies demonstrates a multidimensionality. The sociologist belongs to one group or to several, each with its own tactic and strategy. Science itself has its strategy, of which the scientist is more or less aware, and of which he is more or less the leader. In short, every group we may study will have its strategy and its tactic.

Once it comes under scrutiny, a group may seal itself hermetically in the face of any investigation, or it may welcome the sociologist with open arms. Consciously or unconsciously, both reactions form part of its strategy. If a stranger is given a warm-hearted reception, apparent or genuine, it is because he is expected to bring something with him, such as information or propaganda from outside the group. As for the sociologist, objectivity is frequently and superficially trivialized as being a form of passivity, and this he cannot accept. And yet, he does not want to be biased. Therefore he will have to confront these multiple dimensions: the tactic and strategy of the groups to which he is affiliated or from which he originated (class, nation, intelligentsia, etc.); the tactic and strategy for knowledge and for the insertion of his knowledge into praxis; the tactic and strategy of the group he is studying.

This confrontation will provide a limited, relative but heightened objectivity. During it the sociologist of the everyday will make a comparison between the revealing (signifying) elements of the various projects for action, including language, symbols, attitudes, opinions and behaviour patterns. During this comparison he will disengage himself from his own subjective elements, ridding himself of them by calling them into question. As far as possible, he will free himself from the social contexts upon which he depends. He will force himself to adopt the asceticism which is an integral part of scientific culture: to think on several planes and to organize and structure the transfer from one to the other in a coherent way.

Axiom of mediations: It will be to the advantage of the sociology of everyday life and of empirical research in general to avoid groups which are too small or too large. It is equally to the advantage of sociologists engaged in empirical research if they parenthesize concepts which are too narrow and too precise, in terms of how they can be understood and to the connotations they have.

Comments. This axiom stipulates a regulatory rule or hypothesis rather than a form or a formal definition. It has links with the previous axiom. The sociologist of the everyday will not lose sight of the fact that he is acting as a rational 'medium' or intermediary between groups in society as a whole. Despite the many mediations and communications which exist between them (including language), these groups are partially external and opaque to each other.

There are occasions when this rule needs to be flexible. For example, the study of interindividual relations within the restricted framework of family life, and the description of individual roles and their relation within this framework, would fall more within the purview of psychology or social psychology. However, (private) family life in an overall context – the bourgeoisie, farmers, the proletariat, French society, etc. – is within the purview of the sociology of everyday life as we have defined it. This does not mean to say that it does not exist within even larger groups, where standards of living and lifestyles, etc., can be determined by the relations within them.

If we consider a very large group, for example the working class in general, i.e., on a world scale, it is a reality which goes far beyond our investigative possibilities. It is a matter for sociology in general: beginning with the concept, it seeks to define the link between this concept as accepted and current praxis, and thus to grasp the current situation of the working class within a specific social entity. However, it will be very difficult to study so vast a reality empirically – in its everyday reality. As an overall entity, society itself is very difficult to grasp.

It is in our (scientific) interest to move among intermediate realities, employing modest concepts which are not too wide and not too narrow. It is in our interest to begin our investigation with those realities which act as mediations and *means*, and which consequently are neither too secret nor too publicly manifest: tactics and strategies in so far as they become manifest in action; symbols and signs in so far as they are practically effective; communication groups, villages, neighbourhoods, towns, businesses, trade unions, etc. The macrosociological and the microsociological, the whole and the restricted, none must escape scrutiny. However, the restricted, the local and the 'micro' have limits and an opaqueness which resist investigation. In the pursuit of the whole and the total, sooner or later thought will be brought to a halt by the political decision which determines them, by the options which have been taken or are in the process of being taken, and by the ethic or the aesthetic which is in the process of making (or breaking) itself – invention, creative activity, *poiesis*. Now knowledge can offer them its contribution and its arguments. It cannot presume to command them.

As a working hypothesis, we will elaborate certain propositions which are linked to the previous axiom: *The sociological unity of a group and the social consciousness which links the consciousnesses of its constituent individuals to it are never more than intermediary states, mediations or means to an end. Tactic and strategy determine this and are determined by it. In phases of extreme tension, turmoil and intense social activity, the existence of a group becomes historical. Its structures burst asunder. Its everyday life is suspended, shattered or changed. It coincides with the historical. In the phases of complete relaxation and stagnation, interindividual and psychic relations predominate; the group tends to fall apart and everyday life tends to show only its most banal and trivial side. Thus it is indeed the medium, intermediary, mediating phases which we are considering here as providing privileged testimony.*

Thus, setting out from the medium zones, our study would go in one direction towards the broader zones, and in another towards the narrower ones, not in order to separate them from each other, but to reach them.

Our study holds no presuppositions about the complexity and the contradictions on these (micro and macro) scales, and this is what distinguishes the previous rules and axioms from Cartesian thought, which uses the simple to assemble the complex.

These givens underline the prudent, limitative and relative character of a research programme which nevertheless opens a vast field of experiences and knowledge. Every statement acts equally as a safety barrier and as a positive heuristic rule.

2 The role of hypothesis

The role of hypothesis in the sciences in general has been examined many times. We feel it could be useful to return to it in order to clarify its role in the social sciences and in our own research.

Let us remind ourselves that in all dogmatisms the process of knowledge is bound up with systematized philosophical arrangements, thus devaluing the role of hypothesis and the invention of hypotheses.

Dogmatism quite correctly gives prominence to the presuppositions inherent in the way facts are perceived, as well as in scientific observation, in conceptual links between phenomena and in theoretical developments, but then it extrapolates. It tries to reduce these implications to general, and thus philosophical, *postulates*; this would allow it to police the use of hypotheses. However it is clear that hypotheses which are subordinated to a systematized philosophy (to an idealist or materialist ontology) lose the characteristics of hypothesis, and are imposed a priori as absolute truths. This is the way the materialists (contradicting dialectic) and the idealists (totally in agreement with themselves, which guarantees them the benefit of coherence) proceeded. When knowledge is regulated in this way, the first thing to be compromised is the invention of hypotheses. This leads to sterility.

On the other hand, a certain subjectivism (equally philosophical in inspiration), a certain relativism and a certain positivism have stressed the hypothetical character of every science. The use of hypothesis would make knowledge conjectural. In its way, this tendency extrapolates as well. The invention of hypotheses and the very requirement for hypotheses may originate either in the elusive complexity of the real, or in an a priori inherent to the human mind, such as determined categories or a general (logical and formal) principle of identity.

Going farther than previous methodological work,[3] and with the desire to make room for imagination in the knowledge of the human 'real', we will maintain here that the role of hypothesis is connected to the *complexity* of the phenomena under scrutiny and also to their *random* character (both aspects being interdependent).

We are not using the term *random* in a pejorative way to mean whatever knowledge is unable to grasp, in other words pure chance, a radical contingency or an indeterminism. The thesis of an absolute indeterminism both in nature and in historical and social reality, as opposed to the thesis of an absolute determinism, is certainly untenable. Here as elsewhere we are trying to clarify a way of thinking dialectically. There are determined biological, historical, economic, sociological *conditions* (which are taken over and modified by their own creative praxis), which constitute the 'real' in its accepted sense. There are *processes*, which contain the evolution and forward movements of the real. These conditions and processes point towards *possibilities*.

It is itself a necessary requirement that a choice, an option or a decision (a tactical and strategic commitment) be made regarding these possibilities. Free actions – collective or individual, short term or long term – do not escape determinism; they are based upon it; they have their inner determinisms; they unfold; they are born premature or they come to full term; they are enacted with varying degrees of awareness and effectiveness, sometimes blind, sometimes calculated; they modify their determined conditions and create new ones. They modify and reorientate processes but they do not eliminate them.

We rule out the idea of absolute necessity along with the idea of absolute chance and the purely fortuitous. Absolute necessity, i.e., determinism, belongs to ideology, not to knowledge. It excludes dialectical movement, relative chance and relative necessity, the relatively predictable and the relatively unpredictable. From this viewpoint, there is a certain unpredictability (and thus the advent of something genuinely new) which does not come simply from not knowing the causes and limits of knowledge. It also comes from chance per se, and also from freedom. We cannot calculate a priori what the limits to predictability are, but knowledge can never predict everything, nor can practical action prefigure and control everything. By using formal theories (games and decision theory, information theory) we can even *predict the unpredictable per se*.

Thus this notion of randomness is based on a few recent acquisitions to the field of knowledge, and notably on *information* theory. If we are careful not to confuse 'information' with 'knowledge', this will facilitate the inclusion of information within knowledge. The concept of randomness in information theory profoundly modifies the concept of statistical probability which derives from the natural sciences (statistical and quantic theories). It implies an exploration of the *field of possibilities* (whereas statistical probability infers predictions based on the past). Above all – and this is its principal interest in so far as this study is concerned – it implies the idea of a *widening of the field of possibilities*. To our mind this widening is essential if we are to understand the life of groups and individuals in 'modern' society. In a sense it characterizes it. It is what makes it imperative to have increasingly more finely honed and conscious *tactics* and *strategies*. It is what makes it essential to *opt* more and more frequently.

The widening of possibilities is accompanied by contradictory phenomena: pressures and constraints, models and norms, checks, gaps and imbalances. Moral or ideological pressures and constraints maintain a sort of static equilibrium within individual or collective consciousnesses which run the danger of being swamped by possibilities. Thus *realization* can lag behind *possibilities* to a vast extent. In the random field of what is possible, realization – subjected to objective and restrictive rules – is itself random. The real, i.e., *realization*, can only be understood through the possible and the random.

Let us go beyond formal methodology and illustrate this statement by a few examples, i.e., a few *hypotheses*.

a) An individual can imagine himself to be a nebula (a cloud) of virtualities (*possibilities*). This representation is not a carbon copy of quantic theories of matter, which speak of a cloud of *probabilities*. The process of his practical life consists of a sort of condensation of possibilities. From being a nebula or cloud of virtualities, he becomes a constellation of actions and powers (capacities). He realizes himself, more or less completely. Complete realization, the exhausting of possibilities, is immobility and death.

The same is true of groups. They too make their way through randomness: they take chances, they wager on their future, or they stagnate. They come into being, they manage to survive, or they die.

b) The entry of *women* into industrial production has not resulted in a massive increase in the number of women in the active (productive) population. It has allowed for a redistribution of female jobs: fewer women employed in domestic services and more employed in commercial services and office jobs, etc. Above all it gives women – to a certain extent, and according to social class and country of residence – the chance to *choose*. They can educate themselves, take up a profession, give it up as soon as they marry or have a baby, or go on working. Possibilities require options – not irrational options, but ones which are motivated and thought through. Thus the determined economic and social process (the entry of women into industrial production and more generally into active life) has not revolutionized the female condition, as it was expected to do. It has increased the number of possibilities and choices, and the degree to which women

112

can be free, both as individuals and as a social group. This produces obvious paradoxes. In the working class, many women choose, more or less freely, not to work in factories or workshops. In the comfortably off classes, many women choose to work in offices and to take up professions.

Thus the ideas of determinism or of necessary process, and of possibilities and options, are not ruled out either for groups or for individuals. The same applies for the idea of chance and of regularity (or determined tendency). If a group is to establish what its relations are to be, hypotheses are inevitable. The way options are shared out within a group is not completely predictable. Any study of the situation of women today will contain hypotheses about the grouping under consideration, the contingencies and possibilities of choice, and the variables within projects of choice which help to explain frequencies.

This brings us to the idea of *social options*. Individuals are not alone in making choices. Very large or restricted groups alike point themselves consciously or unconsciously in an irreversible direction, and select a particular solution for their problems, either collectively or in the person of their leader. Any given solution was not imposed by an absolute necessity. Other routes were possible. Sometimes we (individuals and groups, the masses and their leaders) realize this too late. In any event, a bifurcation has been reached, possibilities have been separated, and one possibility has been adopted to the exclusion of the others. Thus in the so-called 'West' we have opted for a durable consumer item: the car. We have given it an important place in our everyday lives. Though it was taken in the past, today this option controls the development of industry, causes traffic problems, and makes it necessary for towns to be restructured, etc. The example of countries of the East makes it clear that this was a social option and a collective choice (not a necessity). This option is an integral part of a comprehensive society: economy, culture, lifestyle. It helps to compose and to typify it. Just like important political decisions, collective options introduce *discontinuity* into the historical and the social.

c) When dealing with a sociological problem, it is sometimes possible to use the following formula: 'let us suppose the problem has been resolved, and let the person answering be x . . .' Given a virtual population or the virtual rise in an existing population, we may find ourselves faced with a problem such as the following: 'If x is the possible structure of the town which contains this population, what properties should we attribute to this possible structure to enable the population to draw predictable advantages from it?' Then, we will try to find a representation for x, i.e., to *imagine* it in function of the desired result. Generally we will find variants x, x, x, each one of which we must examine and criticize. Thus we will use the method of imaginary variants. It is obvious that these variants can be relatively daring, according to the quality of the imagination constructing them. The examination of solutions and variants may often force us to reconsider the problem, its terms, and the notions which allowed it to be formulated.

This is how the sociology of everyday life can consider the problems of *urban development*. It can contribute to the search for optimum formulae. The problem is a practical one. We have a great many experiences at our disposal to help us resolve it: the experience of old towns (spontaneous, historical), which were relatively successful, and of new towns, which have been more or less a failure. We are working on a *virtual object*, which must be brought into being. How can we achieve this without the use of images? If we are to move from received experiences to the construction of the virtual object, there are a certain number of steps we must take: the formulation of a problematic, the elaboration of *hypotheses* and propositions about what is possible, the invention of images, etc.

Therefore we must bring hypothesis into general use. No hypothesis must be excluded a priori, no matter how arbitrary, risky, extreme or even dangerous it may be. By introducing both chance and imagination into knowledge of the social real, we are making room for chance in the way we invent hypotheses, and for a kind of free play in the process of gaining knowledge.

The sociologist's investigative abilities are linked to his capacity to invent hypotheses. Consciously or not, he explores what is possible by using images just as much as concepts. Therefore, in the specific culture which follows the 'catharsis' we spoke of earlier, there is a form of imagination which has its part to play. The role played by imagination and hypothesis will have consequences in terms of styles of thinking, and the sciences of human and social reality will use imagination more or less consciously and deliberately to find an original style.

If hypotheses which share the random character of the phenomena under scrutiny are used extensively, this is also due to the *problematic* character of these phenomena. This term no more means 'irrational', 'uncertain' or 'impossible to formulate' than the term 'random' means 'indeterminable'. On the contrary! Human groups have problems, real problems which make up part of their total reality. Possibilities are answers and solutions – more or less good, near or remote – to these problems. To get close to a group, or to the individuals within a group, and to understand it, is to determine what that group's problematic is, at a given moment and in a given situation or set of circumstances.

The 'problematic' cannot be confused with the 'absurd'. In real life, human problems arise with contradictions which demand and imply solutions, opening up possibilities. The problems men set themselves are not insoluble (if it were true that humanity only set itself insoluble problems, and that its problematic is indefinite and undetermined, all present and future humanism would collapse, and nihilism would take over in its stead), but nor do they have ready-made solutions. Therefore it is the problematic side of a human group which enables us to grasp its reality, its possibilities and the (tactical and strategic) way it can achieve them. In this way we avoid yet again the false dilemma of either pure empiricism and the collection of unconnected facts or philosophy, dogmatism and presuppositions. Finally, we are connecting the social sciences as a whole to a general but determined problematic of man; the problematic of everyday life and of its radical transformation. By formulating specific problems (the problems of groups) and trying to see how they connect with the general problematic, we will stimulate projects, hypotheses and possible solutions.

In its turn, the confrontation between these possible relations stimulates the invention of hypotheses about phenomena. So what we are doing here is looking not for a method for formulating 'sociological problems', but rather for a method for connecting each given and each partial reality to the more general problematic we are concerned with. In our opinion, the common expression 'sociological problem' contains an illusion. In one sense, all problems are sociological, since every sociological reality can only be grasped in relation to its problems. On the other hand, no problems are sociological, since problems can only be formulated in relation to a general problematic of historical and social man which goes beyond sociology as a specific and particular science.

Propositions concerning *what is possible* must be scrutinized, confronted and argued. When projects are confronted with 'real life' (with practice) it is imperative that the interested parties participate. It is impossible to impose a solution. Whoever decides for one particular solution (and consequently integrates it in his strategy) is obliged to examine the counterproposals. He must bear in mind that his solution may fail.

Therefore the hypothetical character of this process, and the way its method is linked to a determined general problematic, has profound connections with the *democratic* character of social life and the free scientific study of it.

So to the generally accepted types of hypotheses we will add a new one: the *strategic hypothesis*. Taking the most distant possibilities as its starting point, it returns to the present in an attempt to extend the force lines and the tendencies of the real towards this extreme point of what is possible. Its aim is to be more precise than the other hypotheses in the way it mediates between facts and concepts, and between givens and solutions to problems. It connects all the fragmented empirical facts with the concepts it is elaborating and constantly calling into question. It has the classic qualities and properties of hypothesis: it keeps in contact with the facts; it discovers new facts; it organizes the facts without forcibly systematizing them; it is verifiable. It is verified within praxis.

The hypothetical character of the procedure and of its object will become even more apparent when we examine the following extreme case: the creation of the object (the construction of a new town or the development of a new kind of town planning informed by the ideas provided by the sociology of everyday life). We are no longer talking about the usual kind of case, i.e., where the observer modifies what he is observing and is himself part of what can be observed. The extreme situation we are examining seems both more dramatic (because it involves more responsibility) and more capable of founding a broad practical rationality. This practical rationality would not exclude the so-called irrationality of images, emotions and feelings by ignoring or harrying them.

As we have said, the sociologist of everyday life has his strategy. Moreover, what he discovers and makes public can modify certain other strategies, namely those of the groups affected by the problems posed. This gives knowledge an entry into creative praxis. By emphasizing the role of hypothesis, randomness and newness, and by making the procedures and the object of knowledge more hypothetical, rather than invalidating this knowledge, we are confirming its rational and scientific character.

The importance attributed to hypothesis does not authorize us to fetishize it in favour of an 'approach' theory by which approaching facts and problems would be more interesting and far reaching than actually grasping them, which would immediately be suspect. Such a confession of powerlessness would be incompatible with the will to enrich research and to open it up to new perspectives.

The importance of hypothesis does not exempt us from the need to look for *proof* and to scrutinize it. A mass of facts can only prove anything in cases where reality is static, in a process of becoming which does not experience any serious accidents. In such cases, it is the logical coherence of the hypothesis and the way it harmonizes with a set of phenomena which provide the proof.

Much more interesting is the case of a dynamic reality, racked by problems and possibilities, where the convergence of several privileged testimonies proves more than any amount of empirical observations. The real proof is to be found on the level of the *practical* verification of a hypothesis. We are therefore talking about two distinct types of proof, one formal – coherence – and the other experimental – realization within praxis.

3 Transduction and transducers

The classic operations of reasoning can no longer suffice. Induction turned fact into law, the particular into the general, and the contingent into the necessary. To draw its conclusions, deduction went from the general to the singular, from affirmation to implication, and from the necessary to the necessary. To these rigorous operations we would add the notion of *transduction*, which builds a virtual object using information, and which uses givens to arrive at a solution. We can also say that transduction goes from the (given) real to the possible.

The theoreticians of information talk about 'psychological transducers' in order to designate the psychic modalities of this operation, revealed by their theory. In a similar way, we will introduce the idea of *sociological transducers* to designate the operation carried out unceasingly by social groups (and the individuals within those groups). They go from the present to the virtual and from the given to the possible in a never-ending prospective operation which the usual psychological ideas of achievement, prediction and uncertainty cannot exhaust.

Theoretical transductions and effective (practical) transducers derive from the same theory.[4]

4 The idea of level

The idea of *level* is rapidly becoming widespread. As well as being adopted by scientific terminology (the terminology of the social sciences and even of the natural sciences), it is also entering into day-to-day vocabulary. This empirical usage in no way clarifies its scientific usage. On the contrary. Essentially it derives from the hierarchic structuring of modern bureaucracy, which expresses itself in the following way: 'At managerial level, prefectorial level, ministerial level, cantonal level, departmental level, regional level, etc.' Levels of authority are also degrees in the hierarchy. In the army, they tend to use the term 'echelon', which is similar. Therefore there is a meaning behind the generalized usage of the word: the astonishing role played by hierarchy and bureaucracy in the structuring of society. Are its scientific meaning and this popular meaning the same? If they are, the word is clear but worrying. If we use it carelessly we will risk validating a certain practice and ideological representation of the social. If they are not, then it will require elucidation.

In truth, the scientific meaning of the word is rather obscure, for sometimes it is used subjectively (on the level of good sense, on the scientific level), sometimes very objectively (at subatomic level, at molecular level, at the level of gravitational field) and sometimes in a mixed way (at infraconscious level, at linguistic level, at supralinguistic level). I have collected these terms from a variety of scientific journals. If we read the recent *Entretiens* between Lévi-Strauss and Charbonnier, we will come across even more obscure turns of phrase, such as 'level of participation' and 'level of authenticity'.[5]

Earlier we located everyday life rather summarily as a *level* within praxis and society as a whole, and we added several observations. Scientifically speaking, the concept of *level* is no longer distinguishable from several other concepts, i.e., *stages* and *degrees* or *planes*, such as *sets, frames of reference, perspectives* or *aspects*. And yet these concepts are not identical. They all contribute towards expressing a complexity which is differentiated and yet structured within a whole (a totality). A *level* designates an aspect of reality, but it is not just the equivalent of a camera shot of that reality. It allows for it to be seen from a certain point of view or perspective; it guarantees it an objective content. In a reality where successive implications can be seen, it represents a degree or a stage, but with more consistency and 'reality' than symbols or models, for example.

Taken in its widest sense, the idea of *level* encompasses the idea of *differences between levels*. We could even say that the actual or possible difference between levels is the criterion by which levels are determined. Wherever there is a level there are several levels, and consequently gaps, (relatively) sudden transitions, and imbalances or potential imbalances between those levels. Therefore this idea excludes the idea of the *continuous field*, although it is not incompatible with the ideas of general context, globality or sets. Levels cannot be completely dissociated one from the other. Analysis may determine levels, but it does not produce them; they remain as units within a larger whole.

The schematic of a scale or of a formal hierarchy of degrees is much too static. Although by definition they are distinct and are located at different stages, *levels* can interact and become telescoped, with differing results according to what the encounters and circumstances are. As one level mediates another, so they act one upon the other. At one particular moment of becoming, in one particular set of circumstances, one level can dominate and incorporate the others. The idea of a structural set of precise and separate levels is untenable. It would invalidate a concept which is indispensable: rigid concepts do not capture the real in some vast, flexible net, they let it escape. Thus the level of the everyday and the level of the historical can interact. Level must not be thought of as being incompatible with the process of becoming and with mobility. Realities rise to the surface, emerge, and take on substance momentarily at a certain level. At the same time, the concept implies an internal determination, a relatively stable situation overall. The fact that we can speak of a 'level' makes it clear that everything is not in everything; there are not only differences, but also distinctions.

The concept of level makes the concept of *implication* sharper and more concrete. Each level is the result of an analysis which brings out the content of the other levels, and makes it more explicit. To use a turn of phrase we employed earlier, each one of them is therefore both *a residual deposit* and *a product*. But these propositions are not sufficient. Each level contains others, in a state of possibility. It analyses itself and makes itself more explicit. Thus every level is a 'level of levels', although the analyst does not have the right to suppose that they are limited or unlimited in number, or whether they are finite or non-finite. Each level implies others. When the analyst has singled out two distinct levels, he may be able to find others in between them. By analysis and experiment he should be able to discover *thresholds* leading from one to another; the threshold confirms the level. Finally, multiple 'realities' coexist on each individual level, implying and (mutually) implied, enveloping and enveloped, encompassing and encompassed, unmediated and mediated (unmediated in themselves, mediated in relation to other vaster or more restricted levels). Thus, in a succession of dichotomies, the logic of genera and species begins to take shape and ramify, through its contact with the 'concrete' it helps to define.

This representation may be approximative, but it has the merit of uniting mobility and structure. As it becomes more explicit it stands increasingly apart from frameworks of social origin, such as military and bureaucratic hierarchies. It can stretch out towards the universe, which henceforth we will not imagine as an architecturally rigid edifice, or as a flowing river, but as a colossal interaction of *levels*, from the subatomic to the galactic, from microcellular organisms to living species, from small social groups to the large sociocultural formations we call 'civilizations'.

To make the representation more precise, we can turn to *physics*.

Spectrum analysis of light and harmonic analysis of sound make distinctions and discontinuities apparent within what are apparently continuous phenomena. In a spectrum, there are both stationary (or relatively stable) and mobile transients, periodic global formants and partials. Spectrum analysis, and even more so harmonic analysis, can offer us a guideline for the analysis of overall or periodic social phenomena which are apparently continuous and homogeneous.

There are certain branches of modern mathematics which may help us to get a tighter grasp on this representation. Let us write a random series of numerals:

$$8 \quad 1 \quad 9 \quad 2 \quad 5 \quad 8$$

Between these numerals we can write more at random, and so on, and similarly we can add more in vertical columns, above or below the original numerals:

$$8 \quad 87493 \quad 162199 \quad 0753$$
$$7 \quad 2193 \quad 829772$$

The sequences of numerals do not constitute a number and yet each one of them is a set. It has a structure, but this structure is not rigid as in numbers and numerical sets. It can be called 'semi-rigorous'. The set forms a grid (or trellis) to which we may add as many columns or lines as we wish. Thus the set is neither finite nor non-finite (or rather, like the sequence of numerals and numbers, it is non-finite virtually, but always finite). This set is never completed, and we can always add new elements to it in between any of its elements.

Instead of vertical and horizontal rows of numerals, let us put straight lines (see next page). This makes the trellis more concrete, more determined and mobile.

Although we can start from any line or column to begin the trellis, its structure is not arbitrary; we can insert any horizontal or vertical straight line we have previously drawn. The beginning is arbitrary, and so is the end (when analysis stops). Therefore we can start the analysis of levels where we wish and where we can, and still come up with something determined. The construction of the trellis determines the squares or rectangles implied within one another, and which are

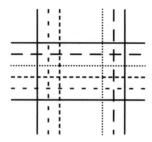

homologous or identical and spatially distinct. Thus the trellis (or lattice) represents *implications* of identical levels in distinct times and places. We will call these successive implications in the two possible directions – the broadest (macro) and the narrowest (micro) – *levels* with arbitrary starting points.

The broadest implication we can attain will always come within the scope of an even broader figure, and vice versa. The trellis makes us aware of the existence of *thresholds* and also of their mobility. It also makes us aware of the existence of differences between levels and their variability. There is nothing absolute about the split between them, and yet their relative variability is incontestable. Between any two implications there will always be an *interval* which is impossible to bridge.

To grasp the idea and how it may be used, we would do best to confront it with something concrete. So here are some examples of grids which present levels in their relative situations and their active reciprocities.

These examples by no means exhaust the fruitfulness of the idea and they only partially make what it means more explicit. In particular, they fail to make the distinction between *levels of reality*, *levels of abstraction* and *levels of meaning* completely clear. Nevertheless we can see a rule emerging: 'If the highest level of abstraction does not correspond to the deepest level of reality, the object of knowledge will become confused.'

The first table is a condensed version of material borrowed from various chapters of Robert Francès's book *Perception de la musique*. The other 'grids' deal with our own subject: everyday life and the analysis of it.

The schematic of levels has the disadvantages of all schematizations. The mobile network (trellis or 'lattice') of squares is by no means absolutely or definitely superior to any other representation. The problem of what is distinct (the problem of units, whether they are ultimate or signifying, or not, etc.) will crop up yet again.

In spite of its deficiencies, the schematic of levels has incontrovertible advantages. It demonstrates how a level which has been *chosen* as the starting point for analysing a set of phenomena defines a frame of reference. The level at which we begin restricts the horizon of our analysis. It will require other concepts on a corresponding level, it will stipulate the use of procedures permitting us to pass from one level to a neighbouring one, and it will forbid us to skip over levels, etc. Thus the schematic takes subjective or arbitrary elements of the analysis into account, while not insisting that the starting point must determine the object (which would lead to a hypersubjectivism, or to a pure probabilism, which would dissolve the object per se).

Levels of musical perception

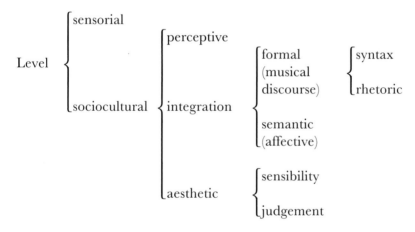

Note that:

a) Intensity, timbre and pitch in sound – melody, rhythm and harmony in musical composition – are not exactly *levels*, but elements, formants or 'dimensions';

b) the sensory level is a (necessary, non-sufficient) *condition*;

c) the perceptive level is the *foundation* (of the set, which the other levels return to);

d) There can be gaps, according to the people and the cases involved, and it is precisely these gaps which demonstrate the levels;

e) their hierarchy can change, as can the hierarchy of the dimensions, when one or other of them is emphasized.

f) there are still other levels which can be determined, for example levels of fullness of perception.

Level of analysis (in structural linguistics)

A) *Two levels of analysis* (and reality)
$$\begin{cases} \text{phonemes (non-signifying units,} \\ \text{objects of phonology)} \\ \\ \text{morphemes, words} \\ \text{(signifying units)} \end{cases}$$

(Liaison between the two levels: the principle of the *double articulation of language*)[6]

B) *Level 0*: the extralinguistic world, objects

Level 1: speech as a system of signs and sets of words; language as a system of signs with rules for their use

Level 2: a metalanguage, logical system of metasigns, referring back to the signs in level 1

(This is based on the work of various logicians and semanticists.)

Fragment of a grid of levels in everyday life

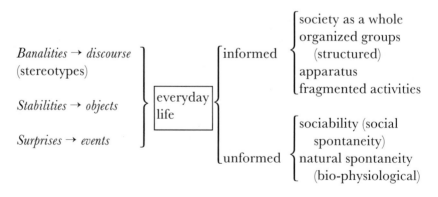

124

Another fragment of a grid of levels in everyday life

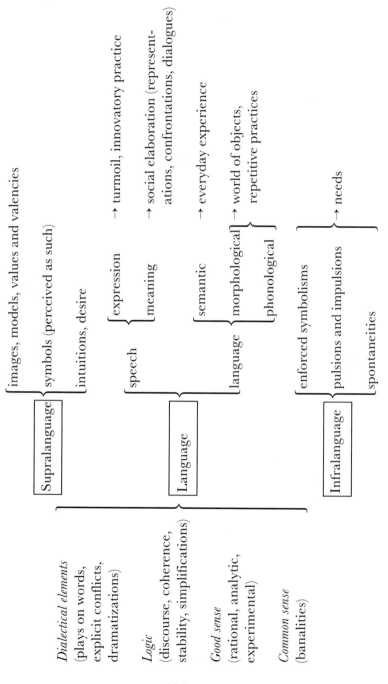

5 Continuity and discontinuity

The links between these two categories affect every area of knowledge. In this respect, considered per se, in the way they interact and in their links with objects and contents, and finally in terms of the operational techniques they bring into being, they should be granted prominence in any treatise on dialectical logic (which is a mediation or intermediary level between formal logic and the theory of concrete dialectical thought).

Here, however, we will merely offer a few methodological observations. Analytic reasoning, or understanding, which is an essential process of knowledge, examines continuity by using discontinuity (and vice versa). A straight line is the result of a cut made by thought in two- or three-dimensional space. To study it, I make a further cut; I select an arbitrary point of departure (point zero) on the line; I segment it; then I bring in an unlimited number of other cuts, which I can count (enumerate). I fragment it in enumerable sets of pieces, each with two ends. However, I know that this line still escapes me; every segment has the power of continuity, and enumeration cannot exhaust it.

On the other hand, if the study of a phenomenon – analysed in variables – gives me a series of discontinuous values, and consequently distinct points on a graphic representation, I join these points together by a curve; I look for the function best able to make this join. If necessary I extrapolate. Continuity will join the discontinuities together.

In this way, in so far as we can determine it, the unity of what is continuous and what is discontinuous is located first and foremost in pure abstract logic (where what is continuous is defined by what is discontinuous, and vice versa, the one referring to the other), and so on, concretely, dialectically, to infinity. Were it possible to grasp this unity concretely and to determine it fully, knowledge would come to an end, and the object, the universe itself, would be exhausted. We can only determine this dialectical unity by considering it to be inexhaustible. For knowledge such as ours, which proceeds by using categories and by applying concepts which have previously been developed with 'the real' as their starting point, 'reality' is not inaccessible or transcendental; and yet it can only be considered as a *limit to the* (asymptotic) *infiniteness* of finite knowledge. The infinite, which is the ultimate object of finite knowledge, manifests itself successively as an aspect of continuity (a mathematical example: the power of content in set theory) and of discontinuity (a mathematical example: a space with an infinite number of dimensions). On this point, it is surely bad dialectics to make the mistake of thinking that the *idea* of this unity constitutes effective knowledge, whereas in fact it merely indicates the vanishing point of our knowledge, which is only determined by the direction in which it is going. In our view this *idea* orientates knowledge, i.e., the use of concepts. It is less rigorous than an axiom but more demanding than a simple regulatory idea or aheuristic principle, as it is usually understood. Its content is more than an abstraction, and is less than concrete. It only becomes (apparent) knowledge when, as if by magic, an ontology changes it from being an idea or a distant and inaccessible horizon into a thing, a 'being' which has been possessed.

The result is a *relativization* of the knowledge obtained by the use of concepts. Inherent to dialectical thought, this relativism has always been fought by dogmatics, and above all by those who purport to be dialecticians. The 'grain of truth' (Lenin) contained in a statement or in a series of propositions is never anything more than a grain, and its truth only becomes apparent later on, when the grain has germinated and prospered, thanks to its own fertility. However, there is indeed 'a grain of truth', and we are not adopting an absolute relativism. Knowledge has points of impact and connections. To use a metaphor, it has anchorages.

We analyse the continuous using the discontinuous as our starting point, and vice versa. However, discontinuity enjoys a kind of privilege, which is malignant but at the same time benign (to use more metaphors). We set out from it, i.e., from the finite. The small whole number is still the springboard of science. Discontinuity constitutes the beginning and the stability of thought, the point from which its far-flung expeditions set out, and to which they return with their plunder. In praxis, there are distinct and stable *objects*, and analytic reason purports to know that these objects exist, and what they are, but then realizes that they are not particularly stable or distinct, and that it does not know what they are, which leads it to ask questions about their stability. These objects constitute the point at which knowledge applies itself, because this is what they are in everyday practice. Basically, to *produce* is to create well-defined implements and objects which are strengthened in the process of becoming. Knowledge always aspires to reduce its object to a *finite* number of answers to a finite number of questions, each question eliciting a *yes* or *no* (and thus logical) answer. Thus there is nothing immediately ontological about the privilege of discontinuity (even though it is connected to human finiteness and to what is *finite* in discontinuity). It derives from everyday practice and from the process which leads from ignorance to knowledge, from what is near to what is far away, from the unmediated to the mediated, from the small whole number to limitless sets, from solidity to randomness. Dialectical thought has not the right to compromise with vague propositions (there is continuity and discontinuity, and the two interact) by transforming them into absolute truths. It must establish a firmer grip on ideas and processes. Nor has it the right to identify the object of knowledge – marked by a certain relativity and a historicity of knowing – with an absolute objectivity to which it holds the key and with which it shares the privilege.

Dialectical reciprocity demands that thought should analyse the continuous by starting from the discontinuous, and vice versa. Concepts and categories do not coincide with reality. They illuminate it, and in doing so to a certain degree they 'reflect' it. As a result the application of categories such as *continuity* and *discontinuity* to a content (a set of phenomena or empirically verifiable facts) involves an element of contingency, subjectivity and relativism. In a sense, and up to a certain point, to illuminate something is to give it a certain *perspective*. However, one particular perspective implies another, and the confrontation of the two creates new problems; it brings forth the 'grain of truth' each one of them contains, and makes it grow. The objectivity of the object constructed according to each category is revealed; it takes on new shapes. Objectivity is heightened.

Georges Gurvitch believes that sociology establishes a perspective which sees human facts according to the category of *discontinuity*. It emphasizes distinctions and reveals irreducible diversities; it discovers types, genres and dichotomies. It traces the outlines of groups (such as classes and nations) and describes conflicts between structures. The historian, on the other hand, focuses on the same inexhaustibly diverse facts, but from the perspective of *continuity*. He emphasizes transitions and transfers; he thinks according to a pattern of continuous becoming, a single time, the time of history.

This ingenious and profound thesis strikes us as being acceptable, up to the point we indicated previously. In our opinion, the sociologist's perspective interacts with the historian's, and vice versa. Their mutual antagonism is intellectually fruitful, and the one must constantly take the other into account. The confrontation of their perspectives enables us to contemplate a unity between them. This is a path which leads us towards new truths. Could it be possible to alternate from the one to the other while leaving them mutually separate? Even if the difference between them proves insurmountable, and if the unity cannot be achieved and exhausted, it is nevertheless a process which must be attempted. Without it the sociologist's discoveries (of types and structures) and those of the historian (epochs, periods, processes and events) would become fixed unilaterally and would hinder the development of knowledge, i.e., of concepts and the dialectical movement of their effort to heighten objectivity.

So the sociologist reflects on the limits of history as a science, and tries to discover how it relates to his 'object'. We already know that sociology has formally recorded the unevenness of developments in history. We also know that it has observed historical 'drift': the gap between effective actions and intentions, and the results of events provoked by tactics and strategies. In this way sociology becomes a rational part of history, but in our view without having to relinquish the historicity of the human being. The relations it brings out differ from those discovered by the historian, but this does not eliminate the process of historical becoming.

Critique of everyday life emphasizes certain aspects of human experience, i.e., of *praxis*. It separates them out and classifies them according to type. The situation of the everyday in praxis and the level it occupies within it depend on society as a whole. In the monopolistic state capitalism which we know from experience, the gap between everyday life and the other aspects of praxis reaches a maximum; everyday life is subordinated to an extremely basic hierarchy of functions (such as norms, values, roles, models and apparatus) at the top of which come technology, bureaucracy and personal power. Sadly, it is *almost* the same in state socialism, which we only know from a distance; the difference – noticeable but not absolute – lies in the importance of politics and the understanding of politics in the social structures of state socialism. The idea of a *possible* transformation of the everyday and consequently of a radical critique of everyday life is the equivalent of opting for a decentralized socialism which would subordinate production to social needs which have been recognized and detected preferentially, thus placing knowledge and the recognition of other people, desires, creative freedom and the poetics inherent in social practice at the top of the hierarchy (of norms, values and models, etc.). Finally, we know that in archaic societies, the everyday was much less separate from culture, religion and ideologies than it is today.

Nevertheless, although we may emphasize differences, this is not to overlook homologies, analogies and above all transitional *processes*, in other words history and human historicity. In so far as it is sociological research, critique of everyday life will not be satisfied merely to emphasize and draw certain outlines for bringing what is empirically real into general social and rational contexts; it is concerned to discover where and upon what it can bring its influence to bear in order to transform everyday life. It sees itself as practice within praxis. It has a certain will, without which it would degenerate into poetic lamentation (like Rilke's, for example). It opts; it determines the stake and the risk; it gambles and wagers on history. In a sense the historicity of man can be defined by moments of great turmoil: revolutions. When these turmoils occur, the sociological and the historical, the everyday and the global, come together and fuse. Revolutions are total phenomena, essential events, or at least they are so in the modern world, the world where historicity asserts and confirms itself. After turmoil comes calm, drift, then divisions and gaps. We will come back to these processes, and when we do so we will give the category of *continuity* pride of place. It does not create them. It enables us to grasp them more effectively, while the (implied, reciprocal) rival category enables us to grasp the results of the process of becoming and of human actions.

Let us now consider another aspect of this question, namely the relations between the continuous and the discontinuous. Let A and B be two living or, better still, thinking and acting 'beings' (individuals or groups). A space separates them. If this space is impenetrable –

forests, uncharted mountains, seas – they must each go their own way, regardless of whether they want to meet or to avoid each other. If the space is completely penetrable and offers a continuous free field, A and B perceive one another, and walk forward either to fight or to love, or simply to get to know each other.

The most interesting cases are those where the intermediate space is neither completely penetrable nor completely impenetrable. There will be obstacles, and so there will be several paths A can follow to reach B and vice versa. These paths are distinct, yet they intersect, or merge. This is when discontinuity intervenes. A must choose a certain path. He sets out towards B (or towards where he thinks B is), and at each crossroads he must make a new choice. Every option obeys tactical considerations. A supposes that B is in a certain direction and that the path he chooses will lead him closer. If the series of choices is articulated according to coherent considerations, we say that A has a strategy, and so has B.

And so the theoretician can place A's and B's strategical choices in a matrix. Calculation comes into play. It reveals the mutual *chances* of the pair (they may be lovers or bitter enemies – what is important is that we know whether they want to meet or to run away from each other, or whether one wants to meet the other, and which of the two this is).[7]

Let us suppose A and B to be enemies. If the space is opaque and inpenetrable, neither has a vantage point, and they will have to trust to chance. The *alea* is complete. If they can see each other from a distance, they can challenge each other visually and run towards each other in a luminous, transparent space. The *agon* is complete. Therefore the *agon* and the *alea* represent two extreme cases and two characteristic polarities in the pure state. Between the two there stretches a vast mixed region where the *agon* and the *alea*, opaqueness and transparency, fear and daring, risk and chance combine in a variety of ways. In this vast region, *numbers* (small whole numbers, in the simple cases at least, the first numbers to be tackled by analysis) are in charge. The possibility of enumerating actions and events depends upon a certain number of choices, options and decisions, and how they are linked together. This enumeration must not lead our analysis to overlook the deeper dialectical movement: the relation between the *agon* and the *alea* – of the *continuous* (objectively, space;

subjectively, the will to strike the enemy) and the *discontinuous* (the coherent series of decisions).

To put it another way, distinctions (distinct units) must have a foundation. They cannot be taken as absolute, for this would be to overlook the fact that they are providing a momentary form or structure to something. After having made a distinction, analytic thinking makes connections. After having made connections, it makes further distinctions. Then, dialectical reason reconstructs the process of becoming and *tends* towards totality by heightening the object and objectivity.

The theory we are considering – the theory of tactics and strategies – is not limited to games, to warfare or to business relations. It is applicable to all temporal consecutions of distinct (discrete) units: sequences of regulated gestures, of words and utterances, of images, of symbols; dialogues with questions and answers, etc. As soon as a dialogue ceases to use the conversational register and rises above triviality, it has started to employ a tactic and a strategy. The same is true for regulated exchanges, be they nothing more than words or gifts exchanged between groups.

Be they extreme cases or mixed situations (with their context: love or intimacy, rivalry or alliance, the transparency or opaqueness of the distance in between), the *agon* and the *alea* appear in whatever becomes formalized or ritualized, or whatever unfolds in a distinct and successive manner, including liturgy, ceremonies, stage acting, and the set phrases of poetry or love.

During these processes (affective, subjective and spontaneous) *content* does not disappear; it survives in *continuousness*. However, it is the discontinuous which governs the form or rather the formalization which operates in the situation in vivo, in the relation between the protagonists: approach, challenge, meeting, confrontation.

Thus, in response to the concrete demand of a given situation, social modalities of *repetition* appear. These cannot be reduced to mere repetition of simple mechanical gestures, pure stereotypes, but rather are the repetition of the process and its development both subjectively and objectively. Analysis projects these periodicities like a spectrum, immediately distinguishing between them or between their 'formants' as they rise above triviality like the tides or waves of the sea.

To establish or re-establish the rights of the continuous as against those of the discontinuous (and vice versa) would be to agree that one had a privilege over the other. It is certain that nineteenth-century thought, inspired as it was by evolutionism and the philosophy of history, privileged *continuity* (although this statement is not valid for Marx and Marxism). Next the category of discontinuity was brought to the fore. This period produced a number of useful discoveries. Language is constructed with differences, incompatibilities, disjunctions and exclusions (short-term or long-term, on both the phonemic and the morphemic level). *Structuralism* takes these observations on, but develops them to a disproportionate degree. Here, as before, we accept the concept of structure, but in a limited way. What we are seeking is to follow the movement between continuity and discontinuity in depth, taking all the interactions and all the conflicts into consideration.

Seen from this angle, we can say that there are processes of becoming and development which are relatively continuous. We will need to highlight one particularly important type of process, the *cumulative process*. We will also show how processes, and especially cumulative processes, fall prey to discontinuities, obstacles, bottlenecks, halts, breaks, gaps and imbalances. However, a process per se never brings about decisions or events. Decisions belong to forces (for example, *social forces*) which come into being by means of a process, or as it is sometimes put, on its 'base' (for example, on the *base* of the *economic process*), but which cannot be reduced to that process. As regards events, it is men who produce them, men who formulate the tactics and strategies of social forces (or in the case of interindividual relations, of psychological forces) and put them into action.

We can discern three levels of analysis and reality: processes, forces and events. By passing from one to the other we will attain a greater complexity, more freedom, more randomness.

This is all to repeat propositions we have already presented, but more clearly and more intensely. All social groups from the 'micro' to the 'macro' scale have a conscious or unconscious, latent or formulated (openly demonstrated) tactic and strategy. So have individuals, in their unmediated or mediating relations. Why? Because, be we individuals or groups, we all have a relatively uncertain future which we must face up to, and for which we prepare in a relatively lucid way. We all have our problems, in which our existence is more-or-less completely involved. Complete societies and partial groupings interconnect, maintain each other, disappear or collapse. Lucidly or not, they know this.

There has never been a human 'substantiality', be it of a sociological, psychic, psychosociological, ideological, economic or political nature. The ontological category of 'substance' is disappearing from our horizon. The secrets of groups, their opacities and their ambiguities, which are what give the illusion of substance, are made up of anxieties or audacity with regard to *what is possible*, of entrenchments and offensives, of retreats and advances in relation to other groups, of courage or of weakness of will in response to problems. Human groupings see – or choose not to see – the results of 'conditions'. The spontaneity and vitality of these groups are reflected in representations (symbols, norms, models, images, etc.) or are formulated by means of ideological representations. However, it is individuals who reflect, who formulate opinions, and who define attitudes and crystallize patterns of behaviour. Individuals show the group to which they belong images of what is possible and what is impossible. They calculate and compute; they are spokesmen, deputies, 'elected' representatives: family heads, trades-union leaders, rural dignitaries, city administrators, party leaders, statesmen. There is no substance here, only men, actions, relations and (individual and collective) consciousnesses. In the beginning was action; in the end action is recognized (although the classic concept of act, action or experience does not exhaust the idea of *praxis*). Every human life is a progress or a process towards a possibility, the opening up or closing down of what is possible, a calculation and an option based upon random events and the intervention of 'other people'.

Beneath their ambiguities, critical study of everyday life will reveal the tactics and strategies of partial groups (such as women, young people, intellectuals, etc.) in society as a whole. Whether these tactics and strategies are manifest or concealed, it will be capable of detecting them and the ways they express themselves. The study of the everyday will grasp the relations between groupings which make their contacts opaque, or which make them mutually accessible, in spite of misunderstandings, tactical manoeuvres, disguises, strategic openings and adventures.

When groups become isolated, they degenerate; they cease to exist 'through action'. Continued existence in itself implies action and struggle, and therefore relations. The *agon* only disappears when groups and individuals go into decline. When they degenerate, groups break up into scattered elements, minigroups and individuals. The everyday lapses into triviality. As for the moments where strategy predominates, these are the great historical moments of revolutionary turmoil. Strategy gives a sense to groups and to their lives. 'Sense' – direction, orientation, expression, goal – is not some comfortable, speculative entity for a specialist, such as the philosopher, to elucidate philosophically. Sense is drama. It is constituted by strategy – the strategy of the group. The strategy of the group creates it.

Therefore the level of the everyday as a 'reality' would be the level of *tactics*, lying between the level where there are no more actions, where reality is stagnating and coagulating, and where triviality dominates, and the level of decision, drama, history, strategy and upheaval.

Once again we are repeating statements we made earlier, but from a different perspective. However, these statements must not be taken literally. In so far as the everyday is a reality which must be metamorphosed, challenged and made challengeable by critique, it can be observed on the level of *tactics*, of forces and their relations, and of stratagems and suspicions. Its transformation takes place on the level of events, strategies and historical moments. Therefore we will not allocate a statistical level to everyday life and our study of it. This would draw us down into triviality, or up towards factuality (in the stipulated sense).

Therefore we will try to discover how each group we examine responds to 'stimuli' (such as challenges, propositions and provocations, threats, claims and offensives) from some other group, and how it resolves tactical problems. Passing over to the level of strategy, we will try to see how groups tend to minimize the chances of maximal gain for their partners or adversaries – or conversely how they maximize their own minimal gain.[8] In a random series of an unlimited number of questions (with yes-or-no answers, and so of the kind which could figure in everyday conversation), it is the second of these strategies which produces the largest number of correct answers. On the other hand, the minimal strategy would determine a tactic of dissimulation, retreat, denial and misunderstanding, which would become apparent as such in the everyday.

Knowledge per se has its tactic: to know, to make known, to make the everyday known as an object of knowledge. It has its strategy: to bring about the dissolution of the everyday and to reduce it indefinitely – to provoke its metamorphosis by inferring the maximum number of options in this sense – by demonstrating the possibility of narrowing the gap between the everyday real and what is possible, by investing in what is (relatively) superior and by elevating what is (relatively) inferior. This strategy involves the use of philosophy while at the same time pushing it from its pedestal and realizing it as a vision of transparency in everyday human relations. This self-same strategy involves the struggle for the rights of science to be one of the elements of an overall (political) strategy.

We must distinguish between the theory of the *wager* (of Pascalian origin) and the theory of *strategies*. The individual can gamble and lay wagers. A group is never aware that it is gambling on its future, or that it is placing bets and running risks. It is to the 'distanced' observer on the outside that the activity of a group can appear like a wager. A group will only enter upon an action for gain, and with the certainty of winning. We call this certainty 'confidence'. It is the opposite of 'mistrust' and of the attitude of 'challenge' towards other groups. Only leaders can be aware of risks, i.e., the chances of failure and success, and usually they are careful to keep these to themselves; the 'confidence' groups have in their goals is also confidence in their leaders, something which the leaders themselves take every care not to jeopardize. Here ideology plays an ambiguous role: it fosters ambiguity. Both an illusion and a stimulant, ideology creates representations which belittle 'the other' and overexalt the self. Collective units gamble, but do not know they are gambling. A troop of soldiers which can see clearly that defeat is on the cards, i.e., that it is involved in a gamble, is already demoralized and half on the way to defeat. Only the chief receives exact information and transforms it into orders. He alone assesses the chances. He alone knows that he is gambling and that his wager is serious and at the heart of the drama. This is one of the most scabrous aspects of 'leadership' and of ideology. Raising morale by concealing the possibilities of failure effectively increases the chances of success. The chief assumes all responsibilities, for misinterpretations, misunderstandings, even for ideological lies and for the elimination of overperceptive individuals. In everyday life as well as at moments of crisis, the way men behave is frequently Machiavellian. What is more, the pursuit of any good and the fulfilment of any desire, no matter how incomplete, always incurs risks and dangers. Could bets and wagers be the prerogative of a few individuals who alone are capable of bearing the situation when they come face to face with randomness? This would hardly be encouraging for democracy, but, as Marx and Lenin have told us, democracy contradicts itself, it thrives on contradiction, and this self-destruction only comes to an end with politics, that supremely serious gamble, drama of dramas, destiny of destinies.

Critique derives not from theory, but from praxis. If we emphasize the tactics and strategies of groups, this is not to fetishize them. Only if we formalize them will they tend to become fetishes, since formalization would transform them into the objects of a higher science.

The traditional idea of destiny as elaborated by traditional (classic) culture contains and mixes together several contradictory elements which games and strategy theory helps to clarify somewhat. The idea of destiny, i.e., the tragic, contains the idea of the (inevitable) failure of every intention and every project. It contains the representation of a game which is weighted against the hero, who (inevitably) makes mistakes which lead to his downfall, while his opponent (god, determinism, mechanism) necessarily plays well. Finally there is the idea of an act which concludes in a way *other* than that which the participants expected and wished for. The tragic is nothing other than gambling, in all its breadth and seriousness.

In this sense, the everyday is both the residual deposit and the product of the tragic and of destiny. It is the tragic which has been smothered, undetected and unrecognized. It is destiny awaiting its hour and which the people it concerns await without knowing it, or more exactly without recognizing it. It is tactics and strategies which go their own way, without 'us' knowing it, since 'we' are caught up within it between the object and the subject: in an ambiguity which is never completely resolved, we are the object of the action and at the same time we are its subject. Therefore the everyday is also the non-tragic, the source of the tragic and its naked remains, and the empty place of Destiny, filled with an amorphous mixture of necessity, chance, freedom, dangers, assurances, risks and securities.[9]

Seen in this light, the everyday is on the one hand an *empirical modality for the organization of human life*, and on the other a mass of *representations which disguise this organization*, its contingency and its risks. Hence the impression given by everyday life as 'reality': inconsistency and solidity, fragility and cohesion, seriousness and futility, profound drama and the void behind an actor's empty mask.

Has not every distinct (individual and group) human unit been led or conducted to *somewhere it did not want to go*, and dragged to *somewhere other than it wished*? The experience of history and historicity weigh down on the present in a confused manner. Every human unit has a memory and a fund of information – good or bad – which are mixed together in the everyday. It cannot see everything and it cannot know everything, but it knows and sees something. If it cannot know its destiny as such (and the main protagonists are themselves ignorant of it because of all that is unforeseeable in the outcome of conflicts between strategies), every entity senses something which shows through or is revealed (or both at once) in the symbols, the sayings and proverbs, the images and the myths it uses. As well as concern for the future, as well as anxieties, symbols and memories, there is work, the pressing concerns of the moment, goods and satisfactions, ordinary pleasures, ordinary pastimes: the present moment or the actual (to avoid using the suspect word 'reality' with all its burden of fetishism). Present moments do not coincide exactly with the conditions or the results of data, and even less with possibilities. They are part of them; they are more than them; they are less than them.

Theory has revealed the importance and the penetration of *play* in everyday life and in social practice in general. Several distinct levels and dimensions of play are apparent. There are games of a spontaneous character, games with rules and games with tactics. Strategy can be a *serious game* although it may not be perceived as such. And there are others, such as games which are blindly unaware or ignorant of themselves (an extreme example: alienation through destiny and the tragic), objective games, which accept risk (an extreme example: adventures outside of an everyday context), and subjective games, with formal rules (an extreme example: frivolousness). These are various distinct and yet inseparable ways and stages of taking randomness into account, and to limit and control its freedom.

Thus play would be a (frequently disguised and misunderstood) dimension of everyday life and of praxis. It contains within itself several degrees or levels, several dimensions, according to how it relates directly and consciously to randomness per se. Could play be the starting point from which we could envisage the metamorphosis of the everyday?

6 Micro and macro

The distinction between the 'micro' and the 'macro' appears in most of the sciences, at the same time as the idea of level. It originated in mathematics, when Riemann conceived of large spaces with properties different from those of small-scale spaces. Subsequently physicists adopted it (i.e., the distinction between microphenomena and the macroscopic scale), followed next by sociologists, geographers and economists, etc.

In every field, and most especially in our area of research, the 'micro' and the 'macro' appear to be mutually irreducible. We say this warily, because it implies serious consequences: after having rejected Aristotelian epistemology, which changes the act (here, the act of the social group) into substance, we have rejected Cartesian epistemology, which uses the simple to construct the complex and deems that an exhaustive analysis leading to total synthesis is possible, on condition that the process is logically ordered.

In the everyday, on the microsociological level, unmediated relations are carried on between one person and another (via blood ties, or neighbourhood and socially contingent relations) which are complicated by ties of direct dependency and rivalry (i.e., husband/wife, father/children, employers/servants), and accompanied by rebellions which are just as direct. On the macrosociological level, these unmediated ties and subordinations are survivals which prolong archaic relations (of consanguinity and territoriality) or feudal relations (of subordination and vassalage). On this 'macro' level, such relations are mediated; they pass via 'the thing' – reified and reifying, alienating and alienated: commodities, money, language.

As a result the 'micro' level is ambiguous and the 'macro' level is abstract, and yet no sooner have we formulated this statement than we need to turn it on its head. If it is ambiguous, the 'micro' level is also the level where the question of authenticity has a meaning: the unmediated can become authentic, either in spontaneity or in truth; at least this is what we suppose and what we demand of it. If it is abstract, the 'macro' level is also heavily present. We need to emphasize this paradox. Because it is ambiguous, the 'micro' can be accused of being false. And yet only the 'micro' can become authentic, in other words transparent, through the mutual recognition of relations. The 'macro' which seems, and indeed is, so 'real' is also the realm of falsities and fetishes. And yet, if we are to validate and authenticate the 'micro', we must first transform the 'macro'.

Therefore there is a distance and a gap between the two levels. Any attempt to miniaturize social science by using the study of limited groups would soon come up against this obstacle. It is a barrier to analytic reason, which reduces the complex to the elementary and the compound to the simple. The 'micro' level is just as complex as the 'macro' level, but in a different way. As regards the reverse procedure, which would attempt to grasp the 'micro' via the 'macro', this leads to a sort of untenable and dangerous sociology which would define the everyday absolutely by the whole.

Gaps and differences between levels do not authorize us to dichotomize any one of them, and even less to 'scotomize' it.[10] Irreducibility is not the equivalent of separation. There is a multiplicity of relations, correspondences and homologies between the 'macro' level and the 'micro' level. Both levels 'reflect' the society which encompasses them and which they constitute. Thus, the correspondences between family (private) life and society as a whole are almost self-evident. Society as a whole acts, becomes apparent and intervenes through the ambiguity of direct ties which are simultaneously biological and social, or, perhaps we should say, because of that ambiguity. The contradictions and conflicts within families represent or reflect those of society as a whole (be it feudal, capitalist or socialist) and those of the classes (the bourgeoisie and the proletariat). What is more, in a sense, the unmediated character of direct relations is nothing but a mirage. These direct relations are also mediated: by language and by money, etc. On the level of these relations, the unmediated is as much of a reconstruction as it is a constituent. Perception of others also implies a network of mediations which determine it and limit it. The 'macro' level appears to be the level where the 'micro' is integrated within the whole, a process which leaves little room within its empty spaces for marginal, abnormal or 'deviant' elements. The 'macro' does not determine the 'micro'. It encompasses it; it controls it; it penetrates it and imposes regulations upon it, which are themselves at differing levels of depth and effectiveness: norms of conduct and behaviour patterns, models and roles, etc. Using and abusing the limits of the 'micro', the 'macro' brings all its weight to bear upon it.

Are these relations dialectical, in other words conflictive, polyvalent, mobile and multiformal? Doubtless they are. On one hand, the 'macro' makes every effort to contain, to absorb and reabsorb the 'micro' (but by means of the actions of privileged individuals, its leaders). It succeeds, but never totally. In spite of its ambiguities, or maybe because of them, the 'micro' puts up a resistance. The social and the cultural never reabsorb the biophysiological, the unmediated or the natural. The sector which is rationally controlled by praxis never eliminates the uncontrolled sector, the sector of spontaneity and passion. Once separated off, the 'macro' atrophies: mediations no longer have anything to mediate, and the means of communication no longer have anything to communicate. Isolated in turn, the 'micro' lapses into irrationality and meaninglessness.

When they are not governed by laws, spontaneity and immediacy lose direction. Conversely, without spontaneity, laws and norms resemble death. It is on the level of the 'micro' that life has rights, and spontaneity feeds into practice and culture; it is the living root of the social. However, it is on the level of the 'macro' that the decisions which eradicate ambiguities are taken, that the division of social labour is organized, and that norms and images are developed.

The existence of the 'micro' level implies and supposes *neighbourhood* (or *contingent*) *relations* in a social space. Distinct, but not separated, the sides and facets of microelements come into contact with each other. The fact that they are mutually distinctive should not disguise the homologies, correspondences and analogies. Families, villages, towns and businesses live side by side in social space and their 'internalities' interconnect. Considered from the point of view of the *continuous*, these relations in social space give rise to representations and mathematical formalizations (such as topologies, transformations and groups). From the point of view of the *discontinuous*, they also give rise to representations and formalizations (such as networks and graphs).

The *tree* offers a good representation of relations of neighbourhood and proximity within a larger unit. Small branches spring from larger ones, which in turn spring from the trunk; they grow in forks which produce distances but not separations. The leaves grow side by side at the end of the branches and only communicate via the branches and the trunk, i.e., via the tree as a whole.

Thus the interaction of distinct and inseparable units can be represented in images and forms which lend themselves to rigorous formalizations. This is a mode of thinking and investigation which makes use on the one hand of images and the imagination, and on the other of mathematical research.[11] Thus the tree is more than a physical reality transposed on to society; it is more than a symbol and something other than a symbol. It is a *formal instrument* with an original relation to the concrete. Is it a form or a structure? Let us leave that question to one side for the moment. The tree stretches out without losing its cohesion. As it grows it retains a particular and characteristic form. It presents a number of remarkable points – ramifications, bifurcations, disjunctions – which are also fragile points, points of fracture, changes of direction. It illustrates a dynamic and relative stability, a growth which is coherent, but always under threat. Would it resolve the problems of 'continuity/discontinuity' and 'the elementary/the total', in material nature and in society? In a sense, and up to a certain point, it doubtless would. In any event, it offers an illustration of social space and social time, and of relations of proximity and distance.[12] However, there are certain characteristics of society as a whole, such as alienation through money and commodities, which it does not represent. Nor does it demonstrate that (provisional) balances and self-regulations in social consciousness and society, and within determined social frameworks, are brought about not by mechanisms, but precisely by the intermediary of representations.

7 Indexes, criteria, variables

In these methodological considerations, we never separate the abstract from the concrete, or form from content. On the contrary: we use every occasion we can to demonstrate how the abstract already contains aspects of the concrete and how form is already an aspect of the real. However, if we do not separate them, this does not mean that we should conflate them, and to avoid this we will start from the most formal and the most abstract and progress towards the most concrete.

We must now point out the indexes, criteria and variables in this progression.

A social fact designating more and something other than itself: such could be the definition of an *index*. It has a meaning which is a content; it reveals, it indicates. Often, at first sight, an index is non-signifying; and therein lies one of the traps in the idea of 'signification'. An index refers to something hidden, or conversely, to something so obvious that the observer is unable to see it within the mass of evidence before him. Therefore the index is a sign, but is not intended as such, and consequently it is not arbitrary. It is part of the phenomena it reveals; it is linked to them as they are linked to one another, one expression among many others. It is as close to the symptom as it is to the sign. A symptom can be considerably far removed from the actual location of an illness or its causes; and yet the connection exists.

Therefore the index is only of use as a part, aspect or element of the phenomenon being considered. Its relation to this phenomenon is not generally clear, or easy to establish; some indexes are deceptive or disappointing. When an observer or experimenter first makes contact with a social group he begins by looking for certifiable indexes. At this level, only rational instinct is brought into play: the scientific culture which is sometimes called intuition. A social group presents a sort of face, an (open or concealed) presence, where indexes can be copious or scanty. Using indexes which are frequently secretive, the scientist makes things up; he uses his imagination. As Picasso is quoted as saying, 'First of all I find something, then I start to search for it.' This remark reinforces an old paradox; it brings to the fore certain characteristics of the dialectical movement of thought. An excessive concern for rigour and logical coherence makes thought inflexible; valid in

143

itself, this concern already presupposes the object without knowing it; it constrains thought to invest the object with the characteristics of formal rigour, which it assumes to be purely objective. This is to disregard the subjective aspect of formal rigour. It formalizes, it quantifies; or again, whenever it approaches a concrete object it grinds to a halt, unable to reach it.

Occasionally an index will reveal something other than was expected. Occasionally it resembles a clinical symptom. It indicates a crisis, tension or vitality, a failure or a decline. Sometimes what is most internal comes to the surface and reveals itself in what is most external, namely the index; what is most profound shows through in what is most superficial and fleeting. Conversely, research will sometimes show an index to be invalid.

The need to scrutinize the index in depth means it must be measured against *criteria*, some of which are general and formal, others specific. A good *index* shows itself to be relatively constant, within the limits of the observations or experiments being undertaken; it permits us to grasp a certain number of facts and to group them (by classification). No longer a mere appearance, it reveals the hidden reality; it translates it or it traduces it. In this way it supersedes itself to become a *criterion*. In fact the criterion is not external to the index; the index becomes a criterion when it becomes precise and heightened; at that stage the attentive observer or experimenter will distinguish it and separate it from its initial context, to apply it to other phenomena or other groups. The index becomes an analytic implement for penetrating and classifying. The *indexical criterion* changes into an objective criterion, which in turn joins forces with a set of criteria which are always *specific*. As for general criteria, they stipulate the use of specific indexes and criteria; they regulate the successive procedures and levels of this process: discovery and invention, the transfer from the fleeting index to the indexical criterion, the constitution of a coherent set of criteria characterizing a phenomenon.

An excellent illustration of these procedures would be the *criteria of underdevelopment* to be found in Lenin's *The Development of Capitalism in Russia*, and in his subsequent writings.

Let us consider the *criteria of underdevelopment* as Lenin has already defined them:

- the splintering of economic units;
- virtually autonomous local markets which are poorly integrated in a national market linked to the world market;
- low concentration both in industry and in agriculture;
- weak contradiction between the collective character of production and the individual (private) character of appropriation;
- forms of personal dependence in social relations;
- economically backward forms of productive relations with the predominance of agriculture and the slowing down of transfers of population;
- poor needs of association and archaic forms of association;
- weaknesses of the large groups (classes) occupying different situations in production;
- weakness of class antagonisms;
- traditional forms of moral life and social life, etc.

More recent authors have added further criteria to these economic and political ones: *demographic* (high birth and death rates); *technological* (poor per capita use of energy); *cultural* (high percentage of illiteracy); *sociological* (limited mobility, rigid structures along with poor overall integration, etc.).[13]

These new criteria modify and complete the set established by Lenin (which was limited to the economic aspects of the question), but they do not invalidate it. The general criterion of economic development and the criterion of social and political 'progress' is the reduction and disappearance of one or several specific indexical criteria of underdevelopment.

This set of criteria sheds a remarkable light on everyday life in a poorly developed society, i.e., a society *which must be transformed* by guided (planned) economic growth. Each criterion is like a spotlight, pinpointing a specific trait.

In accordance with our programme we will now complete the above list by adding the *criteria of the underdevelopment of everyday life in the developed countries*:

- the backwardness of 'services' essential to everyday life compared with production in general (production of the means of production or production of 'privately produced goods');[14]

145

- the manipulation of the consumer and of his needs by advertising and propaganda;
- the backwardness of techniques applicable to everyday life compared with production techniques, military techniques, and techniques for the exploitation of space;
- the splintering of local and territorial units (such as families, neighbourhoods and towns, etc.) and excessively powerful means of integration;
- an inextricable mixture of archaic forms of moral and social life and modern forms of communication and information;
- the backwardness of town planning as the form and context of everyday life compared with needs and technical possibilities, and compared with the social life in towns in the past;
- forms of personal dependence (consumer/producer, private/public, citizen/state, woman/man, etc.);
- a slowing down of possibilities;
- a reduction of possibilities involving spatial movements (so-called social mobility, tourism and travel);
- a relative erosion of certain sectors (such as cooking, housing and leisure, etc.) in various countries;
- a fragmentation of technology and an incoherence of the 'world of objects' and 'goods' in the everyday;
- illiteracy and 'cultural' backwardness in terms of the art of living and lifestyle, love and eroticism, sex and family planning;
- the abstract and mechanical character of the idea of happiness (reduced to the idea of comfort) . . .

This list of (indexical and specific) criteria is not intended to be restrictive. We would be happy to make the disappearance of one of these indexes a general criterion of progress, and the elimination of them all as a criterion of revolution . . .

As far as *variables* are concerned, at this stage we will merely point out the difference between the idea of *strategic variables* and the concept as it is usually understood. We would define the variable generally as an aspect or constituent element of a complex phenomenon, which possesses a relative independence, allowing it to vary separately, and by means of that variance to modify an overall phenomenon which is governed by a limited (i.e., countable) number of other parameters. The index should enable us to grasp a variable in its relative independence. The use of criteria should enable us to verify variables and their connections within a set which constitutes the phenomenon as a whole. Here the role of the index is analytic, and the role of the criterion is synthetic.

This classic idea supposes the existence of a *continuum* determined by parameters (thus possessing a certain number of dimensions). However, the strategic variable introduces discontinuity. It focuses on the future. It points to inevitable options, with all the (long-term negative and positive) consequences and risks choice implies. Of necessity there are several strategic variables, all mutually incompatible (and if they were not, there would be no options, no clear-cut decisions spelling out what is possible, committing the future and unfolding in a preplanned sequence: no tactic and no strategy). If they fail to determine their position in a specific conjuncture of their strategic variables, businesses, local groups and political parties will be unable to grasp what and where they are. Analysis of these strategic variables is interesting in two respects, theoretical and practical. What it uncovers will help us to get to know and to understand the problems facing the groupings and units, and consequently the changes in the offing. It will also allow us to act upon them, by modifying their strategic variables, options and shifts in direction.

Thus, by distinguishing between *structural* and *conjunctural* variables more precisely than before, we are introducing discontinuity. As it happens, this distinction is already known and accepted, but in a way which is frequently rather vague. In principle, structural variables affect the most stable part of the phenomenon under consideration, its centre or 'essence', its regulated nucleus, i.e., the part governed by laws encompassing in a general way the processes of internal balance and self-regulation, and thus of stabilization and structurization. Conversely, conjunctural variables are a matter of links and relations, accidents and interactions. In short, they are to do with the consequences of the process of becoming, and with the context beyond the whole phenomenon we are considering. By breaking structures up (by destructuring them), these consequences may modify the phenomenon; they may even change it completely. These conjunctural variables are sometimes subordinated, sometimes dominant and decisive; in the first case, the unit under scrutiny will be maintained and consolidated; in the second, its unity will be broken up and it will lose its wholeness as an entity or nucleus.

We will return to the relation between 'conjuncture' and 'structure' later. For the time being let us observe that we envisage a dialectical movement between the two terms: a conflict during which one controls the other or is controlled by it. The conjunctural is more than a mere sequence of events and contingencies; it is the pressure of the process of becoming on structures and their necessary inclusion in strategies. In a word, it is history, it is (relative) stability, the (relatively) defined, the (briefly) fixed, the diachronic; thus it is whatever the process of becoming will form, and then destroy.

From this angle we have established that one characteristic of the everyday is the fact that its strategic variables are misconstrued, disguised and *latent*, so to speak.

8 Dimensions

The concept of *dimension* comes from mathematics. Social scientists use it widely and somewhat arbitrarily. Sometimes they use it to formulate generalities (the human dimension or dimensions, the historical or the sociological dimension, etc.), and sometimes to calculate and list all the 'dimensions' of the phenomenon (its variables) they are researching.

In mathematics, the term has a precise meaning. A space has one, two, three, four . . . dimensions, or, when it satisfies certain well-determined conditions, an infinite number of dimensions. Dimension is defined very rigorously. Moreover, the mathematician knows that he can *conceive* of, but not *formulate*, a space with more than three dimensions (even though in science fiction four-dimensional space-time passes from the conceptual into the imaginary!). The correspondence of mathematical calculations with physical reality poses a certain number of problems, many of which have not yet been resolved – far from it.[15]

On the pretext of rejecting or limiting formalism, should we forbid the social scientist to take a distinct human unit and attribute 'degrees of freedom' to it, or to include some specific human event in a set of probabilities which have been calculated from hypotheses determining the field of possibilities and fixing the distribution of probabilities with *x* number of dimensions across the set as a whole? On the contrary. Nevertheless the social scientist must realize that these considerations remain within the formal domain and are a window on to the reality under scrutiny, rather than a means of exhausting it.

The question of 'dimensions' has been obscured by the veil of obfuscation which has shrouded and distorted dialectical thought. Never before has so much been said about dialectic and never before has it been so little understood. Before, thought was often spontaneously dialectical, and thus it was working in the dark. The passage from analytic understanding to dialectical reason was effected without any considered awareness, and yet there was more dialectical movement in thinking and in the way concepts were used[16] than there is today, when dialectic is the fashion among philosophers and elsewhere (above all 'elsewhere').

There appears to be a misunderstanding underlying this obfuscation, and it is important to clear it up. *Dialectic* and *dialogue* have points in common. Now dialogue, like dialectic, is in fashion, and with good reason. Who does not engage in dialogue, or does not try to? Who does not talk about dialogue? Who does not try to communicate, to communicate what they think, to enter into communication? Without developing the idea any further here, we would make the observation that this emphasis on dialogue comes with a profound doubt about its possibility; its means and mediations – and these include language and reason active within Logos – are brought into question and their limits are revealed. Is not language as opaque as it is transparent? Is it not a place of misunderstandings, misinterpretations and misrepresentations? Could not perfect and perfectly coherent discourse, total discourse – the discourse of the philosopher as it is traditionally perceived – be a metalanguage? Are there not several levels of communication and realization, with language being just one of these levels of experience, which is not self-sufficient and does not suffice in order to communicate, and even less in order to realize what has been said (and what has not been said) in praxis? In our view the privilege accorded to language in contemporary thought, and also in art, is the equivalent of a fetishism. Language is something other than a means of communication: something more and something less. The Word is not a 'being'. Taken as a simple means or considered as an absolute, language manifests itself as alienating and alienated; privileged, hypostacized (with or without communication and meaning), it changes into a thing. It reifies and becomes reified. This fetishism disguises real human relations, first that of communications, and second that of the realizing in everyday life (and in the 'lived') of what is said and what is meant.

Supposedly, dialogue unfolds between *two subjects* (any other terms are means and mediations without a specific reality). These two subjects are thought to determine each other grammatically and structurally: I and you, we and you. Quite simply, this model forgets that there are *never only two terms* (two subjects) involved. The third, the *other*, is always present. Why speak, why employ forms of communication and language in the act of utterance, if it is not to rid ourselves of an uneasiness, i.e., of hidden or recognized intentions, challenges and suspicions, so that the act of comprehending emerges from an incomprehension, which in fact is never completely eradicated? Living dialogue illuminates a misunderstanding, without which there would be nothing to say in any case, and which provides the 'matter' the subjects work on in a dialogue situation. This 'matter' is both the 'material' which is being expressed (hidden emotions, poorly revealed opinions, symbols) and the 'material' means of expressing them (the way words are used, intentions, intellectual operators, visible procedures, manifest patterns of behaviour).

This misunderstanding renders dialogue essential and yet difficult, possible but frequently doomed to failure. Where do its hidden roots lie? First, in language, in the words used and in the way they are used, in the symbols used and the intentions behind their use. And also in the systems of reference, which generally remain unclear. And also, and above all, in the *other*: the spectator (real or fictitious), the listener (present or virtual). Between 'you' and 'me', between 'we' and 'you', there is already another, 'he' and 'they', 'she' and 'they', 'they' and 'one'. Some people call this Other 'society', or the 'moral dimension' or 'values'. Believers call it God or the Devil, and psychoanalysts call it 'the Father'. It is close in language and distant in 'systems', 'frameworks', 'regulatory behaviour patterns' – and again, in the formal rules governing opposition and confrontation, the rules of tactics and strategies. As for philosophers, they have some very beautiful names for this included, excluded Third Party: transcendence, mind, thought, being, totality. All of these are correct: there can be no dialogue without a third party, there can be no relation between two without the other. But they are also all incorrect: none of the names is adequate.

Once it is restricted to two voices, a dialogue ceases; words are lacking, there is no common meeting ground. All that remain are cries and silence, cries which may express solitude and silence which may express a profound understanding, or its opposite. Into the two terms (with the second) I introduce the Third Party. It is part of the 'presence'; it takes part. Even in the most delicate conversation between lovers, it 'is' already there: the call of fear or of desire, fear of society (for its approval and consent), fear (or hope) of having a child, waiting for destiny, for passion. As for the monologue of challenge, adventure or desire, it is already a dialogue with a real or fictitious partner, and also a dialogue between the *agon* and the *alea*, which introduces death as a third term. The third term is always that which is possible, and it is this possibility that creates the common measure between the two terms or distinct subjects in 'the real' (the actual, what is present, presence), that both enables and compromises their mutual understanding by simultaneously creating misunderstanding and the possibility of eventual agreement.

How could there be art, poetry and theatre if dialogues in everyday life were limited to two voices? If this were the case, the words of two lovers, two allies or two rivals, two friends or two enemies talking to each other on the stage in front of the third party (us, the public), would scream of mendacity. If this were the case and if pure dialogue had any sense, 'them' and 'us' would take place in one world, and 'I' and 'you' in another; there would be neither society nor language; communication would not be a form of social practice. Or else communication would be a form without content: with nothing to say, without the barrier of opaqueness to overcome, without any misunderstanding to clarify. Or else communication would constitute its own content: speaking for speaking's sake, reflecting its own verbal reflection.

The Other and the Third Party are inherent in dialogue; they determine it and limit it. Forever invoked and forever discarded, evocative and evoked, the Third Party never completely enters into the actuality of the interview, in the presence and the present. It never exhausts itself. In itself, the Third Party is infinitely complex. It is infinite analysis – a hypothetical idea which must be handled with care, we should add. The characteristics of the Third Party are becoming more apparent; it is more, or it is less: more or less important, imminent, oppressive. Sometimes models dominate, sometimes symbols, sometimes one particular image or representation, and now and again 'something' more obscure. This imminence weighs down on the dialogue, directing it and regulating it. It is stronger than the minds which are exchanging words, i.e., it is something more than words alone, something more than 'being'. The Other always spills over from the act, i.e., from the reality of the dialogue. The lover, the poet, the actor – they all exhaust themselves in their effort to exhaust the possibilities of dialogue. They would like the act and the words, the real and the language they are using, to coincide; as if by magic they would like to make Logos effective and to tear it from its limits to make it coincide with life; but here too they are still acting: they resort to overdramatic gestures. If they were to achieve their aim, they would kill off their source of life: expressivity. All would be silence.

Through an initial and predictable misunderstanding, dialectic presents itself as dialogue: with *two* terms, two *dimensions*. Thus analytic understanding reduces dialectical movement to an opposition. In Hegel, however, whenever there are two terms or two voices – the master and the slave, for example – their conflict always contains a third term, born within and from that conflict, an active supersession: consciousness itself. The reduction of the dialectical relation to two dimensions is accompanied by a confusion between dialectical thought and logical thought, which has its own methods (disjunction, dichotomy, distinctions between genus and species, etc.). This confusion has sterilized dialectical thought, which has become unable to grasp movements concretely; on the other hand, it has been very fruitful for logical thought, which has superseded Aristotelianism and has created a multiplicity of operational techniques in which binary (two-term) oppositions and relations, including complementarity, interaction, reciprocity, etc., play a major role.

To eliminate this confusion, we will use the idea of *level*. We need to distinguish three levels: *formal logic* and *pure formalization* (including

axiomatization); *two-dimensional dialectical logic* (including the operational techniques of complementarity, polarization, reciprocity and
interaction); and *three-dimensional dialectical movements*. Analytical and
logical thought may attack these movements in a variety of ways in
order to reduce them to silence, but it never succeeds in exhausting
them.

When we examine the breadth and depth of praxis by operating a
vertical section (which cuts through and reveals the strata superimposed by time: the diachronic) and a *horizontal* section (which cuts
through and reveals the actual: the synchronic, the structured), it will
only afford us knowledge if we relate it to a third term: a process.
Only a movement like this, a *growth* or a *development* for example, can
make such operational procedures permissible, given the dangers of
randomness and the damage that such sections can do. Only the
third term can give meaning to analytical techniques which reduce
destiny to two dimensions or a single one.

We can now sum up the question of dimensions:

a) *Dimension* ONE. This is the dimension of analytic understanding
and formal logic. Analytic abstraction only comprises one aspect, one
element, one variable. When applied to an object, formal logic leads
to unilaterality. In what purports to be an in-depth exploration of
the selected aspect, the tendency is almost always to privilege it, and
to transform it into a mechanically dominant 'factor' or an ontological 'essence'. It is thus the favourite dimension of dogmatism;
dogmatism sets up home there; it reduces everything (the totality) to
a single dimension: to unilaterality, where supposed clarity is in fact a
mutilation.

However, analysis of any comprehensive multidimensional phenomenon must break it up into 'formants'; this operation is essential.
We are duty bound to make discrete studies of social time, social
space, ecology, demography, norms, models, regulatory behaviour
patterns, everyday life, etc. Nevertheless, certain methodological
principles are imperative: to fight against unilaterality; to restore
analysis in its entirety; to make distinctions without separating but
also without muddling. Not to think that everything is in everything,
and not to think that everything is external to everything. Not to
overemphasize difference, and not to overemphasize unity; to handle
analysis prudently and synthesis with suspicion . . .

b) *Dimension* TWO. Above all else, this is the dimension of dialectical logic, the realm of disjunctions, mutual exclusions, dichotomies, i.e., those operational techniques which enable us to define and to grasp polarized relations, reciprocities and interactions. In our opinion, the study of (relative) stabilities, structures, and (relative) constants should give priority to these two-term relations.[17] They allow us to grasp and to define (relative and momentary) balances and (provisional) self-regulations. They also explain why scientific knowledge makes use of binary arithmetic, matrixes and double-entry tables, grids, alternating (opening and closing) techniques, questions with yes-or-no answers, etc. This area is not purely formal; more exactly, the formal is also part of the real, up to a certain point. Dichotomies and oppositions on an abstract plane correspond to practical operations: bifurcations, shifts of direction, alternations, the presence or absence of a thing defined as a thing (as a stability). More broadly, there is a logic of action, of will, i.e., decision logic. There are options and choices. 'Either this or that.' As we know, language alone requires me to pronounce one phoneme as opposed to another, thus excluding the other by enunciating a different one in its place. To be effective we must make clear distinctions between possibilities and between relations (but this does not mean that there will not be waiting periods during which situations change and 'mature', or delays and temporizations, impatience, attempts at compromise, conciliation, synthesis, etc.). Decision logic has been developed by operational research and by games theory. Information theory has explained an aspect of social practice in communications which is formal, and at the same time real. At this level a *discontinuous* aspect of praxis becomes evident, which comprises calculations concerning discrete units (qualitative mathematics) and the concomitant operational techniques. This discontinuous aspect can be enumerated, and thus it can be exhausted. Every reality which is considered to be made up of a determinable number of discrete units can be exhausted in a finite number of questions with yes-or-no answers, and consequently in a finite number of signs or of words.

c) *Dimension* THREE. Tridimensionality is the level of dialectical movements, or more exactly the level where reality itself is grasped. Time and time again we have determined tridimensionalities in the knowledge of human reality: need–work–pleasure, do–say–live, the controlled sector – the uncontrolled sector – the mixed sector, etc., and we will have cause to do so again.

Nevertheless it would be incorrect to state that with tridimensionality knowledge fully grasps the 'continuous', the 'concrete' or the dialectical movement per se. Such a statement would fetishize tridimensionality and would be metaphysical or theological. What is more, the distinction between dimensions already implies analysis. Tridimensionality encompasses a formal framework: the three dimensions of space, the three dimensions of time (before, during, after), the three pronominal groups in the grammatical expression of social relations (I and you, we and you, they and them). This formal framework remains relatively constant and structural at the heart of a seemingly infinite mobility.

Human reality makes itself known tridimensionally. In the philosophical tradition, triplicity appears from the very start: body, soul, mind; sensibility, understanding, will, etc. These classic triplicities reverberate in every domain: feeling, perception, conceptualization; colour, intensity, saturation of perceptions of light; pitch, volume, timbre; rhythm, melody, harmony, etc.

In fact, action also has three dimensions. A decision cuts; it sections; it reduces a complex situation involving the past (which is irreversible and irremediable, but which has allowed for the gaining of a capability or an empowerment), with all its possibilities and impossibilities, to two dimensions, to the choice between two possibilities. The conflict between the controlled sector and the uncontrolled sector is constantly resolved by the acquisition of new knowledge and new empowerments, which moreover are always limited . . .

Grasped tridimensionally (thus by means of a certain form), dialectical movement extends beyond analysis; it cannot be calculated. It even eludes language, since the efforts made when people speak are nothing more than attempts to bridge the gap by inventing unexpected words and turns of phrase. Tridimensionality is not exhausted by finite knowledge. It forbids us to think that we can proceed only by asking questions which require yes-or-no answers. Sooner or later the moment comes when these questions and answers will lose all meaning, and when someone will reply: yes and no. Exhaustion is death, but before that it is defeat and failure, rupture and finiteness. In every domain, tridimensionality points to a determined movement, encompassing internal conflicts and proceeding by a succession of supersessions.

d) *Multidimensionality*. This becomes acceptable providing we refuse to fetishize tridimensionality. In a dialectical anthropology, man would be multidimensional, and we would be happy to grant games, for example, the theoretical dignity of a dimension. Each 'dimension' would correspond to a degree of freedom. However, if we accept this, we should be wary of substituting the constituent relations of a *presence* by a *representation*. We must not substitute the concrete space and time of praxis by a 'configurative space' analogous to the one physicists used in their formalisms. A configurative space is nothing more than an abstract representation of three-dimensional practical space.

e) *Infinity of dimensions*. Here we pose the problem of non-finite analysis. If totality or 'reality' – including possibility, and taken on all levels – proves itself to be limitless in complexity and in depth, then surely we must imitate the mathematician and introduce an infinity of dimensions. If 'the real' cannot be exhausted in a finite series of limited questions formulated in logical and precise terms, to which the interviewee can answer yes or no, and if in one way or another we must qualify it as being 'non-finite', surely we should take this into account in the representations we use.

The problem goes beyond our frame of reference. There is a law which knowledge still obeys: 'I must stop.' Sooner or later it comes to a halt before an obstacle which also acts as a support: an object. Praxis overcomes it; analysis dissolves it using other means. Knowledge and praxis perceive the non-finite as a possibility, a 'horizon of horizons'. We must not see it as actual infinity. We must make infinity relative.

9 The idea of structure

This idea was rapidly accepted by the sciences. Now it predominates. There is a widespread representation of reality as a structure, from which it follows that science is nothing more than the knowledge of structures and the truth of these structures.

Where does the idea originate? How could it have come into circulation so rapidly? Let us limit ourselves to a few initial explanations.

The idea of *structure* comes as much from the social sciences as it does from mathematics and physics; Marx used it before Sophus Lie who introduced it in mathematics in the study of transformation groups, and almost at the same time as Spencer in sociology. The term started to become widespread around 1930. It corresponds with a general preoccupation among scientific thinkers, which grew in opposition to the predominant concern of the previous period. This was continuist and evolutionist; its thought developed according to the scheme of a continuous process of becoming; it introduced the process of becoming into immobility. It studied forms and formations. The twentieth century has grown increasingly preoccupied with the discontinuous. Instead of introducing the process of becoming into what is stable, the question is asked as to how stability is possible at the heart of the process of becoming. Other aspects, the 'structuring' and 'structured' aspects of the real, become apparent. Driving analysis farther and in a different direction than hitherto, the search for structures reaches the discrete and stable elements of realities.

It is reasonable to think that these aspects – the process of becoming and stability, formation and structure – will lead to a more profoundly dialecticized knowledge, of which Marx's thought provides the model. It is equally reasonable to suppose that a certain stabilization of the world round about 1930 (with capitalism holding its ground, and socialism becoming frozen in the face of this persistence) played no small part in these 'structural' preoccupations, which facilitated and continue to facilitate certain discoveries, while preserving a certain unilaterality in comparison with a totalizing dialectical way of thinking.

The idea of *structure* has been highly elaborated, and has had many uses, but today it is rather shop-worn, and is becoming something of a blunt instrument. It is becoming confused. It is noticeable that the word has accrued a multiplicity of meanings and that when people use it they are never completely sure what they are talking about. Even the old and popularized distinction between *form* and *structure* has been lost sight of. In day-to-day language, a sphere and a circumference have a form; a polygon has a structure. Put more precisely, this means that there is a connection between form and continuity. Now what is continuous cannot be enumerated. On the other hand, when a totality is made up of discrete, distinct and discontinuous units, it has a structure; the discrete units make up a countable grouping, which can be exhausted in a finite series of questions answerable by yes or by no. It is extremely curious to see analytic thought pushed to extremes of sophistication and ending up with very fine differences and extreme distinctions, yet at the same time maintaining some very serious confusions. In this light, we are already seeing form and structure in opposition to each other. Grouped under the heading 'reality', the confusion between *form, structure* and *function* will soon reveal itself to be one of the weaknesses which impede knowledge of the everyday, the understanding of its problems and the imagining of its possible metamorphoses.

From numerous passionate discussions, symposiums and seminars on 'structure', three main conceptions emerge:

a) Structure is *what is intelligible*, it is *essence* in a thing or in a set of phenomena. Sometimes this 'essence' is represented philosophically as a sort of substance, and we have an Aristotelian epistemology. In this case it is an organic unity, as G. G. Granger demonstrates.[18] In this conception, form, function and structure become complete equivalents, since these terms are considered as being more or less the same as the existent 'whole' or totality.[19]

b) Structure is a construction, with reference to an object or a set of objects. By studying them we extrapolate a *system* of coherent relations, together with the transformations which enable us to pass from one system to another and to grasp their relations. Thus structure is located on a certain level above phenomena, but it allows us to grasp them in so far as they have an inner coherence and present combinations of finite and defined properties, i.e., probably in so far as they answer to certain functions (for example, marriage, to perpetuate society). In this conception, structure is therefore the formal representation of a group of relations which has been constructed with a view to studying a set of phenomena and a particular problem which concerns them. There is a confusion between *form* and *structure*, but it is no longer on the level of reality, but on the level of abstraction. Structure is the model, an unconscious or supraconscious representation in what exists.[20]

c) To conclude, a final conception places *structure* neither on the level of a substantial 'reality', nor on that of a constructed abstraction. It conceives of it as an intermediary and a mediation, and also as a relative constant at the heart of the real, as an unstable balance between opposing forces. Therefore structure is not self-sufficient. There are forces which carry it and support it from beneath, so to speak; other forces, higher units, maintain and control it from above. It is a temporary balance which can only be conceived of in reference to the other levels, to the forces and contexts. Isolated and taken per se, these considerations of balance bring us back to the initial conception of structure.

There are structures, and structures conceal forces which modify them in a perpetual movement (of destructuring and restructuring).

> Be it partial (the structure of a group) or total (of an entire society), every social structure is a precarious balance, which must be permanently re-established by ever-renewed efforts, between a multiplicity of hierarchies at the heart of a total social phenomenon with macro-sociological characteristics, of which it only represents a single sector or aspect . . . This balance between multiple hierarchies is strengthened and cemented by models, signs, symbols, social roles, values and ideas, in short by the cultural works which are specific to these structures.[21]

If we look back at Marx's thought in *Capital*, we will notice that he does not exclude any of these meanings and conceptions. In accordance with the programme he set himself in a well-known text, the Preface to *A Contribution to the Critique of Political Economy*,[22] Marx defines the production *relations* which make up the economic *structure* of society, the 'foundation' on which a legal and political superstructure is built, and to which the *forms* of social consciousness correspond. Here structure is the essence of a society, capitalist society, defined and determined by certain production relations. Structure and form are not synonymous. Legally elaborated and systematized property relations form part of the superstructures which carry out certain functions in a determined society. Social consciousness adopts 'forms' – of ideas, of ideologies, of civilization – which should be studied in terms of their formation in history. Structure *forms itself* in the course of a history. Knowledge of capitalist society implies knowledge of its history in so far as it is a 'socioeconomic formation'.

However, to study capitalist society in actuality supposes a series of analytic operations and abstractions (which grasp elements and which penetrate inside concrete totality). Not only does Marx begin from an abstraction in relation to real economic actions, exchange-value, but he also constructs an abstract capitalist society reduced to its essential forces and polarities: the proletariat and the bourgeoisie. Only then does he reintegrate all the aspects, all the intermediaries, all the elements he had momentarily left out of the concrete totality. Thus *Capital* constructs a model. Structure becomes an implement of analysis and dialectical synthesis. Finally, after a long analysis, this synthesis (which Marx left incomplete) reveals the forces which undermined the society in question from within, and led it to its downfall. Both negative and positive, these forces prepare for destructuring and destruction at the very centre of the structure, in its nucleus, at its heart. Structure is therefore never anything but a precarious balance between the opposing forces of momentary stability and revolution.

Thus we can recognize the three concepts of structure in Marx, but they are arranged hierarchically, and the third predominates. Marxist thought distinguishes (markedly, although not very clearly) between form, structure, function, system and totality.[23] All in all, is not structure the stabilizing factor, stability itself, by which a 'being' (an individual or a set of individuals, types, species, social groups, etc.) preserves itself until time bears it away? In short, is structure not its armature? Is not that the role of the skeleton, and of the shell?

In our opinion, the quite excessive emphasis on this concept in present-day structuralism overlooks everything structure contains which is dead or capable of dying. Certainly, in its way, structure has life. Let us take a skeleton, for example. It is born and develops within the individual and is his inner link with his species, its history and its struggle against its environment and within its environment. And yet, although it supports life, the skeleton itself is not alive. It is fixed, it survives the individual. When we examine the skeleton we will not find the living being; all we see is the anatomy, not the physiology. To privilege the skeleton is to proceed like a palaeontologist, a classifier who sees his studies as a convenient way of classification, and is more concerned with nomenclature (although this is essential) than with grasping what the human really is. It is a process in which death grasps the living. The human skeleton has a function, or several functions. For example, it facilitates the upright stance, and maintains it. It cannot achieve this without the help of the muscles or the circulatory system, etc. It is not synonymous with these functions, nor with any other determined function. The various functions (circulation, secretion, etc.) act upon each other, suppose each other and superimpose upon each other. Each makes up a partial fact, the cause and effect of a certain cohesion and self-regulation within the organic totality. The totality of these functions – life – is not synonymous with any of them and cannot be defined by any of them; as it is a totality, it is multifunctional or transformational. As for the form of the human body, it is a demonstration of life itself, i.e., the entire set of functions, the totality of functions and structures. It cannot be reduced to a series of distinct and discontinuous units, like the bones of the skeleton. It is nevertheless true that the skeleton becomes formed, and that, when normal, this form demonstrates a precarious but satisfying balance between the various physiological functions, producing the normal form of the living human organism.

We suspect intuitively that there are complex relations between these various terms (structure, function, form, as well as systems, totalities, coherences). We cannot separate them, but nor can we merge them; we cannot reduce them to each other, but nor can we isolate them. Could the way they interconnect be a matter for dialectical thought? What is certain is that the relation of these terms creates a problem. This problem disappears if we merge them, and even more so if we see them as being synonymous; as we shall see, this is what characterizes *structuralism*.

Before making our definition, let us consider the following image, which follows the concept very closely. I pick up an empty seashell on the beach; I examine it; I find it beautiful, fragile, perfect in its way, and it satisfies my mind like a materialized Idea. I see that it is endowed with a prodigiously delicate *structure*: symmetries, straight lines and curves, grooves and ridges, lobes or spirals, serrations, etc. It really is a structure where discontinuities stand out (in spite of the importance of continuous lines), notably in its symmetries and dissymmetries. I admire its delicate details; in each one I discover new details and new delicacy. I am lost in admiration. I decide to describe these structures carefully and to use them to learn about the living beings these shells once contained. An excellent method, since the shell is there, in my hand, stable, solid and precise. However, am I going to forget that it is nothing more than a piece of work and a 'product', and the product of a relation, the relation between a living being and its environment? If I find that living being in another shell similar to the one I have picked up, I will see that it is soft, sticky and (apparently) amorphous; taken out of its shell, how different the two are! And yet it is the shellfish which has secreted the shell; it has taken on the form of the shell; it has given itself that form. The living being and the living form make up the whole: the shell and the tiny, sticky animal I have separated with my knife. This mass of cells has functions – of which secreting its shell is at least one (or several) – and the shell has a function (or several). If I consider the shell in isolation, I emphasize the definite, fixed, and also mortal and dead, aspects of life. Part of the process of becoming and yet eluding it, the shell – a product or a work made by life – is not alive. Its description enables us to *classify* types and species, according to clear distinctions (logical ones: according to specific differences). And yet the shell is never anything other than a thing, the witness to a moment when life stopped, abandoned by death on the dead sands, exiled from the unflagging life of the sea, of the living space which goes on and on. It is perfect, it is beautiful, it illuminates life and the works of life, it illuminates beauty, but the light it sheds on the world is a cruel one. Why cannot life do without this framework which is more 'beautiful' than life itself, and which persists after it has passed away? So is there anything mortal in perfection and beauty?

With a question like this we bring dream and science, knowledge and art together in a shared borderland. But it goes too far in one direction. In its way, by privileging mobility and amorphousness, it romanticizes. Not for a single moment must we forget the extent to which the shell and the 'being' which secreted it are different. Not for a single moment must we forget the problem which this question helps to formulate in all its forcefulness. At the heart of the universal process of becoming which creates and which destroys, which asserts and negates, how and why do we observe (relative) stabilities, defined and relatively constant contours, regularities, forms which are born and survive, which produce and which reproduce, at the heart of innumerable interactions? Among the shapes of the continuous process of becoming – the circle and the spiral – how is it that there are discontinuous *structures* endowed with defined properties –

polygons, polyhedrons, groups, tree diagrams, networks? In the cosmic process of becoming, what is the secret of the Earth, that stable sphere betrothed to death? In the history of man, what is the secret of everyday life?

In the light this has shed upon our research, houses, neighbour-hoods and towns themselves – in a word, morphology – resemble the image of the seashell. The economist may perceive them in a differ-ent way, and link this morphology to other concepts, that of productive force, for example. He is right from his point of view, and this point of view is something to which we can refer, in that some-times it can be considered of paramount importance. For us, morphological description enables us to classify; it sends us off in search of those living beings – hidden, (apparently) amorphous, sticky and soft perhaps – comprising the groups which have secreted these shells, it helps us to grasp them in their everyday reality. This every-day life is hidden; when the shellfish is alive, it closes up when we touch it. Dead or dying, it yawns wide open. But let us not overwork the image . . .

We have already partially linked everyday life to the idea of the amorphous or unformed. In a sense, it is part of the *astructural*, to use the expression employed by Georges Gurvitch in discussions and polemics against contemporary 'structuralism', with the precise aim of showing the limits of the concept of *structure*. For Georges Gurvitch, forms of sociability are astructural. Structures appear on the macro-sociological scale, but on that scale phenomena cannot be contained by structure, since they encompass non-structural elements.

However, it is not sufficient for us to identify the everyday with the astructural. A more detailed analysis is required. Whatever is appar-ently unformed can conceal a form or be part of one. Let us look at the seashell image again. The everyday differs from what the descrip-tion of its external forms (its morphology) tells us, but cannot be separated from it. It must not be confused with a pure, unconditional spontaneity, a kind of absolute effervescence or primordial vitality, which is what the term 'unformed' conjures up. Could it be that it has no function? On the contrary, there is a multiplicity of functions which are carried out in the everyday and which play their part in defining it. If we are to get to know it, we must first distinguish between form, function and structure, and then look for their connections. If there are spontaneous, unformed and astructural elements in the everyday, there are also elements which are 'structured' by determined and fragmented activities, and by functions associated with society as a whole, and finally, there are elements which are organized by apparatus existing on the 'macro' scale in society as a whole. What is more, by using models to scrutinize what is apparently amorphous or unformed, we may discover forms or structures within them. Thus what appears most contingent and most accidental in the everyday can contain and translate – and sometimes traduce – group tactics and strategies. Analysis is never faced with an entirely irreducible residual deposit. In this sense we would accept some (but not all) of G. G. Granger's conclusions. In social phenomena, form and the formal intervene in the very depths of content (but without absorbing, reabsorbing or exhausting it). They bring logic with them (oppositions, disjunctions, polarizations) via the various effects of language or decisions. Therefore there are hidden structures which formal thought can grasp by reconstructing them according to diagrams or models.[24] What at first sight appears unstructurable can reveal structural determinants which are of paramount importance in the concrete process of becoming, namely strategies, options and choices. In short, the 'conjuncture/structure' relation is profoundly dialectical. Not only does structure refer us to conjuncture, with an implied reciprocity; not only should knowledge place itself now in the perspective of structure (of relative stability), now in the perspective of conjuncture (of the process of becoming); in a sense, structure is also conjunctural, and conjuncture contains structural elements. From the point of view of structure, conjuncture is made up of luck and interactions. From the point of view of conjuncture, structure itself is nothing more than a precarious and momentary success, a win or a loss in a complex gamble. Each term can be considered alternately as necessary and as accidental, as creating a free act and as prohibiting it, as failure and as good fortune. When a structure is broken up (by destructurization, which begins deep within structure), other structural elements appear, for which we may use the following terms: strategies, options, decisions, information, etc. Thus on every level, on every rung of society, the *event* is not irreducible. Even a revolution – that total phenomenon and creative turmoil – is prepared; strategies take it on board, or it overturns them; there is nothing unconditional about its origins. 'The lived' and the everyday can never be completely separated from totality. What appears to be conjunctural in the one can appear to be structural in the other; what looks like a simple event in the one looks like a strategy in the other. A notable example of this would be the confusion we have pointed out so many times between the *public* and the *private*, which caricatures their supersession in and by revolutionary praxis as predicted by Marx. This confusion has personalized and 'privatized' power and has made private life public by 'reprivatizing' it. On the level of society as a whole, this is a conjunctural situation which arises from the interaction of state-controlled powers with the new means modern technology has put at their disposal. On the level of the everyday, a multiplicity of events are dependent on this, as is the form they will assume. This is the way the social functions of information and communication work. The form they adopt and the social function have no relation of absolute necessity.

Once more we find ourselves with the 'conjuncture/structure' relation. We have by no means exhausted it in all the concrete situations in which it can be found. Conjuncture appears to us as a (non-finite and continuous) pressure on structure from the process of becoming, and as the virtual shattering of structure. Conversely, it also appears as a rigorously determined object, related to a logic (decision logic, strategy theory) or to a formal theory (information theory). Structure appears to us in turn as the solid, stable element, or as something fragile, constantly brought into question, constantly compromised, the precious and momentary result of the process of becoming and of history. It is the fulcrum of action and freedom, and thus of a disalienation, but from the moment it becomes fixed and made into a representation it becomes a force for alienation; but from that moment too, the process of becoming has already begun to dismantle it.

Let us try to push the analysis of the 'conjuncture/structure' relation a stage further by applying it to a specific case. 'The lived' in the everyday can and should be described using language. Now language does not have the privilege of expressing the lived comprehensively. Language is a conjunctural work, the work of a society, but it is heavily structured, and is a means of action and communication. At one and the same time it is more than a simple instrument at the service of a conscious will and a conscious purpose, and less than one. For these reasons alone it would be difficult to see language as the embodiment of universal Reason. It corresponds generally to a level of experience which has already been socialized and filtered, and specifically to what is lived (individually). It is not the equivalent of a Reason capable of grasping everything and of saying everything on the spot, nor of a social medium by which an individual consciousness might be able to express 'the lived'. Consequently the lived belongs to a broader 'living'; when formulated verbally it illuminates or focuses on a zone (a level) at the heart of living. In one sense the 'lived' is the work of an individual, the realization of a project in a 'living' constituted by social praxis, a general work by groupings in relation to one another. The 'lived/living' dialectical relation in which language intervenes as a mediation and a third term is partially beyond the scope of language, and thus beyond the scope of our logic and our analytic implements (which means we must make them keener). Why? Because language enters into this relation; rather than encompassing it, it is encompassed by it. Thus the 'lived/living' relation remains *unconscious* (except in the case of the mediation which assumes an exaggerated realness and which, in a spontaneously produced and constantly reproduced self-delusion, appears to coincide with the relation by absorbing its terms). We do not know how we live, and yet our consciousness can only be defined as consciousness of our lives and how we live them, and of our individual actions in social praxis. The term 'unconscious' refers no longer to a substance, but to a situation. It becomes relative and 'sociologized'. In this sense, *the unconscious is consciousness*. Conveyed by means of language, or rather linked immediately to language and coinciding in fact with 'what is said', it remains locked within itself, even when it falls silent when threatened by the 'other', since it consists not only of 'what is said' but also of 'what is not said'. It splits into two: 'the lived', what is experienced, the nucleus of that experience, and the 'living', the context and horizon of 'the lived'. From then on, consciousness seeks itself through the 'other', even though it is itself 'what is'. This paradoxical and permanently tense situation of a reality which coincides both with itself and with its mediation and its implement – language – and yet which hounds itself remorselessly, acts as a stimulation; it must forever 'become conscious' of living, of the 'other' and of itself.

Language must always open itself up; it must go farther and deeper in order to grasp something else, both in the luminous and sombre nucleus of 'the lived' and on the chiaroscuro horizon of 'living'. For the speaking, self-speaking consciousness, this search for 'something else' is the only way it can avoid succumbing to the alienation of taking what has been said as accepted (as its 'being'), and of considering the mediation to be the reality, and language to be a defined and defining entity. The result is that what is prior to what will be said and spoken is also subsequent to what was said (or not said). What is subsequent to what has been said and what has not been said is prior to what is going to be said. The 'prelinguistic' or 'unconscious' level is also 'supralinguistic' at the same time. The two levels, the infra and the supra, intersect. They are always relative one to the other, and the one defines the other, in an ever-repeated conjuncture.

Possibly there is a key which will enable us to grasp this highly complex relation: the grammatical structure of our statements. Practical statements formulate the lived, and pronouns provide these statements with a structure: *I, you* (sing.) *and he – we, you* (pl.) *and they – I and me – one and them*. The elements of this group enter into various configurations and constellations which are sometimes binary and disjunctive, sometimes three-dimensional. When brought together the terms are mutually inclusive and exclusive. In the I/you (sing.) relation, the third term 'he' is sometimes excluded or parenthesized (but is still there!) and sometimes explicitly present. The same can be said of the I/we relation. We can make a list of the possible oppositions and constellations:

- I/you (sing.)/(he) – (*he* parenthesized)
- I/you (sing.)/he – (*he* included)
- I/us/(he or they) – (*he* or *they* parenthesized)
- I/us/he or they – (*he* or *they* included)
- I/you (pl.)/(he or they)
- we/you (pl.)/(he or they or them)
- we/you (pl.)/he or they
- we/you (sing.)
- we/they
- one/I
- we/me, etc.

These constellations are finite in number. There are not even very many of them. Could they be similar to the well-known studies which determine and limit the number of situations in theatrical drama? It might be amusing to try to demonstrate this. However, the practical situations they become involved in are inexhaustibly changing, varied and mobile, and full of unexpected moments. Thus *structure* would be the finite (determined and logical) aspect of a movement whose infinite, mobile aspect would be *conjuncture*. Conjuncture is expressed in a structure, and structure signifies a conjuncture. However, when the conjuncture is modified the structure is transformed, and even shattered. Structure tends to maintain and to stabilize conjuncture. For this reason they have a dialectical relation in which neither term has an absolute pre-eminence, but in which a third term – the process of becoming – plays the primary role. Encounters, conflicts and possible reversals are of prime importance. The process of becoming does not burst forth from pure and unpredictable spontaneity. The form it adopts is that of the future, i.e., of projects and possibilities. Here too we can analyse conjecture: it conceals the tactics and strategies of the 'I's and the 'we's, the 'you's (sing.), the 'one's and the 'they's.

Let us note that each structural element contains all the others, potentially or in the present. In particular, the 'I' and the 'me' encompass 'we's and 'you's (pl.), 'you's (sing.) and 'them's. They cannot be isolated. They cannot be determined by themselves. Between and within 'I' and 'me' and the relation between them is language, society and the world. A particular structural element can become polarized or focused, and it can pass into language. It can become a nucleus or a focal point – or else, conversely, it can grow increasingly faint, blurred and obscure. In the latter case, the region which is emphasized (polarized or focused) changes place; it shifts elsewhere. If something loses weight and emphasis, this is not to say that it has stopped existing and being active.

When I emphasize my presence, my will or my thoughts by saying 'I', the 'we' (the interaction between individuals, or the social group of which 'I' am a part, along with its consciousness, its norms and its values – or again society as a whole with its regulatory representations and patterns of behaviour) becomes blurred; the social becomes 'unconscious'; it continues to be active; in my mind I can reproduce a social representation by endowing it with the warmth of a personal presence; without me even realizing it, my decision can be founded on a norm or a value, and I can believe in all honesty that something which has come from elsewhere really is my own. In this case the 'we' is the content and, more than that, it is the *law* of my consciousness and of its 'being', bearing in mind that we are not using these terms in any ontological, substantial or absolute way. The 'we', or rather the 'we's, are simultaneously internal and external to 'I' and 'me'; they determine them, but not in a crude, external way. And it is only at the heart of 'we' that 'I' can be distinguished from 'me', to the extent that the 'we' authorizes this split, making it possible and indeed inevitable. It only appears at certain stages of history, and in certain societies (such as ours!). The distinction between 'I', 'me' and 'we' operates in a specified 'us'. The 'I' takes the dominant voice; it illuminates certain fragments of the 'we' and focuses them. The 'me' encompasses the deep plurality of the 'we', or rather, of the 'we's.

But what happens if I speak out in the name of a group (family, friends, associations, etc.) or if I make an important decision justified by the norms and values of the group, and by the regulatory representations and patterns of behaviour of society as a whole? In this case, 'I' am speaking and 'I' am deciding; and yet, 'I' and 'me' become blurred. Whatever I am becomes unconscious. I can even misinterpret my feelings and my interests, and disregard what is closest to my heart by failing to recognize it. The 'we' becomes localized and focused. It becomes the centre and the nucleus of consciousness. 'I' and 'we' do not disappear. They still figure in the constellation. They remain active. It really is me who is speaking and making decisions, but only in so far as I am part of us. The 'I' and the 'me' lapse into relative unconsciousness.

The same thing happens when the 'I' succeeds in placing itself in the perspective of the 'you' during a dialogue. In this case the 'we' links the 'I' and the 'you' and takes front stage: preconscious but supraconscious at first, it becomes the focal point or centre of conscious activity, while the 'I' per se becomes 'unconscious'.

This dialectic of consciousness (i.e., of infraconsciousness and supraconsciousness, of the passage from relative unconsciousness to relative consciousness) corresponds to dialectical moments: 'the lived/living', 'conjuncture/structure', 'the everyday/totality'. It is clear that *signs* (words: I, you, he, etc.) play an important role. They are relative constants, crystallizations, nucleuses both of consciousness and of communication. Do they create what they signify? Yes and no. Taken absolutely, this idea is an extrapolation. Taken relatively, however, it is true. Language is a social fact, and plays a part in all social facts. It is a part of them. It is therefore the active element of every social phenomenon. It helps to bring it into being and to fix it. Realness and possibility, the project and its realization – they all pass through language. It enables works, but does not create them historically. In societies such as ours, where the individual manages to express himself (not without difficulty) because he manages to exist (not without difficulty), individuals have created their way of expression. Once it has been constituted, it becomes active. It creates individuals. Signs per se intervene. In this way the dialectical movements we mentioned above become interwoven with an even more complex movement: 'expressivity/signification', which unfolds at the heart of society as a whole.

Thus we are able to relativize unconsciousness, and to conceive of it socially by linking it to the idea, rather vague in itself, of 'the lived', i.e., in this context, the everyday. Given the importance of signs, we could connect the study of unconsciousness thus defined in the 'conjuncture/structure' relation for the conscious beings we are, to a general semantics and a general semeiology, but with the proviso that we do not assume that this way of studying language will have the privilege of delivering an essence.

Using this model, we will immediately be able to discern a concrete form of alienation in the everyday. Alienation does not only come from the norms and models we ourselves determine. It does not only come from the inventive patterns of behaviour and the fascinating images which distract us from ourselves. When it is born from a misunderstanding of the level on which consciousness is situated, it is the child of our own initiatives and our own actions. If I confuse 'I', 'me' and 'we' – if I merge them, if I overlook the distance between these levels – I introduce an alienation. 'I' thinks it is 'we', and even worse, 'them'. If I forget the gap between these terms, if I leave one of them in blind necessity by opting for another, if I disregard unperceived conflicts by accepting the set as cohesive, then 'consciousness' and 'unconsciousness' become blurred and their roles become reversed. 'Misconsciousness' triumphs. Now when social practice teaches us language it also teaches us how to pass from 'I' to 'we', and vice versa. It is a rather crude cultural apprenticeship, a structuring and structured verbal technique. In this context there is a risk that the terms 'structure' and 'technique' may lead us astray. They conjure up a sense of solidity. But in this context these techniques are random, and the social structures of consciousness which we are trying to delimit are both strangely vigorous and curiously fragile; effectively, on the individual scale, they are founded on words. Hence the constant possibility of a *misuse* of words and an *unawareness* of what they relate to.

In the preceding pages we have carefully distinguished the concepts (of form, function and structure) in order to grasp their connections more effectively. We can proceed in the same way for *system* and *structure*. The way the word 'system' and the word 'structure' are used is as vague as it is obscure. There is a tendency to make them synonymous, particularly when certain characteristics of structure are emphasized, such as coherence, inner logic, and the whole in which elements are distributed and maintained according to an immanent logic. The term 'system' used to be misleadingly clear, because it was used indiscriminately to mean 'the real' (the system of consanguinity, according to Morgan),[25] conceptual constructs ('legal systems', for example, or 'political systems') and pure abstractions ('philosophical systems'). In every case, the most important characteristic is balance and inner cohesion. And we need to know where this characteristic originates: from logic, from the real, or from both. If this question remains unanswered, the concept will be equivocal. This would perhaps explain the ambiguity of the idea of structure, which is understood sometimes as a construct (a model) and at other times as given (an essence), or as a mixture of these two polarities.

It would perhaps be feasible to keep the word 'system' (in the social sciences) for structures which reproduce their own elements with periodic regularity, thus imposing cyclic form on social time. This is a form (among others) of coherence and temporality, characterized by a circular process: the elements change, but their connections do not. Let us take one interesting case: *systems of agricultural cultivation*.[26] This has been the object of some significant work (more in Italy and Germany than in France), but it has been somewhat neglected, so that similar research has subsequently been greeted with a great deal of surprise. It is obvious that since land settlement and the growth of villages, peasant groups have had to take every element into account when organizing production: soil, climate, population, labour needs and resources, and techniques for plant cultivation, etc. Of course, in archaic peasant communities, this organization was not carried out according to our own rational and operational way of thinking. The indispensable balance was achieved by empirical trial and error, in the guise of representations and symbols, according to the order attributed to the cosmos and to the human community, and under the leadership of elders, chiefs and priests. Mistakes were very costly: famines, crises within the community. It is probable that mechanical self-regulation came too late, and that the prevention of mistakes and the prediction of errors was a matter of informed guesswork. In any event, balance was achieved in a situation of permanent change, which involved the reproduction of elements and their relations in a social practice as yet unaware of itself. The system of cultivation itself grouped a series of productive elements together in a coherent set: woodland (for gathering, breeding, wood); steppe, pasture (for livestock); arable land (for cereal production); gardens (for vegetables); orchards (for fruits), plus other less essential but in certain cases important elements (places for fishing, rivers, ponds, etc.). It is clear that these 'parameters' gave rise to defined conditions (notably by way of the techniques involved) which combined in ways which were sometimes viable, sometimes optimal, but sometimes destined to die out.

The balanced distribution of the various 'elements' establishes a system. The term becomes valid when we consider the balance and the necessary cohesion of the whole. When an agrarian system is well defined – notably by the implements and agricultural techniques it uses – it determines the landscape, and the structure of the village and its relation to the soil. It also determines a periodicity, i.e., a cyclic time scale made up of small cycles. The large cycles were biennial, triennial, quadrennial (in other words, at the end of two, three or four years or more, the same crops reappeared on the same land). The large cycle of crop rotation was made up of smaller cycles: years, seasons, months, weeks.

In a general context, the ways of adapting to a terrain were always flexible. Using wisdom and knowledge, experience and determination, human groupings have always used the land to enormous advantage (so much so that even brutal interventions by conquerors or landowners failed to shatter their representations of the cosmos and their sense of organic balance). There is nothing infallible about this wisdom; it is brought into effect to remedy mistakes which come in the wake of catastrophes, rather than as a sovereign cure for them. Therefore, given the diversity of concrete situations, the problem of classifying systems of cultivation is fairly difficult to resolve. Once again we are faced with indexes, criteria, typology and models. In spite of their unquestionably 'systematic' character, these systems do not coincide with other, more logical systems. For this reason agronomists and agricultural historians have suggested a great many typologies, using different indexes and criteria. Some – particularly in Germany – begin with the predominant element (woodland, pasture, ploughed land, fruit or vegetable cultivation) while not overlooking the dynamic aspect the system frequently adopts (for example, itinerant cultivation, or crop rotation and the burning of woodland, etc.). Others take a negative criterion: the extent of uncultivated terrain or of land left fallow. They draw a distinction between relatively discontinuous cultures and relatively continuous ones. Others base their classification upon the results of techniques; thus the famous agronomist Gasparin classed systems of cultivation into 'physical' (natural), 'androphysical' (a stable habitat, man's active intervention in nature, but with cultivation interrupted by fallowing) and 'androctic' (the increasing predominance of continuous cultivation and of techniques characterized above all by the contribution of independently produced fertilizers). One could even begin from a purely economic criterion (barter and the commercialization of products), from a purely technical one (the implements used), or from a purely quantitative evaluation (gross vegetable or animal product per unit of land or head of livestock).

Despite the rigorous character of these systems, a methodological problem remains, namely that of *type*. There is also the problem of the relation between historicity and structure. 'Systematicity' by no means eliminates the complexity of the facts. Moreover we should note that new techniques ('technical progress') do not always merely modify existing systems and structures. In many cases history proceeds by explosions, by sudden mutations which bring crises and dramas in their wake. Sometimes the leaders of a given society think they have achieved a definite equilibrium (as in the case of the average development of cereal cultivation from the eighteenth century up to the present day, which has been rationally managed). Sadly, modern techniques have purely and simply broken up the systems, the structures, the periodicities and the rhythms. Under favourable conditions (technical means and the amount of land available), freedom of initiative becomes such that nothing in nature stands in the way of options, choices and projects. Questions of profitability, yield, financial means, market, planning, tactics and strategy replace the old 'rhythms' imposed by the relations between man and nature. In this day and age, the ancient rhythms, cycles and regularities, all our ancestral representations of the cosmos and of human actions, are falling to pieces.

And yet, the old systems have not disappeared. They perpetuate themselves and carry on in a great many ways, not simply as survivals, but actively (unless one defines everything which is not the result of the latest techniques as survivals). Even in rural areas of the industrial countries, apart from regions where specialized cultivation has been developed using the most recent techniques (like the Corn Belt in the USA), we may observe many traces of ancient systems of cultivation. In so-called 'underdeveloped' regions and countries, they are in the majority. Nor have the corresponding representations disappeared, especially not those linked to cosmic cycles and rhythms. Doubtless their persistence is connected with other human phenomena, and these need to be studied.

What we have just said about agricultural systems could also be said *mutatis mutandis* of other systems. Relations of consanguinity have already been studied extensively, so let us leave them to one side. Instead we will look at musical systems. History reveals the existence of many musical systems (the segmentation of the sound continuum, scales, etc.), all of which are coherent. This characteristic – coherence – becomes conscious and predominant in the West during a rationalization which begins with the Greeks and reaches a peak in the eighteenth century. The system of tonality elaborated at that time is an integral part of a remarkable rationalization taking place in all areas and all relations. It truly is a system, with an ultimate logic (namely tonal harmony) which governs the other aspects of musical creation, song, the use of instruments and voices, and the rhythms and periodicities of repetitions of sounds and their combinations. From then on the system of tonality spills over into social life: popular songs and melodies obey the laws of tonality. Then we witness a twofold phenomenon, both sides of which are equally remarkable: the persistent echoes and revivals of archaic systems, and the shattering of all previous systems under the technical impetus of tonality.

These observations suggest a hypothesis (which in fact we have already formulated using other words, and which we have retained for further use). The system of tonality contains partial systems, which sometimes manifest themselves on a dual plane, that of aesthetics and that of day-to-day life (we do not consider songs to be external to everyday life; a symphony belongs to learned art, whereas a popular song is part of the dimension of the everyday and of the social which involves play, which is a dimension we are attempting to shed light on). These systems are remarkable for their coherence, even when this is obscured by everyday trivia; it is thanks to this coherence that they are able to go on surviving for so long, like the agricultural systems we can still observe in our own so-called 'under-developed' rural areas. In practice, these systems appear as vicious circles which emprison: A supposes B, which supposes C, which supposes A. How many times in our everyday lives do we hear the remark: 'It's just a vicious circle!' It is a characteristic of systems to be circular and cyclic, with periodicity and repetition. So what we are attempting is to make an inventory and a count of such partial systems: agricultural systems; logic and discourse in general, and the use of language; music, painting, and especially architecture, in so far as it enters into everyday life; links of consanguinity and relations; systems of ritual, gifts and barter; systems of signs, or semeiologies, in manners and dress, etc.

In one sense, the everyday is made up of such partial systems, juxtaposed without any rational links, and each with its own implications and consequences: temporality, rhythms, periodicity, recurrences and repetitions, specific works and symbolizations. These systems are distinct and disconnected. Some of them reproduce or prolong former dominant 'systems', such as agricultural systems or ceremonial systems for example. Most if not all are out of step with 'modern' techniques, which tend not only to reject them as anachronistic, but above all to dismember them. It will be our task to describe the remaining debris, which still retains visible traces of the vigorous structures which once supported it and are still legible within it.

Structuralism proceeds by privileging structure absolutely, and by absorbing within it the other terms we are considering, along with the relations they designate. Without admitting to do so, it substantifies it, presenting it as an essence and as something intelligible, thus acting as a belated marriage broker between Aristotelian ontology and a Platonism which dares not speak its name. Stability becomes both active and formal, the prototype and model for the real. In this way a certain elasticity or plasticity of structures, their inner contradictions, and the profound action of negation, i.e., of time, are marginalized.

The (relatively) permanent structures which 'succeed' after a period of time have survived the effects of time. They persist. But at the same time how can we suppose that during this same period certain structures (such as living species, social groups, patterns of behaviour and mental attitudes) have not disappeared, and perhaps in much larger numbers than the structures which have survived, either flourishing or impoverished? The negativity of time is at work. The gaps in our classifications are highly revealing and we cannot reduce the prehistory of life and mankind to a juxtaposition of biological and social fossils, like a display case of empty shells and pieces of bone. This hypothesis is impossible to ignore, that is, unless we confuse structuralism with a theological formalism. Following this line of enquiry, we discover chance not only in the inner combinations of structural elements, but externally in the way in which the combinations relate to the environment. If a given combination is relatively successful and permanent, this is not simply the result of its 'essence', its stability and its inner coherence. The secret of success is also to be found externally, in exchanges with nature, with other species and with other groups. However, sooner or later chance itself appears as necessary and determined, both in its elements and in the way they combine and 'succeed'. The inner coherence becomes clearly apparent when the other structures have been worn out or broken up, and have disappeared. It can also happen that coherent, and therefore stable, groups remain stagnant. As Hegel might have put it, we may measure their losses by the size of their winnings. And gambling is not entirely conscious or entirely unconscious; it leaves room for intelligence and stupidity, wisdom and madness. It would be possible to use these observations to draw up a schematic for a specific historicity and a sketch for a dramatic history which would leave room for rationality (including the rationality of numbers and of gambling).

If it is limited and delimited in this way, structuralism contains many truths. It has discovered a few. Moreover, we are not suggesting a conjuncturalism as an alternative doctrine to structuralism. By giving it a place and a part to play, we are not lapsing into eclecticism. What we are trying to do is to place unilateralities in a progressive dialectization of concepts. The preceding arguments confirm views we have already formulated. We accept the idea of structure, but in a limited way. What we say is: if the value of structures is exaggerated, the idea itself is compromised. (In a nutshell: 'structuralism versus structure'.) Despite its efforts to the contrary, pure structuralism loses touch with historicity and with social realities in all their diversity. Its favourite areas are to be found in archaic groups and survivals. It cannot cope with *processes* like the historical modalities of a process of becoming which smashes through obstacles. From our way of thinking, purely structuralist method (if indeed the words have any meaning) cannot tackle the problems of the modern world. Just like empiricism, it tends to exclude dialectical thought (although it does not succeed in so doing). By exaggerating the importance of stabilities, it also tends to reject the concept of alienation (including its extreme form: reification). It reifies actions and works precisely because it does not have a precise idea of what alienation and reification are. The structuralist school ratifies certain unfortunate consequences of the extreme division of labour in social practice and in knowledge. By separating them and then identifying them, it crystallizes and congeals them.[27]

We will continue to employ the methodological concept of *the model* by setting out precisely what its attributes and properties are:

a) It refines certain characteristics of the concept in general, and of conceptual elaboration or conceptualization. By summing up an experimental and practical given, the classic concept turned too much towards the past, and also towards the simple. The *model* is a more flexible tool, capable of exploring the complex and the random. With it, thought becomes 'propositional' in a new way: programmatic. However, if the 'model' refines the concept, it cannot dispense with it. It presupposes a conceptual elaboration.

b) Like the concept, the model is a scientific abstraction and a level of abstraction. It is always revisable, and cannot be taken either as a reality or entity immanent to the real beneath the appearances of phenomena (the ontological temptation, which structuralism finds hard to avoid), or as a norm or value (the normative temptation). The methodology of models forbids their fetishization.

c) The model is constructed in order to confront 'reality' (experience and practice). It is useful, not least because it helps us to appreciate the gap between itself and the facts, between the abstract and the concrete, between what has been certified and what is still possible. The model is useful: it is a working implement for knowledge. Only the concept has the dignity of knowing.

d) As far as a set of facts is concerned, there can be no question of a single model. If we are to grasp the actual and the possible, we must construct several models. The confrontation between these will be as interesting theoretically as the confrontation between one of them and the concrete element it represents. In this way diversity and discussion during the process of knowledge take on added value. No one model can be sufficient or pretend to be sufficient by bringing research to a halt. So we are faced with two alternatives: ontology or criticism, dogmatism or empiricism (or pure relativism).

e) The concept of the *model* also helps to refine the concept of hypothesis. Every model encompasses a hypothesis (in the broadest sense, theoretical or strategic). Every hypothesis concludes by constructing a model, which is the halfway stage between inventing the hypothesis and proving it. So the model assumes the qualities of hypothesis: provability, creativity. As Politzer said, it should enable us to move from philosophical luxury to the economy of philosophy, by separating the hypothesis out from speculation.

f) Because it must prove its creativity, the model must have an operating or operational character. However, this trait must not be fetishized. The operating techniques linked to a particular model must be examined with care and suspicion. Fetishization of this characteristic, which blows it up out of all proportion, is the feature of a certain well-defined ideology, namely technocratism. The operational model becomes the practical and theoretical property of a bureaucracy and a technocracy. This brings us back to the most disturbing aspect of structuralism. The fetishization of the concept of the 'model' is part of the strategy of the social group of technocrats.

In the pages which follow, we will construct and propose two models of everyday life in society as a whole: a model of needs and a model of communications.

3

The Specific Categories

1 The concept of totality

In the preceding chapters our examination of the formal tools (the intellectual implements) of the social sciences has led us time and time again towards concrete investigations about our object of study: everyday life. Now, in this inventory of the specific categories which this contact with the concrete has helped us to elaborate, we will sometimes find ourselves obliged to look back once more towards the formal. There can be nothing surprising about this. Surely that is what dialectical movement in thought is. We study specific categories and concepts in order to determine their relative importance and the limited spheres in which we may apply them. The specific does not preclude the formal, and the particular does not preclude the general. Overall we must have a precise and flexible set of mental tools at our disposal.

We cannot do without the concept of *totality*. When we are dealing with human reality, both theory and practice encompass a conception of totality (i.e., of society and mankind), implicitly or explicitly. Without this concept, there can be no frame of reference; no generality, and even more, no universality. Without it, knowledge itself ceases to have a 'structure'. It becomes scattered into fragmented studies which replicate exactly the division of social labour instead of controlling it and understanding it. In the best cases this is no more than the equivalent of a hypercritical self-destructive attitude (since the universal reappears with different names, and often dogmatically: globality, nihilism or postnihilism, culture, civilization, etc.). In less favourable

cases the fragmented studies and disciplines dissolve into myriad isolated, empirical facts. In the final analysis, there is no longer any
obstacle for thought to struggle with. That temporary barrier and
limit to analysis, the real, has been removed. Thought has been
engulfed and buried under a mass of facts which, to add insult to
injury, it respects and sanctions. It no longer has a criterion or a hierarchy of facts and concepts; it no longer investigates the essential
(because the essential is no more!). The very idea of knowledge as
totality – as concrete universality – becomes blurred and disappears.
For an empiricism without concepts, one fact is as good as another.
When we try to particularize knowledge, we destroy it from within.
The 'concrete' we have sought for so long eludes us. The hyper-
concrete is as abstract as any other philosophical generality.

Over and beyond the methodological use of totality, we must also
consider its practical use. Without an (illusory) representation or a
(true) knowledge of social totality, without a participation in the
social totality (an illusory or true *participation* – but the latter is preferable to the former!) in social totality, no specific group has any status
or certainty. It feels it has no place. It lacks self-confidence in its own
vitality. Its everyday experience breaks down into interindividual,
socially contingent relations. As a result it has no confidence in its
leaders, i.e., those of its members who enable it to face up to the
future and who hold its strategy in their hands.

This highlights an aspect of democracy. Without the effective and
well-founded (genuine) participation of citizens in totality, there can
be no political democracy. In democracy, partial groups are forever
confronting each other; each has its tactic and its strategy. Nevertheless they are participating in a totality which their confrontations and
rivalries ('non-antagonistic conflicts', to use a widespread but rather
vague formula) do not destroy. If there is no insistence upon totality,
theory and practice accept the 'real' just as it is, and 'things' just as
they are: fragmentary, divided and disconnected. Activities, and
therefore individuals, become 'reified' like things, and, just like things,
are separated one from the other. This insistence upon totality is
nothing more than another aspect of the participation we mentioned
above.

Without the concept of 'totality', how can we possibly formulate,
or even conceive of one of the principal laws of social and human

development? This is that law: once it has taken a definite shape in social practice, each human activity wants the universal. It aspires to universality. It wants to be total. It tends effectively towards totality. Therefore it comes into confrontation with other activities. In its quest for totality, it tries to make them its subordinates. It invents tactics and strategies. It makes itself real through *works*, and each work is the result of a momentary totalization through the predominance of a particular activity (aesthetic, juridical or legal, scientific, philosophical, even poetic, or through games, etc.) and consequently of a particular representation or tendency. Therefore, during this bitter struggle, each activity achieves a totalization of which it is the generative nucleus and the effective element. It is precisely in this way that it shows itself to be partial. Limits become apparent. The moment it becomes totalized is also the moment when its immanent failure is revealed. The structure contains within itself the seeds of its own negation: the beginning of destructuring. Achievement is the harbinger of its withering away, it announces it and provokes it. Totalization imposes doubt, collapse and disintegration. Every trial must be carried out, every hypothesis must be hazarded, every attempt at totalization must be put to the test before the irreducible residual deposit – the everyday – can claim its demands, its status and its dignity, before we can consider raising it to the level of totality, through a process of conscious metamorphosis . . .

What activities are we talking about? Religious representations and religion in general, which once aspired to universality and which compromised themselves in their struggle for control. Philosophy, which criticized religion and sought to supplant it, creating its own representations and concepts, but coming to grief as an absolute system. Science in general, which translated its ambitions and pretensions into scientism and technicism, thus demonstrating its own limits. Each particular science, and notably history, psychology and sociology, took turns in inventing totalizing hypotheses and 'structuring' representations. Political economy takes the human and reduces it to the status of a tool for production. The state, that coercive power, aspires to universality in a way which is apparent today on a world-wide scale. Finally art and culture produce aestheticism and culturalism.[1]

It seems to us that this conception of fragmentary totalities (each one of which empties itself of human reality after having sought to occupy that reality completely and in fact after having effectively contained and enriched it) does account for one aspect of history. On a vast scale – that of *Weltgeschichte*, world historicity – it makes the concept of *alienation* concrete. Each activity which creates representations shows itself to be both productive and alienating: productive at first, then alienating, as much for itself as in its efforts to absorb other representations or to exterminate them using a pseudo-critique which slips very easily into terror and violence. At their birth, many of the major works of culture and civilization could be characterized – in their structuration and inner balance – by the predominance of one representation which does not destroy the others, but which subordinates them. Works are determined by the hierarchy of all their elements, the result of an effort and a creative struggle, rather than by the fact that they may belong to a discrete and circumscribed domain such as religion (and the history of religion), philosophy (and the history of philosophy), or knowledge (and the history of knowledge), etc. From this perspective religion, philosophy, art and knowledge appear as *types* of works rather than as domains or regions. Works are linked to a typology which already possesses its own vocabulary. Each undertaking is an endeavour based upon a hypothesis. This hypothesis is not represented as such, but is presented as a truth, which, with the general backing of a group, one man tries to bring into language, and then to the absolute. No matter how close it gets to success, every endeavour is destined to fail in the end. Every endeavour is an attempt to realize mankind and its goals by determining them, i.e., by creating them. Every endeavour is an attempt to disalienate mankind and its goals by realizing them in a total work. Until such time as everyday life becomes the essential work of a praxis which has at last become conscious, every endeavour will lead to a new alienation.

With the dialectical movements of 'alienation/disalienation/new alienation' and the 'realization/fragmentary totalization/breaking of totality'; the concept of negativity gains fresh impetus. Every totalization which aspires to achieve totality collapses, but only after it has been explicit about what it considers its inherent virtualities to be. When it makes the illusory, outrageous and self-totalizing claim that it is a *world* on the human (and thus finite) scale, the negative (limitation, finiteness) this 'world' has always borne within itself begins eating it away, refuting it, dismantling it, and finally brings it tumbling down. Only when a totality has been achieved does it become apparent that it is not a totality at all. Unlike those practical systems and structures which shatter, leaving their debris in the 'lived', these semi-fictitious, semi-concrete ideological worlds die slowly. With the occasional burst of energy, their death throes go on and on. Even as they wither away, they remain active. They have the prestige of having been achieved, the prestige of perfection. They are great works.

This schematic, which we have presented as a sort of world law (of the relation of the finite to the non-finite or of totality to elements), originates in philosophy. Hegel applied it, but incompletely, since on his own admission his own system and the state eluded him. Originating in philosophy, our schematic contains a fundamental critique of philosophy. We are replacing the philosophical idea of an achieved totality and a complete system with the concept of *totalization*. In our view, philosophies were attempts on the part of philosophers to carry a representation (i.e., something which was as much an interpretation of the 'world' as it was of the real life of mankind) to the absolute. Taking their hypotheses from real life, they have attempted to transform them into a 'world'; they have tried to metamorphose everyday life by 'worldifying' this or that, in a semi-fictitious, semi-real way. They have proposed an abstract way of living, a project, a semi-Utopia, a more or less delirious wisdom, while artists were offering works of art: an immediately habitable 'world' for the senses and emotions to live in.

In his critique of Hegelianism, Marx turns the Hegelian conception of the process of becoming against philosophy, a theoretical system, and against the state, a practical system. For philosophy, the process of *world becoming* is the law of the world and of the state; but philosophy or the state only become a 'world' by a process of supersession which comes when they wither away. Philosophy and the state were proclaimed to be 'worlds', while the real world – the everyday life of mankind – was left to one side beneath them. If philosophy and the state are to be part of the real world, if they are truly to become 'worlds' by summoning the real world up to the higher spheres whence they proclaimed themselves, they must die. This is the philosophical meaning of Marx's so-called philosophical writings. These have been called philosophical, but wrongly so, since they state that the death of philosophy is a necessity. It would be a creative death, a kind of battle, with all the pain a battle brings. World law decrees that all activities must end once their goal has been achieved and they have come full term, i.e., once they have reached their limits. In fact, Marx did not follow his thinking through to its conclusion. Just as Hegel exempted philosophical system, religion and the state from the law of the process of becoming (from the world law), Marx is reluctant to draw certain conclusions. In several texts he sometimes exempts art and the moral sphere from world law. He often accepts that when the economic, the political and their alienations come to an end they will be superseded by art, or by the realm of ethics. We do not wish to exempt art and the moral sphere from world law. The metamorphosis of the everyday demands that these ways of metamorphosing the everyday fictitiously must also wither away.

If Marxist thought since Marx has completely forgotten 'world law', if it is regressing (and with it philosophical thought in general) to system and to the fetishizing of politics and the state, there is all the more reason for us to get down to work again, and with renewed efforts. And so we are replacing philosophy with another form of investigation, which nevertheless contains and uses its concepts. We are aware of the theoretical experience of the last fifty years, and for this reason we say that the tenacious efforts of certain philosophers to maintain or revive philosophy have compromised it (in short: 'philosophism versus philosophy').

This theoretical experience demonstrates that the concept of *totality* has as many disadvantages as it has advantages. Without it, theoretical thought would be impossible. With it, theoretical thought risks losing itself in dogmatism. The idea of *totality* (or even of *totalization*) brings with it certain imperatives. Once put into place, it is in command. It demands *all* thought, *all* knowledge, *all* action. It directs knowledge; it orientates investigations and plans them. It tends towards immanent structure. It desires power. How can we conceive of totality if we do not share its point of view? Once it becomes dominant, the most general category tends to absorb particularities and specificities, and therefore to neglect differences and types. If I conceive of the world, mankind and society on the basis of a broad and creative hypothesis, I subsequently verify my conception. With an inextricable mixture of good and bad consciousness, in bad faith or good, I tend to eliminate whatever does not fit in, whatever does not suit my purpose. After this, I start to develop arguments. I reject difficultly acquired partial knowledge for a superficial encyclopedism, which is all I need to crown my ontology. If there are any problems left, they are secondary ones. After I have found everything, i.e., the whole, even if I go on seeking I will find nothing. Once my totality is established, dogmatism is nigh. We are the whole, I am the whole. The total man belongs to us.

In *History and Class Consciousness*, Lukács wrote that 'The primacy of the category of totality is the bearer of the principle of revolution in science.'[2] This statement seems both true and false. It was true when Marxism was the only powerfully structured set of ideas at a time when the concerns of non-Marxist thinkers were completely fragmented. Since then, from the Marxist point of view, the dangers of this category have become apparent; as for the non-Marxists, they have adopted it. Structuralism and culturalism have taken the category up, and they have even turned it against Marxism. The former totalizes structure and enables it to absorb the other concepts and realities. The latter constructs a coherent whole, 'culture', using a variety of elements taken up from praxis: tools, implements, symbols, models, etc. It highlights their relations, and establishes a cultural totality. So Lukács's statement seems obsolete. We will subordinate the category of *totality* to that of *negativity* or dialectical negation, which strikes us as being more fundamental. What is more, we consider that the revolutionary principle is essentially critical (negative), and that today it applies more to everyday life than to knowledge in general or to society in general; this is our way of reintroducing science into praxis.

Today, methodologically speaking, the category of 'totality' plunges us into almost insurmountable difficulties. Are we *inside* a totality? Which one? Bourgeois society? Industrial society? Technological society? Society in transition (but to where)? How can we determine a totality *from inside*? In order to think of bourgeois society as a totality, Marx began by determining *what was possible* – socialism. He then turned back towards the real, seeing it in terms of the process of becoming, as a totality riven by inner contradictions and destined to be shattered by revolution in the near future. For us this process of thought is increasingly difficult to follow because, contrary to all expectations, capitalism has not been shattered under the pressure from the proletarian masses in the most capitalist countries, and equally because the very idea of socialism has become obscured by the way it has been put into practice. While we continue thinking along the lines of Marx's plan (from the possible to the real and from the real to the possible) we are not confident that it will help us to clarify the real and the possible which surround us. In any event, how could we validly determine a totality if we take up a position *outside* it, be it from this side or that? The recent concept of *signifying totality* aims to modernize the concept we are considering here. We have already pointed out how vague it is. For whom and by whom is the signification of the totality under consideration elaborated?

Consequently, in so far as it marginalizes the critical (negative) moment and has been handled in an ontological, normative and speculative manner, we are abandoning the category of *totality*. At the same time we are adopting it again, in a dynamic sense. We are dialecticizing it, on the one hand by introducing the concepts of *partial totality* and of *totalization*, and on the other by distinguishing between the *total* and the *universal* (the universal is thinkable in so far as it becomes created), but without separating them. If the will for totality remains an imperative in terms of theory, it is equally so in terms of practice (the demand for totality and for the supersession of scissions, divisions and dispersals). Without this initial option – the *will for totality* – there can be no action and no attempt to achieve knowledge. Without it, we accept whatever is empirically and fragmentedly 'given', we accept a real which has been split into two and dichotomized; we ratify the social division of labour; we give our blessing to the analytic fragmentation of activities, functions, actions and gestures; we make the accepted '*thematizations*' and pseudo-worlds into laws, and we establish them as truths. In doing so, we are sanctioning separations.

Thus one initial act distinguished knowledge of social man and of praxis from the natural sciences: the will for totality. The mathematician, the physicist and the biologist can do without it (although no doubt it continues to be an implicit element of their research). In the investigation of the human, this inaugural act – which aims to recapture a fragmented totality – is already total, or rather, totalizing. It has nothing to do with individual or individualist subjectivity. It implies a culture. It comprises a sensibility, a way of perception, an intellectual certainty, a *claim*, a movement of radical critique towards assertion and action. We see all this as part of the critique and the transformation of everyday life.

This initial act sets up a strategy. It is conceived within a strategy in which it plays a role and which contains complementary aims: to develop knowledge as an element of praxis, and to refuse to accept separations within praxis. In the name of this strategy, whoever exercises it will not be prepared to accept that knowledge is powerless, nor that those who possess knowledge should be conditioned, nor that the keys to knowledge should be surrendered into the hands of those who happen to be in power at any particular time. Moreover, their struggle is not against differences and diversities, but against pluralisms which beyond a certain point of affirmation split totality (for example: reformist and revolutionism; divisions in labour and the trade unions; the separation of the everyday and society as a whole with respect to immediate claims concerning the details and organization of practical life, and political claims concerning the state and social life as a whole, etc.).

Thus the idea of *totalization* is formulated not ontologically, but strategically, i.e., programmatically.

However, the 'bottleneck' which is hindering knowledge has still not been resolved. How can we avoid being trapped in a dilemma? Where do we start from, from the whole or from the parts? From the general, or from particularities? . . .

Would not the way out and the solution be to determine a *total phenomenon*, which would reveal a totality without granting it any theoretical or practical power, and without allowing it to be defined and controlled? To pass from phenomenon to essence is a speculative operation which leads to philosophism and ontology, and we must avoid it at all costs. We take the phenomenon as it is: a set of observations, i.e., of certified differences, which we link together without any ontological assumptions. Therefore, rather than having the wholeness of an 'essence' or a 'substance', the total phenomenon diversifies when scrutinized intellectually in terms of social practice. However, this diversification does not mean that it collapses into fragments. Thus it would open the way for dialectical reason, which is forever striving to reconstruct a whole from the differences and conflicts of its 'formants'.

In this way we have grasped a totality via aspects or 'formants', each of which is itself like an open or partial totality, so that nothing can be determined in isolation. But what should we call it? Man, or the human. Thus, using a process which is observable in praxis (and not simply in abstractions and theory), we will grasp a 'total human phenomenon' through its various determinations, each of which refers to the others. To put this another way, the aspects or formants of the total human phenomenon will constitute a theoretical structure; at the same time their practical relations and interactions will constitute the basis of a process of becoming and a historicity. Within this frame of reference we will observe active differences, relations and conflicts. By determining them we will be able to define historical and social particularities without assuming the supreme (and always illusory) power of capturing the universal and of exhausting 'being'.

We have already indicated what the initial dimension of the total human phenomenon is: need. Man is a being of need. He shares this fate with all living beings. It is only with human needs that man becomes human. In relation to nature, they are artificial, but they are the product of the process of human becoming. How does this happen, by what mediation and by what means? Labour. Other possible ways of specifying the relation of the human to the natural (culture, knowledge, etc.) presuppose that man has a certain power over nature, were it no more than an ability to detach himself from it. Therefore they imply labour; if we do not accept this mediation, then the arrival of man and his relation to nature are based on an ontology or a theology (the 'sudden appearance' or the 'abandonment' of man in nature). As well as being a mediation, labour is the second dimension. It has a reality of its own; taken simply as a concept it does not explain everything. This reality demands careful scrutiny; without that we will mistake it for an entity and not perceive it as a phenomenon and a set of relations. Labour characterizes social activity, with its conditions and attributes: tools, language, the (biological and social) division of labour, manufactured or consumed materials, formed and stabilized produce. If it is true that we find analogies with human labour in nature (such as hunting in groups, the work of the spider spinning its web or the bird building its nest), only man confers an existence of their own on the means and mediations between himself and nature: implements, materials, language, techniques, products and objects. If, at first, labour has the purpose of satisfying elementary and natural needs, it also contributes to their transformation. The needs of work and of the worker, the need to work and work as a need – these modify sensory activities, and even the sensory organs themselves. The 'human world' which is created in this way is composed as much of human bodies and their physiological activities as it is of the range of works, products, objects and goods. It has no precise limits; it excludes neither inert objects nor the obscure forces of nature: there is no frontier between the sector controlled by technology and labour and the uncontrolled sector. It is a vast, uncertain and highly populated region, the region of everyday life.

Once transformed, need becomes human and social need. But then the term 'need' is no longer appropriate. It is no longer adequate as a description of the real. It still evokes want. Now from one angle, once it becomes social, need becomes *capacity* and power. Man *is capable* of this or that action, creation or work in order to satisfy himself, or at least to try. The doors of what is possible begin to open. Although he has no alternative but to choose, and although society makes every effort to control his choices, it is always from the range of what is possible that the individual man will select them. On the other hand, once it has become individual, we call need *desire*, and it develops through controls, authorizations, inhibitions and possibilities. With acquired capacities and powers on the one hand, and the uncertainties of desire on the other, a dialectical movement is born, which fills everyday life.

As much as any other, and more, sexual need becomes modified and these modifications enable us to understand the others. It can be argued that it loses the characteristics of instinct and need, such is its attachment to symbols, images, rituals and ceremonies, i.e., forms which are external to nature. And yet it never manages to separate itself from sex per se, even in the wildest Platonic Utopias, even though it disrupts sex drastically (and not without damaging it), and metamorphoses it. The sexual act becomes a social act, and even the quintessential social act, in which an entire society recognizes itself, with all the orders and interdictions, the pressures and demands, the open possibilities and the closed ones. At the same time, the sexual act cannot be seen as one simple, coherent action; it is a microcosm with thousands of changing aspects. It crosses over disconnected areas: body and soul, spontaneity and culture, seriousness and games, covenants and challenges. The act of love between a man and a woman summarizes a society, and even in its clandestine and hidden aspects; but this is because it is consummated (lawfully or not) in secret, outside of that society. In a novel dialectical movement, *it is an extrasocial social act*. It is consummated in society and, if needs be, despite it and against it; and this is how and why it reflects society like a mirror. Hence its importance in the world of (aesthetic and ethical) expressivity. It is the most cultured of needs, the most refined of desires, with its social content which it supersedes in its search for the absolute, and yet it still plunges into the depths of nature, and into the profundities of dialectical contradiction.

Could need and labour be the two determinations of the total phenomenon we are seeking? Were we to reduce man to needs we would be forgetting the metamorphosis of need into power (and we use the word here not to mean power over things or over men, but the capacity to carry out determined activities at will). We would be guilty of overemphasizing the sordid side of life. We would be neglecting the important difference between *privation* (need which has become power, and the will to make demands) and *frustration* (need which has fallen back to the level of want, without hope of fulfilment), and this difference merits detailed examination. On the other hand, were we to define man by labour, we would be moving towards a fetishizing of productivity and the work ethic, or even regressing towards the archaic sanctification of craft and peasant labour. In short, we would be mutilating the human being by neglecting *pleasure*. Once need has become power and will, once it has been metamorphosed into desire, it demands pleasure, explicitly. Labour loses meaning and reality if it does not culminate in pleasure or open the way towards it: labour is social and collective; it is individual and interindividual power. Labour is indispensable if man is to *appropriate* nature, but pleasure alone makes this appropriation effective.

Three determinations, three 'formants', three dimensions: need, labour, pleasure. Each has its own reality; not one stands alone.

Without losing its own determination, each one refers to the other two, influencing and transforming them, and suffering the repercussions of this transformation. Thus we have a coherent triplicity, but in which the coherence – which is not without its contradictions and conflicts – does not result in immobility. So distinct are the three determinations that, in social practice and in history, they are allotted to different and even conflictual individuals and groups (classes). We observe the man of need (who is out of work), the man at work (who has few needs and little pleasure), and the man of pleasure (which does not mean that he achieves fulfilment). This lived unilaterality is unsatisfactory and it must not be transformed into representations, as is often the case; more exactly, every representation deriving from unilaterality must undergo radical critique; moreover, theoretical critique leads finally to practical critique. Those individuals and classes which demand pleasure pure and simple are doubly degraded: they are socially parasitic, and pleasure eludes and disappoints them. The worker whose life is devoid of pleasure and the glowing rewards it brings can only aspire to a dreary existence for which the work ethic is an inadequate reward. As for the man of pure want, if he is unable to grasp the lifeline of productive activity, he will rapidly relinquish all his humanity.

These many forms of alienation, privation and frustration, these voids and empty spaces, go hand in hand with large-scale conflicts and their innumerable ramifications.

The three dimensions are distinct, even disconnected, but they are nevertheless linked together and bring each other forth in an ascending spiral which crosses history and establishes man's historicity. We are speaking of a *spiral* here, and not a *circle*. When determinations fall outside one another they only do so relatively, momentarily and partially. And when they do so, the human will be mutilated in a manner which they imply and foreshadow, and which 'is' within them both virtually and actually. This certainly is a totality, but one perceived by the senses rather than by the mind. This human totality allows us to understand what constitutes the specificity of man compared to nature, from which he separates himself without detaching himself, and which he enters without discarding his artificialities.

In what way is this reality perceived by the senses? Could it be that without realizing it we have defined man's 'being', the universal, or have attempted to do so? Could we have elaborated an ontology, dressed up as an anthropology and a sociology? No. The totality we have defined does not purport to exhaust man's 'being', or to define it. It does not preclude other determinations and other dimensions, i.e., other degrees of freedom. On the contrary, it invokes them; it is a necessary and non-sufficient condition for them. It will be present in every human fact, on both the level of analysis and the level of reality, and will enable us to discover supplementary determinations. More-over, it does not coincide with any one concrete observation (and for example it would be incorrect to identify the 'family life/professional activity/leisure' triple determination with the tridimensionality we have presented above!). Let us consider *play*. It springs from the depths of spontaneous living and natural activity: animals play games, and so do children. As an attribute of the human being, it does not coincide with any of the above-mentioned dimensions. Play is part of every human activity. In a sense life in its entirety is play: a risk, a game or match lost or won. From childhood onwards there is a need to play (and moreover want and privation themselves can be acted, simulated and disguised: in asceticism, and in privation which has been accepted in order to delay fulfilment or increase pleasure). Everything becomes a pretext for playing, even effort itself; serious games and work are often very similar. And so, the relations between play and pleasure are not easy to discern. If it is part of all activity, play soon relinquishes this ambiguous role and becomes distinct: it establishes itself as something separate; it adopts forms and rules; it becomes organized socially. It is impossible to imagine mankind without play activity, or society without underlying or manifest games. Could this therefore be a fourth dimension: human time joined to the three other spatial dimensions? Why not? But let us be careful. Let us avoid straying too far into the realm of paradox. But it is certainly rather surprising that it should be our era, the era of func-tionalism and technology, which has discovered *homo ludens*.

2 The idea of reality

This idea presents as many difficulties as the ideas we have already examined. The 'real'? It is the object and the objective of knowledge, the fulcrum of action. We reach out to it, we try to grasp it, either to observe it, or to transform it. The real demands realism. Is there anyone who does not want to be 'realistic', to be anchored in the real, to know it and to have a hold over it?

Sadly, those empiricists and positivists who merely want to observe it are frequently satisfied with small beer. Armed with their specialized techniques, they hunt down little facts. They discover a portion of reality, and the flimsier the observation, the narrower and more precise the comment they make; the more fragmented the fact itself is, the happier they are. The more realistic the realist is, the more blinkered he becomes. It is even worse when the philosopher defines the real in advance – philosophically – either as matter or as spirit. Taken per se, and fetishized, the idea of *reality* (even when adorned by adjectives such as 'concrete' or 'human') shrinks and shrivels. The real reveals its profundities to those who wish to penetrate it in order to transform it, and who attack it with determination, and a multiplicity of implements. But whoever wishes to transform the real has apparently lost touch with it. He is tendentious. What about objectivity? And why change the real rather than merely noting it down? In whose name and for what? To what end? For common sense, in day-to-day language, whoever wants to change the real is an 'idealist'. He sets out from an idea or an ideal.

Hegel has taught us that the real is more profound than existence or what can be seen to exist; would this profundity be metaphysical? Marx has taught us that there would be no knowledge (and no need to know anything) if the apparent and the essential coincided at the heart of the real, or if they were completely (metaphysically) separate. But if this is so, why are there so many appearances in the real? Why is there so much that is abstract in the concrete, and why are there so many forms in content? Why and how is the formal also concrete, and real? Sometimes the everyday appears to be the sole reality, the reality of realists, dense, weighty and solid. At other times it seems that its weight is artificial, that its denseness is insubstantial: unreality incarnate.

To dispel these obscurities, perhaps we need to clarify the terminology and to distinguish between the *actual* and the *real*, or again, between the *present* and the *real*. Maybe then it would be easier to link them together. In any event, we should certainly dialecticize the idea of 'reality'.

Let us begin by reintegrating the possible within the real. Usually a distinction is made between them – and quite rightly so – and then they are separated. The possible is seen as abstract and vague, while the real is seen as thick and weighty, as 'being' or 'existing'. But the possible enters the real. It appears there: it announces and invokes its presence within it, and then sets about destroying it and negating it. As for the real, it is a possibility which has been made effective or actualized. In one way or another, and regardless of what we imagine the link to be, we must conceive of a connection between the actual and the virtual, the potential and the possible. The actual and the virtual have a dialectical relation, even in the case of natural phenomena, but even more so in the case of human phenomena, where a consciousness of what is possible always intervenes. Human actions always define themselves as choices, as a means of access to what is possible and as an option between those various possibilities, regardless of whether the actions are individual or collective. Without possibility there can be no activity, no reality, unless it be the dead reality of things in isolation, which have a single possibility: to maintain themselves as they are. If we join the category of *possibility* to it – which, like the idea of totality and the idea of structure, is a philosophical legacy – the category of social and human *reality* can be retained. It becomes dialecticized. It continues to guarantee heightened objectivity to knowledge while avoiding superficial objectivism and illusively profound ontology. It eradicates a few false and insoluble problems, notably those which come as a result of the dissociation of fact and value, and of the real and the ideal. Why change the real? Because it does change, of necessity, and if knowledge begins with what is possible it can help to direct this change, and control it. The flat realism of the immediate strives desperately to prove how spacious it is. When it is dubbed 'materialism', its victory over an even more abstract and shrivelled-up idealism is an easy one.

We maintain that the possible demands a choice and an act, and therefore demands a yes-or-no answer. Given the 'real' with its problems (its contradictions) and the solutions proposed, sooner or later we decide unequivocally for one particular solution, and act accordingly. This is why an option involves a strategy and a series of options which amount to a series of bifurcations and disjunctions. Decisions have their logic, their mathematics and their calculus.

These calculations revolve around the 'possible/real' relation, in so far as it produces a form which, despite its formal character, is part of the real. However, this statement itself runs the danger of provoking a theoretical illusion: that of the superfluity of the formal. When dealing with possibilities per se, and with the coming forth of virtualities, we cannot answer the questions they pose by a yes or a no. Possibilities, i.e., solutions to problems, are discovered and invented; contradictions within the real are themselves heightened, or are evaded. It is a history, a dialectical process of becoming. Practical action itself differs from (mathematically) formalizable series and frequencies in the following way: the stake is constantly changing, and the goal becomes modified as do the number of players. Will-power makes what is initially impossible possible, while modifying both the means and the ends. Action does not transcend calculation and form: it encompasses them by superseding them. Quantitative or qualitative (ordinal) mathematics cannot grasp the 'real' completely. However, we do not know in advance exactly what it is that eludes them. Only the philosopher believes he can draw boundaries and demarcation lines. So the new mathematical implements enable us to perceive the human 'real' more effectively, and to penetrate it. But they do not exhaust it. It is in the everyday and its ambiguous depths that possibilities are born and the present lives out its relation with the future.

Is this a reason for replacing formal logic (which is binary: true or false, inclusion and exclusion, opposition, contrariness, etc.) by a logic with more than two valencies, three for example: the true, the false and the random (or the possible)? In our opinion, no. Decision logic justifies the old formal logic, and extends it. To choose is to exclude all the possibilities except one. To opt is to act so that the impossible becomes possible, and so that things which are possible become impossible. This implies a logical 'possible/impossible' relation subordinate to a deeper dialectical relation. Logic, which is the concrete form of a set of questions which are answered by yes or no, occupies a certain level. Consequently, this level must be that of games and strategy theory, of operational research and of information theory. Dialectical reason occupies another level, which encompasses the former. This relation (which is not always easy to grasp) is part of the 'real'.

Once it has been fetishized, the category of 'reality' has enormous disadvantages. It destroys specificities and differences. Under the umbrella of this concept, and with the misuse of the epithet 'concrete', the human real is considered to be on a par with nature, or the real of nature is considered to be on a par with the human real. Confusions are created, fodder for philosophical overindulgence. By dialecticizing the concept we can begin to answer questions about the *reality of consciousness*.

Consciousness does not appear to be 'real' in the way a substance or a thing is, nor does it appear 'unreal', like a reflection or an epiphenomenon, the accidental substitute for something else. Social consciousnesses are born, grow, wither away and die like individual consciousnesses do (and from which they cannot be separated). Social existence and consciousness (like every existence and every consciousness) have something *transitional* about them. They come into being and go towards something else or other than themselves. Every consciousness lights up or switches off, becomes transformed or stays the same (never for long, even when it is embodied in a work). It is born of a problem, when what has been accomplished – the 'real' in its narrow sense – has become inadequate. In this sense, it negates the 'real' concretely and specifically. It is born along with a possibility arising from the practical question the possible asks of the real, and vice versa. An appearance or an apparition, it changes itself into action, i.e., into 'reality', in so far as it resolves the problem posed. Therefore one of its conditions is the undermining of the 'reality' which has already been accomplished and structured. In the solidity and substantiality of a self-sufficient, self-satisfied 'real', consciousness falls to sleep. It 'is', and consequently it is no longer consciousness. We do not say, 'All consciousness is consciousness of something', but, 'All consciousness is consciousness of a possibility'; this is what gives it its acuity, its good luck and its misfortune. Without possibility there can be no consciousness, and what is more, no life. Presence implies what is possible in the present, and for the present; the future is an indispensable horizon and guiding light. Consciousness can never be at home in the real, in anything which has been stabilized or satisfied; and yet it seeks the real, or rather realization, as well as stability, and satisfaction.

Consciousness is born of problems, contradictions and conflicts, of

Critique of Everyday Life

options and choices which are both necessary and free. One must choose between various possibilities: that is what is necessary. One must take risks, wager on randomness and gamble: that is what is free. Thus consciousness presents itself as a specific 'reality', but not given, and not unmediated. Self-consciousness is born in the other, of the other and by the other. It 'is', and yet it is not. It 'is' action and relation, and not substance; it 'is' the confrontation between the consequences of problems, the demand for solutions, clarity of expectation, perspective and choice between possibilities (and impossibilities). It is born in action and action brings it into being. It is born in works, and works bring it forth. It is productive, it is self-productive; it resolves the problems embedded in what it creates. It is its own work, and yet it escapes as soon as that work is accomplished. It negates and it supersedes, but cannot be defined as absolute negativity alone.

Fully real in its way (but not like a 'region' which could be described separately from the 'real'), consciousness has necessary and non-sufficient conditions in other realities, whether they be biological and physiological, or economic and historical. It cannot be reduced to these 'real' conditions. As soon as we mould the idea of reality around any thing which has substance, we become trapped in a dilemma. Either consciousness eludes the category of 'reality', something caricatured in those theories which derealize it and reduce it to pure reflection, or to pure negativity; or else it conceives of itself as a thing which has substance and which segments into (historical, psychological or sociological) processes or into (individual or collective) states and representations.

We have already criticized and rejected several confusions, notably the confusion between 'reality' and 'structure'. There is another which is no less frequent, and just as dangerous for knowledge: the confusion between *function* and *reality*. Function is seen as the criterion of reality, biologically and socially speaking. According to a certain neo-Hegelianism which is as widespread as it is unaware of its origins, one of the philosopher's famous statements could be transcribed in the following way: 'Everything which is functional is real, everything real has a function.' Rationality and functionality are seen to coincide. Function would create reality (including the sensory object with a 'reality' that would apparently bring functions into play which would vary according to the culture and the civilization involved).

These formulations define a *functionalism*, a corollary of structuralism and of various realisms in contemporary thought. Functionalism decrees a rational balance and harmony between nature, culture, and society considered as a whole. It postulates a situation whereby, in itself and by itself, representations are completely aligned to actions, and what is real is completely aligned to what is true. For a functionalist sociologist, if something does not have a function it cannot exist. At the very most it can be seen as an offshoot of a real function. Families have functions. The working class has functions. Bureaucracy has functions (especially because it is mainly composed of 'functionaries'). As for the state, it obviously possesses many functions, by definition. In other words, functionalism eliminates critical thought. According to this criterion, since anything without a function is superfluous, it must disappear. Of what use is everyday life? What is its function? It has none. If we cannot suppress this regrettable residue, at least let us cast it aside. How easy it is to pass from observations to diktats, and from ontology to the normative. And how quickly doctrinaire functionalism brings a functionalist ethic and even a functionalist aesthetic in its wake.

Critique of functionalism has important implications for what we are talking about. The new towns have demonstrated the undoubted merits and the even more undoubted shortcomings of functionalism when it tries to create the framework and conditions for an everyday life. The errors and illusions of the doctrine can be grasped in action, in the work itself. Moreover, it is a question of a general tendency, linked to the importance of technicians and to the formation of a technocratic ideology in every present-day society. Like anyone who possesses a skill and who exercises a fragmented activity, the technician has a function in an overall unit. The technocrat oversees this unit, organizing its functions and supervising them. Therefore there is a link between integral functionalism and ideological and practical technocracy.

The idea of 'function' derives from several sciences and also from social practice. As far as mathematics is concerned, it seems possible to rationalize and formalize the functional completely; it can be analysed into variables and reconstituted in objective processes. As far as biology and physiology are concerned, they give the functional a kind of life-giving promotion. We are no longer dealing with abstract trajectories or units, but with organisms and organic totalities. So we can add the representation of utility, and of an indispensable system within an organism, to that of mathematical necessity and rigour. At the heart of every living and coherent entity, every part which is not the result of a destructive analysis of the whole and which maintains its integrality in the face of attacks from a relatively hostile 'environment' – in other words, every 'real' part – corresponds to a function and to an organ. From then on it seems impossible to dissociate function from organ and function from structure. Theoreticians may have rejected a certain simplistic organicism, but this has not led to a heightened critique of the concept of function. In so far as a society constitutes a whole and possesses a specific life, could it not be seen as a sum total, or a synthesis, or a totality of 'functions'?

This representation contains elements of truth and elements of error, and the latter predominate once the representation becomes systematized. Critical analysis discovers a mixture of fetishized determinism and of finalism, as well as an underlying tautology. Given what it is, an organism is made up of organs. Each organ perpetuates itself by acting upon the others and consequently by directing its own activity back upon itself. By definition, every organ perpetuates itself by 'functioning'. Thus every organ has more or less complex self-regulations (such as feedbacks, scannings and homeostases, to use the vocabulary of the cyberneticists who have helped to elaborate these concepts). The idea of self-regulation helps us to clarify the idea of 'function'. We imagine an organism to be a self-regulating ensemble composed of functional self-regulations which perpetuate both themselves and the organism. Thus, while changing, it maintains a stability and could be said to possess its own inner logic. This does not rule out chance or disorder, and so consequently it can become disrupted. Every self-regulation has its limits. The connections between partial self-regulations seem vague. A living organism is flexible because it is vulnerable. Complete adaptation would lead to lethargy and stagnation as surely as complete inadaptation would bring about its demise. So how can we know whether better results might not have been obtained with other adaptations or inadaptations, or other combinations of organs and functions? Perhaps a function is nothing more than a successful mistake, a non-functional element which has changed (since the conditions themselves have changed), or the result of a stroke of good luck. Today's dysfunction could be tomorrow's function. Functionalist finalism evades the issue; it is untenable.

Our objective conditions change and we change our conditions. If our consciousness can lag excessively behind these conditions, surely our body can too. The optimum would seem to be a halfway house between adaptation (indispensable but sterilizing) and maladaptation (creative, stimulating, but deadly). Exactly what is the relation between modern man and contemporary society, and the conditions they have created? How can we distinguish between the functional and the non-functional? At this point we would tend to argue that 'modern' man and society cannot go on neglecting everyday life and leaving it behind for much longer, and that its non-functionality will be transformed into supra-functionality. And perhaps this is one of those rare predictions one can make about the future without too much danger of getting it wrong.

It is quite amusing to observe the antics some highly intelligent, hyper-realistic and clear-thinking social scientists get up to in order to save functionalism. They cannot avoid admitting dysfunctions, and so surely they must accept 'survivals' or 'time lags'. This would add even more fuel to the argument against integral functionalism.[3] The dialectical trick (if we may call it that) is to absorb and resorb dysfunction within the functional by maintaining that dysfunction is the condition and inevitable reverse side of any function. When Merton looks at political bosses in American towns he finds they have many 'functions', including the function of attending to specific interests – the needs of their constituencies, or of the poor and the marginalized. The only means available to these wretched people is to exercise their civil rights by speaking to the local boss to obtain a few favours. In short, via its own 'dysfunctions', the political and bureaucratic machinery of American democracy can get its hands on something which might have eluded it: everyday life. It is true that the 'apparatus' and the 'machine' stifle news which might offer any encouragement. In doing so, they hinder communications, paralyse consciousness and society, and forbid any active criticism (not to mention a few other little irritants, such as gangs and rackets). Who cares? And this is the way the functional penetrates into the very heart of the everyday, absorbing it and integrating it into society as a whole.

Merton's realist and functionalist arguments are flawless. Why criticize 'dysfunctions'? Perhaps they fill in gaps in reality, albeit badly. Why consider them as symptoms of its deficiencies? Why use them to make a critique of the 'real'? One might just as well list the functions of the liver, and then complain because it is prone to illness, exclaiming: 'Ah! If only we didn't have livers!' To put it another way, social functionalism is not without its paradoxes. These highlight the disturbing side of the doctrine. Functionalism and 'integrationalism' make ready bedfellows. In society, as in a living body, the highest functions are probably the ones which exercise control and integration from above. The ideal kind of control and integration would leave no room for the unforeseen, the marginal or the 'deviant'. It would know how to predict randomness and to absorb it per se. Finally, the real and the rational would coincide in a social truth, that is unless the dysfunctions did not intervene to bring a little disorder and creative dissymmetry into all this well-established and well-controlled order. What an unexpected stroke of luck that would be!

The amusing thing is that this functional realism avoids philosophical generalities and is unaware of its own reactionary neo-Hegelianism.[4] It derives from the same radical critique: the real encompasses the movement which negates it, providing it is grasped in all its profundity. The actual comprises the possible and the negative operates within it. The real is the ephemeral and superficial side of reality ('existence'); it hides the deeper forces. 'That the rational is real is contradicted by the irrational reality which at every point shows itself to be the opposite of what it asserts, and to assert the opposite of what it is.'[5] This fully reinstates Marxist thought and method. It is not because we want to change it that the 'real' – the everyday – eludes us. We are not setting out from another reality external to the reality we are studying. We are setting out from its inner movement, and from what is possible. Then and only then can we grasp it and know it completely.

Biologically or socially speaking, could play have a function? In our opinion, it is impossible to answer this question by yes or no. In nature, since animals play games, it would appear to correspond to the need to get rid of excess energy, to an almost pure spontaneity, free from the pressures of the immediate 'environment' (which is not to say that it is undetermined and unregulated). Could we say that play is basically useless? No. It is practice for activities; it anticipates and prepares for practical situations, or presents them as potential risks and difficulties, in a diluted form. So it is useful, very much so, and perhaps the more 'useless' it appears the more useful it really is. It is useful because it is redundant, in that it owes itself to a redundancy of vital energy, implying the relief of elementary needs and functional requirements: hunger, thirst, fatigue.

In social life, play has a use. What is it? Relaxation and entertainment, yes, but more than that, it is rediscovered spontaneity, and even more, it is activity which is not subjected to the division of labour and the social hierarchies. At first sight, humanly and socially speaking, play seems to be a minor, marginal activity, sidelined and tolerated by the important functions of industrial society. Compared with the reality of practical life and the truth of representations, it seems to be an illusion, a lie, something phoney. On closer scrutiny, the reverse is true. Play recalls forgotten depths and summons them up to the light of day. By making them stay within the everyday, it encompasses art and many other things as well. It uses appearances and illusions which – for one marvellous moment – become more real than the real. And with play another reality is born, not a separate one, but one which is 'lived' in the everyday, alongside the functional. It may seem that we are regurgitating the old apology for the *acte gratuit*, but no. We are protesting against the loss of grace and gracefulness. Play is a lavish provider of presence and presences.

One can do without it. Austerity has no time for it and social order is afraid of it. Integral functionalism tries to eliminate it (as is so clearly demonstrated in the new towns and housing estates!). And this is one of the paradoxes we must highlight. For surely it was a dialectical movement within integral functionalism itself which gave rise to the study and the rehabilitation of games, at a time when 'industrial' and 'technological' society was at full throttle.[6] It could be that poetry and fiction are part of the same protest against the functional, in that they liberate a need for something marvellous, fantastic and even freakish.

Functionalism finds play hard to tolerate, because the territory it occupies cannot be defined in advance. It is a domain without limits, like that of (free) critical thought or of art (when it is truly free), which can and must appropriate matters which do not concern them from the point of view of social integration and the functional. Everything becomes play, in the theatre and in acting for example, including the most important matters and the most dramatic circumstances. Everything should be able to become a game, in the conscious simulation of tactics and strategies, in light-hearted imitation (and *homo ludens* has a host of tricks and dodges we will not mention to help him get involved in serious matters and to see them *sub specie ludis*). Games use many ancient magic, cosmic, religious and technical objects which formerly were important and serious, but they also provide a practical method for stripping anything too serious of its overimposing gravitas, and thus of its power, reducing it to the everyday by not allowing it to set up home above everyday life.

Did cathedrals have a use? Yes, and in many ways: a cathedral was a muster station in serious circumstances and a meeting place for ceremonies; it was a symbol of the community, of the medieval town and its territory; it was a politico-religious centre. Were they built functionally? No. Over and above their functions, they *presented* an image of the world and a summary of life according to a certain vision of the world and of life. The builders started from this symbolic representation (which was obsolete in itself, but vigorously spontaneous as far as they were concerned), endowing it with richness and embellishments, which are the attributes of spontaneity. Going beyond mere social function, they metamorphosed spontaneity into style. But then, through style and symbolisms, the cathedral became a monument which was always *present* in the town, active not only at exceptional moments, but also at the heart of the everyday.

Thus critique of functionalism leads us to new ideas. In the first place, the mechanisms of self-regulation in society are inadequate. Their balancing and 'structuring' mechanisms are always precarious. On the level of society as a whole, mechanisms are replaced by *representations*. The mechanisms for correcting imbalances are active on various important levels, but never on comprehensive or total ones. On the economic level, for example.[7] We can use the words 'function' and 'functionality' to qualify them, i.e., as processes operating through a kind of semi-awareness or even lack of awareness on the part of those who contribute to them. On the level of the state, of strategies and of society as a whole, functions are entrusted to 'apparatuses' which act by means of representations: ideologies. What is more, symbolisms introduced from elsewhere can prove very effective. Representations (ideologies) and symbols are passed off both as truths and as realities. Like symbolisms, the 'apparatuses' (which are constructed on the level of society as a whole, i.e., of the state and of political strategy) are redirected towards the everyday, grasping it in all its dereliction, and integrating it. In this way the highest level returns to the lowest (which does not stop the 'lowest' eluding it). Functionalism is itself a representation and an ideology, which consciously aims at exerting control and integration in conditions which are ipso facto given, accepted and recognized.

In the second place, we have highlighted the concept of 'polyfunctionality' and, more importantly, the concept of 'transfunctionality'. Certain 'realities' have several functions in social practice, towns for example (a place of everyday life, rest, family life, non-professional relations, neighbourhoods, etc.). After separating them analytically, functionalism projects them on the ground, and the result is a parody of 'reality', even though all the elements of the 'reality' are there (and even though, by its interest in the elements of the 'real', functionalism is in advance of those theories which ignore them, voluntarily or not). With functionalism, analytic understanding takes its labours to the bitter end, and at the same time goes to the bitter end of the social division of labour. It 'institutionalizes' the results, and there they are on the ground in the new towns, implacably 'real', inert and lifeless.

What would life be like for an organism which exercised the functions of each of its organs simultaneously and in isolation? What would our lives be like if – and the idea is horrendous – we had to use our consciousness and our hands to control the functions of our stomachs, our hearts, our livers or our kidneys? Functionalism leads to a dead end, the kind of false world nightmares are made of.

The multifunctional exists, and so does the transfunctional. By the latter term we mean whatever we cannot reply to by 'yes' or by 'no' when asked the question: 'Is that useful?' Play, for example, is transfunctional, and so is art, or the work of art, because they contain a play-generating 'yeast' (which does not exhaust them and which they do not exhaust). More generally still, what distinguishes a work from a *thing*, an *object* or a *product*? An inert thing (a pebble, a piece of wood) has no function, a product has at least one, and an object has several (for example, a chair, which helps me to do my job, to rest, to have a chat . . .). As for works, they are transfunctional; they have many uses, which they supersede.

Whether it is functional or not, an ornament – tolerated by functionalism as long as it remains ornamental – is a sorry caricature of the work of art. Whether it is durable or not, the transfunctional is a work. Play is momentary transfunctionality which consists of its own unfolding: the ephemeral work of an individual or several individuals, successful or not, perfect or not, marvellous or not. A town is durable transfunctionality. Brought off or botched, it is the work of a social group and of an overall society. Towns were no more than the vaguely conscious or even 'misconscious' work of everyday life. They must become a fully conscious *work*, with the purpose not of 'integrating' an everyday which has been cast aside at the lowest of levels, but of metamorphosing the everyday into a work, on the highest level the level of art and of freedom. Then, as social man nears a goal which today is Utopian (and consciously postulated as such), the everyday and the whole will be works which cannot be dissociated, and the real will no longer be split up into the 'real' and the 'true', in other words into 'true' versus 'false'.

3 Alienation

Since it was taken up again some thirty years ago, the idea of alienation has been studied many times. There would certainly be every reason to write an in-depth history of it. This history would allow us to resolve the following theoretical problem: 'The idea of alienation is a legacy of philosophy, and perhaps its essential patrimony. In what ways can we use it as an analytic implement to help us understand the modern world? In what ways does it introduce philosophy into the social sciences?' For the time being we will tackle the problem per se, rapidly and succinctly, without becoming waylaid by historical considerations.

Our first observation is that the way the idea is generally used seems quite clear: 'man' is alienated, torn from his self and changed into a thing, along with his freedom. However, at the same time, there is something vague about this. Too often alienation has been seen as a single unit and as an entity: the alienation of man. In fact, there are many alienations, and they take many forms. Too often 'disalienation' has been taken as an absolute, and as the end of alienation in general. In Marx's so-called philosophical thought, the alienation which Hegel presented speculatively becomes a historical fact. So does its disappearance. However (although we find many indications that his thought also moved in the opposite direction) Marx tended to push the many forms of alienation to one side so as to give it one specific definition in terms of the extreme case he chose to study: the transformation of man's *activities* and relations into *things* by the action of economic *fetishes*, such as money, commodities and capital. Reduced to economic alienation within and by capitalism, alienation would disappear completely and in one blow, through a historical but unique act: the revolutionary action of the proletariat. In this historical and revolutionary perspective, there remained something of the philosophical absolute from which it derived, in spite of Marx's critique of Hegelian philosophy and of philosophy in general.

Before we apply the idea of alienation to the social sciences and especially to critical study of everyday life, we feel we need to formulate several propositions. We have put these propositions (which are somewhat more than hypotheses and somewhat less than established truths) to the test during our research.

First proposition. We must particularize, 'historicize' and relativize the concept of alienation completely. To put this another way, alienation is only conceivable and determinable within a (social) frame of reference, and in relation to a whole which is both real and conceptual. Therefore absolute alienation and absolute disalienation are equally inconceivable. Real alienation can be thought of and determined only in terms of a possible disalienation. Conversely, disalienation can be thought of and determined only in terms of a complete alienation or of another possible alienation. Alienation is not a 'state', any more than disalienation is. Both are conceived of in movement.

Second proposition. Once relativized, the concept becomes dialectical. There is a perpetual dialectical movement: 'alienation–disalienation–new alienation'. Therefore an activity which is disalienating and disalienated in relation to what has gone before can lead to an even greater alienation. For example, to become part of a collectivity can 'disalienate' one from solitude, but this does not preclude new alienations which may come from the collectivity itself. Leisure activities 'disalienate' from the effects of fragmented labour; however, when they are entertainments and distractions, they contain their own alienations. One particular technique may 'disalienate' human activity from nature or from another, less effective technique, but it may bring a technological alienation which can be much deeper (such as fragmented labour, or the social imperatives of technology, etc.). The 'reprivatization' of everyday life disalienates from the state and from history. It alienates by bringing forth a deeper 'privation', that of private life established within an everyday context. Thus alienation and disalienation characterize concrete situations, taken in movement and not considered in a motionless way along fixed structural lines. More exactly, the 'alienation/disalienation' dialectical movement enables us to determine a structure within concrete, changing situations. Thus a disalienation can be alienating, and vice versa. Only by precise analysis will we be able to distinguish between the aspects of this movement, rather than muddling them up together.

Third proposition. The worst alienation is when the alienation itself is non-conscious (or unrecognized). Awareness of an alienation is already disalienation, but it can become changed into a yet deeper alienation (when failure, privation or frustration become fixed in the consciousness). So the option which brings one alienation to an end, by going towards a possibility, can create another mutilation and a different alienation.

Fourth proposition. The reification of activity (when activity and consciousness become 'things', and allow themselves to be taken over by 'things') is an extreme case of alienation. This situation constitutes a polarity and final frontier for alienation, but it does not exhaust the concept. Taken per se, reification disguises the many forms alienation adopts.

Alienation within and by the state (political alienation) must not be confused with economic alienation (by money and by commodities), although there are links between them. The alienation of the worker differs from the alienation of women and of children. The ruling class – the bourgeoisie – is alienated by artificial desires and phoney needs, whereas the proletariat is alienated by privations and frustrations.

The alienation of social groups, which stops them from fully 'appropriating' the conditions in which they exist and keeps them *below their possibilities*, differs from the alienation of the individual within the group or by the group (families, towns, nations, classes, etc.), which 'derealizes' the individual by subjecting him to external rules and norms. There is a technological alienation (which can be superseded, but not without bringing additional risks) and an alienation as a result of a low level of technology. There is an alienation through escapism, and a different one through non-escapism. We also need to be aware of alienation in respect of the other individual (subordination), alienation in respect of society as a whole (scissions, dualities), and alienation in respect of oneself (failures, privations, frustrations), etc. And so alienation is infinitely complex.

At this point we need to look for a criterion enabling us to orientate ourselves through all this complexity, and to give a precise and objective definition either of alienation or disalienation, or of the exact moment in the process of becoming, or of the essential character of the situation and the way it is developing. Using this criterion we would be able to perceive what alienates and what disalienates, what is alienated and what is disalienated.

It would seem that this criterion can only be situated within dialectical movement. It comprises dialectical movement per se. But since it is a matter of grasping this movement, can we really speak of criteria? The worst alienation of all, absolute alienation – in so far as that makes any sense – is when movement is blocked and is brought to a halt. Now this coming to a halt can seem beguiling, like a definitive solution to the problems posed, like a state of supreme satisfaction. There is nothing more comfortable than a 'state'. And this is how reification, an extreme case and a clearly determined 'state', both defines and disguises all alienations. As far as the movement itself is concerned, it can take the most disturbing forms, such as dissatisfaction, anxiety or crisis. Contradictions, which we tend to confuse with alienations, are creative. Contradictions give rise to problems, and thus to a set of possibilities and to the need to find a solution, and therefore to the need to make a choice. The solution may be optimal, mediocre, bad or phoney (i.e., illusory). A good solution resolves the initial problem by modifying the givens against which it is reacting and which it is transforming. When the movement stops the givens of the problem are frozen; even if it is not insoluble, it becomes so, in the name of a phoney solution, which is generally the result of a mis-understanding about the givens and an unawareness of what is possible. Thus the idea of the 'problem' and the 'problematic' no longer gets lost in the clouds, but nevertheless there is probably no general criterion which would enable us to reveal and classify problems in specific terms.

Let us give some examples, or use some of the examples we have already given, but in more precise detail. Innumerable human beings have been tortured by innumerable conflicts since abstract (rational) social processes became detached from the systems governing the immediate and direct relations between individual people. Such immediate relations prolong archaic relations before the advent of the major processes such as the formation of the state or the accumu-lation of capital, etc. In essence, processes develop well above the lowly realm of direct and immediate relations, which is situated in the everyday. However, the major processes and systems of relations are not completely external one to the other. Although there is a gap, they interact. As long as the Father was nothing more than the agent of biological life, of strength and direct authority, conflicts were prob-ably frequent and brutal, but they were never insoluble. When the Father becomes the agent of the law and of the state within a family, conflicts are forced underground. No longer can a child avoid ani-mosity towards the Father, who becomes an image and a model which bring together in a conflicting way the child's need for protec-tion and wish for security, and its reliance on him as a mediator between the closed system of family life and society as a whole. At the same time, these contradictions stimulate the development of individ-ual consciousness. Systems of 'private' relations are disalienating with regard to external pressures, and yet they make an even greater alienation possible, the alienation of the child by the Father (when the child identifies with the Father). The major social processes are disalienating with regard to the narrowness of systems of private rela-tions; they offer horizons, open spaces and freedom. And yet, in so far as they are abstract imperatives, they are alienating. Movement and conflicts are creative per se. Contradictions are always preferable to the absence of contradictions.

Let us consider 'women'. The term itself seems to suggest a kind of alienation in which half of the human race is considered or considers itself to be like a different species. What is this alienation which subjects women, stopping them from fulfilling themselves, subordinating and degrading them, tearing them from their true selves and dividing them up the one against the other? Would the alienating power be love, or motherhood, or housework in everyday life?

It is as difficult to answer these questions as it is to deny that there is a general alienation which determines and damages the 'feminine condition'. The love which alienates – passionate love – is not thick on the ground, as they say; as for the love which disalienates – elective love – it is more frequent and more normal, and does not fetishize either the lover or his loved one, or their physical or spiritual relations. It disalienates with respect to loneliness, while imposing several obligations for the two elements of the couple. And what of motherhood? It means freedom from sterility and is alienating only when it is physically debilitating. As far as housework is concerned, sociologists observe that proletarian women do not dislike it as much as middle-class women say they do. The latter want to work 'outside the home', and preferably professionally. Proletarian wives do not find housework any more tedious and tiring than working in a factory. If they can, they choose housework. So can it be the drudgery of housework which alienates women? It appears that the alienation of women represents a heightened image of the general alienation of our own specific society; thus if we are to understand it we must scrutinize society as a whole. Furthermore, there are certain 'situations' to consider, such as the women for whom having a baby shatters their future, ruins their plans, and condemns them to poverty and failure; the mother is sacrificed on the altar of maternity.[8]

Could not certain very profound reasons for the alienation of women be found in representations and symbolisms, and thus on the level of society as a whole and of 'ideological superstructures'? In this case, these reasons would be as hidden as they are profound. They would intervene in the motivation of individual desires as much as or more than in the material conditions of activity (although the one does not exclude the other). Therefore we cannot define alienation in the everyday until we have revealed symbolisms, and described and analysed motivations. What is really interesting is that there are veritable treatises on female alienation which present it as inevitable and beautiful, which systematize it and raise it to the absolute and take it to the absurd. Thus in Gertrud von Le Fort's *La Femme éternelle*, to become someone else, through someone else and for someone else, be it man or god, to 'be' in turn Virginity, Spouse, Motherhood, to annihilate oneself to become the instrument of Providence, to appear as silence beside male voices, as fluidity at the feet of male rocks, to wear symbolic veils, to unveil, to offer oneself – such would be the destiny of Femininity . . .

Let us conclude with some less lachrymose examples. On many occasions we have pointed out the importance the car holds in our everyday life (or should we say, in our culture and in our civilization? We will keep such weighty words for later . . .). This importance is the result of a social option, taken without full knowledge or awareness of its reasons, and above all, of its consequences. This option has set a process in motion which is probably irreversible and which threatens to dominate a wide sector of the 'real', to disrupt towns, etc.

A car is an item of goods, an object whose use brings satisfactions and which has a functional utility. The relations forged between individuals and this object go far beyond mere use and sheer pleasure. There are many individuals who 'realize' themselves by driving their car. They deploy qualities which lie fallow elsewhere; daring, virility, mastery of self, energy, and even sexuality (or so they say) would all be part of this relationship with the car. It is laden with ideology. And then the pathetic comedy begins: conversations dominated by the car, anecdotes, stories about accidents, etc. It is plain to see that drivers identify with their cars, and become aggressive, coarse, brutal, and of course these qualities are not apparent only when they are driving, far from it. Where is the alienation located? In the usefulness of the goods and the pleasure it provides, or the manner in which pleasure is taken from it? In the attitude, which has become a pattern of behaviour? The answer is obvious. Thus here, contrary to the alienation of women (which refers us to society as a whole), we can grasp alienation, i.e., the alienating–alienated situation, on an unmediated level.

Sociologists in America have recently discovered a most exceptional man, not least because of his exceptional banality: the other-directed man, one of the other-directed people.[9] This remarkably trivial man possesses ultrasensitive psychological antennae via which he detects other people's opinions (principally important people's) and conforms to them. He is energetic in affirming his personal integrity. He chooses to integrate within the social group and society as a whole, because he believes in it and because he is morally sound. It is not imposed upon him. A man like this has principles. His judgements and his moral convictions are his own, and do not come from an external moral code or a religion controlled by an all-seeing, spiteful god, to whom the depths of his consciousness would be like an open book. So this new man has retained the mannerisms of the 'inner-directed man', but only as some kind of superficial joke. This social phenomenon is the product of the manipulation of individuals and consciousnesses by modern technology, along with the ever-increasing importance of bank accounts and credit, the growth of suburbs and new housing estates, the rising cost of setting up home (mortgage, furniture), and more generally, 'consumer society'. Sexual relations and marriage are the only sectors in which free competition persists. However, even here, it is the men who come closest to the current model who will get the bonus points in the sexual and matrimonial contest.

So this individual does whatever his group tells him to do, but without having to be told. He obeys the imperative representations and models of society as a whole, but from the bottom of his heart. Moral order is freely and democratically accepted. Only groups have an active reality; but groups and individuals are equally depersonalized, abstract and artificial.

And so recent American sociology gives us an excellent description of alienated man in an alienating society, at a time of monopolies, (monopolistic) state capitalism and bureaucratic overorganization. It does not use Marxist terminology, but it presumably is aware of the theory of alienation, even if it does not mention it. Is it surprising that, apart from a few short stories and novels which broach the theme, there is no equivalent critical analysis to inform us of the specific alienations in the socialist countries? Such is the fate of Marxist thought in the twentieth century . . .

The diversity of these situations shows the extent to which it is difficult to find a simple, objective, general criterion for alienation. This diversity equally shows that it is possible and indeed indispensable to elaborate a *typology* of alienation. We can determine *types* of alien-ated–alienating situations. Alienation in everyday life would appear in this typology and would constitute a part of these types (but not their entirety, because there are other alienations: the alienation of society in its entirety, political alienation, for example). New forms of alienation, unforeseen and unforeseeable only a few years ago, would also be included in this typology, for example technological alien-ation. As for 'reification', it would only be one of the types, the simplest, the clearest and the easiest to define. Perhaps this typology would re-employ the terms used by Hegel and Marx, while giving them a precise content, but without extrapolating a classification: *Entfremdung* (to become 'estranged' from oneself), *Entaüsserung* (to be torn from onself), *Verwirklichung* (to find in fulfilment the principle of one's decline and loss), *Verdinglichung* (becoming more thing-like), etc. Alienation in the (psychiatric or psychosomatic) philosophical sense could also be included in this typology, probably under a variety of names.

Fifth and final proposition about alienation. It is appropriate to make a clear distinction between the *other* and *otherness* (in order to make their connection, their dialectical unity and perhaps a dialectical move-ment from one to the other more clear).

Maybe this difference is one of the reasons for the problem facing us. Alienation is the result of a relation with 'otherness', and this rela-tion makes us 'other', i.e., it changes us, tears us from our self and transforms an activity (be it conscious or not) into something else, or quite simply, into a thing. Now there are many thinkers who consider the relation with 'otherness' to be a creative one. This is profoundly true. No self-consciousness can close up upon itself. Man is a con-scious being, conscious of what he is (of his being), but only in, by and through what he is not, otherness and action upon otherness, con-frontation with otherness, want, privation, desire, work on external material, works (products or works in the strict sense of the term), and finally, what is possible. What a consciousness 'is' is hidden from it, and partially eludes it. This self-consciousness 'is' consciousness of not being the object of which it is conscious. Without consciousness of otherness, every consciousness will come to a halt, and become blocked (so that, in the theory of alienation, non-consciousness of oth-erness is precisely complete alienation, the immobility of alienation).

214

Consequently it is beyond doubt that 'otherness' is fundamental to human perception – and yet, that 'otherness' fascinates us per se, disturbing us and plunging us into the depths of uncertainty, and even more deeply into anguish. Where are the limits of otherness? There are none, neither in nature and in the 'world', nor in the depths of the body and of consciousness. These depths are bottomless; and 'I is otherness',[10] i.e., the separation between 'I' and 'me' is already complete. Therefore could otherness be the transcendental, the irreducible outside, given with the inside (self-consciousness) in an inexhaustible relation? In a hypothesis like this, alienation disappears; there is nothing to enable us to discern the tearing away from the self and the normative influence of 'otherness' as the transcendental, the 'world' or the thing 'in itself'.

The philosophical imbroglio seems inextricable. Indeed, it is. The concepts become tangled together in a Gordian knot. What makes 'being' and what makes 'the being' at the same time makes nothingness, and the nothingness of this 'being'. Transposed into an ontology which purports to describe the 'lived', everyday experience clouds over and the simplest differences become blurred.

Let us be bold. Let us cut through the Gordian knot by introducing a simple distinction taken from everyday life.

Let us use '*the other*' to mean whatever is near enough to us to enable us to be its accomplice. The other is something (possibly) friendly and accessible; the other offers itself to us, up to a certain point. When it looks at us, we do not feel at all uneasy, except perhaps for a fleeting moment. It is our fellow-man.

Otherness is distance, an inaccessibility which threatens us and drags us away. Ipso facto, otherness tears me from my self. It attracts me, it fascinates me.

Therefore there would normally be a dialectical movement, a never-ending passing from otherness to the other, and vice versa. The passing from otherness to the other is called knowing, gaining power over otherness and vanquishing it; what this means is that I approach otherness and bring it closer to me. It is a disalienation (which can entail risks of further alienations). To pass from the other to otherness is to discover something unknown; it is to discover something distant in what is near. What we knew and what we were familiar with moves away from us and makes us feel uneasy. It is an alienation which can also contain a certain disalienation. But should otherness come to dominate the other, should we lose contact, should we become tightly embroiled in mistakes, misunderstandings and misinterpretations, should we lose all control, then alienation will take over, i.e., otherness will tear us from our selves, otherness will make us lose both the other and our own selves. What is essential is the movement, the passing, the supersession. To come to a halt and become blocked is the greatest alienation of all.

In this sense, the concept of alienation could be brought closer to the 'lived'. The 'lived' could clarify the concept of alienation, and conversely, the concept of alienation could clarify the idea of the 'lived', which is still a vague one.

4 Lived and living

If we have included and continue to include the idea of the 'lived' among our specific categories, it is on one precondition: we must make it dialectical. If not, the 'lived' will remain on the level of a phenomenology, oscillating between a description of the immediate and a Platonist ontology of essences.

We have already used an image to determine the idea of the 'lived' dialectically. It is a focusing of practical consciousness, a centre of density and of heat, if not of light. This focusing or localization moves about. It changes level, with the gaps and imbalances these changes (which are differences in level) entail. Thus in no way can so-called personal or individual consciousness be a given centre, a fixed focus or a closed sphere. It – 'I' or 'me' – sees itself lit in a variety of ways. Sometimes it is the psychological or biological level which appears in close-up; at others it is the strangest motivations of the subtlest of desires. Sometimes it is interpersonal relations (the recognition by 'me' or by 'I' of a consciousness of otherness, or of the desire of another) which are brought into focus, sometimes it is the 'we'. At other times it glorifies norms, symbolisms, representations or general regulatory forms of conduct, on the level of 'they' or 'them', or 'one'.

Our individual and social consciousness is no less complex than the smallest fragment of material nature or the social totality itself (which consciousness reflects, or rather, *refracts*). To put this another way, it is infinitely complex, and yet at every moment there is a certain lighting, a focal point, a close-up, a creative determination. For all that, every dimension, every horizon and every level will always be present, and active.

We call this ensemble the 'living' (and we have described it using visual images, which are the subtlest kind of image in this imperfect language of ours). We will attempt to reconstitute the 'lived/living' dialectical movement, which encompasses the everyday and social consciousness. The traditional theory of consciousness, which con-geals it by reducing it to the 'I' (thus to a congealed form of the lived) disregards this conflict. The 'living' has no precise frontiers, either on the dark side (nature and spontaneity), or on its social horizon. Always vaster, always virtual, it summons the 'lived' and provokes it. At the centre of this unstable, volcanic and tempestuous landscape, the 'lived' is like a nomad's tent. It is always what has been accom-plished, or what 'is' in the process of being accomplished, and thus superseded, because it is always disappointing and in decline even while it is being realized.

Hence the inevitability of the conflicts between the 'lived' and the 'living', which make up the life of (individual and social) conscious-ness. They are to be found on various levels, and give rise to a great many tensions. Although they are not yet fully distinguishable from the images we have used, and despite their approximative character, these concepts enable us to represent consciousness as actuality and as a work. In one sense, the lived is what has been accomplished, it is therefore the real and the actual. And yet, with its multiplicity of vir-tualities, the breadth of its horizons and its low-key lighting, the 'living' is just as much of a presence, and thus an actuality. The 'lived' cannot be seen as the inert result of living, nor as its vague consciousness. The lived is the present, living is presence. The lived is also the work – be it alive or dead – created by living: it is whatever I do, whatever I know, in my own light and within my own horizons: it is the part of a 'living' which does not belong to me, since it is quintessentially social, but which I have been able to appropriate. Despite the close links between them, the lived and the everyday do not coincide exactly. 'Living' is not located outside of the every-day. In the everyday, moments of drama are stifled. Now *the lived is essentially dramatic.* However, we must make a distinction between its real drama and the dramatizations which it accrues. Just as there are always elements of sophistry and rhetoric in language, social living always becomes inflated. The dramas of individuals and the dramas of groups become magnified. In fact what happens is that real drama and artificial dramatizations reinforce each other in a mixture of serious mise-en-scène and natural theatricality. This is the case not only for art, but also for many 'demonstrations' of social life, which use symbols and representations widely in order to magnify the lived. Let us think of mourning, funerals, marriages or encounters. The incessant passing from the lived to the living and from the living to the lived is an aspect of the everyday.

5 The spontaneous

The category of the 'lived' permits us to rehabilitate the category of *spontaneity*, which has long been disparaged, thanks to the attitude both of rationalist and of transcendental philosophy. Neither culturalism nor structuralism can admit the spontaneous and the unformed.

However, the rehabilitation of the 'spontaneous' does not rob critique of its rights. Quite the opposite. Are we about to make an apology for the spontaneous which would fetishize it?[11] Certainly not. Spontaneity has no privileges in any domain, be it everyday life or politics. When it is lacking, 'something' fundamental is missing; there is a gap, like a sterile little vacuum in the tissue of life. However, spontaneity is not always creative every time, with every risk it takes. It makes mistakes, and it fails more frequently than rational prognostication and calculation. Neither the idea of it nor its reality offers a criterion for existence or for value. Authentic per se (but how can we know this?), it eludes control and integration. And yet it imitates and mimics itself. In the spontaneous, it is difficult to make out what are dramas, dramatizations, de-dramatizations or super-dramatizations (which procedures of social control and integration encourage, and then repress). In periods of intense ideological control, the spontaneous and the non-spontaneous become merged, as do the natural and the artificial. This means the members of a particular group discover ideologically saturated values, norms and symbols 'spontaneously'.

To put it another way, whether it be in our consciousness or in the outside world, we never attain pure nature or any unconditional 'being'. The spontaneous is already part of the social, although it is not the social per se. Everyday life gives it a place and a consistency, and is the level on which it expresses itself. The spontaneous is nothing more than an element of the social, on a certain level. As such, it exists. It is active, it grows, it withers away, and as such it dies, in everyday life.

6 The idea of ambiguity

Once we have rid it of any ontological preoccupations, this concept has a wide area of application.[12] Outside of critical periods (when anything problematic has more importance than acquired stability, when conjuncture dismantles structure, when strategy takes the ascendancy and when the need to choose becomes apparent and marks a moment of bifurcation in the process of social becoming), human groups live in the mode of ambiguity. As long as problems are not immediately pressing, or if they are yet to be posed, human groups can ignore them. This has an impact upon consciousness (and as always we use the term to mean a consciousness which is simultaneously individual and social, although at times the two aspects may well be in conflict). It is satisfied with an appearance of definitive stability; it swells up like a cyst, and becomes an untroubled reality and a 'being', rather than pursuing the possible and 'being' pursued by it. And so the dramas fade away, the tragedy of the whole is obscured by a comedy of little details. Because nothing vital is at stake, everything is acted out in a ponderous or flippant manner. The relations between individuals within groups, and the relations between groups themselves, become dedramatized. They oscillate between blinkered attitudes and hollow opinions: envy, jealousy, pacts and squabbles, ceremonies which serve to disguise mutual rivalry or admiration. Instead of passion there is an (illusory) impartiality and a (misleading) objectivity. Trivial representations suffice. Anything contentious is pushed to one side, although this does not neutralize it. People talk about such things as little as possible and the spread of banality goes unchecked. The realm of ambiguity is also the realm of everyday triviality. At every moment the elements of the lived and of the living seem on the point of splitting up and going their separate ways: groups within society, individuals within groups, patterns of behaviour within individuals.

It is not always easy to distinguish between the ambiguous and the ambivalent. At this stage we would tend to emphasize their differences, placing ambivalence within the purview of psychology. Ambiguity, however, is a sociological category, a lived situation which is constituted from contradictions which have been stifled, blunted and unnoticed (unrecognized) as such. In the case of ambivalence, it is within the consciousness of an active individual that the problem or conflict emerges; with his back to the wall, he has to choose (this or that, love or hate, subjection or freedom). Sometimes he will already have made his choice, but is unable to make it explicit or effective. Ambiguity, however, is a condition offered to an individual by a group. Faced with differences he finds difficult to explain, he adopts a kind of temporary and undisciplined indifference; one day, soon perhaps, he will have to opt; but the moment of choice has not yet arrived; he has still not reached the fork in the road. Ambiguity is a complex situation, but it lacks mindfulness, and is made up of several virtual polarities. Ambivalence comprises a conflict which develops between feelings, people or representations.

There is no shortage of cases or examples of ambiguity in everyday life. So much so that one could say that ambiguity is a characteristic of the everyday, and that the everyday is the sphere of application and content of ambiguity, taken as a category (i.e., a specific concept). The *family* has a biological and physiological reality; in the first instance it is located on the level of immediate person-to-person relations: husband and wife, children and parents. Does it possess social functions? This has been contested, and it has been seen as a 'residual deposit'; twenty or so years ago it was thought that industrial society and the proletarian revolution would dismantle the family and share out all its ancient functions across 'society'. But it would appear that, against all expectation, the family has been given new functions, provisionally or permanently, in consumption and in culture. Have these new functions restored the old ones? Has the family regained its educational function? This is open to doubt. What is not in doubt is that, throughout history, society as a whole has given the family a range of forms: the patriarchal family, the feudal family, the bourgeois family, the proletarian family, the socialist family. It is influenced by ideology and culture: we can talk of the Islamic family, the Christian family or the secularized family. Institutions intervene vigorously to prohibit cases of deviance, blatant survivals and transitions towards anything new: they impose a defined structure upon the family. At the same time, the family retains unmediated links which originate in the distant past, before the development of modern society, such as patriarchal links and feudal relations of subordination. In this complex interaction, it never becomes separated from its biophysiological 'formants', even when it has been elevated to the dignified status of a higher ethical or cultural value, with the concomitant representations and symbols. However, if its situation is de facto ambiguous, it also accrues defined motivations and recognizable attitudes. The 'modern' and the 'archaic' confront each other in the family, in a mutual recognition of differences which, once recognized, tend to be disregarded. Various symbolic representations or psychosociological motivations are used as theories of the family: emotions aroused by the immutability of human nature, by the maternal instinct, by virility in its role as protector of feminine vulnerability, etc. In its very basic principles, the family 'is' ambiguous. Hence the general ambiguity of everything which happens or which does not happen within it: love and rivalry, confidence and mistrust, suffocation and protection, use and abuse.

Together with the family, woman belongs to the category of ambiguity. As an informal social group, the only way 'women' can be understood and situated is as the embodiment of ambiguity. We have already mentioned the paradox that half the human race and organized society constitutes a group defined by gender, which is to a certain extent distinct, with its own aspirations, demands and strategies. Biologically creative, 'women' have always been ipso facto the natural mediators between social groups, generations, culture and nature, and individuals. They mediate – in other words, they generate conflicts and divisions even when carrying out the conciliatory role their 'functions' attribute to them! Biologically creative, and probably the creators of the first human realities at the dawn of history – agriculture, the village, the house and its basic equipment, the hearth, cooking utensils, furniture, fabrics – women have subsequently been demoted to carry out inferior tasks, making them relatively unproductive economically and relatively ineffective socially. And so they 'are' the illusory substance of the everyday, its unreliable depths, its terrain and its climate, and yet they are endowed with the attributes of the human race (intelligence and rationality) as well as with the specific qualities of the groups to which they belong. Nothing stops them intervening in the gamut of public or private situations, but everything forces them to use indirect methods if their interventions are to be effective. The consequence is a profound and permanent conflict which can never reach a climax, i.e., it can never become the kind of overt, explicit antagonism which would endanger society. So the conflict is contained in a state of ambiguity: a blunted, ever-rekindled, ever-stifled contradiction. There are times when 'women' as a social group are able to wipe away the traces of their historical defeats, and when, after exerting gradual but constant pressure, they finally gain the promotion they have so long waited for. At these moments ambiguity bursts asunder in contradictions: possibilities longed for and disappointingly fulfilled, the serious side and the frivolous side of 'femininity', 'femininity' per se and its harsh ethic, which women both desire and reject. From these moments on, the ambiguity of the past and of the present becomes explicit, whereas when it was in control it was 'unconscious' (unrecognized), hidden under representations and symbols which maintained and disguised it. From time immemorial and up to and including the present day, women have been the custodians of a treasure chest of norms and representations. How prosaic and tedious these norms and representations are, but also how tenacious in praxis, and how profound: everything involving the house, the 'home' and domesticity, and thus everyday life. At the same time, both symbolically and as conscious 'subjects', they embody the loftiest values of art, ethics and culture: love, passions and virtues, beauty, nobility, sacrifice, permanence. But these come into conflict with other supreme values: sensual delight, total pleasure, luxury and lust. These conflicts are profound but disguised, reduced to ambiguity and hidden beneath it, but nevertheless, and in spite of the mind-numbing nature of housework, women are less likely than men to be stultified by the specialization and fragmentation of labour. So superiority becomes inferiority, and inferiority contains the seeds of superiority (although they are reluctant to germinate). *Therefore, women symbolize everyday life in its entirety. They embody its situation, its conflicts and its possibilities. They are its active critique.*

We (i.e., in everyday or 'modern' life) are flooded by a generalized ambiguity, which perhaps explains why certain philosophers have used it to extrapolate a philosophy, changing what is a sociological category into an ontological one. Now this improper generalization finds itself challenged by an obstacle and one overriding objection: ambiguity prevents awareness of ambiguity. Sociologically, it is a category of unawareness and ignorance, or rather of misunderstanding and lack of knowledge, where appearances merge with the 'real'. As appearance and illusion on a massive scale, 'consumer society' has become stronger and stronger. Modern capitalism would appear to produce for social and individual needs; it therefore appears to correspond to Marx's definition of socialism (and this appearance in itself is enough to make our situation paradoxical). In fact, 'consumer society' manipulates needs; the masters of production are also the masters of consumption, and they also produce the demands for which and according to which they are supposed to be producing. Deliberately or not, they leave other equally valid needs and other equally objective demands to one side. It is not very often that a voice makes itself heard[13] to criticize this illusion which is not entirely an illusion, this appearance which is not absolutely an appearance, since needs – even if they are provoked and prefabricated – can not all be equally phoney and artificial. Ambiguity between individual and social needs and desires papers over unperceived contradictions, blunting them and coinciding with the three-dimensional 'realness' of the everyday. Only when there is this ambiguity can the illusion and the appearance be sustained.

From the moment we begin to scrutinize them, mass culture (together with mass consumption) and the effects of the mass media reveal an enormous ambiguity. Using highly sophisticated techniques, mass communications bring masterpieces of art and culture to everyone; they make history in its entirety, the 'world' itself, accessible to all. They bring the past and even the future into the present. By continually improving their manner of approach and their means of distribution, these techniques circulate what is most refined and most subtle in the works of mankind, those painstaking creations to which men devote their lives, and in which epochs and civilizations are embodied. Modern techniques make taste more sophisticated, raise the level of culture, instruct, educate, and bring an ency-clopaedic culture to the people. *At the same time,* they make their audience passive. They make them infantile. They 'present' the world in a particular mode, the mode of spectacle and the gaze, with all the ambiguity we have already noted and which we continue to emphasize: non-participation in a false presence. This distribution lives off the past, it cuts it up and wastes it. Producing images and representations, the techniques of the mass media create nothing and do not stimulate any creativity. They consume the precious goods accumulated over the centuries, exacerbating by their own actions this more general historical fact: history has forced many creative sources to dry up, and will go on doing so indefinitely.

The mass media shape taste and cloud judgement. They instruct and they condition. With their saturation of images, current affairs and 'news' devoid of anything new, they fascinate and they nauseate. They expand communications and they threaten coherence and thought, vocabulary and verbal expression, language itself. Will they reach the extreme point where the 'world of expression' is exhausted, where everyone will be a spectacle for everyone else, where the event will be broadcast while it is happening? We call this extreme point the Great Pleonasm, the Supreme Tautology, the Final Identification of the real with the known, surprise annihilated by the illusion of per-manent surprise – ambiguity annihilated by its own triumph. Here too ambiguity presupposes and produces appearances which disguise it; never to appear to be what it is – that too is an aspect of ambigu-ity. Everything takes place as though ambiguity were only apparent and manifest in the supersession which is destroying it.

Even more generally, the way the members of one group perceive or apprehend other groups and other human beings takes place first and foremost in the mode of ambiguity: amazement and curiosity, repugnance and rapacity, retreat and generosity, desire to assimilate and need to repel. It is a kind of 'apprehensiveness': grasping yet fearing, discovering a vague threat, seesawing between a reassuring present (the other 'is'; we can hold it, distance it and define ourselves in relation to it) and a disquieting future. All that we know about our possible relation with it is this one useless detail: it can harm us or it can help us. There comes a moment when we must make up our minds and make a decision: we must make a judgement and take a choice. Options are decisive. They shed light on all that is hidden in the twilight world of ambiguity. Ambiguity cannot last long. It is not permanent. It has a time limit.

Rightly or wrongly, and according to the circumstances and conjunctures, decisions begin with an assessment, which to a certain extent runs the risk of making a mistake in the present and of failing in the future. After assessing the situation (which hitherto was ambiguous, and thus impossible to judge) we go into action; we dive in headfirst; there are no more discussions. The best man of action is the one who chooses his moment well, who discusses the pros and the cons at length, but not for too long. He waits for the situation to be ripe, but not rotten. He takes his time, and avoids hasty judgements and interventions, but by no means does he drag his feet. He replaces the 'yes and no' of ambiguity and the suspension of judgement (the 'perhaps' or 'why not?', and the 'what's the point?' of caution and hesitation) with the dilemma of action. He answers a question either by yes or by no. He opts. His decision simplifies the complex situation and the ambiguity, and by the very act of simplifying them, transforms them. One sharp blow, and ambiguity collapses. And that is when ambiguity reveals itself to be what it is: uncontrolled complexity, confusion, opaqueness. Ambiguity leads us towards a decision which will negate it and reveal it, bringing it to an end and unmasking it. The sword of decision cleaves continuous time into a *before* and an *after*. True time – many-sided, continuous and discontinuous, way-marked by the forks in its paths, mapped out by decisions and options – is revealed.

So we see yet another dialectical movement emerging before our eyes: 'ambiguity/decision'. Once we have discovered it, we will no longer be able to fetishize ambiguity and to see the everyday and the ambiguous as being synonymous. We will no longer be able to behave as if this category – ambiguity – defined a situation of the human or within the human, irreducibly and irrevocably.

As an aspect of this movement, the act of decision itself becomes an object for theory and even for a particular science, a fragment of a general theory of praxis, similar to logic: 'praxiology'. This theory can no more be identified with critique of everyday life than it can with knowledge of praxis. It touches only one aspect of them. It completes the theory of ambiguity.

The essential point here is that the theory of ambiguity foreshadows and calls for the end of ambiguity itself. It gives rise to a general problem (together with its complement, decision theory). To study the everyday is to wish to change it. To change the everyday is to bring its confusions into the light of day and into language; it is to make its latent conflicts apparent, and thus to burst them asunder. It is therefore both theory and practice, critique and action. Critique of everyday life encompasses a decision and precipitates it, the most general and the most revolutionary of them all, the decision to render ambiguities unbearable, and to metamorphose what seems to be most unchangeable in mankind because it lacks precise contours.

7 Challenge and mistrust

If there is a category among today's social facts (i.e., a set of facts denoted and connoted by a category) which corresponds in our modern world to what Mauss described as the total social phenomenon, namely gifts in archaic societies, would it not be the notion of *challenge*? Today, challenge appears openly in all areas and at every level of social reality. It is becoming a recognized, explicit, conscious and almost everyday mode of social relations between individuals and groups (genders, ages, classes, peoples and nations, institutions and organized apparatuses, political regimes and modes of production).

In our resolve to make the scientific research in which we are engaged deliberately 'neutral', impartial and objective, we might well sometimes overlook these sociodramatic categories. In its beginnings sociology's favourite areas of study – and perhaps to an exaggerated extent – were the manifestations of challenge in archaic societies: potlatch,[14] ordeals and 'judgements of God', competitive forms of exchanges and gifts, ritual declarations of friendship or hostility. This tendency has been disowned, too much so. Let us reinstate the study of the social forms of challenge, while at the same time bringing it up to date and modernizing it.[15]

Once the importance of challenge in archaic or historical (Promethean) societies has been reassessed, its sociological study and its specifically historical study become complementary. The light shed on social practice is dramatically revealing. Thus the eighteenth century saw groups and classes with increasingly clear-cut contours throw themselves in the face of a multiplicity of challenges, in all areas, including culture, art and morality. ('We, of this particular group, are and will be more cultivated, more refined, more moral, more civilized and more reasonable than you, members of another group; or we will appear to be, which more or less boils down to the same thing.')

Challenge is part of tactics and strategies. It reveals them, while at the same time concealing them. Noisy, provocative, silent, there is a period of mutual challenge in every confrontation. Challenge is polyvalent. Thrown down on a certain level (economic, cultural, ideological, political, etc.), its presence comes to light and reverberates in other areas, and on other levels of praxis. It is a means of exerting pressure, and so it is an action rather than a declamatory and gratuitous mode of expression or an impersonal figure of speech in social reality. Challenge is a means of exerting pressure beyond the group, but its actions reverberate within it; it rallies elements which have been scattered, and regroups them; it puts an end to periods when collective life breaks down into individual preoccupations and trivialities. For this reason, it enters into the everyday and elevates it, by ridding it of part of its triviality. It gives it colour.

Seen in this light, the social groups reveal well-determined characteristics. The bourgeoisie has always lived in the mode of permanent challenge to its adversaries: feudalism to begin with, then the working class. It was able to include challenge as one of the apparently universal values, so that ideologically speaking it is more of a challenge to time than to men, whose lives are ephemeral. These values – reason, nationhood – belong to a class-consciousness which does not present itself as such. Every statement with the words 'reason' or 'nation' in it contained a challenge, but not expressed as such. The bourgeoisie sought to unite challenge with confidence, a most volatile mixture. Whenever it stops living on this particular mode, it becomes slack, unleashing fear, and even panic. Conversely, as a social group, technocrats avoid challenge, and provocation even more so; they work in silence, deep underground, and this distinguishes them from the other class fractions from which they derive or which they serve. The rowdy, provocative challenges hurled by intellectuals at general opinion (romanticism, surrealism, existentialism, for example) mark certain periods of culture, and certain other periods are marked by their silence. These differing attitudes can imply a confession of powerlessness, or a possibility of action. As regards the challenge of the proletariat to bourgeois society and to the bourgeoisie, it can be silent and mistrustful rather than provocative.

Critical periods, i.e., acute forms of confrontation and revolutionary moments, always seem to be preceded or followed by periods when tensions and challenges are less extreme. But challenge can be more far-reaching, and much more profound. It could be said that economic growth and the development of technology throw down a series of challenges – long suppressed – to the individual, to art and to the moral sphere, and to modern man in general.[16]

Could peaceful coexistence be an idyll, could there be fraternization without an ulterior motive, could there be mutual toleration with a pluralist ideology in both camps, in an unruffled juxtaposition of opposed regimes? Unthinkable! Interaction is a law. We must not confuse official declarations, which are often most perfidious when they are at their most diplomatic and skilful, with the dialectical movement of the real. Peaceful coexistence is a perpetual mutual challenge. Objectively, and in the mode of challenge, overt incompatibility makes way for a compatibility which is not without its own risks. With its component of randomness, a challenge replaces a threat. It is based on a situation – the possibility and fear of mass destruction – much more than on the will for anything. It comprises a volatile relation of forces within boundaries fraught with danger. We should not imagine it to follow any archaic model, like some kind of generalized 'potlatch' of nuclear or conventional arms; that would be too tidy and too simple. The challenge is many-sided, and will continue to be so: it is economic, political, military, cultural and technological. We are well aware of what its contents are: industrial growth, aid to underdeveloped countries (whose weight may well prove decisive) and unrestrained technical development.

And so challenge puts the solidity of existing structures permanently to the test, and at the same time it tries their ability to adapt to circumstances. When it is explicit, challenge resembles intimidation; when it is covert, it resembles tolerance and understanding, and therefore flexibility.

Can there be a challenge without mistrust, i.e., without fear? Not often. And if so, we would call it arrogance. When challenge became generalized it brought mistrust in its wake, and this fosters an immense and terrible uncertainty. We have learned a lot from the new concepts it has brought us: the ubiquity of randomness in the modern world, the importance of tactics and strategies in social 'reality', etc. Mistrust determines a specific alienation: it clouds things over, it creates panic and it stultifies; at the same time, it stimulates energies. The climate of challenge and mistrust is prodigiously uplifting, but it is as unbearable as it is stimulating. Mistrust also determines a disalienation, the vague anguish which comes when we are confronted with the innumerable questions randomness raises. 'Why this? Why that?' Perhaps when the need for security becomes less important it will lead to a mutation in social consciousness. With the current degree of anxiety and tension, the human mind becomes detached from nature. It demands that the tranquillity of nature and the restlessness of culture be superseded. Would this mutation open the way for a demand for a radical metamorphosis of the everyday? We can only hope so. If not, yet another failure will be added to the list, and it is already much too long as it is . . .

From the start of their coexistence, the two opposing 'regimes' or 'systems' have reacted one against the other, and in a very profound way. This is not the place to study this dialectical movement: the pressure of one 'system' upon another and the way the systems respond to that pressure, with all the repercussions and exaggerations which ensue. This interaction gets broader and more intense, with each side maintaining that it alone keeps all its promises (and even other people's promises, as someone notoriously once put it) and the ability to fulfil mankind's aspirations. In this interaction, *the image of the other* (the result of an unstable combination of information and propaganda) is already playing an ever-increasing and contradictory role. It is the image of challenge, an image we challenge and which we mistrust.

Thus a 'world' or 'planetary' unit is under way, contradictorily, dialectically, i.e., in a way which is both necessary and random, determined and aleatory. As we go beyond our own planet, and as the adventure of space opens up before us like a chasm, 'globality' enters into the dialectical movement of man and of history. But what will this globality be? We have no means of predicting it with any accuracy. The most we can do is to draw up a table of possibilities, chances and options. A highly complex interaction is unfolding before our eyes, and within us, on the mode of challenge. It is not mechanical, and is full of random elements. The way this challenge works is changing. At first it turned the bourgeoisie into wild beasts (fascists), and then – without making it any the less ferocious – it shook it from its lethargy, and, to a certain extent, from its stupidity; the bourgeoisie tries to rid itself of its old Malthusianism, to plan ahead, to 'harmonize' production and consumption; it succeeds to a certain extent, but without transforming the fundamental conditions and categories of bourgeois society, and without suppressing the class struggle or the proletariat. In the other camp, the capitalist challenge initially prevented the socialist state from withering away; it was one of the causes of Stalinism, perhaps the main one; then it shook socialism from its dogmatic slumbers, and it shook up state doctrinairism and crude centralized planning; and now socialism is at last beginning to take social needs into account.

We now know that, in their challenges and their contradictions, the two modes of production present some similarities and some curious homologies. Notably, on both sides, everyday life is neglected and abandoned to its backwardness, in the USA because of the inadequacies of the 'public services', and in the USSR because of the priority given to heavy industry. On one side, there is a dearth of statism, on the other there is too much of it. On both sides technological alienation has produced results which are in many respects comparable. The challenges of the two sociopolitical regimes concern the same category, the category of everyday life.

The regime which carries the day will be the one which produces the most wealth, the most means for action, the most freedom – in a word, the most possibilities. Will it triumph by the pleasure it offers mankind, or by power over it? Who can say?

This is why we have not taken any one idea (the idea of 'globality' for example) to guide us through the complexities of the modern world and its problems. One idea alone would not have enabled us to make predictions and to take options. To guide us through the labyrinthine world of challenge, we have chosen one humble and essential requirement: the transformation of the everyday through critical knowledge of it.

8 Social space, social time

There exist social time or social time scales which are distinct from biological, physiological and physical time scales. There is a social space which is distinct from geometric, biological, geographic and economic space. Everyday space differs from geometric space in that it has four dimensions, which are in a two-by-two opposition: 'right/left – high/low'. Similarly, everyday time has four dimensions which differ from dimensions as mathematicians and physicists would define them, namely the accomplished, the foreseen, the uncertain and the unforeseeable (or again: the past, the present, the short-term future and the long-term future).

The more deeply we analyse them, the more subtle and the more differentiated these ideas become. With respect to *social space*, we will distinguish between subjective aspects and objective aspects. Subjectively, social space is the environment of the group and of the individual within the group; it is the horizon at the centre of which they place themselves and in which they live. The extent of this horizon differs from group to group, according to their situation and their particular activities. Objectively, the idea of social space is not synonymous with the currently accepted idea of 'social mobility'. Taken in isolation, social mobility remains an abstraction; it implies networks and channels via which it is established, if indeed it constitutes a lasting phenomenon. Social space is made up of a relatively dense fabric of networks and channels. This fabric is an integral part of the everyday. We will study it later, in our model of communications, where we will try to see if we can give a precise meaning to the terms 'social distance' and 'social field'.

As for social time, let us emphasize once more the difference between cyclic time scales and linear time scales, and their relativeness. We know that the former have their origins or their foundations in nature; they are connected to profound, cosmic, vital rhythms.

The latter are connected to knowledge, reason and techniques; they correlate not with vital rhythms and processes, but rather with processes of economic and technological growth.

We will look closely at the results of the interactions between cyclic rhythms and linear (continuous or discontinuous) time scales in the everyday. Therefore we will be proposing a rhythmology or a sociological 'rhythmanalysis',[17] and we will attempt to distinguish between periodicities and to study their relations and superpositions, taking either mathematical harmonic analysis or physiological research as our model. Moreover, each group has its 'tempo', which is relatively fast or slow, and which varies between work and everyday life outside work. In this way we would hope to develop a theory of the multiplicity of social time scales.[18]

9 Praxis

We now come to the simplest category, and the most difficult to elucidate. It is the most abstract and the most concrete, since it applies both to the everyday and to the wholeness of society. It is the category of *social practice* or *praxis*.

Since Marx's early writings (which are also called philosophical), the idea of *praxis* has been distorted and impoverished. Before we try to reinstate the idea in its entirety we will look quickly at the restrictive ways it has been interpreted.

Making[19] reduces social practice to individual operations of the artisan kind on a given material which is relatively pliable or resistant. During this operation, the producer or creator – part artisan, part artist – discovers himself. By means of the object, he recognizes his work and his own abilities. As he works, he forms his own abilities. This is as true for traditional potters and weavers as it is for painters. When they make something, they also make themselves.

At one and the same time, the idea of *making* is narrower and vaguer, more deceptively precise and more equivocal than the idea of *production*, which as yet is not broad enough to cover the idea of praxis completely. In spite of its apparent precision, the idea of 'making' is without contours. Is play a 'making'? If it is, the idea can be used to include whatever one wants. If not, it becomes restricted to productive work upon an object, work which is of a determined kind and, moreover, somewhat antiquated. As soon as we fail to stipulate the limits of the idea and the frame of reference in which we are using it, it can result in misuse, namely deceptive values. In modern industrial labour, the direct and unmediated contacts the operator has with his tools and his material are diminishing, and with automation they actually disappear. An analysis of praxis based upon this idea would be in danger of overlooking many facts. It lags behind reality, and the clarity which comes as a result of this lag is deceptive. We think of labour in the industrial era along artisan lines, and the labour of the present era – the era of automation – along the lines of 'classic' industry. Fragmented labour has altered the relation between work and life outside work, and automation has altered it even more. When he 'makes' something, the individual is no longer 'making' himself. He is 'made' in a complex totality of which 'making' is only one part and one aspect. For all that, on the scale of society, production and production relations remain determinants. Moreover, whenever there is a 'work', no matter how modest – and not a 'product' – the value bestowed on the individual act by the 'making' remains valid (including when it is in the caricatural form of a hobby, or do-it-yourself).

Here are some other reservations about the idea of 'making'. It does not help us to pose the problem of inventiveness in practice, nor does it help us solve it. It treats the technique as though it were the material, and tends to relegate both to the background, as general givens of all activities which make anything, without examining the implications and conditions or the consequences and results in themselves. In order to give more value to the agent's individual initiative and skill, it emphasizes the zone of indetermination (the margin of freedom) which the technique and the material put at his disposal. This does not help us to make a clear formulation of the problems of freedom, with all their implications, or of the problems of individuals and of the groups to which those individuals belong. And what happens to alienation in this schematic?

The narrowness of the way in which empiricism and pragmatism interpret the idea of 'practice' has been stressed so often and so vigorously that it is hardly worth reiterating. By only considering individual practical action and its result, by replacing breadth of theoretical vision (which they present as simple abstraction) by practicism and the vulgar practical mentality, by extolling success as the criterion and principle of judgement, Anglo-Saxon empiricism and pragmatism eliminate the drama, the profundity and the problems from individual life and from social life. They have proved attractive because they are simple, i.e., they simplify. They reveal the absence of a philosophical tradition, or more exactly the absence of an effective tradition which has penetrated culture. If they were able to spread their ideas it was thanks to the great crisis of philosophy, when the withering away, the supersession and the absence of philosophy all became merged in an inextricable confusion. The image of praxis they present is all the more false for being more 'realistic', more precise and more in line with the experience of fragmentation. They have even contaminated Marxist thought.

Against Anglo-Saxon pragmatism and its apologia to success, several philosophers – with little awareness of the situation or of the role they are playing – have made a virtue out of failure. They have rehabilitated drama and the tragic, but excessively so: only failure has any meaning, since success or victory simply demonstrates the platitude of the intentions and the goals which inspired them. So today the derisory sociological apologia to success is countered by the no-less-derisory idea that humanity only sets itself insoluble problems, that men play to lose, and that the magnitude of the aims and the profundity of the goals are measured by the extent to which they fail. We are now leaving this dilemma behind us.

Pragmatism disregards the fact that decisions are based on logic and that actions are dialectical. It disregards the theory of choices, possibilities and risks. It eliminates concrete problematics: conflicts, contradictions, openings. It thinks of praxis not as something concealing a complexity of movements, but as a cold, naked concept of the real, with the density of a stone. The atheoretical conception of human activity goes hand-in-hand with a functionalist conception of the real. Emphasizing one specific formant of activity – technology – the transition to a technocratic positivism which considers itself to be broad, deep and of course 'realistic' is easy.

An analogous restriction has occurred in dogmatic Marxist thought, in tandem with similar divisions. Using a different terminology, specific sides of praxis have been emphasized such as productive labour, the action of man on external nature, and matter as the object of the activity which precedes conscious activity. Ipso facto there is equally a tendency to give value to technology, productivity and success. We jump from productive labour, identified with praxis, to some other aspect (the planning of productive labour, political practice, the practice of the state or of the party) without worrying too much about piecing these multiple fragments back together again. Hence an ideological confusion which makes it possible to transfer the rather vague quality attributed to praxis in general to a determined (political) practice: the ability to achieve good results from an action, control over spontaneous or unwitting processes, technology, knowledge, and control over the forces of nature. This ideology does away with the need for a strictly political theory which would describe and analyse the means of state power and the sources of specifically political action: apparatuses, propaganda, methods of direction and command, techniques of distribution and constraint, in short, the penetration of globality and statism, and the marked separation between them, into the everyday.

In terms of its inability to analyse and its hostility to knowledge, so-called Marxist practicism is just as bad as pragmatism. Its idea of praxis is just as blinkered and just as obscurantist. It sidesteps the issue by presenting its own 'praxis' as an ideological (philosophical) representation rather than *reflecting* its truth in a critical fashion. Dogmatism has been able to present the total liberation of mankind and the blossoming of its freedom as having been accomplished, but it has done so within a framework which in fact makes this impossible: statism, the requirements of primitive accumulation, dissatisfaction, and the restriction of needs and pleasures. By dint of stressing specific aspects of praxis, or ideology (and notably matter and philosophical materialism), it has succeeded broadly in blurring and parenthesizing other aspects, and in excluding them from the idea of socialism: notably everything concerning everyday life.

After such a lengthy and effective obliteration, only by making a considerable effort will we be able to reinstate the idea of *praxis* in its entirety.

The action of social man on nature (the outside world) is only one aspect of praxis, but it is already a complex one, since when we analyse it we find a large number of formants: techniques (tools and knowledge), natural forces, resources and raw materials, the organization and division of labour (the *social* division and the *technical* division of labour are not the same thing, particularly in capitalist society), etc.

The relations between human beings – groups and individuals – are obviously part of praxis. Action upon nature (productive forces) implies social relations (production relations) and explains them, up to a point. Conversely, social relations cannot be established or conceived of outside action upon nature (productive forces). Social groups, and notably classes, are simultaneously productive forces and social forces. However, social relations and production relations are not the same thing, and praxis cannot be defined comprehensively either as a sum total or as an interaction: 'productive forces/production relations'. This representation fetishizes economy. It ends up as a simplistic productivism, as perfunctory as the functionalism we have already refuted: a productivism of material production. It forgets or refuses to listen to Marx's argument against Adam Smith's bourgeois productivism, which recent economists and sociologists have taken up again in the fight against vulgarized Marxism: all societies comprise and imply a non-material and yet practically creative production, namely the various 'services'. Now these services are woven into the texture of social relations, production relations and property relations. They make them more complex. They represent social needs *generally* and the *specific* social needs which have been accepted and controlled. They help to articulate production and consumption in the everyday (whether it be distribution, transport, health and medicine, education and training, leisure activities, advertising, specifically cultural works, etc.). Although simple and unmediated in appearance, everyday life reveals on analysis the presence of a range of effective representations, symbols, regulations, controls, models and norms (ideologies and 'superstructures') which intervene and mediate it. Conversely, these multiple mediations of everyday life take on an unmediated existence within it, albeit unevenly. Mediations of the everyday do not all intervene simultaneously.

Praxis reveals an extreme complexity on very varied *levels*: from the biophysiological level, which comprises relations with nature other than that of material production strictly speaking (as much within the family as in the village, the town or the nation), to the abstract and formal level of symbols, culture, representations and ideologies. The so-called 'superstructural' elements and formants react on the 'base'. This classic postulate of Marxist theory will be incomprehensible if we fail to perceive that there is a level in praxis which is relatively distinct and marked per se, the level of everyday life. Symbols and representations react first and foremost on unmediated relations, between which they intervene as mediations: the apparently direct relations between persons and things (goods) which are precisely what the everyday, as well as the apparently simple modalities of social consciousness, is made up of.

But praxis also reveals itself as a totality. We would maintain that the idea of totality derives from praxis. However, this totality never appears to be other than fragmentary, contradictory, and composed of levels, of contradictions on differing levels, and of partial totalities. How do we reach totality, i.e., society itself, from within? Precisely, via these partial totalities and levels which cross-refer to each other, and via these fragments which presuppose a whole and which necessitate the concept of a whole of which they are the evidence and the elements, but not the entirety. Fragmented in one sense but already total in another, every act of thought or social effectiveness refers to the totality via the other levels. It reveals a total praxis, and points the way towards it. Only by restoring this mobile and contradictory (dialectical) profundity to praxis will we be able to understand and reinstate certain of Marx's famous postulates. Social life, the life of society and of the individual, is in its essence social practice: praxis. Production produces man. So-called 'world history' or 'the history of the world' is nothing but the history of man producing himself, of man producing both the human world and the other man, the (alienated) man of otherness, and his self (his self-consciousness).

This is an ideal point at which to protest once more against the ideological operation which reduces praxis to production, and production itself to economic (material) production. Praxis encompasses both material production and 'spiritual' production, the production of means and the production of ends, of implements, of goods and of needs. To produce and to reproduce is not simply to cast a certain number of produced objects (implements of production or consumer goods) into distribution, exchange and consumption, or alternatively to invest or accumulate them. It is also to produce and to produce again the multiple *social relations* which enable production and the *appropriation* of goods (and which also limit or hinder them).

In this way, and in this way only, do we become aware of the coherence of a determined society (its structures), and of the incoherences which the coherent structure dominates and subjugates until such time as it disintegrates. To detach the productive forces from action on material nature, or more generally to single out certain categories from praxis by giving them a privileged status, to consider certain objects separately and to turn them into fetishes (commodities, for example, or money) – these are precisely the procedures which Marxist critique refutes. And this is how the foundation of all critical thought, including critique of religion, critique of philosophy and critique of everyday life, becomes manifest.

In production, it is not only products which are produced and reproduced, but also social groups and their relations and elements; members, goods and objects disappear while groups persist or crumble away, remaining active, playing their games and developing their tactics and strategies. Beneath an apparent immobility, analysis discovers a hidden mobility. Beneath this superficial mobility, it discovers stabilities, self-regulations, structures and factors of balance. Beneath the overall unity, it uncovers diversities, and beneath the multiplicity of appearances it finds a totality. Analysis must maintain these two sociological aspects (incessant change, the disappearance of elements, nascent conjunctures – the structuring of the whole, relative stability) and grasp them in the wholeness of a single history.

Praxis produces the human 'world', our world, the world of objects and goods, the world our senses perceive and which therefore seems a gift of nature to the organs and body of an individual. The expression 'outside world' is deceptive. It groups together *things* (e.g., a pebble), *objects* (e.g., a house), *products* (e.g., a pencil) and *works* (e.g., a painting). Through the mediation of language, the outside world 'is' also the inner world which reproduces the human world of objects, products and works by means of verbal structures. (Individual) consciousness 'reflects' a world which seems external and which social praxis has created. Up to a certain point (but this determination does not exhaust it) this consciousness can be defined as the place – the field – where significations and symbolisms left by praxis in the world of objects come together.

We must distinguish between repetitive praxis and inventive praxis. This distinction is essential if we are to make the idea of praxis more dialectically profound, and reinstate it in its entirety. Repetition plays a considerable role on every level. Sooner or later productive and technical actions end up as reiterated gestures, and this is an important if not essential aspect of labour. As for operations entrusted to material devices (such as tools and machines), they always involve many to-and-fro movements: oscillations, rotations, alternations. As Marx pointed out before our contemporary economists and sociologists did, products per se differ from works and natural objects by their capacity for unlimited production. We know that a large part of everyday life is made up of stereotyped and repeated actions. This repetitive praxis keeps the human world going, and helps to produce it over and over again. It underlies the human world and constitutes its stability. Is it intrinsically alienating? No. It will only alienate in definable conditions and situations: when 'something else' becomes possible.

However, we should not separate repetitive praxis from creative praxis. There are several types of repetition, and we will have cause to examine their differences at a later stage. The stereotyped, mechanical repetition of gestures and signals differs from the rhythmed and periodic starting and restarting which characterizes vital activities. Let us remember that in mathematics repetitions of formal operations (such as adding or subtracting an element from a set) – iteration and reiteration – are fundamental and prodigiously creative acts.

Therefore we can expect to find transitions and mediations between the repetitive and the creative. This is why we did not think it possible to define the everyday by the repetitive alone, but rather as the place where repetition and creativity meet and confront each other. Social praxis cannot be confined to supporting, maintaining and reproducing. In our arguments we have tried to demonstrate the relative character of structures, stabilities, constants and balances. Praxis is not confined to the everyday, nor is the everyday confined to a mechanical and unlimited recommencement of the same gestures and operations. Repetitive practice is necessary, but it is not enough per se. It never attains the definitive, automatic balance, a balance without contradictions. This would be the supreme alienation. It is the 'base' of the inventiveness which undermines and modifies it. Praxis is creative. On the frontiers of inventiveness, we sense the coming of acts which disrupt praxis and transform the everyday: revolutions, total phenomena which introduce a multiplicity of possibilities which the unfolding of history strives unsuccessfully to exhaust . . .

Other less garish and strident forms of creativity are much more humble. Creativity is not only produced outside the everyday, on the higher plane of representations and symbolisms. At first commencement and recommencement are indistinguishable, and their difference only becomes apparent after time, and as a consequence of it. We would go so far as to say that all inventiveness is born from the everyday, and is confirmed within it. Where and how is the act of creativity accomplished? We know that in terms of the norms and received frames of reference which govern higher activities it is often marginal, bizarre and deviant. Its creativity is only apparent later, in what follows. The inventive action is often similar to gambling: it comprises a wager and a risk of loss. The history of the sciences proves these assertions as much as the history of art and of political doctrines do. In our opinion, the most inventive people are individuals who are not isolated, but who have the backing of small groups. Certainly large-scale groups and society as a whole are essential in offering the necessary if inadequate conditions for inventive practice. Individuals in small groups achieve what praxis makes possible, on a comprehensive scale. Inventiveness makes its way from mediation to mediation through ponderous repetition, through the stimulations of conflicts and the enticements and interdictions of social values and controls. Could not inventiveness – or the seeds of inventiveness – be a product of the limited and daring praxis of small-scale groups: sects, secret societies, political parties, elective groups, laboratories, theatrical troupes, etc.?

Our analysis leads us to introduce a multiplicity of differences, levels and partial totalities into the idea of praxis, but without abandoning the idea itself. We will distinguish between the following:

a) *Total revolutionary praxis*, the praxis Marx dealt with in his so-called philosophical writings (which contain a radical critique of philosophy while perpetuating traditional philosophy). Total revolutionary praxis would overturn what exists from top to bottom. It would bring an end to alienation in one total historical act. It would reveal contradictions, and then it would resolve them. It would overcome scissions and separations, first and foremost those between *being* and *thinking* (consciousness), the *private* (the everyday) and the *public* (the state, politics), *need* and *desire*, and *nature* and *culture*, etc. It implies the supersession of philosophy and its fulfilment, as well as the withering away of the state.

Today the idea of total revolutionary praxis seems Utopian. And indeed it is. In so far as all philosophy has (directly or indirectly) presented some kind of half-aware Utopia, and in so far as Utopia stimulates action by achieving itself through a succession of approximations, we will retain the idea, and we will even foreground it. Whatever appears as a Utopia also appears as an Idea. The idea of *total praxis* is nothing other than the idea of *revolution*. When we introduced the idea of a metamorphosis of the everyday we stressed the twofold character of this programme: it is both Utopian and realist. Changing the world rather than interpreting it means not only changing the outside world but, above all, changing the everyday. This total praxis becomes possible as soon as it is thought, and because it is thought. However, given the real conditions (production relations, and the historical and political conjuncture), it is not possible. We return to Marx's idea of a dialectical unit comprising the supreme Utopia and the supremely real. Would not the idea of total revolution be as vital in determining the field of possibilities as the idea of absolute (achieved) knowledge is in determining the path of science and the sense of the relative?

b) *Partial revolutionary praxis.* The economic development of a country and the general growth of production (as opposed to an uneven and incoherent growth) represent a partial revolutionary praxis, a fragment of total praxis which can conceal it and even cheat it. It is not always easy to distinguish this partial revolutionary praxis from the reformist praxis which accepts and submits to the 'real' – i.e., production relations as given – rather than bringing pressure to bear on their contradictions, in order to transform them.

c) *Knowledge as practice* (in so far as it has its reason and its content in praxis) and conversely *practice as intervention and embodiment in knowledge.*

Knowledge is in no respect an abstract activity. It may have its theories and its concepts, and it can be host to the conflict between theory and practice (in their dialectical unity, i.e., a creative conflict), but nevertheless theoretical knowledge cannot be separated from praxis. It is an integral part of it.

Even the 'purest' knowledge uses techniques and implements, be they material or formal. It is therefore inseparable from the productive forces, from the social forms of the organization and the division of labour, and from the political forms which sanction and direct social forms of organization. Thus the foundation and, even more, the *content* of scientific objectivity are social (and thus relative, up to a certain point). To say that science is objective is to say that science is part of praxis. Sectors of knowledge can develop only if they serve the needs and the interests of a determined and relatively large social group (such as a class or a class fraction, a country, or a social and political regime), even if their theoretical foundations have been long established.[20]

d) *Political practice*, on the scale of society as a whole, but which is only one level of praxis at one particular stage of the process of becoming, which means that we have no right to fetishize it. 'Political practice' may have (momentarily) refuted Marx's ideas on total revolution, the withering away of the state and the end of political practice, but to present this as a definitive truth would be pure empiricism, and it would also 'ideologize' Marxism, which sought to be a radical critique of ideologies. At the same time, this attitude confirms that radical critique is a necessary aspect of Marxism. Ideology is part of political practice, but praxis contains the social truth of ideology, of politics and of the state.

e) *Repetitive practice*, an indispensable resource for the everyday. It is both irreducible (impossible to suppress) and reducible (in that it can be reduced indefinitely). It can be analysed according to different types of repetition (mechanical, periodic, cyclic, etc.).

f) *Inventive* (creative) *practice*, which derives from repetitive practice. We can already distinguish between practice which creates material works and practice which creates practice, i.e., which modifies human relations (including their ethical dimension).

g) *Specific practices*, uneven in terms of their technicality and of the extent to which they penetrate the uncontrolled sector. They belong to the skills and professions which act upon natural or human 'material': education, medicine, art, architecture, trades unions, farming, etc. In this category we will also include the social practice of small groups (elective or neighbourhood groupings, learned societies, theatrical troupes, and determined 'publics', etc.) which support and back an individual capable of inventiveness, until such point as he escapes them or they themselves reject him. On this level, and according to cases and situations, the historical can become what is most internalized (accepted) or most externalized (cast aside as unimportant).

These limited practices cross-refer to each other, and to the entirety of the set they constitute: existing practice as a whole. Via the groups we can grasp fragmented totality; passing as it does between practicism and speculation, this is perhaps the best route of access. However, this passing from the fragmentary to the total is not without its difficulties, as a careful reading of Marx's authoritative *Capital* will show.

h) When linked to the idea of praxis, analysis of the everyday reveals several formants. Not only do we find the various forms of repetition and the seeds of possible creativity, but we also find utilitarian and fetishist practice, which manipulates things on the level of analytic understanding (which disguises contradictions and dissociates dialectical movements into defined and isolated 'elements'). In the everyday we observe empirical thought at work, with its belief in commodities and money as things. Empirical consciousness takes things and objects from the everyday, and separates them from activity and social relations. It confuses products and creative works, things and objects, with no concern whatever for basic analytic distinctions (while proceeding according to the laws of logic and analytic understanding, which are also those of trivial discourse and day-to-day language). This empirical consciousness uses means as ends: goods, money, commodities, capital. It champions fetishism as a valid consciousness. This is the level on which it establishes itself: the reality and (apparently) unmediated positivity of accepted needs, representations and symbolisms. On this level, received representations, which are not recognized as the results of a history and as functions of an entire society, and are indeed unrecognizable as such, impose themselves unchecked. Inadequately aware of its link with totality, and based on the fragmentary division of labour and on class relations (themselves misunderstood, i.e., treated with suspicion and parenthesized), fragmentary practice is accepted as the real, in all its opaqueness and clarity.

It is precisely this 'realness', this 'positiveness', this 'practice' that critique of everyday life disturbs and dismantles (at least on the theoretical plane, the plane of concepts) by proclaiming *the possibility of its radical metamorphosis*. First of all, critique poses the problem: 'What is it that supports this realness and makes it appear as a solid and valid reality?' Therefore its first targets are the representations and symbols active within this apparent 'realness'.

10 Logos, logic, dialectic

Now it would be easy to illustrate the use of dialectical thought, and there are thousands of examples to choose from. Here are a few, and our selection is not without its irony.

France is the fatherland of eternal theoretical and practical reason, the country of Descartes and of Classicism, of the three unities, of the system of tonality in music (Rameau), and of the metric system, etc. The French system of road signs embodies and materializes pure reason for the senses of modern man, and provides a model for technicians the world over. France is the land of the hectometre.[21]

However, if our Frenchman is Cartesian, he also likes his life to be lively and volatile. He gets carried away by odd obsessions. France is also the fatherland of fashion, of ephemerality, of frivolity, fragrances and frills. It is the fatherland of femininity.

If we juxtapose these two aspects of the French genius, the resulting picture will be lacking something. We hope (in vain) that they will coexist peacefully; but the picture is in monochrome, the colours of drama are missing. It is the same when we make the euphoric suggestion that they can complement each other. On the other hand, to confront them as being logically incompatible would be to brand French culture as regrettably absurd, and our judgements would become increasingly disenchanted.

In truth, these two 'aspects' do indeed have their conflicts. They pose problems. On the one hand, they penetrate the most ordinary details of French everyday life, in the general context of modern life. On the other, they refer us back to history, to one particular history.

The fact that these specific characteristics penetrate everyday life (with their contradictions, and in spite of their contradictions) leads us to hope that they will endure. History tells us that probably they will disappear.

In so far as we know anything about it, the sixteenth century in France reveals an exuberance and a lust for life which was to be swallowed up by the Wars of Religion. Then came the century of classical rationality and the bourgeois bureaucratic state of absolute monarchy; the state made use of this rationality and imposed it, mutilating and alienating spontaneity. When it came to levelling out differences and originalities, state rationalism was as effective as state capitalism and administrative socialism! In the eighteenth century there was an attempt to reinstate our lost spontaneity; this attempt reached its critical point with the romantic rebellion, which was doomed to failure, as it was powerless to halt the effects of centralization, the predominance of the Parisian head on the provincial body, and many other phenomena.

In France today, the conflictual 'aspects' of the French genius coexist and affect different groups. Administration (which transforms rationalism into bureaucratic ideology) is the domain of rationality on the practical level, and the universities are its domain on the abstract (speculative) level. A section of the intelligentsia and the feminists represent the volatile aspect, sometimes in the form of rebellion, at others as a pure and simple caricature of spontaneity. The appropriation of these contradictory aspects by differing groups does not stop contradictions and conflicts from emerging, but it blunts them and plunges them into ambiguity. Because of this, the French everyday might be described as a volatile and ambiguous mixture of rationality and empiricism, of positivism and sentimentality. This does not stifle the demand for a supersession which would reinstate spontaneity without losing the clarity of reason, on the contrary, but it does give us reason to fear Americanization, that ideological commodity imported in the name of technical progress, 'consumer society' and the mass media. A socialization peddled by ideology and political models would be no better.

But there is more to be said about dialectical thought than these illustrations tell us. Let us return to another problem, a difficult one, and as yet not satisfactorily resolved: the relations between logic and

245

dialectic. We have already stressed the distinction between *levels* of thought: *formal logic* (logic of similarity), *dialectical logic* (relations of difference, opposition, reciprocity, interaction and complementarity), *praxis* or *dialectical reason* (the exploration and the grasping – never completely – of real dialectical movements). Moreover we have granted logic its own level of reality: the study of relative stabilities, self-regulations, structures and momentary balances in a process of becoming at the heart of which structurings and the dismantling of structures (destructuring) succeed one another. It may be that we failed to stress sufficiently the relative, provisional and momentary character not only of concepts in knowledge, but also of stabilities in the real and in structures. If we are to get a clear understanding of the situation of the everyday within a comprehensively structured society, it is imperative that we return to this question.

Why is the problem so acute? Because post-Hegelian philosophy (including dialectical materialism) has too often taken Hegel's formulations about the emptiness of the categories of formal logic literally. Accordingly, logic is considered valid for 'domestic use' only, as Engels put it. This is to overlook the fact that there is nothing insignificant about everyday usage, and that the use of discourse – language – in everyday life precedes its use in knowledge and philosophy. And another little fact is frequently forgotten: mathematical science operates on the plane of formal rigour, i.e., logic, and dialectic is not an overt feature of it. Philosophical critique may discover some dialectical movements in mathematical thought (the finite/the non-finite, the continuous/the discontinuous, etc.), but nevertheless the rigorous techniques and operational procedures of mathematicians remain irreducibly logical and formal. So they are useful 'concretely'.

Certain people were led to imagine dialectical thought to be at one and the same time a subject ('dialectics'), a rejection (a pseudo-supersession), and a pure and simple reflection of the dialectical realities active in things, and which operate in the manner of things. This is to confuse dialectical contradiction with logical absurdity, because no distinction between logical contradiction and dialectical contradiction has been made. This presentation of philosophical thought as though it were higher philosophy degrades it and comes dangerously close to sophistry, but without any of the merits attributable to the critical thought of the Greek Sophists. In fact it did allow for a great deal of sophistry, and as an implement for analysing stabilities and dialectical movements it was worthless.

In this pseudo-philosophy, dogmatic sophistry consists of an appeal by the human to nature to 'found' historical and social dialectic by giving it a political (and therefore empirical) use, and then to legitimize it in this debased form. When the human is projected into nature without any prior critique, it is one particular way of acting within the human which is sanctioned, and not the human itself.

Galilean, Cartesian and Newtonian physics pushed geometry and mechanics to their farthest consequences. It was a science of trajectories, and gave very little houseroom to questions concerning the stability of mechanical systems. Once several general laws had been accepted, among which were the so-called 'universal' laws of gravity, stability was a logical conclusion. This science presented a single model of reality, *the planetary model*: at the centre, the sun, on the periphery, its retinue of satellite bodies, and a single force linking them together. This model constituted a defined, closed and stable physical system. Given gravitational forces, Newton's law and the tangential impulsions at the initial instant, it became increasingly difficult to calculate orbits, but the fact that they were stable was virtually assured. In passing, we should note that the planetary model appeared to be universal. For more than a century every effort was made to imagine human (psychological and sociological) reality according to this image: a central, primordial element, with subordinated elements gravitating around it.

When Bohr conceived of the differentiated atom of microphysics, he imagined it by analogy with the planetary model (the principle of correspondence): a nucleus, some electrons. However it quickly became apparent that the stability of the system conceived of in this way was no longer self-evident. The interaction of positive and negative electrical particles could not play exactly the same role as gravitational interaction; although the active forces were in proportion to the masses (electrical charges) and in inverse proportion to the square of the distance, negativity and repulsion came into play. The stabilization (self-regulation) of the system posed a problem. At the same time and correlatively, microphysics was moving from one model to another. It was abandoning the planetary model (on the microscopic scale) in favour of the *harmonic model*, which we will now explain. In this model, the atom is analogous to a vibrating spring or string (a linear oscillator). Like a string when it vibrates, it presents static states within a spectrum. Fixed at its two extremities, the vibrating string takes an infinite number of transitory positions between those two terminal limits. Within this infinite number, certain well-defined positions can be observed, which become consolidated, so to speak, during the vibrational movement, excluding other intermediate positions as they do so. Not only are these static states determined, but they are also determinable on the basis of numbers which are whole (harmonics), and therefore distinct and finite, although the number of harmonics remains unlimited. This relation between the finite and the non-finite gives rise to some precise calculations (Fourier's series and integrals, Freedholm's theorem, etc.). Where does this physical reality come from? From the remarkable fact that the initial impulse – the plucking of the taut string – exerts a *double* action: it displaces the string from its position of equilibrium and it also transmits a perturbation (a wave) along the length of the string, which seeks to regain its position of equilibrium. The law of perturbation must be calculated together with the law of the return to equilibrium. The first acts in relation to the distance on the string (frequency) and the second in relation to the square of the distance from the ends of the string to the position of equilibrium (amplitude). The force of gravity does not have this duality. It is a single force and the gravitational field is only influenced by the dynamic effects of a single force in opposition to the inertia of material masses. Therefore the harmonic model enables us to represent something which the planetary model could not: *dual* interactions (positive and negative, attraction and repulsion). Via this model we can turn our minds to representing a veritable *complex field*: spectrums, transitionals, static states, harmonics, the determinable relation between the finite and the non-finite (between the continuous and the discontinuous).

We should point out here that the concepts of equilibrium and of rest, immobility or inertia, are not the same as the concept of static state. This state stands out from transitionals, of which there are an infinite number, but there is nothing definitive about it. In a sense it is itself only a transitional; the string's final position – and its initial one

– defines the equilibrium at the beginning and at the end of the movement. However, there is another side to the question. When two sides of a set of scales are equally weighted they offer an equilibrium which the slightest addition of weight on one side will break for ever; the mechanical equilibrium disappears, because it has no capacity for righting itself or for self-regulation. Conversely, when a string vibrates it moves in a stable manner, and the movement itself creates a relatively stable form, although static states stand out from the continuous background provided by the transitionals; the force of the initial percussion or plucking and the actual place of impact modify the subsequent overall form and its distinct elements (harmonics) *relatively little*. Mathematically, in the case of fairly small oscillations, frequency does not depend upon the initial conditions of the movement, but is defined by the properties of the determined system per se.

Bohr used his planetary model to formulate his 'stability postulate', a mental process in which, precisely, stability was grasped as a problem. At around the same time, Planck published his famous hypothesis according to which an oscillator can only emit or absorb radiations in discrete and discontinuous quantities, measurable by whole numbers (energy particles: quanta, photons). This useful hypothesis also demonstrated the usefulness of the 'harmonic model'. We know that Planck's hypothesis contradicted Bohr's, but that eventually the two became merged. It was demonstrated that an atom (made up of a nucleus around which electrons with negative electric charges circulated) can only assume certain relatively stable configurations, and that when it shifts from one static state to another which has less energy, it loses a quantum or a whole number of energy quanta.

From then on, *double determinations* (continuous and discontinuous, positive and negative, finite and non-finite, etc.) come into play in microphysical material reality. Wave mechanics and quantum mechanics were to develop the harmonic model. The propagation of light waves allows for static states, relative stabilities, trajectories and discontinuities, in short, corpuscles. If continuous waves appear in corpuscular form, the corpuscles themselves will in turn become part of the vibrational movements (waves). The energy contained in the wave associated with a corpuscle spreads like that corpuscle. The 'wave/corpuscle' dichotomy and the 'continuous/discontinuous' dichotomy can no longer be separated from the idea that matter and the field occupied by physical (material) forces are dynamic.

And so it became possible to interpret these discoveries (which revolutionized physics) as a brilliant vindication of dialectical methodology and of dialectical materialism as a philosophy, and there were many who had no hesitation in doing so. The old geometric and mechanistic physics of continuous trajectories, simple fields, and discontinuous physical bodies posited without any concrete link with the surrounding continuousness, became old-fashioned. Although, on a rough estimate, this appeared to be quite correct, it was limited by its own logical character. If we are to grasp objective, material nature in all its profoundness, we need to make our concepts dialectical and to introduce dialectical ideas and movements. Is it not imperative to admit or to reaffirm a dialectic of nature?

And yet, is it really that simple? Are we not going rather too fast? Let us pause to think. How can the 'continuous/discontinuous' relation and the 'wave/corpuscle' relation be determined in microphysical reality? To begin with, determinations were posited as different and oppositional, and thus were seen as mutually exclusive. Then connections were discovered. These discoveries took place at the beginning of the era of classic physics: the study of optical phenomena (spectrums, rays, diffusion and diffraction) and of vibrating strings. From then on it became impossible to say that concepts and objects (fields and bodies considered as physical realities) can be grasped by thought and consciousness 'without reciprocal contact', which for Lenin and for Hegel is the essence of antidialectic. We can even say that the unity discovered between opposites or contraries modifies their relations and turns them into contradictions (dialectically). Thus we can talk about a dialectical movement of thought just as we can about the making of concepts and operational techniques dialectical. Moreover, these movements have a relation with objective reality, i.e., with movements in reality; this vibrating string, this tuning fork whose properties I am studying, 'exist'. They are fragments constructed from matter which existed before I did, which exist in front of me and outside of me; when I invent the formal implements which will allow me to define them and up to a certain point to demonstrate them, I am not creating their properties. In particular, the link between these properties and simple whole numbers and countable sets, static and distinct states, discrete units and relative stabilities, is an objective one.

And so can I cast caution to the winds and move from 'gnosiology' to cosmology and ontology by attributing nature with the dialectical movement I have just described? Can I make dialectical movement objective in knowledge without further process? This would be jumping the gun, and would pose problems which the philosophers of institutionalized dialectical materialism have failed to notice or have parenthesized. The scientists who revolutionized physics had no knowledge of dialectical thought and proceeded using experimentation on the one hand and formal rigour on the other. In so far as they had an 'ideology', it was a bourgeois one. But there is a more serious issue. Could the macrophysical material world be beyond dialectic? Could microphysics be governed by the dialectic of nature? The latter *is* dialectical and the former *is* non-dialectical, such is the effective conclusion of the official philosophy of nature, which serves it all up in a recklessly systematized mishmash of dialectical methodology and philosophic materialism. Now macrophysics is the world of our senses, of objects and of things, and of our social practice. *It is the world of the everyday.* According to this view, it would be perfectly stable, governed by logic and logic alone, like classic mechanics, and thus beyond dialectic! . . .

As it happens, the only way the science of physical reality can progress is by using the principle of correspondence (between levels of reality). If there is no longer any correspondence and analogy between the macrophysical level and the microphysical level, how can the latter be grasped? Only by reference to analogies and homologies can knowledge demonstrate differences. By granting it an absolute and abstract stability, the dialectic of nature not only makes the 'human world' of relative stabilities, discourse and logic incomprehensible, but also severs the correspondence between its different levels.

What exactly do we mean when we talk about a 'dialectic of nature' and of 'matter' on the microphysical level, the level of waves and corpuscles? Do we mean that there is a mobility, a movement of matter, a process of becoming? That is certainly true of classic mechanics and of trajectories. Do we mean that although they are distinct, the terms we use – matter and energy, wave and corpuscle, continuity and discontinuity, etc. – have a relation and a unity?

Although it is obvious that they do, what that relation is remains unclear. Are they identical? In that case we would seesaw between clarity and logical identicalness, and the absurdity of an absolute identicalness between terms which *a priori* are distinct and mutually relative. Are they contradictory, a set of contradictions? But that would imply the stability of a 'system' which becomes difficult to understand. It is true that stabilities are always provisional, and that they have critical moments. It is true that every structure collapses, or has the potential to do so. These considerations do not eliminate the very general and creative problem of stability and (relative) constants in the process of becoming. Moreover, the concepts of conflict, contradiction and antagonism do not exonerate us from the need experimentally to study critical moments and moments of rupture, the collapse of structures, and 'destructurations'.

So long and in so far as a 'system' remains stable (presenting static states, constancy and 'bodies'), can we talk about 'dialectic'? Only if we take great care. It is true that we do not really know what happens between the plucking of a string and its return to the stability of a static state (i.e., harmonics). To a certain extent and until further notice, transitions and transitionals cannot be calculated using mathematical implements. Equally, it is true that the string may snap. That is not our concern here. As long as our study highlights static states, constants, relative stabilities and the numbers which express them, we will remain on the level of logic, and we will not have the right to 'transcend' that level. All we can do is patiently to make the concepts dialectical, while avoiding the *philosophical* operation of creating an ontology: an 'in-itself' dialectic of nature. To do so would be to abandon our model; we would be turning our concepts into representation and turning provisional conclusions drawn from our model into absolutes. Stability (and this is almost a paradox) is much more related to discontinuity than it is to an 'existential' or 'ontological' continuity. Here, dialectical thought consists of a study of stabilities and structures which does not overlook the process of becoming, and of a study of the process of becoming which does not overlook stabilities. In short, it is a question of grasping structurations without omitting the process of becoming which dismantles them and which is already active within structuration per se. Thus our answer to the question about dialectic in nature will itself be dialectical, i.e., not 'yes' or 'no', but 'yes and no' (perhaps yes, perhaps no!). We will develop the harmonic model until we have exhausted it, and we will refuse to use philosophy to transcend it.

It is a truism that the achievements of contemporary physics have resulted in a promotion of logic and a dialectization of concepts, and thus in the consolidation of a dialectical logic as a level of thought.[22] The logical *formalization* of thought in mathematics and physics has become more profound in that it has been accompanied by a gradual *dialectization* of logic. But (unless we use a philosophical postulate which we must declare as such, and which greatly exceeds both the content and the form of knowledge) we have no right to go straight to the absolute by decreeing a dialectic of nature which our mind can immediately grasp. The official Marxist theory of *reflection* not only admits a dialectic of nature, but also supposes that our minds can seize it fully and exhaust it, since they 'reflect' it.

The concept of *complementarity* which comes to us from microphysics is in no way privileged. To grant it a special importance would be to set it up as a philosophy; we would soon be replacing the old determinist philosophy with a non-determinist metaphysics. The concept conceals the model and stops us finding the unknown elements which the harmonic model contains and to which it is a pointer (notably whatever happens between the initial disturbance and the static states in the transitionals). Thus the concept of complementarity is no more important or essential than those of reciprocity, interaction, contrariness or contradiction and antagonism. It does not account for the formation of stabilities (structuration), or for transitions, breaks or critical points. And yet, in so far as we can observe interactions between 'dual' properties, and relative stabilities, structures or forms deep within interactions, we can no more dispense with complementarity than we can with difference, contrariness, polarity, oppositeness and reciprocity of action, etc. With an extraordinary confusion between levels of thought and of reality, contemporary philosophers have believed in the dialectic of complementarity, while at the same time affirming the incompatibility of this concept with dialectical thought. With the same inextricable confusion, philosophers tried to remove stability from dialectic,[23] and then by some kind of miracle to extrapolate stability from antagonistic contradiction.

And so, when speaking about material nature, would we say: '*There are dialectical movements and processes, and there are stabilities which are based upon a refined logic'*? No matter how cautious this statement is, it cannot satisfy us completely. How can we separate logic from dialectic?

And could we distinguish between regional ontologies, by saying: '*There are regions for dialectic and for the process of becoming, and others for stability and logic. Similarly, nature is one region of being, and history or consciousness is another; dialectic may have a role to play in nature, at least in terms of region and species, but alienation never can. In history, consciousness and praxis, specific dialectic and alienation can both have a role to play*'? But how can we place these regions or regional ontologies in relation to each other? The idea of totality collapses. But totality is the inspiration behind our research, in which – above all and against all odds – we are striving to be systematic.

Would continuousness be the world's ontological background (or as someone who is 'listening in' on being might say, its background noise), against which objects, things, action, events and relative stabilities stand out? That is nothing more than a metaphysical thought; only in science fiction does an absolute 'continuum' in space and time, which is revealed only in so far as it is inaccessible, appear as a serious object of discourse. There are philosophers who draw their imagery from science fiction, but without really realizing that they are doing so.

Finally, could we say: '*The non-dialectical position is imperative for dialectic, that is its background and its foundation. When that position is present, dialectic enters into contradiction with itself. It posits and presupposes stableness in order to conquer and destroy it*'? This would be going back to Hegel, or even farther, to Fichte.[24]

Therefore we are finding the transition from methodology (or gnosiology) to an ontology extremely difficult to achieve. And yet, reliable sources – social practice, language – tell us that knowledge and method correspond to 'something'. This 'something' is revealed subsequently, in the history of knowledge. None of the schematics available to represent it in advance is satisfactory. In these conditions, there is only one way in, and only one way out: to abandon the system (momentarily, but probably for quite a long time), to abandon the comprehensive picture of the universe, and to abandon ontology – while making sure not to return to empiricism, positivism or simplified logicism.

Rather than exploring 'being', we must explore what is possible (and this includes the exploration of space, and the transformation of everyday life). Would not 'being' reveal itself in what is possible and by what is possible at the same time as it realizes itself historically? Is this not what the idea of total praxis implies? From this perspective, classic ontology would harbour a serious error, namely the wish to reach 'being' after the act, via the past and via what has been accomplished and made actual, in a metaphysical repetition, a new beginning or eternal return, a resurrection, a reminiscence. It tries to use thought to reduce the double determinations of the actual, and primarily by the rift between thought and reality. It ends up in a dilemma: it must either admit divine creation, or endow matter with a quality or property which already contains consciousness and spirit. Now these two affirmations are unacceptable. What right have we to attribute to the *non-finite* universe qualities and properties which only have a meaning in our *finite* world, at a fleeting moment of the development of mankind on Planet Earth?

Ontology is worn out. Let us use the exploration of what is possible and the development of knowledge to discover modalities of thought with which to replace it. Let us develop a metaphilosophy. In the meantime, let us make a careful distinction between the levels of reality and thought, while taking care not to merge whatever is linked together and not to separate whatever appears distinctive.

Will this detour (which is brief but at the same time lengthy) through the labyrinth of so-called philosophical questions be a digression from our subject: everyday life? No. It will enable us to draw up a series of propositions.

First, we must not overlook the constancies and (relative) stabilities of everyday life, but nor must we fetishize them. The everyday per se does not have the viscous consistency which is often attributed to it, nor the evanescent, fluid mobility which is a corollary of that representation. Stabilities are definitive in appearance only, and we must avoid confusing them with 'the real', the 'existential', 'being', 'substance' or 'human nature'. Once we penetrate a stability, its limits become apparent on all sides. We may think it is compact and durable. The critical thought inherent in knowledge dissolves this illusion.

Second, the solar–planetary model has long been presented as universal, and it still has an influence in the domain of the social sciences. Does it not underpin representations of hierarchies in the family and in the state? For our study of everyday man, we prefer to use the harmonic model, in so far as any physical model can be of help to us. Not only are we to trying make a kind of spectrum analysis of the everyday; we also consider that stabilities and periodicities emerge from a set of fleeting and profound phenomena: transitionals and transitions. Forms and structures, or static states, are born and prosper against a background of fleeting states which works select and consolidate. The actual and the potential are united in an intelligible way. Static states can extend towards limitlessness – towards formlessness. Whatever is fleeting and transitional receives forms and structures which deform or transform it but which do not abolish it. There is much that is unknown or unforeseen in these relations and connections, which are yet to be defined with any clarity. When we use this model we will often employ the terms 'formants' and 'partials' as used in harmonic analysis, rather than the word 'element', which is used in conventional analysis. However, we will not use them to hide 'dys-harmonies' and conflicts.

Third, we will say: 'In nature, history, society and knowledge there is a multiplicity of dialectical movements, each one distinct and specific.' Transposing the physical principle of the superposition of small movements and oscillations, we will go so far as to say: 'There are as many or more dialectical movements in social consciousness as there are waves on the surface of the sea.' We will never say: 'Dialectic wants . . . dialectic does . . .'. We will only employ the word 'dialectical', i.e., as an adjective, never as a noun. Moreover we will know that a dialectical movement of thought (or in thought) never coincides absolutely with a dialectical movement in nature, history or thought per se. This last proposition may seem paradoxical, but it means that thinking never exhausts the content of a concept or of a thought, and that there is a dialectical relation between all movements. Such a coincidence – which the vulgar representation of *reflection* postulates or suggests – would exhaust any objective dialectical movement by a thought or a concept, and would be 'exhausting' for human thought and for praxis. The identicalness of two dialectical movements is an *idea*, and can never be anything more than an idea, pointing to a convergence at infinity which is both necessary to postulate and impossible to attain. However, if there can never be an absolute coincidence of two dialectical movements for human thought (i.e., identicalness between an objective movement and a subjective movement of thought), nor can there ever be mutual externality. Dialectical thought grasps objective movements *partially* (fragmentarily, in approximative and provisional propositions), and in its own particular way (the way of knowledge – the process and the history of knowledge – through the specific contradictions of knowledge, which are not completely unconnected to the contradictions of society, history or nature, but which are resolved in another way). *The result is that a dialectical movement never takes place entirely within language.* Discourse can never express it adequately. Would not the idea of a total discourse also be an idea taken to the limit, to infinity? Discourse must make several approximative attempts before it can 'say' a dialectical movement, and even then it will never be exhaustive. The verbalization of praxis and the use of (day-to-day or sophisticated) concepts are both equally inadequate for the task. In short, just like concepts, language must use thought and knowledge effectively to make itself dialectical. Language is a work, the work of a society.

Discourse is an important if not essential fact of the everyday. It is controlled by logic (although in everyday life it never achieves the formal rigour which a logician's mind can draw from it). It is controlled by 'the world of objects', by concerns about stability, by effective stabilities, by questions which require yes-or-no answers. Dialectical movement reveals itself in the gaps and breaks in coherent discourse. At times the gaps and breaks or, so to speak, the holes within discourse, give rise to irrational obscurity or formlessness (the 'infralinguistic' level), and at others to the irruption of deeper movements (the 'supralinguistic' level). Thus we can define dialectical thought neither as incoherence nor as a higher coherence (discourse on discourse, or total discourse). Often it starts with play on words (including the most famous one of all, *aufheben*, to abolish and to construct, thus to supersede). It must stimulate discourse in some way, assaulting it even, in order to force it to say things which language would not put into words, and would even conceal. When Hegel brought dialectical movement in general to language, he achieved something unique, but he did not exhaust dialectical movements, nor did he make discourse absolutely and definitively dialectical.

257

And so we need to note a sort of unceasing dialectical movement between Logos (logic, discourse, the everyday) and dialectical thought per se. To elevate or bring a specific aspect of praxis (and the everyday itself) to language, to pass it into language, is an essential task for thought; it is a creative endeavour, and even a revolutionary act. To speak actions, events and objects – to put them into words – is the only means for conceiving of them (for developing concepts). However, language and discourse are not self-sufficient, and are always inadequate. The philosophical privilege granted to Logos by contemporary thought tells us much about the difficulties of philosophy: it is much more a position of retreat than an impregnable fortress. One level of experience and one part of the (everyday) real are passed off as being equals to totality. No doubt is cast either on the object of knowledge or on its reflection within the mind: they coincide, or almost. This implies a postulate: that the part is appropriate to the whole. But this implication is ignored. The mistake is so obvious that the philosophical and almost ontological privilege invested in the Word comes in tandem with a profound social crisis of language, expressivity and the 'world of expression'. It is as though praxis itself were refuting the appropriateness of the part to the whole, by destroying it! Language and discourse are valid only in so far as they are superseded by a tense and concerted effort, on all sides and in all directions: towards the everyday and towards the poetic, towards logical rigour and towards dialectic, towards the 'infra' level and towards the 'supra' level.

Therefore dialectical thought implies a permanent critique and autocritique of discursiveness, of logic, and of their categories. Let us repeat something we have said many times before. Dialectical contradiction is radically different from logical contradiction (or absurdity). It is reason on a higher level of intelligibility. Once grasped, it founds itself both as fact and as concept. Although it is inexhaustible, it is not irrational, arational or transrational. It develops on the conceptual plane where, in an ever-repeated process, concepts are rendered dialectical. As such, dialectical thought is clearly indispensable for all the sciences as well as for knowledge of praxis, but this does not confer any kind of a priori upon it. Dialectical thought avoids empiricism and it avoids rationalist construction. The moment of critique (the negative) is essential to it.

Therefore although language and discourse are facts of everyday life, a great effort will be needed to make them express the everyday. Language and discourse are part of everyday life, but this does not mean that we can put the everyday into words easily. To experience banality is not enough to tell us what banality actually is. Thought about the everyday tends to be limited to thought about everyday discourse (language). So it tends towards a simple semantics, a logic of the everyday, or simply a description of banality, whereas the aim should be to discover certain hidden movements: need/desire, private/public, natural/artificial, serious/frivolous, work/outside work, alienation/disalienation, etc. With their particularized movements, their specific contradictions and their interactions, these resonances and dissonances deep within the everyday are revealed only slowly and with difficulty.

Fourth, since we have not projected dialectical contradiction, logical identicalness, contrariness or complementarity on to being, nature or the absolute, we can discern *types* of contradiction. This is the kind of typology attempted by institutional Marxism, which distinguishes between contradiction and antagonism (in a way which purports to be linked rationally with practice, but which in fact comes straight from political empiricism).

Let us take the typology a stage further. First we distinguish an initial type, which is the contradiction to be found in concepts and representations, and which is resolved essentially by an effort of consciousness. Supersession always operates within a form or a structure of social consciousness. Principally, it modifies representations or concepts. Supersession takes place in and through language, by means either of a promotion (which delivers certain things into language) or of an invention (of words, images or symbols), but this does not mean that it becomes completely separated from practical action. This kind of invention of words, symbols and images – in short, of ideologies and representations – has its quota of effectiveness, and does not purely and simply 'reflect' accomplished facts with the aim of justifying them. It creates something: a unit within the whole. Since contradictions *between ideas* can be resolved in and through an effort of consciousness, this effort is itself an action. As soon as it resolves conflicts between representations in a *work*, it creates a unity. In this sense, any cultural, philosophic or aesthetic work is a highly complex social product, and quite distinct from material products. It does not simply reflect or express contradictions; it supersedes them and resolves them 'through ideas' or in and through a proposition, i.e., a unifying hypothesis. If this proposition brings forth new conflicts, we only notice this later, during a historical process. In itself, the *work* is a unit and a whole, and it also creates a unit and a whole: a specific unit made actual within the whole. Its content is indefinitely analysable, and thus inexhaustible. It contains the (provisional) unity of the non-finite and the finite.

We will distinguish between this first type of contradiction and those which, in the way they are represented, are insoluble by the effort of thought (knowledge) alone, but which are apparently *possible* to solve by means of creative praxis. The interested parties see the problems arising from the process of becoming, and in what these problems bring they see the actions which may modify them. By making the problems real, they resolve the conflict by establishing a higher unit. Then they must grasp profound dialectical movements which demand to be superseded: conjuncture and structure, problematic situation and categoric givens. In this case, no intellectual or cultural *work* – or no philosophical, aesthetic or ethical one – can offer or even suggest a solution.[25]

The distinction we have proposed is not exactly the same as the theoretical (methodological) difference between contrariness and contradiction, for it is well and truly a matter of *conflicts* between representations (ideologies, symbols, concepts). Moreover, no representation can remain purely 'representative', and all representations are represented in the real (practical) world. These conflicts stimulate the creation (production) of works and are momentarily resolved in a work. In 'real' life, every work is transformed more or less profoundly into a way of living and of acting.

Nor is the distinction the same as the political (practical) difference between reform and revolution. It is true that the second type of contradiction corresponds to the revolutionary situation. People can no longer go on living as before. They can no longer use representations to resolve their conflicts. So the question is one no longer of interpreting 'the world' – the human and natural real – in an (aesthetic, philosophical or moral) work, but of changing it. Therefore the change must be achieved within the context of the way of life and living conditions: in and through praxis. However, the changes which come about as a result of such situations do not always revolutionize ways of living. If they can affect 'real' life – ways of living and of acting – they can also express themselves in works and in simple changes of representation.

Finally there are the contradictions which at the moment are insoluble, i.e., whose resolution does not even appear *possible*. However, we cannot say for certain that such a situation will last for ever. Marx wrote that humanity only sets itself problems it can resolve, as though every problem already implied the burgeoning consciousness of solutions (possibilities). But surely this formulation is too optimistic. As for the pessimistic and nihilistic formula: 'Humanity only sets itself insoluble problems', it is untenable. The deepest contradictions are tenacious; the problems they pose can only be solved in the long term. Applying our thought to praxis, we will be able to distinguish between what is immediately possible and what is possible in the long term (but impossible for the present), and between the possible impossible and the absolutely (and ipso facto inconceivable) impossible. Therefore there is a profound analogy between the effort of an artist or a philosopher to express and resolve contradictions on the plane of 'ideas' (but in a 'real' work) and the general effort of individuals in social practice to formulate and resolve their problems. In the first case, the activity of creative consciousness produces a work which disalienates in relation to certain experienced contradictions but which produces another specific alienation (which may be ideological, philosophical or artistic, etc.). The work is a product, although not all products are works. In the second case, activity realizes individual possibilities; at first these are nebulous, but during his history the individual makes them actual in a generally limited series of choices; he becomes what he was; he produces and is what he becomes. His everyday life is a work of creativity. It is far from being a free and conscious work. It can sometimes transpire that the creative effort ends pathologically, in neurosis or psychosis. In its way, a pathological state is the creative work of an individual, elaborated, systematized, coherent and everyday, which resolves – badly – the inner contradictions of his consciousness (but without 'reflecting' the brutally objective, psychological or social external conditions which are shared equally by all the individuals of a class or an era). The pathological state is a lived work of creativity: a personal product, a bad solution to a conflict between what is possible and what is impossible. The pathological state disalienates in relation to the initial conflictive situation, but plunges the mentally alienated individual into a deeper alienation, by the fact that he imagines that the initial contradiction has been resolved by the creative work he is living through: the delirium, the pathological state itself.

One corollary of the typology of contradictions is a typology of negativities. In one case, negativity attacks representations; in another, it undermines situations; in a third, it challenges and dismantles the totality of what exists. The univocal and general negativity (the ontology) of Hegelianism – in its diluted version, contemporary existentialism – cannot satisfy us; it is of no use to concrete analysis (except perhaps in formulating the problem of analysis per se, which as we know implies general negativity, since if used without due caution it breaks, dissociates and isolates, taking differences to the point where they become separate and analogies to the point where they become merged). Beyond a certain limit, the negative becomes a fetish, a vision of nothingness; radical critique becomes hypercritique, and nihilism is established as a truth without that truth having been legitimized. Like dialectical movement, negativity or negation will always appear to us as particularized and specific: sometimes as a lack and a gap, sometimes as a (perceived or unperceived) absence, sometimes as a breakdown or a point of disintegration. We will see it at work in a variety of ways: challenges, disturbances, disintegration.

Should we attribute any 'functions' to negativity? Only with a great many reservations. For example, certain thinkers consider that terror has a sociological 'function', namely to drive the masses into an action of which it is the cause and the effect. Terror could be seen as the embodiment of the negative in political and historical action. Now on the other hand we could agree with Marx and Lenin that when the masses genuinely enter political life the need for violence and terror is reduced and even eliminated in favour of concrete democratization.

In any event, the ideas of specific negativity and supersession bring with them the radical rejection of one particularly tenacious fetishism which we will never stop criticizing, and that is the fetishism of 'the real' and 'the positive'. To present the negative in all its profundity, we shall use the precise concept we have used before: the concept of the *possible* (equally specified and concrete). Between the world which is chock-a-block full of realism and positivism, and the gaping world of pure negativity and nihilism, our aim is to discover the open world, the world of what is possible. We are not confusing this with indeterminateness, although it is not without chance and randomness.

11 Logic and characterology

We previously mentioned a dialectical movement within methodology itself. The formal already contains specificity (content and concreteness) and vice versa. Where specificity is concerned, it encompasses the formal because the formal also has realness, socially, in praxis. Thus the level of logical thought cannot be isolated and pushed to one side in an abstraction external to reality in general and to stabilities in particular (provisional balances, self-regulations, series of decisions and choices, etc.). Therefore when we pass from the abstract to the concrete, we must already be taking on 'the real' and recognizing it. The way we are going to apply this theoretical notion will seem paradoxical. In effect, to bring something which appears to be completely irreducible to logic – i.e., individual character – into logical patterns deemed to be inherent to the everyday real is almost attempting the impossible. Nevertheless we shall attempt to determine the logical frameworks of such a characterology.

It is easy to discover relations of opposition, of polarity, and even of complementarity between individualities. Every historical period offers types of individuality, the relations between which can only be understood by means of these formal concepts. Let us recall the feudal baron and the knight who devotes himself to defending the widow and the orphan, the faithful knight and the treacherous knight; the giant of art and knowledge in the times of da Vinci and Michelangelo, and the condottiere; Savonarola the mystic and the Machiavellian mind; the saint and the adventurer; the militant and the arriviste, etc. The opposition of these types does not exhaust their connections. Once we have analysed the way they are polarized, we must try to understand historically how such opposing types came into being simultaneously. The ways in which they relate would appear to be more complex than the ways in which they oppose and complement one another.

Correlation, complementarity and the division into opposites are transferred into the 'soul' and the individual consciousness. As Kierkegaard wrote in his Journals, it takes at least two men to make up a single one: Pantagruel and Panurge, Sancho Panza and Don Quixote, Leporello and Don Giovanni, *Jacques le fataliste* and his master, Faust and Mephistopheles (and the latter is a bit more than half of one man, and a bit less too!). Several great works have projected the parts (or formants) of the human soul into opposing and complementary individuals. As a result, every 'soul' seems to be made up of at least two individual souls. However, what is presented in art as a lively dialogue between two complementary individuals occurs in the 'lived' in the guise of a more or less profound conflict. The logical relation of opposition does not exhaust the real relations. Moreover, we have not yet reached the limits of the logical connections.

Let us leave history now and consider existing (bourgeois) society. In this society, the relation between the individual and the social exists. How could it not exist? The mutual exteriority of the individual and the social has never been anything more than a deceptive representation: even when the individual thinks he is separating himself from society, he remains a social being. And so the relation exists, but social reality is such that this real and incomplete relation lies hidden; for this reason it can be misunderstood. It is neither conscious nor unconscious in the sense that an occult or obscure substantial reality is. It is hidden beneath representations which render it effective and efficient: norms, attitudes, symbols, values. The present-day conformism which lies at the heart of everyday banality is happy to accept norms and models as though they were the true 'individual/society' relation, rather than an effective mediation of it. An essential element of the structure of this society and of the 'individual/society' relations within its frameworks is that there be a lack of knowledge of them. And if the real relation does become apparent, it is always in an incomplete and mutilated manner. Is this not what happens in the large economic and bureaucratized organizations within monopolistic state capitalism? The individual firmly believes in 'society', and sees himself as a member of it; but this society is nothing more than a limited company, in the capitalist sense.[26]

Because the 'individual/society' relation is not known or recognized as such, because it remains opaque and because certain of the socially imposed ways it is represented do not tally with the 'lived' (the individual within praxis), the individual tries to find out what this relation really is. His lack of knowledge gives rise to a fundamental uneasiness which is as stimulating as it is destructive, and this is the context in which he reconstructs the relation. But he does so using representations which have been developed for this very purpose. The 'individual/society' relation becomes the object of a variety of theorizations which employ elements borrowed on the one hand from the lived and from society as a whole, and on the other from institutions and ideologies. Ignored or misunderstood, the real relation becomes completely alienated and fossilized (reified) in a deceptive and limiting representation. Instead of participating fully and consciously in social praxis, the individual constructs himself on the basis of a particular form and a representation of that form. In his effort to rediscover the hidden relation he strays even farther from it and loses his powers (his possibilities). He becomes imprisoned within himself. This attitude by which he is formed as a conscious individual, and which will soon become a mere collection of behaviour patterns and stereotypes, implies some deceptively creative postulates: the 'individual/society' relation must and can be created – society has a coherence and a unity, since its inner contradictions are not of prime importance. Thus in all good conscience, good will and good faith, the individual will build his 'soul'. The basic materials of this 'soul' will be representations, and these will come up against other, previously accepted representations, which they will either challenge or reinforce. In all good conscience, the individual will believe that he is living to the full; his 'soul' will be his own creative work, and even a kind of cultural work in which creativity and representations are lived as everyday facts. In so far as they are stable realities, these 'souls' enter into a logical structure within dialectical movement. This determination interacts with the other economic and social determinations. It superimposes itself on them in a complex relation of resonance or dissonance. It does not supplant them and does not destroy them.

In the relation thus put together, i.e., constructed, let us observe three (logical) moments:

a *general, abstract, metaphysical:* the relation of the 'soul' with society in general, represented as a whole;
b *particular, positive, pragmatic:* since he perceives society as a given, the problem for the individual is to establish a determined relation with this given society, in given conditions;
c *singular, mystic, personal:* the representation which the individual has of himself as difference and in-difference, as irreducible originality and as personality.

Thus the active representation and the 'lived' which it represents enter into the logical pattern of classic syllogism: general/particular/singular. Each logical 'moment' implies another, and they all assume substance and reality independently of each other. Thus in the everyday reality of existing (bourgeois) society we find the general type, the particular type and the singular type, each one emphasizing a logical element or moment; what is more, at the heart of each class or type we rediscover all the other moments, in a subordinated or recessive state. For example, in the class (in the logical sense of the term), i.e., in the general type, we will recognize one general type (or subclass, or subtype), another particular one and another singular one. Thus we will have a formal combination: A.B.C.; A (a,b,c), B (a,b,c), C (a,b,c); A (aa, ab, ac . . .) with implied types, subtypes and sub-subtypes.

A. *The general type.* This is the highest class or type; he considers the relation with society consciously and takes it as a constant object of thought and meditation; however, his consciousness of the social remains abstract.

A.a. *The Utopian.* Utopianism poses the fundamental problem of the individual/society relation in such perfectly clear terms that the absurdity of formulating it abstractly by means of two mutually independent and external terms becomes blindingly obvious. The Utopian knows that the truth of praxis consists in a conscious oneness: the everyday/the whole, the individual/society, or even the individual/the human race. However he sees this truth as a pure ideal outside the real, something to be created *ex nihilo*. He cannot see that this oneness already exists, but in an incomplete way, mutilated, alienated, mainly because it lacks conscious expression. Thus the Utopian in the classic sense of the term wishes to create a new society and an entirely new life, with new men, individuals united in their desire to sign up to a new social contract. He thinks this is easy to achieve, since it relies merely on the consent of a certain number of minds similar to his own. He is not very aware of the practical conditions and problems. For him, the principle of the identicalness and oneness of the 'individual/society' relation remains general, logical and abstract, rather than being concrete and dialectical. Devoid of means, the pure aim becomes a false one. Mankind will fail, but the failure will be a noble one.

Subtypes: 'Idealists' in the commonplace sense; dreamers, reformers and founders of sects; leaders of literary or artistic movements, etc.

Sub-subtypes: the misunderstood, martyrs, minor poets . . .

A.b. *The man of action.* The opposite of the Utopian, and his complement, he gives priority to the real, realization and means. For him, the data of problems are solid ground. He uses them as a foothold. He has little concern for what may be in the distance. He accepts goals which come from beyond himself and his own thought. He spends little time mulling over the goals and a lot of time on the interests and on the solid means of action. In the case of the Utopian, only the ends counted, and without means, the true goal became a false one. In the case of the man who wants action for action's sake, good and genuine means become dubious if the goal for which they are used is an uncertain one. He thinks he is free, but he is the unconscious slave of real historical forces. If genuine freedom can be defined as knowledge and mastery of necessity, the freedom of the pure man of action can be defined as ignorance of his own enslavement. Among the humbler representatives of this type we find agents and hired men – among its more illustrious representatives are enlightened despots, and certain captains of industry and kings of finance. They can only 'succeed' by exploiting the stupidity of other people; their careers end tragically and they cannot understand what has happened to them.

Opposed subtypes: the activist and the militant; the organizer and organizational man; the politician; the boss; the male 'Rastignac' and the female one (a recent species).[27]

A.c. *The thinker.* He despises the Utopian because the Utopian is not a man of action. He despises the man of action because the man of action is not a Utopian. He is a thinker, therefore he thinks. He is particularly fond of problems of method. He tends to emphasize personality, which he understands to be the opposite of the social, but he tries to reconcile this opposition by being adaptable. In fact, the thinker is a subordinate of the Utopians in ideological terms, and a subordinate of the men of action in practical terms. Deluded by his own methodological or 'intellectual' efficiency, he effortlessly combines the inactivity of the former with the lack of awareness of the latter. He interprets the world, and thinks he has transformed it. He comes to believe that ideas act by themselves, or ends up adopting an ideology which justifies his real life.

Opposed and complementary subtypes: the systematic philosopher; the essayist; the eternally misunderstood; the resigned woman; the embittered cuckold, etc.

B. *The particular type.* The 'individual/social' relation ceases to be perceived as such. If there is any awareness of the social, it is as the postulate of a limited practical activity. Thus the relation is reduced to the particularity of the individual within a limited group. In the words of this individual, philosophers are not practical, and there is no social problem; everything is a mere question of force and adaption, whether by constraint or by consent.

B.a. *The civil servant (the bureaucrat).* With a bit of preferential treatment, a little savvy, a serious attitude and a couple of qualifications, all will be well. Remember the respect we owe to the hierarchy inside which we are on the up and up. Things being what they are, all we need do is to be virtuous in principle, i.e., to make virtue the principle of the state and to make decency the principle of bureaucracy.

Subtypes: the conformist; the specialist; the well-informed man who has his finger on the pulse of things; the pedant (the policeman of knowledge); the citizen; the matron or eternal mother; the member of the *Académie française*.

B.b. *The middleman or the bohemian.* The reverse and the complement of the bureaucrat, this ersatz civil servant tries to occupy every available hole in the social automatism to which he owes his appointment. Although this has no status, and comes to him from outside, he considers it to be the freest and most internalized act of his own personal initiative. Although his function is to act as a safety valve or conductor, he sees himself at the summit of the hierarchy. He despises bureaucracy for being too staid and too pragmatic, and thinks he is using it. In fact, by sweetening its brutal methods and by adapting it to local conditions, it is he who is being used by bureaucracy.

Opposed and complementary subtypes: people in 'public relations' and 'personnel management'; publicity agents; literary critics (benign ones); lawyers; well-meaning little priests; brokers; masters of ceremony; detectives, etc.

B.c. *The independent man*. He believes that conscientious work is the only road to success. 'After all, we need right-minded folk who do an honest day's work and who are not there merely for the show. Maybe us lot aren't famous, but at least we're our own men. The state, civil servants, thinkers and what they think, art, religion – what's it all for if not to be made use of and to make our lives that little bit more enjoyable . . .?' Such are the independent man's thoughts as he sets up his little business. A good husband and a good father, off he goes to war to get conveniently killed for his country. Is he the unknown soldier? He certainly is. On fixed days of the year he remembers that he is a citizen, and goes to vote. His life may revolve around himself and his relationships, but he has a clear conscience, for surely his way of life is essential not only to himself but also for the well-being and existence of society. 'If everyone thought only of themselves, and if God thought of everyone, what a wonderful world it would be.'

Opposed and complementary subtypes: the criminal; the scab; the professional double-dealer; the expert; the pure glance and the voyeur.

C. *The singular type*. In the previous two classes of types, the relation with the social existed, but in a mystified form and reconstructed misleadingly in a representation. So in A.a, the relation appears as goodwill, followed by an inability to make it real. In A.b, the relation is as sharply presented as it is in A.a, but in a negative form: the strength of this *positive* character comes from his *negative* completeness. This type of individual has sold his goodwill in exchange for success. He imagines that the structure of society is there to serve him, and that by exploiting it he has overcome the 'individual/society' division or the 'private/public' division to his personal advantage. In fact, although he is using society for his own ends and is controlling it for that purpose, he is allowing himself to become enslaved by the reactionary social forces of that society, without knowing how, and without even realizing it. In A.c, the relation degenerates somewhat more, both in practice and in its representation. Rather than being negative, it becomes indifferent. The individual puts himself 'above society'. This is why the philosopher finds it so easy to imagine that he has overcome the fundamental contradictions, in the Mind, or in his system.

In the B groups, we no longer find society as a whole, either as a practice or as a representation. The relation is between delimited spheres, and society as a whole disintegrates into particular groups. Every individual in these groups enters into contact with one or several 'circles' which he takes to be society as a whole. In this way the civil servant, or even the professional intellectual, believes in the generality of his experience, whereas in fact all he has experienced is a sum total of particularities and particular groups. The middleman imagines that he has a strategy for overcoming the fragmentation and the division of labour: to travel everywhere, to see the world. He thinks he has grasped the totality, whereas in fact he is fulfilling a function: he links people together. As for the independent type, he buries his head in the realness of a fragmented activity and thinks he has resolved the same problem.

In group C, we witness the complete degeneration of the 'individual/social' relation. Not only does it become blurred; it also dissolves and vanishes. The term 'society' disappears from consciousness; but the only way it can really disappear is as a result of a pathological state. Thus society appears to be completely disguised, and the return to generality is achieved by the invention of completely phoney representations. So logical structure does not stop alienation. This is two-sided, and consists of a weakening of any concrete link, and of a series of arbitrary representations (ethical, aesthetic, etc.). The individual man of type C sees himself facing the 'world' alone, and he tries to attain it without the mediation of the social, of history and of practice. An intuitive sense of a pure 'self' leads him from a lived, everyday situation into irrefutable fetishisms. Here, character per se disappears. Everything becomes attitude, role-play, theatricals, acted out on the theoretical stage of a vulgar empiricism.

C.a. *The fanatic.* A coarsely egotistical 'self' disguises itself under cosmic banners: god, nature, 'world'. This individual sees himself facing the universe, and his only relation is with the 'world'. Thus he believes himself to be universal, whereas in fact nobody could be more singular. He asserts himself hypocritically by using the 'world' as a sphere of influence and self-justification. This character, or rather this attitude, encompasses various stages and variants, from the cold-blooded calculator disguised as a Kindly Soul to the religious fanatic. This type is forceful and ferocious in equal measure.

Subtypes: the Lady; the pseudo-poet; the Kindly Souls.

C.b. *The oppositionist.* In C.a. there is a conscious emphasis on the 'world'. In C.b., the emphasis is expressly on the Self. C.a. says yes; C.b. says no. C.a. is a hypocrite; C.b. is a facile cynic. The type whose character is oppositional defines his 'self' as the contrary of someone or something, and often as the contrary of everything which is not him. He is 'pro everything anti, and anti everything pro'. He thinks he is more sharp-witted and human than the fanatic; and yet although his disposition is the complete opposite, he performs the same kind of social (i.e., antisocial) actions. Deep within his consciousness– unconsciousness he is often frustrated. Of all the types, this is probably the most unstable. Sometimes his relation with praxis sinks even lower, i.e., even farther from that of a genuine consciousness. Sometimes he finds a way out; he escapes from the prison of his own character. We can often detect traces of infantility in him, as well as many flagrant contradictions (for example, the superstitious atheist).

Subtypes: the ostentatious anarchist and the ostentatious anticleric; the hypercritic.

C.c. *The pompous idiot.* This one is well anchored in the everyday; he collects its most commonplace contents and inflates them crudely. He uses triviality to discover wisdom, a philosophy, a vision of the world. For example, he extracts proverbial sayings from their ironic context, their mutual oppositions and corrections, and turns them into eternal truths. There will always be rich people and there will always be poor people. Those people don't suffer as we do. Money can't buy you happiness. There will always be wars. You can't make an omelette without breaking eggs. We aren't choirboys. I'd rather be a happy pig than an unhappy Socrates. There's a nip in the air, etc. . . . .

The pompous idiots are so stupid that they seem harmless. Because of their retarded and blinkered individualism, they are easy prey for demagogues. Through the inertia and mechanical nature of their stupidity, they go farther than others more treacherous or more intelligent than themselves in disintegrating the social and the human.

Subtypes: these are innumerable: the sententious sage; the sermonizer; the avid reader; the 'public-spirited' man, etc.[28]

12 The total field

Throughout this book we have challenged the right of the particular and fragmented sciences to encompass the whole. Not one of them can claim sole right of access to 'totality', but each is entitled to continue pushing its investigations farther and farther, without barrier or impediment. But they can only grasp partial totalities.

Moreover, we have accepted the idea of a 'field', while rejecting the idea of a 'continuous field'. Areas, sectors and regions cannot be in pure and simple juxtaposition. However, the concepts of level, unevenness, hiatus or gaps rule out the representation of an immense, coherently constructed set of sub-sets: the Whole. Gaps, holes, shadows and reflections, absences – these too form part of the total field. Therefore we reject the idea of a vast continuum which the fragmentary sciences can methodically and analytically carve into pieces. We also reject the idea of a sum total of areas. Each specificity constitutes an area, but the distinctions are relative, and we have no right to carry them to the absolute.

While we recognize the difficulties inherent in the concept of 'totality', we cannot do without it. However, only if our methodology is scrupulously prudent have we the right to use it. How can we develop a more-or-less coherent model to represent the entire range of knowledge and the situation of our own specific science within it?

Would levels and stages constitute a hierarchy, from a low level (the physical level of inert, material nature) to the highest level of all (the ethical and aesthetic level)? The representation of a hierarchy like this is still much too simple. What criterion should we use to classify these stages and levels, in order of importance? Every stage can break away from its initial position, overturning the entire set and taking prominence both in reality and in thought. For instance, demography can invade the social and influence the course of history, or even modify it. The historical (such as a war) can disrupt the economic, etc. The pattern of an ascending series of stages is too much like a clumsy metaphor – a ladder or a flight of steps – to be acceptable.

Should we group the areas and sectors into a circular pattern, with each area going from the centre to a section of the circumference? Should we imagine a circle made up of circles, a ring made up of rings? This would be more useful than the ladder pattern, by bringing us closer to one important truth: namely, that everything is in everything and everything is total – and yet nothing that is, is in anything other than itself. Within oneness, there are differences and disjunctions; both actively and potentially, there is multiplicity. Every human 'being' is physical, biological, economic, social or sociological, but unevenly, according to the aspects and the moments, sometimes this one more than that one, sometimes that one more than this one, but without ever losing unity completely. So it is not simply a question of lighting, or of perspectives, but of a 'reality' which must be understood.

Sadly, the circular pattern is as static as the linear one. If we try making it mobile (by using the figure or form of the spiral rather than the circle, for example) it will become quite imprecise.

And so, just as we have rejected ontologies and cosmologies, let us (provisionally) give up trying to construct a defined and definitive representation, while at the same time making sure not to regress into positivism. The 'total field' we have before us is as rugged as a mountain landscape and as tempestuous as the sea. We have maps to guide us, but they make us forget how diverse and magnificent it all is. They pinpoint regions and small areas in a way which ignores the fluidity of their borderlines. When each discipline tries to attain the universal (the total) it cannot but stir up conflicts, and yet imperialism is mortal. Each one must find a *modus vivendi* for itself and for the others, making pacts which grant self-determination to those who live in the neighbouring sectors. Tensions are fruitful; subservience is sterile.

The total field can only be grasped in a fragmentary way. We look for totality, we aim for it: it is an Idea (like the idea of absolute knowledge). You imagine you have a fragment of it in your hands, you hold it tight, you cherish it, and suddenly it assumes all reality and truth. You have the audacity to claim that what you are grasping is totality itself. Then immediately it breaks into pieces again, and all that remains in your hands is but a tiny fragment.

What we are faced with here is a precise methodological problem: the problem of *relevance*. Given a set of facts, on what level should we place it, and according to what criterion? What lighting and what techniques should we use to get to grips with it?

It is a very general question, but it is of particular interest to us, since in the confusion which typifies everyday life we are faced with physical elements, physiological elements, social elements, etc.

The rules we are about to lay down require us to take certain precautions. They have no ontological pretensions. They are not purely logical, nor are they purely empirical. They are an attempt to generalize a specific experiment. They refer to a praxis, the praxis of knowledge. They are similar to dialectical logic and are concerned with the connection between relevance and irrelevance. The intelligent reader will see why they differ from the (often profound but finally unsatisfactory) preoccupations of phenomenological philosophy. But let us be more explicit. We are making the concepts and the methodology dialectical, and this is where the difference lies.

a) Knowing that we must pronounce on relevance, we must take our time. First and foremost we must suspend judgement, and for a long time.

b) A decision about relevance is never fully acquired and definitive, like a decision in action; it can never answer questions by a yes or a no. Although it acts as a guide for research and investigation, and sometimes on a long-term basis (strategically), its involvement is never irreversible. Sooner or later, it must be challenged. No 'structuration' of the total field can impose itself as an eternal truth or as a logical statement.

c) The only sets which are easily classified are those which have been overelaborated, overconceptualized, and thus exhausted (grasped, counted, and so robbed of any element of surprise).

d) There is nothing more revealing and creative than mixed questions, marginal events, facts which apparently or really contradict acquired and accepted knowledge, and lateral concepts.

e) There is history, psychology, economics, etc. Historicism, sociologism, psychologism, economism are questionable, and every science comes in tandem with its own critique (which sooner or later becomes a critique of competence and relevance).

f) The obstacles in the path of knowledge – irreducibilities – are never definitive. In other words, we must not confuse 'essence' with 'nucleus'. The hard, dense nucleuses of facts and ideas, their nodes or nodal points, are also centres of interest and of problems, and thus of potentialities. Knowledge resolves them or disentangles them. We discover mediations in the apparently unmediated, and vice versa. Every level we observe presents us with several others to analyse. Again, because of this, relevance is never definitive, and neither is irrelevance.

g) Given a nucleus which seems irreducible (irrelevant), every method of attack is valid: classic analysis, arbitrary hypotheses, reduction and provisional parentheses, the full range of concepts.

h) And so relevance and irrelevance are aspects of a specific tactic and strategy, the tactic and strategy of science.

4

The Theory of the Semantic Field

1 The semantic field

The *semantic field* which we will now attempt to develop conceptually, only re-presents (makes present) a part of the total field for us. Language itself only re-presents a part of it. Thus the semantic field and language would be two levels of the overall experience we call praxis or the 'total field'. These levels would be linked together by implied mutual relations.

This conceptual development contains a critique of the fetishism of *signification* which is currently so dominant. We will try to show that together with, or in the margins of, the signifier, we will also find non-signifiers, and these can be effective and important. Maybe what is non-signifying now could be a potential signifier, waiting to be unearthed by the theoretician as he strolls through the semantic field like a sightseer. Admittedly this is possible, but then perhaps once it has become a signifier, the non-signifier may lose a reality and an effectiveness which its non-signification (its unknown or misunderstood signification) bestows upon it. Can the operation of tearing the non-signifier from its non-signification to bring it out into the light of formal and formalized signification be undertaken without modifying it? If we want to search the everyday for the non-signifiers which may be active within it we must catch them in the rough, in their unconscious or misunderstood situation, and not like water-creatures wrenched from the deep and left to die in the light of day.

For this reason we feel we must distinguish expression from signification, and keep the two concepts (the expressive and the signifying) simultaneously, studying their connections and their conflicts, in a word, making them dialectical.

At the same time we will continue the critique of another fetishism, a corollary of the previous one, that of language. Certainly, language is not simply a *means* or an instrument analogous to a hammer or a file. Its use is not simply to help communication between minds which to begin with were separately constituted. It is itself constituent. But between this and the idea that it is a privileged and sacred place, the realm of being or a modality of being, there is a chasm which some philosophers are reckless enough to cross. They are prey to the metaphysics and the ontology of the Word. If it is constituent, i.e., a time and place on the semantic field, language in our opinion is nevertheless a *mediation*, and thus a means and an implement, but not an irreducible nucleus or intelligible essence. We have already pointed out that this fetishist philosophy occurs in tandem with a crisis of language itself. What causes it and what are its effects? We will try to answer the question as quickly as possible. We will reinstate discursiveness in our own particular way, by understanding its current situation dialectically – as an awareness of Logos per se, implying a distance in relation to it, and the determination both of its level and its limits. And so our critique will be directed against the fetishizing of Logos and against the dissolution of language (or discourse). We will continue to 'bring' everyday life into language but in the context of the exploration of a semantic field which goes beyond discursiveness per se.

This theoretical hypothesis forbids us (as we already know) from adopting the *structuralism* derived from contemporary Saussurian linguistics. As we have already tried to demonstrate, structure is a formal implement and a scientific idea, and by hypertrophying and hypostasizing it, structuralism renders it sterile. For us, the arbitrariness of the sign must be seen in relation to the non-arbitrariness of the non-signifier and of expressivity. Structured by a series of disjunctions, implications, exclusions and inclusions on the phonemic as well as the morphemic level, coherent discourse belongs to a broader field. There are other regions in this field, including 'yes or no' questions and answers.

Next, once we have developed the idea of the 'semanteme', we will need to examine what the relation between critique of everyday life

and a universal semantics is, by means of a series of particular semeiologies which are presently conceivable (i.e., the 'communications
model').

2 Signals

In everyone's experience, two lights (red and green) are the prototype
of the signal. Binary and disjunctive, they obey strictly logical laws,
'all/nothing', 'either/or'. They do not allow for intermediaries, transitions or evolution. They open a way forward, or they close it. They
indicate a fork in the road or points on the railway line. They offer an
option, and suppress another. A third term (the orange traffic light)
can intervene to soften the harsh imperative of the signal. This third
term complicates the signal and makes it less effective; it causes
countless arguments.

The signal can only be directed at a single sense organ. It is either
visual or auditory. In signals, ambiguity is unacceptable. Moreover,
the signal has no relation to the command it signifies. It is completely
arbitrary. Provided it has a distinct beginning and end, a bell will
achieve the same results as an optical signal. Theoretically, a spray of
perfume could be equally effective. Signals are entirely external to
consciousness, and leave the active 'subject' externalized and passive,
like an inert object at their command.

However the signal is not completely external to the human
object/subject which it acts upon. It produces a well-defined effect,
namely conditioning. I stop when the lights are red and keep going
when they are green, and I don't give it a moment's thought. I have
acquired a reflex action. The repetitions of the signal have conditioned me, and a good job too. Without this string of reflex actions of
which traffic signals are a part, how could I drive my car? I have
learnt them. They constitute a code. Once I have learnt them, it is as
if the signals pass down from my hands through my body to my feet,
according to a well-determined practice, in liaison with a determined
technique or techniques.

Signals must be simple and obvious (clear and perfectly distinct),
but they must also have a perfect stability. It is disconcerting when
signals are altered; it causes serious disruption to what is a series of

constituted and stable social actions, for example road or rail traffic. Constant and repetitive in essence, the signal is automatic, it is always there. It functions in accordance with a regulated frequency, without the intervention of any conscious volition, at least when it is in full working order. We should note that the signal does not give any information, or very little; it forbids or it permits; it includes or it excludes; 'one' does not always know why, and indeed 'one' does not need to know why. The perfect signal is perfectly impersonal, it repeats itself indefinitely, even when there is no one in front of it. It is defined by its redundancy, and it delivers no information. If it is well thought out and well used, it brings no surprises; it is always in the same place, always reiterating its imperious command or interdiction, never beginning, never ending.

In the signal, signification coincides with the thing, i.e., the sign. Be it a red light or a green light, the given command (or interdiction) is entirely given by the thing. 'One' does not have to give a thought to what is being signified. *In and by means of the signal, signification is joined to and coincides with a thing which has been taken arbitrarily as a signal, but which itself has no signification.* Perfect rationality and perfect meaninglessness come face to face. Should the signal signify another thing – or something else – for me, it will be because I am questioning it instead of obeying it; defying it, and thinking beyond what it 'is', in its entire presence or entire absence, I ask myself what someone to whom I have no access – precisely because they are not there and because I know nothing about them – has intended. 'Why have they put traffic lights at this crossroads?'

Although it functions in isolation like pure things do, the signal is not alone. It is always part of a defined (codified) *system*. For example, take the highway code, railway signals, or other, more esoteric systems, such as forestry or scouting, etc. When it is well thought out, a system can aspire to becoming very generalized, even to a 'worldwide' degree (road signals, or the Morse code, for example). Given that in practice there are so many situations, the pure objectiveness of the (crudely binary and disjunctive) signal within a system becomes diluted. Alongside signals per se, we see other elements appearing (words such as 'danger' or 'parking', and signs or symbols, like a skull, etc.), and this obscures the defined nature of the sign and of the system. These elements carry a certain amount of information (which is minimal, entirely knowable in advance, and admitting of no uncertainty or dubious interpretation, or otherwise the system would not work properly). A system like this must be closed, saturated, coherent and rigorous. There may be a conflict between the requirements of practice and of rigorousness, but this should not blind us to the (perfectly abstract and antinatural) 'nature' of the signal and of systems of signals.

This is not the place to examine the case of highly complex systems, which are already transitionals towards something else. Doubtless we will have to consider them when we deal with the 'communications model'.[1]

3 Signs

The prototype of the sign is obviously the *word*, but it is not easy to define it. The word has certain of the qualities of the signal, or rather the signal has borrowed certain of the properties of the word. The word can give commands. Used imperatively, it transmits an order; it 'signifies' a command. When I hear the word 'Halt!', I stop; but according to the context, the word 'Leave!' evokes a more or less powerful feeling of acceptance or rejection. Although there is no power of words, certain words have power; this is nothing more than a pole or a limit which would hardly suffice as a definition of the sign, but which would be more appropriate for the signal.

The word is auditive but it is also visual. Ever since writing has existed, reading has been closely implicated with listening, and contaminates it. So much so that in order to grasp language as a *form* (a structure), linguists must first carry out the following operation, which is both concrete and abstract: they must separate the language chain from its environment and from its visual context, parenthesizing the latter. In fact, once they have accomplished this operation, they are left with an abstraction: language as a verbal system. Once it is reduced to being a purely verbal sign, the word *as sign* becomes blurred and confused. Reading is a practical experience which children learn at an early stage, although they start learning aurally a little sooner, and it is part of language as an implement for action and understanding. Is it not very curious that today's audiovisual media should be disrupting the practice of language after having played such an important role in constituting it, many centuries ago?

The elements in spoken (or written) language must be clear, easily distinguishable from each other, and understandable, demanding the least possible effort and avoiding the smallest possible chance of error. Thus they must be disjunctive (phonetically and semantically exclusive). However, the final element is never a simple signal. This final element, namely the phoneme, has no meaning (since it is a non-signifier), and does not appear per se in language. Contemporary structuralist linguistics has highlighted these phenomena.[2] Double articulation, which is made up of an internal difference, is what characterizes the linguistic sign, i.e., the word. Thus on analysis it presents two *levels*: the phoneme (in itself devoid of meaning) and the morpheme (which is a signifier). In practice, the former only appears as part of the latter, and the two can only be separated by analysis. This duality of levels means that in spite of their analogies, the sign cannot be reduced to the signal. The sign has a specificity which is demonstrated by its triple determination: the sign, the signifier and the signified. The signal does not have this triplicity. Although these three elements have a content, in terms both of the subject (movements of the pharynx, the glottis, the tongue) and of the object (things and objects designated with their connections, their relations of interaction, of presence and absence, of inclusions and exclusions), they tend towards pure form, becoming what Roland Barthes has called a 'tourniquet'. Thus content does not determine the use of words, their order and their connections, although it plays a part in the logical structure of the way they are used. Moreover, the formal order of signs leaves room for the unforeseen (randomness), and although their combinations are highly structured, since they are structured formally, they constantly provide something new, except in the commonplace discourse of platitude. So repetition makes way for inventiveness, but without actually disappearing (which presents some curious problems). This permanent renewal of possible discourse has its own laws (such as Estoup-Zipf's law on the frequency of the use of words). The order of signs allows for uncertainty, expectancy and surprise, and thus for play and imagination. The sentence has great elasticity, while the word itself has very little. The word must have a defined and conventionally fixed sense, otherwise the speakers will no longer understand each other. Thus every conversation oscillates between two poles. Around one of them, the chances of misunderstanding are reduced to a minimum, but the conversation will always be trivial. Around the other, the increase in chance and in the probability of misunderstandings increases the chances for inventiveness, discovery and mutual recognition, and for the obstacles to understanding being overcome. On the level of discourse, there is a considerable margin of uncertainty and freedom; on the level of signs (words, morphemes), this margin is very small. The role language plays in everyday life is a product of this duality, or double possibility. It oscillates between platitude and rhetoric, between banality and expressivity.

It follows that, with their formal rules of usage (syntax and grammar), signs (repertoire, vocabulary and lexis) form a coherent system, namely a system of language. The efficiency of this system makes it analogous to a system of signals: it gives commands; it organizes feelings and emotions as well as objects, because it contains an order and imposes it upon the chaos of fleeting moments; it enjoins because it joins and disjoins. It opens up possibilities, and then closes them down. Order in a language system determines the order of words and sentences; it is part of a more far-reaching order, in social practice. Imperious and imperative, language uses words to make us recognize feelings and actions. Ceaselessly, it eliminates ambiguities and misunderstandings, only to allow them to return once more, inevitably. In the tumult and vibrations of everyday life, it tends to create stabilities, static states which are determined in spite of their limitless resonances and their dampened harmonics. To speak is to act. When we use words and sentences (even when we are soliloquizing) we influence ourselves as much as the person to whom we are talking. What we are putting into words has been changed by the fact of being said, or rather of having been said. With its blindfold of misconceptions and misunderstandings torn away, what is being said is revealed in the light of discourse. It is discussed, it is clarified, it becomes impoverished and commonplace – and yet it is enriched by the fact of being present in social daylight. In any event, what has been said had to be said, so that what remains of it after its fleetingness and obscurities have been submitted to the test of language can be assessed. Discourse is an event and an act, and a prologue to action; it is a preparation for action; it forces us to act and to choose, unless we are speaking for speaking's sake, in which case the prologue to decision becomes an end in itself. To speak and to put oneself into words is both stimulating and destructive. Because discourses have continuity we are forced into their network and, as a consequence, into the network of the social actions they refract and specify: this action is permitted; that one is forbidden. But discourses are also discontinuous, and their discrete terms act like a sieve, straining the things which rise up from our inner depths. Logos is not simply a means of communication. It acts as a filter for the feelings and emotions which create it and which it regulates. For this reason, it really is a kind of being, a way of being.

When we bring what has not already been said into language, we are certainly winning a victory. In itself, the act creates something and opens up new possibilities; it is the prelude to unexpected creations, and may even be seen to constitute the essence of what is traditionally called 'philosophy'. When praxis permits an important sector to pass into language, or when its problems demand it, it is an important day for knowledge. And yet, how can there ever be an absolute victory without something being lost? What we are putting into words and what we have put into words is there now, facing us. Earlier it was something happening silently, spontaneously, joyfully, even harmoniously – or maybe something painful and muffled which is not happening at all. Once something has been spoken it will never be spontaneous again. We must think about it, and in the case of a requirement (a 'function'), we need to focus it patiently by trial and error until we can consciously carry it into effect. The 'spoken' is now abstract: presented on the plane of abstraction, on the level of language and the sign. As well as spontaneity and innocence, a little bit more nature or 'being' is lost. We all know that we must be prepared to risk losing everything if we want to win everything. But whatever the circumstances, risking and losing will always be risking and losing!

Thus the system of signs (of language and discourse) resembles a system of signals, but because the one is incomparably broader and more flexible than the other, the analogy will not help us to understand it. It is an open system, controlled by a coherence which is *almost* logical. This *almost* is supremely important. Formally, the non-signifying element in language (e.g., the sound, the syllable or the phoneme) is apparent, but is not recognized as such. Actually, however, in practical, social utterance, it is an important and conscious element, acting as interjection and exclamation: 'Oh! Ah!', etc. In this use of the non-signifier (which dogmatic structuralism finds rather difficult to deal with) expression is more important than signification. Now when it is actually spoken, and taken in its complete context – gestures, mimicry, grimaces – discourse is *expressive*. Inflections of the voice give constant support to the formal relations between the terms of discourse. In this way and in this way alone does it enter into the everyday, not as its loom, but as threads woven into its fabric.

4 The symbol

This has certain of the qualities or properties of the signal or the sign, but it differs from both. The symbol includes and excludes, by bringing the members of one particular group closer together, while excluding other individuals and groups. It makes orders or prohibitions, but in complex ways which are dramatically involving and which sometimes imply a conception of the world and of life. It reveals and conceals membership of a group, the reasons for its membership and the reasons of the group itself. It enters into a form, but this form develops concretely around the symbol, in rituals and ceremonies. The symbol initiates and it inhibits.

The symbol differs from the sign and even more so from the signal in that it appears inexhaustible. Effectively, it is. The signal takes place entirely within its own functioning, and is exhausted there; the sign (the word) is only valid in so far as it belongs in the series of signs and in their mutual interaction. Both as a fact and as a value without limits (even when it is not religious and sacred), the symbol is unassailable. It presents itself, it is a presence, it is present, rich with meaning, and as such is somewhat more than 're-presentation'. Does it express as much or more than it signifies? When Christians make the sign of the Cross, the evocation of the Cross itself is more important than the formal gesture; the believer traces the instrument of redemptive suffering on his own body; he sanctifies himself by deliberately identifying with the crucified god. If he is *signing* himself and *signifying* himself externally with a gesture which proves his membership and makes it manifest, he is also carrying out an internal *act* of faith and, more importantly, of participation. He is linking himself with the absolute Word, the Logos become flesh and put to death for him. When we examine it from outside, this gesture reveals a multiplicity of significations, but viewed from within, it is inexhaustible. Thus the gesture in itself has less reality and value than its symbolic content. It is much more of a symbol than a sign in the precise meaning of the term. It expresses, and this expressivity has primacy over what it signifies externally. When the sign is enough in itself, the form and the letter are more important than the 'spirit'. Sociologists and ethnographers have observed the oppositional and complementary properties of symbols (disjunction and inclusion in social practice) in factual terms. It has been left to philosophers to shed light on how symbols differ from discourse and representation. Discourse and representation distinguish between things and clarify them, whereas symbols are inexhaustible; they offer some kind of obscure and magical participation. Notably, in his *Aesthetics*, Hegel gives an analysis of the difference between symbolism, allegory, simile, metaphor and analogy. If I call someone 'a sly old fox' I am attributing the qualities of a fox (as I see them) to him. Obviously, I know that no human being 'is' a fox and I also know that there is no Platonic Idea of Slyness which would apply to foxes in the animal kingdom and to certain human individuals. However, these representations are too clear, and their very clearness betrays their logical incoherence. On an affective level, which takes me back to my childhood (stories and fables), to archaic times (myths) and also to the realm of the imagination (fantastic tales), I am saying that this man actually does share something in common with a fox – so much so that when I am with him I behave as though he really were a crafty, carnivorous animal, a danger to me and to my possessions, and I advise other people strongly (the people I talk to) to do the same. The symbol confers an effective, real and practical communality on two beings who are different both in appearance and in reality, but more so in the former than in the latter. It makes these two beings partly *identical*. It points to their mutual participation. When it refers to one, it evokes the other, and vice versa. Conversely, a simile would leave them mutually external and only brings them together by using comparatives such as 'like' or 'as'. As for analogy, which is elaborated as a kind of reasoning, it highlights differences. Or else it is subsumed by a symbolism, and directed by it.

Is it possible to list these symbols? Perhaps. Can we count them, or in other words, are they limited in number? Probably. Obviously, they include the sun, the stars and the 'signs' of the zodiac, as well as the sea and the mountains, the elements (water, fire, earth, air), spatial directions, the father, the mother, etc.

Taken in isolation, each one has its particular effectiveness and prestige. It immediately triggers off emotions, and even sensations. Surrounded by its own affective and imaginary retinue, it bursts its way into discourse like an exclamation: 'The earth! . . . The sun! . . . The night!' However, symbols do not exist in isolation. Could we say that they constitute systems? The term is only valid for representations which have been elaborated, and thus verbalized and formalized. Symbols come in groups. We will say that they constitute configurations or constellations: cosmic symbolisms, tragic symbolisms, religious symbolisms, etc. As well as being configurations they can be elaborated into symbolic systems. For example, astrology (as we know it nowadays in the press – daily, weekly or monthly – and above all in the women's press) has become an elaborate system for the psychological interpretation of everyday life, with fairly well-defined themes. This system has been superimposed upon some extremely ancient cosmic symbolisms, which have never lost their emotional effectiveness.

Where do symbols originate? From the depths of a collective or individual 'unconsciousness'? From mysterious archetypes, hidden emotional or existential matrixes? From the pristine discoveries of childhood or from the despair of old age and mortality? From archaic magic or from involuntary and spontaneous poetry? From flights of inspiration or from failures? From the 'world' or from mankind, or from the primitive and obscure relation between them? From power over nature or from powerlessness? From the first steps towards power? For the time being all this is of little importance. What is important as far as this project is concerned is that we emphasize the specificity of the symbol, its inexhaustibility for the mind which wishes to explore it, and its direct emotional (affective) effectiveness.

5 The image

Unlike the symbol, the image is an individual work, but is communicable. Unlike the sign, it does not belong in abstractness, any more than it does in sensuousness. Like the symbol, it appeals to affectivity; it is born in and emerges from a level of reality other than that occupied by signs and their connections. On one hand, it has certain of the powers of the symbol, arousing affective complicities and pacts directly, without using representations as such. It makes itself understood by setting emotion into movement, and by arousing it. It exerts an influence, and includes those who understand it within a group which is characterized by a certain tonality. And so to a certain extent it shares the selective and discriminatory power of signs. It is a form of consciousness, or a level, or a modality if you like, but not the emergence of an 'unconsciousness' which might resemble a storehouse of images. However, it is multiple; it appeals to all the senses, and it arouses obscure emotions by travelling back to ancient seasons and bygone ages of the individual, the group and the species. Thus it activates and actualizes a link between the present and the past, something the sign cannot do. In this respect it is an aspect of expressivity. Communicated and communicating, it is original and unique; it carries the hallmark of inventiveness, of spontaneous or cultivated poetry. It needs signs (today's words and graphic or typographic signs) to communicate, but it overloads these signs with its emotional (expressive) content, the origins of which are lost in the mists of time, together with symbolisms. Although it is alien to the (logical and formal) structure of discourse, it intervenes in discourse by propelling it forward and colouring it with its own emotional tonality. The threshold to this emotive content is always vague and hard to delimit. It works by insinuation and suggestion rather than by imposing itself, which is why it requires complicity and pacts; and yet it overcomes obstacles and barriers which hinder precise signification. It creates misunderstandings and dissensions, but it can also resolve them. Thanks to the image and the content which makes up a part of its influence, opaqueness becomes somewhat more transparent. Distances vanish as if by magic. Could this content be limitless? Possibly, although it may be an illusion inherent to imagination. If we speak of limitlessness, it is in the context of harmonics, where resonance goes

287

on indefinitely, perceptible only to the sharpest of ears, although all perception is limited in such matters.

Therefore the image is the opposite of the signal and the sign. Whereas these address action and the present, the image turns towards the past, like the symbol. It rescues the past from darkness (from 'unconsciousness', to use another terminology) and dispersion, bringing it into the light of the present day. However, unlike the symbol, the image also goes towards the future. It strives to attain something not yet present and to 'presentify' or present it. So it is a prospector in the distant territory of what is possible and what is impossible. It prepares choices and indicates them. It arouses emotions, feelings and desires, in other words virtual actions, and compels imagination to wager on a future it foretells and anticipates, and which it helps to determine (through 'projects of choice'). Thus imagination could be seen as the function of what is possible (in so far as we can talk about 'function' in this context; troublesome but useful, demanding but free, this 'function' is something we could well do without).

From the point of view of reflective thought, there is a kind of incompatibility between retrospection and prospection. They are opposite attitudes or intentions. As for imagination, it knows how to use the past in order to invent the future. It projects what it has acquired through experience towards the future, and frequently starts from something extremely archaic to represent the farthest realms of the impossible/possible. This is not simply a reference to science fiction. We also have the brilliant Fourier in mind, whose vision of everyday life in future society was based upon archaic communal life, but enriched with everything that human development can offer, as Marx put it (and Marx owes much more to Fourier than is generally admitted).

The image is an act. In this respect it implies the will to be effective: sometimes to help make what is possible real or to represent the impossible, sometimes to prepare a project of choice, sometimes to captivate and touch another human being. In so far as it is a social act, the image is the image of an action which it deliberately projects towards the 'subject' – the human being it is addressing and whom it wants to influence. Touched and moved, this person responds to the effects of the image and projects it back towards its initiator. This double projection produces a result which is no longer a projection but a mutual presence, and even an emotional sameness. All communication involves images, and the deepest communication of all is achieved through images.

The image is only active when it is 'expressive'. It arouses what it expresses, and provokes it. The image has an inherently provocative character. When we use an image to provoke an emotion, we ourselves do not need to be moved. However, we cannot invent an image without having previously felt an emotion. As the concept of expressivity becomes more precise, it is turned on its head. On the level of the image, expression is active in its effect, as much and more than in its condition or cause. Whoever experiences this effect locates it in the image, which he qualifies as 'expressive', while for whoever employs it, its expressivity may well be far away in the past. The result is a permanent lag between the invention of images and their use, and between the situation of whoever employs them and whoever is influenced by their action. Thus mutual presence does not rule out misunderstandings and dramas, quite the reverse: it encompasses their possibility.

Although it is not up to us to give a theory of imagination (or of language for that matter), since it has been formulated elsewhere, we will summarize it.

The study of archaic magic and its repercussions demonstrates the emotional effectiveness of practices such as gestures, ceremonies and ritualized expressions, etc. The magician *evokes* people who have disappeared, who are absent; he evokes obscure powers; he *resurrects* the dead, and achieves the *repetition* or the renewal of the past. He can challenge what has been accomplished and act as though what is is not. He can influence the future by *bringing it into the present*. He changes his personality by *identifying* it with a wide variety of 'beings' – demons and gods, kings and genies – in a *participation*.

Now imagination and magic share the same categories. More precisely, the modalities of magic have become the modalities of imagination: to evoke, to resurrect, to identify. So we may maintain that, historically and sociologically, imagination is an extension of magic. However, a profound discontinuity divides them. The magician used his procedures (such as spells and dances) on his patient to produce emotional states which were both entirely illusory and

289

entirely real (lived). The purpose of magic procedures was to create real states in a real collectivity (groups of initiates). When it is aimed at individuals, individual imagination produces images, not states of trance. The illusory character of the image is almost always perceived as such, although in the final analysis participation becomes complete again, and imagination joins forces with magic once more.

6 On several confusions

In order to locate the elements or formants of the semantic field as precisely as possible, we have made clear distinctions between them. We have emphasized their specificities.

However, rather than distinguishing between them, people tend to confuse them. Critical analysis reveals that several of today's most widespread theories are responsible for this.

There is absolutely no question of denying the importance of the work of the Pavlovian school, from Setchenov to Smolenski and Bykov. Some of the criticisms levelled against the scientific results of their research are unacceptable. It is irrefutable that Pavlov's work proved a total activity of the cortex in higher animals and in man (higher nervous activity), and not simply the existence of isolated reflexes. In any case, we can hardly expect physiologists to be sociologists and psychologists as well. However, what we can expect of them is not to refute the existence of other areas and levels of reality and analysis. Refusal to accept this may be partially and subjectively justified by the effort required to extrapolate all the consequences from an important discovery, but finally it will result in the dogmatism and subjectivism characteristic of schools (scientific clans), and their members run the risk of endlessly following up a line of research which will finally become exhausted. The Pavlovians simply forget that the relation of the human brain with the outside world cannot be reduced to the connections between the cortex and stimuli or signals. The human world is made up of objects, products and human works, not of things. It is also made up of other human beings and of the language which links them together. It comprises repetition and non-repetition, and the relations between the two are problematic. To a certain extent this human world which is given to the individual (who intervenes in it and can only assimilate it by being active within it) is the work of praxis. How odd it is that Pavlovism should have been adopted in the name of Marxist materialism, when it disregards the idea of 'praxis', which is the very foundation of Marxism! The 'conditioning' of the human infant in its relations with his father and mother (which are much too 'private', narrow and unmediated in the family of today and above all in the praxis of bourgeois society) has some specific and original features. It cannot be reduced to the acquisition of complicated reflex actions and a 'second system' of signalling, the verbal system. All the while it is learning, the child's relations with its parents are doubly ambiguous. They result from the powers of parents to teach and their powers to oppress. The Father is not given to the child as a simple, unmediated presence, good or bad, or simultaneously good and bad. The Father is not merely unmediated strength and authority, he is social authority: society as a whole, law, hierarchy, the state. Thus the Father is both reality and symbolism. God is known as 'our father', or 'eternal father'. The same applies to the Mother, although what she symbolizes is something more archaic and cosmic. Pavlovian theory eliminates the specificities of the symbol, in so far as it is directed towards creating and shaping basic affectivity. By conceiving of it purely as a second system of signalling, it also eliminates the specificity of the sign (which the structuralist school and the theory of double articulation have reinstated). It equates the symbol and the sign with the signal, which it thinks of in terms of physiology rather than sociology.

If the Pavlovian school proceeds by confusing and reducing specificities in a 'materialist' way, the procedures of the 'bourgeois' and non-'socialist' structuralist school are exactly analogous. It gives a privileged status to *signification*, which has the advantage of appearing to be socially real and yet at the same time immaterial and 'in the mind'. Signification can only be apparent to and for a 'mind', a 'subject'. Once this has been accepted, an inextricable confusion ensues. The significations perceived (in phenomenological terms, *made explicit*) by the reflective, thinking subject – the philosopher, the linguist, the sociologist – merge with the significations which are effectively and practically (socially) carried by signs. How are we to distinguish between them? There are no criteria. This has been a marvellous godsend to philosophical thinkers. What they had long since discovered elsewhere they can now observe in the facts; they make it explicit and separate it from signs, and receive it from significations like a kind of gift. Now the signal and the symbol have significations, but these are irreducible to the significations of simple signs, and they impose themselves upon their 'subjects' without the latter having to explain them. The privileged status these thinkers accord to signification simplifies reality. It suppresses the specificity of levels (of existence and analysis) just as much as when the signal is privileged. Their conception of a unitary field of significations (which ipso facto cannot be a genuine 'field') reveals what their attitude really is. By wishing to avoid the excessive realism and the reification inherent to 'processes', they go beyond the 'mental things' which are so familiar to psychologists and sociologists. At the same time the diversity of the real escapes them, and they feel no need to consider the processes and the differences between 'things': works, objects and products, symbolic works, or works laden with symbols which are aimed at emotiveness, or products which act like signals, etc.

More than thirty years ago, in his *Critique des fondements de la psychologie*, Georges Politzer introduced the concept of signification (in place of the concept of the unconscious), while at the same time protesting aginst the postulates of conventional signification in psychology. Taking the same stance, but developing it further, we would criticize the subjectivist philosophy which accepts the postulate that signification should have a privileged status; we reject the mixture of 'conventional signification' and 'real signification' which philosophers use as a phenomenological bran tub for whatever is convenient for them.

The idea of a 'symbolic function' perpetuates this confusion. It enables them to sidestep the difference between the *symbol* (objective content, emotional effectiveness, archaic origins) and the *sign* (intellectual effectiveness, formal, synchronic and non-dialectical reality). To say that the symbolic function intervenes every time a representation is substituted for a thing is to bring the signal, the sign and the symbol so close together that they become indistinguishable. It is also to forget that symbolism is not separate from the 'thing' (the father, the mother, the sun, the plain, etc.), but is joined to it in a mutual participation. On the other hand, when a signal functions, signification is at one and the same time entirely arbitrary and separate from the thing, and entirely identical to the thing. Therefore there is no univocal 'symbolic function' which would be applicable to all three cases.[3]

Signification is impoverished. Fixed, attached to the sign, established, repeated, codified, it 'is' and is active because it is fixed, stable and stabilized. Taken by itself it becomes disembodied: it is the desert of essence (Hegel) attached to words, to discourse, to Logos. *Expression* is far more creative, and creates in a different way. It lives in the voice, we would say, and in gestures, and in the face. Let us reinstate the living (dialectical) unity which structuralist analysis has shattered. This analysis has a threefold aim: to distinguish between levels and between formants, to reveal structures, and to rediscover a higher unity. Expression is speech. Signification is language as form. Speech carries words along in the flow and rhythms of the sentence; it is concealed beneath what in terms of form appears to be word frequency. When emotion and images intervene in living speech, they do not disturb the pure form of discourse, they bring it to life. Expressivity is a thing of flesh and blood; mobile, unexpected, it is for ever breaking through the barriers of signification, informing, communicating by means of acquired significations. When the individual expresses himself (through intonation or mime), he says much more than he puts into words. His activity is almost like a work of creativity: dramatized action, a theatre of mime.

Thus a dialectical movement becomes apparent in dialogue: 'expression/signification', i.e., a conflict between these two terms. Expression struggles to bear the dead weight and inertia of signification and to make use of it as a fulcrum. Signification fixes expression by immobilizing and reducing it; conventional, intentional, stereotyped, it deadens expression, which in turn forever reconstructs itself, breathing new life into signification.

From this conflict comes *sense* (the movement, orientation and direction of dialogue, and its ultimate goal). It is a term which is not immune from the generalized confusion we are at present living through. At times it refers to a direction, at others to a set (a system) of significations. While not eliminating the latter interpretation of the term, we would emphasize the former. Surely the sense of an act lies in its direction and orientation: the future which it is travelling towards, blindly or lucidly, in other words, *what is possible*. Expression is an act, and it takes on a sense in its oneness with established significations and its conflict with them. Every social action which involves a generalized dialogue (of the self with the self, with another person nearby or far away) also has a sense. In the 'expression/signification' dialectical movement, in which sense intervenes as a constantly renewed third term to resolve the first two, expression is forever striving to get the better of signification; to become unmediated, direct, and directly (emotionally) transmitted. It is not always successful, even when it overloads discourse with exclamations, images and rhetoric. Signification goes on playing its stabilizing role of an inert weight, which expression must bear on its shoulders but without which it would dissolve and disappear into the void. On the other hand, signification is forever striving to kill expression and to kill itself with the banality and maximal frequency of trivial terminology. It can never succeed; success would mean its instant demise.

In some respects there is probably 'a sense' in the overvaluing of signification. Maybe it corresponds to a profound deterioration of expressivity and of the image per se (in terms of the imaginary as opposed to the brute force of the audiovisual). Expressivity is already fragile and weakened, and maybe this overvaluing points to a tendency to compromise it further by making it totally trivialized.

We will come up against these problems again when we examine communications theory (the 'communications model'). We will use these analyses to draw up a critical description of conversation – discussions and dialogues – in the everyday.

7 The properties of the semantic field

Meanwhile, let us specify the properties of the semantic field, which is indissolubly constituted – and precisely by means of their differences – by symbols, images, signs and signals.

While being careful not to take the analogy beyond certain limits (which need to be determined), we notice that the semantic field really does have the characteristics of a 'field'. It presents a continuity, and within this continuity, it has distinct and discontinuous elements, specific values and nucleuses. We can single out discrete units, but we can never completely separate them from the unit as a whole. Continuity and discontinuity are in a state of mutual relativity. At every point we observe a force: a vector. Once activated, these points become polarized, determining tensions, static states, momentary balances, and a temporary sharing out of the forces. At every point potentialities reveal themselves, and in doing so, they disappear. This produces stabilities (which, like the discontinuities, are relative against their background tension). The *dual* properties (expression and signification, emotivity and representivity) polarize the semantic field, maintaining the tensions and invigorating them. Generated by these tensions between the extreme polarities of symbols and signs, waves and vibrations run across it like electrical charges. However, the semantic field is more animated and more complex than physical realities, and the levels (of existence or reality) it presents are more varied and more discontinuous, with differences in level, gaps, and perhaps even holes.

Were we to reduce this complexity to a single one of its formants (such as the signal, the sign, the symbol or the image) it would slip through our fingers. What we would be faced with would be a simplified complexity: the 'field of significations', for example. Taken in its totality, the semantic field as we understand it has a structure, but this structure cannot be reduced to the structure of discourse, any more than it can to the formal connection between signs or to the relation between the sign, the signified and the signifier. It is a much more complex structure, which includes a limited number of variations: disturbances, instabilities and propagations. Although we have no wish to contest the importance of structural linguistics, we cannot use it as a model for structure. On the contrary, we want to carry the ideas of structure and stability beyond language, and to give them back their place in the process of becoming. Nor will we use the theories of gravity, electricity or magnetism as our model; in our opinion the theory we will use (and which we will considerably transpose) is broader and more comprehensive: it is the model of harmonics.

Thus defined, the entire semantic field is *open*. We cannot circumscribe or close it, any more than we can the horizon, even though every horizon is determined.

8 Consciousness and the semantic field

Can we say that (social and individual) consciousness is consciousness *of* the semantic field as a whole, or that it reflects it? No. It is not external to the semantic field. Could we say that it is active *on* the semantic field? Yes, but that is not enough. What we can say is that consciousness 'is' the semantic field, but only providing we purge the little word '*is*' of all substantialist content, and especially of all contamination by brute things. Thus consciousness 'is' not this and not that, but this and that taken as a whole. It 'is' in a specific manner: not a thing among things, nor the ideal or mental double of those things (reflected or not). 'Things' and objects are given to consciousness together with their connections and their significations, as an inextricable part of the semantic field as a whole.

Consciousness 'is' receptiveness on a particular (affective) level of the symbolic nucleuses. It 'is' put into the service of signs and of their formal connections. It 'is' receptiveness on a particular level of signals (the level of unmediated practical action). Finally, it 'is' the lived on the semantic field; it is constantly opening out to it, the semantic field is its basis, it coincides with it.

However, this description is only entirely valid for social consciousness. Although individual consciousness is included and implied within social consciousness, it only occupies a portion of it. So alongside levels of reality (of existence), we need to determine levels of experience and levels of analysis.

In the first place, the most solid aspect of the everyday, and the point of departure of individual consciousness and its sphere of activity, is only a portion of the semantic field: discourse, or even triviality in discourse; commonplaces, redundancy, intelligibility through familiarity. Symbols from everyday life intervene, but isolated, one at a time, and are rarely perceived as such. They are perceived as being within things, and not as a double of those things, and as something external to them which has come to reinforce them emotionally. The symbol is an integral part of familiarity. In the everyday, the Father as creative power, authority and law – the symbolic Father – merges with the father who is directly perceived and emotionally submitted to, a man with a particular voice, a particular face and particular behaviour patterns. Signals per se have much more importance in everyday life than symbols per se. This does not stop symbolisms from having a powerful influence, but this is 'unconscious'. The specific structure and dynamism of the semantic field produce the following imbalance, which is specific to the everyday: on one hand it is *determined by symbolisms which it fails to recognize as such, and which it lives as though they were realities;* on the other *it is orientated by signallings which it takes to be the essential elements which determine it.* The everyday takes its consciousness from signals and relegates symbolisms to 'unconsciousness', despite the fact that they are linked to the most profound vital rhythms such as day and night, the presence of the mother and the father, hunger and sexuality. Riven in two, this consciousness will always be superficial, the equivalent of a lack of consciousness. As for reflective consciousness, it distances itself from the semantic field in an attempt to control it. In the effort to see it in all its breadth, it loses contact with it. The danger is that it will select a fragment of it to use as a means of defining it. This is what theory does when it does not go hand in hand with permanent autocritique and does not consciously aim for the open totality of the field: it selects a fragment – a symbol or symbolism in general, discourse, signification, formal structure, or even the signal – and elevates it to the absolute.

Generally, the dialectical movements which are active on the semantic field as a whole (and which give it life) escape reflective consciousness. It observes them from afar, often as though they were anomalies, whereas in fact they are what characterizes the semantic field. In so far as it animates this mobile and diversified field, dialectical movement encompasses it and envelops it. There is no specific spot or place on the semantic field where it can be fixed. For this reason it is greater than the reflective and purely rigorous (logical) consciousness which attempts to articulate the diverse signs and their less-than-rigorous connections which are given in Logos and in discourse. And so we come back once more to what we have previously proposed, but in a different light. Discourse is (and is nothing more than) a level of experience on the semantic field as a whole. Composed of quasi-static states, it is particularly strong and stable. It opens itself comprehensively to this field, whether it be in the sphere of symbols and images or at the polarity of signals. As a level it is both a centre and an intermediary (a mediation).

As for the semantic field itself, it opens on to every sphere of praxis, with creative contradictions, repetition and inventiveness. Discourse and even the semantic field are made up of correlations, oppositions and contrasts. Dialectical movements encompass these terms and prevent them from succumbing to immobility. They breathe life into them, and for this reason, cannot be contained within them.

The first result of this is that the semantic field as a whole (or a 'totality') is a *concept* based on an experience or even on a level of experience which itself encompasses a diverse range of levels. This concept is not given per se in experience. There is no description, no phenomenology of the 'lived' which could grasp it. It is a theoretical concept, and thus forms part of a theory. A (phenomenological) description of it would take experience *partes extra partes*; it would shed light on small areas of it, appropriating them for its own devices and transforming them into private plots of land, rather than grasping the landscape and the horizon as an ensemble.

A further result is that any consciousness which has established itself firmly on the semantic field (or which thinks it has) cannot really be trusted. Just like an individual, society does not see itself as it 'is'. When we want to consult social consciousness, more often than not we come up against individual and 'private' groupings. Individual consciousness and even social consciousness can speak only of the parts of the semantic field on which they have set up home. They cannot bring total knowledge of it, but they do offer material for that knowledge. In particular, the contradictions of a society 'normally' elude consciousness, discourse and especially the everyday (except at moments of revolutionary crisis, or when revealed by in-depth critique).

If we are to grasp these contradictions we will need a theoretical knowledge which takes the semantic field into account but which understands it per se, and which consequently will grasp the praxis of which it is merely a level. Also we still need to mount an assault on the structures of discourse (in spite of the efforts of dialecticians from Heraclitus to Hegel and our contemporaries) in order to seize dialectical movements and 'bring them into language'. We must succeed in grasping whatever tries to slip through our fingers, not as essence (as unknowable) or as nature (irrational or ontological truth) but as it is, precisely because 'that' is what must be seized and what will reveal the process of becoming of knowledge and of the real. And if 'that' is inexhaustible, we will nevertheless succeed in grasping it if we persist in trying.

Thus dialectical thought will be necessary if we are to conceive of the semantic field, both as an entity (with its limits and its openings) and as a set of diverse elements. However, dialectical thought per se does not appear in or *on* the semantic field. And this is precisely how it *conceives* of it, from the vantage point of a higher level of reality (existence) and knowledge. If dialectical thought was available on the semantic field, there would be no more specificity, and differences would become blurred. The formal and the logical would be absorbed into dialectical movements, and would lose their own specific levels. Logos would be spontaneously and completely dialectical (which it is not).

And so we must think of the total semantic field using dialectical reason, rather than thinking of dialectical reason as something within that field. Dialectical contradiction is hidden from view, disguised between oppositions, 'contrasts' of the field, diversities and tensions. The semantic field is a level of experience and knowledge, but also comprises appearances, apparitions and manifestations of 'something' deeper. Being? Perhaps! But first of all praxis, and history. From within, the contradictions of the semantic field are sensed as powerful movements, producing the instabilities which run through it. From outside (relatively) they can be grasped and conceived of. Of necessity – and we cannot stress this hard enough – the same applies to each separate society and to society as a whole. Since the semantic field is located somewhere in between praxis and knowledge, and since it takes an enormous effort to raise consciousness to the conceptual level, only by painstaking analysis, or at a moment of intense crisis, will a society's contradictions be made fully apparent. Without these stipulations, *one* (i.e., social consciousness) will only be aware of certain partial and everyday effects of these contradictions: uneasiness, dissatisfactions, misunderstandings, disturbances. We can say for certain that socialist critique understands the contradictions of capitalism incomparably better than do the people who 'live' them and try to describe them 'from the inside'. But the opposite may probably be true!

9 The laws of the semantic field

The signal was born with industrialization. Sociological analysis sheds light on this proposition by dispelling some serious confusions, and in particular the confusion between the signal and physiological stimuli or signs in general. Before the advent of modern industry, a battle 'signal', a war cry or a raised banner was more of a symbol than a sign, expressive rather than signifying. The same would have been true of a distress 'signal', a beacon, a warning cry or an alarm bell. During the development of what is sometimes referred to in a rather confused way as 'industrial society' or 'technological society', there were more and more signals. At first they were limited to factories and railways, but soon they invaded everyday life in the form of traffic signals, and innumerable signals to permit or to prohibit. In 'industrial society', urban life becomes peopled by innumerable signallings. Each one programmes a routine, exactly like a calculator, regulating patterns of conduct and behaviour. We may well ask ourselves whether one day the entire set of signals will not constitute a sort of gigantic machine which will not need to be built, but which cyberneticists will simply formulate and put into action using existing connections and signallings. This colossal mechanism will already have regulated society and its everyday life. Perhaps it will give the men trapped within the prison of its machine a splendid impression of spontaneity and harmony. And this is what it will be: kindly towards the average socially adapted ('balanced') individual, pitiless towards the 'deviant'.

Not only are signals ever more numerous, not only are they becoming more dense, but bit by bit they are dismantling the semantic field. As the 'signalling' pole becomes more and more intense the magnetic power of signals is increased. They corrode symbols and lessen the tension between the poles of expression and signification to the advantage of the latter. The semantic field becomes simplified and unified, and dialectic is (superficially) replaced by logic. Hence *the law of displacement: in and because of modern industry in industrial and technological society, the field in its entirety is displaced towards the pole of the 'signal'.*

This law has a general significance, and we will try to explain it. To do this, we will come back to the symbol. The most profound symbols, the affective ones which we perceive directly in 'beings' and which seem to us to be inexhaustibly creative because they impose themselves upon us, have distant origins. We imagine that they are archaic, and indeed they are. On numerous occasions we have pointed out that the old sociological concept of 'survivals' is inadequate. Symbolisms duplicate the existence of 'beings' or of 'things' by reinforcing their immediate and fundamental presence. The Father represents robust affection, but he is also the Law, be it divine or human. The Sun is life and vitality per se. However, have these 'beings' and these 'things' always possessed a symbolic character? When the practical experience of human groups was constituted in an unmediated way, it was not duplicated by a symbolism, it imposed itself as a fact. Before the Father could appear as the incarnation of God or the State (of authority and law), religion and the state had to be constituted. The resonances and harmonics which reinforce fundamental reality make their appearance during the course of history. Symbolisms have no extratemporal or extrahistorical value. They too are established, formed and formulated. *They are the result of an initial displacement, an initial broadening of the semantic field.* For us, they are still linked to the fundamental rhythms and affective nucleuses which make up the immediacy of everyday life: night and day, 'private' relations, etc.

In all likelihood there were periods when symbolisms existed in a certain equilibrium with *signs* (such as written language and visual numbers). Would it not be true to say that these periods were particularly great and powerful aesthetically, and that they were the great periods of *expressivity*? Doubtless our present-day aesthetic perception of a whole range of archaic and ancient creative works is nothing more than a weakened version of symbolic perception as it was initially. We can also apply this proposition to medieval works of art. What does a cathedral mean to us? We may admire its elements and proportions, but what has that got to do with the way a thirteenth-century man would have grasped it as a set of cosmic, religious, political and human symbols?

For us there are still symbols in our everyday life, but at the same time they are no longer there. Everyday life immerses itself in them, but they elude it, because they elude us. We know them in diluted versions as allegories and metaphors, the stereotypes of good luck and bad luck, or petty superstitions. We have demonstrated how these symbols conceal dialectical movements which they keep to themselves. They are ambiguous. They suggest and they inhibit, they exclude and they include, they beckon and they reject, they reveal and they conceal, they act, they 'structure' and they disappear, they express and they dissimulate. What exactly? The life of a group, and its relation with nature and with other groups: what is or wants to be; what is not and does not want to be; a part of its secret.

In so far as we can know anything about them, the societies which were controlled by symbolisms were peasant societies solidly cemented by their cosmic rhythms and their human rhythms, and by their traditions, i.e., precisely by symbolisms. These appeared in stories of the kind we now call 'mythical tales', which specified in a very simple way the significance and the relations of the various symbols accepted by each particular society. What we must surely find paradoxical is that in societies such as these everyday life was not separate from symbolisms, and yet it did not merge with them. Our 'primitive man' knew perfectly well when he was dealing with a spring or a mountain as sacred powers, and when he was dealing with them as part of secular and practical life. The sacred and the secular, the everyday and the symbolic were not duplicates, but nor were they entangled together. Hence the astonishment of ethnographers (and of their readers) when confronted with such a 'mentality', and with the fact that primitive man makes excellent, practical use of objects which at the same time he endows with more-or-less occult properties.

What transpired when *signs* became more and more in evidence, and when men became aware of the use of signs as implements in their society? This took place not only with the invention and use of writing, but also with the advent of urban life, aesthetic and political life, and with the conscious use of discourse. The awakening of Greek thought and its history affords a wonderful example of this. It is here that Logos becomes aware of itself, i.e., that men (some of them specialists, grammarians and rhetors, others non-specialists, such as philosophers) become aware of Logos per se, and gain knowledge of it. It all becomes enormously confusing. Symbols and mythical tales are turned into discursive themes which have been liberated from their ancient constraints. The use of discourse comes in tandem with a marked scepticism about discourse. Alongside the philosophers of Logos we find the Sophists with their insoluble riddles. The signs which begin to proliferate (writing, written numbers, etc.) do not coexist peacefully with symbols, nor do they superimpose themselves upon them. The consequence is a twofold movement: a reorganization of symbolisms (which in their diluted version have been turned into objects for art and knowledge), and an appeal to symbolisms (as ethical or political models) as a means of orientation through all this great confusion. And so now, *signs masquerade as symbolisms, modifying and corroding them. A vast displacement of the whole semantic field takes place which both enriches it and overthrows it.*

We could suppose that henceforth the inner coherence of social consciousness (i.e., of the whole semantic field) and perhaps of society itself becomes a *work*. It is no longer accomplished with the rhythmic spontaneity of blissful unawareness. How does Greek thought re-establish a certain equilibrium in all this confusion? By the philosophy of Logos, of Plato or Aristotle? By tragedy? By an appeal to the sacred, in reaction against the dissolution of symbolisms and against the separation of the sacred and the secular, the everyday and the divine, which was already taking shape (and doubtless with great apprehension) in the irony of Socrates? Indeed, did the Greeks find a way out? Was not this great unheaval the harbinger of a very serious crisis in Greek society? This is neither the time nor the place to answer these questions. The fact that we use a historical example does not oblige us to theorize on the example per se; all we need is to be able to refer to history, i.e., to 'diachrony', in order to demonstrate the formation of a (synchronic) structure, namely the semantic field. What is more, reference to Greek thought may be extremely informative, but it has its limits; in our era, it is the signal – not the sign – which has the ascendancy. For obvious reasons, the Greeks never knew this child of technology.

With the period when signs come to prevail, symbols are hidden below signs masquerading as symbols. Modified, but still present and effective, they henceforth constitute a 'level'. Whereas signs intervene on the level of representations, symbols are active on another level of existence and consciousness: affectivity, spontaneity (if there is any left) and emotivity. We could talk about a social 'unconscious' inherent in everyday life, if the term did not bring with it a succession of

303

dubious representations. Misconscious is the term we prefer. There is misconsciousness of what constitutes the individual's affective nucleuses in his social group, and this misconsciousness is part of an uneasiness and an opaqueness which seem to be a prerequisite if those nucleuses are to be effective. The broader the semantic field, the more acute its inner tensions (the manifestations of dialectical movements). Levels cannot be quietly juxtaposed or superimposed, but neither can one level masquerade as another, or encompass it, without being disruptive. Dimly perceived as such, or not perceived at all, archaic symbolism is constantly intervening, creating confusions and tearing through the fabric of signs and of coherent discourse. It bursts forth dramatically, in cries, interjections and exclamations, in slips of the tongue – in short, in expressivity. Therefore there are literally holes and craters in the tumultuous volcanic landscape of the semantic field. Or else, chastened, modified, rationalized, in other words subjected to discourse and to the system of signs, symbolism slips into discourse through proverbs, sayings, fables, the old wisdom or the promise of a new wisdom. We will demonstrate how everyday communications presuppose all these elements.

Up until now we have concentrated on the most obscure and the most profound symbols and symbolisms, those which are linked to cosmic and vital rhythms and which are perpetuated (in liaison with these rhythms) in the profound affectivity of children and in the emotivity of adults. Religious symbolisms would seem to derive from a slow metamorphosis of primary or primitive symbolisms, a metamorphosis which maintains them during the growing predominance of signs, modifying and adapting them (more or less well) to dominant representations, i.e., to historical periods and social forces. Religion has managed to use these continual transformations and displacements of the semantic field to good advantage, or at least until now.

However, the laws of continuity which regulate it are not the only ones. Diachronically (historically), there are also discontinuities. *Every revolution destroys a set of symbols. Or else, in attempting to destroy them, it destroys itself.* It cannot but try to destroy them, because, as we now know, such symbols play a structural or 'structuring' role which is all the more effective for being hidden. As a consequence, every revolution makes enormous efforts to replace the old symbols it has destroyed with new ones (which are almost inevitably political). We can use these propositions not so much to define revolutionary activity as to characterize it, together with its successes, its failures and its limits. We know how violently the French Revolution 'desecrated' space, putting stipulations made by previous scientific knowledge about praxis and social consciousness into effect. It was in this naked, empty social space stripped bare of symbols that the everyday life of the bourgeoisie was to set up home. The same revolution would not withstand the pressures of time and the rhythms of (cosmic and social) time, which it was unable to rescue from the ancient symbolisms resurrected by religion: seasonal festivals, sacred numbers, cyclic organizations. Political symbols (such as the flag, etc.) could not replace and eliminate cosmic symbols. Henceforth, the symbolisms associated with lived (affective and emotional) time persisted, so to speak, beneath a social space which had been occupied first by signs, and then by signals. This confirmed the general tendency of the semantic field to structure itself in levels – with differences between levels, gaps, tensions and imbalances. The everyday life of bourgeois society was never to become established in a tranquil manner, although tranquillity was precisely what it was aiming for. Not only would it be forever shaken by insecurity, crises and wars, but the field upon which it was built was shifting, agitated, apparently stable on the surface, but undermined by forces from below.

Given an everyday life such as this it was useless trying to relegate symbolisms to the status of small gestures (goodbyes, farewells, handshakes, etc.), minor superstitions (touching wood, etc.) or dreams and folklore. Pointless! The bourgeois world – this world made bourgeois – of signs, significations and formalisms was to find itself caught between a rock and a hard place. On one hand, it was inevitable that there would be a resurgence of symbolisms, and that poets and philosophers would try to use them as a bulwark against the triviality of the 'world' of bourgeois significations. On the other, the signal was to attack and threaten the 'world' of signs and significations, in the name of industrial technology.

Furthermore, there were entire sectors of social practice which continued to be governed by symbolisms, although these were not without their conflicts. For example, symbols of femininity would conflict violently with the practical claims of women. And there was one thing in bourgeois life which would never cease: the yearning for the impossible event – a marvellous, omnipotent Word, which would at last subordinate space to time, metamorphosing it and transmuting the real into a limitless, immortal and magical timelessness . . .

For the time being we will put these contradictions to one side, along with the way they developed in 'modernity' together with their many aspects (romanticisms, Utopianisms, philosophies of the unconscious, imagination and dreams; the victory of abstract art and threats to aesthetics in general, etc.).

Displacement now appears to be a general law. But it also becomes more complicated, because there are some genuine transfers, such as the reorganization of one level by another, and phenomena of rupture. Finally, displacements provoke or reveal inverse phenomena: resurgences, returns, recollections.

10 The social text

For the time being we will present this idea without developing its content. In effect, its significance will only become apparent in the 'communications model'. However it also has a place in the theory of the semantic field. To be accurate, the 'social text' is an aspect of the semantic field, and nothing more. It is how we each perceive the semantic field in everyday life, in a non-conceptual or preconceptual (affective and perceptive) manner.

It is the result of the combination of the above-mentioned formants, but in proportions which are infinitely varied: *signals*, which teach us nothing, and make imperative commands using repetitions which are always identical; *symbols*, which are hidden but which show through from the depths of the social spectacle, transforming it into something other than a spectacle. They bring influence to bear, because they demand participation or challenge it, because they are always a source of surprise, and because their reappearances are always unforeseen; finally, *signs*, which only afford moderate surprises and diversities, since to a certain extent they are predictable.

We all find ourselves constantly – on a daily basis – faced with a social text. We leaf through it, we read it. It is via this text and our reading of it that we communicate with the other, be it society as a whole, or nature. At the same time, we are all part of a social text. We are not only readers; we are also read, deciphered and explained (or not). We are all there indissolubly as object and subject (*object primarily*, since the social text encompasses us and we must see ourselves thus encompassed; *then subject*, since we see ourselves within the text, and decipher and read it from inside, and never completely from outside).

Referring to information theory, we would say that *signals* constitute redundancy in the modern social text: banality and clarity, triviality and intelligibility. *Signs* bring information. *Symbols* can be compared to the 'noises' which interfere with the information which pours forth according to a known (codified and conventional) repertoire, surrounding it from all sides (background noises, empty sounds . . .).

Still with reference to information theory, we would say that at some times a social text is more legible than it is at others. When it is overloaded with symbolisms and overflowing with information, too rich or too rambling, it loses its legibility. When it is reduced to signals, it collapses into perfect banality. It is clear, understandable and boring, and repeats itself ad nauseam. It is the triumph of redundancy. A good social text which is legible and informative will surprise its 'subjects', but will not exceed their abilities; it will always teach them a great deal, but it will never overwhelm them; it is easily comprehensible, but never trivial. So we can measure the richness of the social text by the extent to which it can vary while remaining accessible: by the richness of newness and possibilities it offers to individuals.

Armed with these concepts, let us analyse a few forms of the social text as it is available to us all on a daily basis. The day-to-day reader is not aware of things which only analysis can reveal. The well-informed reader, however, realizes that he is looking at a part of structures: one level of existence and reality, bearing in mind that no one level can exhaust reality as a whole.

In *the village* everything remains symbolic and reveals the truth of symbolisms: archaic and powerful, attached to things, and equally attached to rhythms. The house, the field, the tree, the sky, the mountain or the sea are not simply what they are. Cosmic and vital rhythms envelop them, subtle resonances accompany them, every 'thing' is part of a song. Space and the land symbolize the community, and the church with its cemetery defines time and the world, life and death. Poignantly archaic, everyday life offers itself with complete simplicity: it is entirely humdrum and yet inseparable from its deeper resonances. Every gesture relates to 'something' fundamental, a need, a possession, an object, a presence or an absence, and has a symbolic meaning: picking up bread, cutting it, opening or closing the door of the dwelling, crossing the courtyard and the garden, going out into the countryside. In the village, everything is vigorously alive with the life of actions which are made all the stronger by the symbols they embody. And everything is outdated, old-fashioned, far away . . .

The landscape also offers a social text which is generally legible and often admirably composed, and in which mankind and nature come face to face: the symbols of the former, the signs of the latter.

If we look at *the city*, we will quickly notice how difficult it is to understand this masterly work created by social groups and by society as a whole. It bears the traces of struggles which stimulated the force of creativity, and yet this force tends to obliterate such traces. In the city, symbols have lost the ubiquity they have retained in the village. They become localized and condensed. This does not mean that their role is somehow diminished. Quite the contrary: everything which has prestige and influence, or aspires to having it, everything which organizes and controls this enormous mass of humanity, tends to link up with ancient symbolisms so as to exploit their age-old authority, or else to present new symbolisms in an attempt at self-justification. Symbolisms are condensed into monuments: churches, cathedrals, palaces, large public and private buildings are laden with symbols which merge with their decorations and aesthetic style. Monuments are the works which give a city its face and its rhythm of life. They are its memory and the representation of its past, the affective and active nucleuses of its present everyday life and the prefiguration of its future. We will call them 'suprafunctional' or 'transfunctional', but this is to say not that they have no function or that they transcend function, but rather that their functions are so diverse that no functionality can characterize them or exhaust their social function. On the other hand, in working-class neighbourhoods, in the districts near factories and in factories themselves, there are few monuments, if any. Symbols have disappeared (which means that everything symbolizes power and oppression, and in a hideous way). Nature has disappeared and culture is invisible. Here everything becomes a signal: the signal to start work and the gestures while working and the gestures which maintain the workforce.

Alongside its monuments and proletarian neighbourhoods, the city offers its informative text, rich in signs and significations. Here any analytic description should specify cities and typify them: the city of antiquity, majestically organizing movements which are still close to the old vital rhythms around a few monuments – the stadium, the temple, the agora, the forum, the theatre; the medieval city, with its prodigious vitality, where all elements intercommunicate, city and countryside, house and street, productive craft labour and barter . . . Let us make do with a quick word about the *street*, that phenomenon which epitomizes the modern city. It is in its streets that the life of the large industrial city is at its most original and authentic. It is the street which offers those possibilities and choices which are incomparably more numerous in the city than in the village or small town. We say they 'attract' or 'tempt' us, we call them bargains or fancies, whether we are talking about objects or people, encounters or enticements and adventures. As soon as the street loses this attraction, because it is empty or because the weight of traffic makes it unbearable, the city becomes transformed into a lunar landscape.

What this tells us is that in the society we are observing – the society we are reading – and of which we are a part, intermediaries have special privileges which are frequently excessive and detrimental to things which have or could have more reality. This proposition could be based on an economic analysis: the role of commodities and money, these intermediaries which are becoming increasingly powerful, these things which are becoming fetishes, these mediations which take on a determining role by dissimulating and overwhelming whatever they are linking together. We could read this proposition directly, here in the social text. We will find it on the level of good sense and everyday observation; and yet, there is something paradoxical about it. It means that all around us, the places through which we pass and where we meet – the street, the café or the station – are more important and truly more interesting than our homes and our houses, the places which they link. It is a living paradox, and if everyday familiarity makes us admit it, it does not allow us to see how absurd it is. In times gone by, in the city of antiquity or of medieval times, things were different. Traffic – people, commodities, vehicles – did not dominate. The means and the ends of communication, and indeed of everything, were subordinated to human beings. In this day and age, there is a situation which we are tempted to accept de facto, and even to emphasize: when the street stops being interesting, so does everyday life. Now the city is full to bursting with cars. It has been reduced to systems of signals. What will become of it?

Busy, active, its only link with nature the sky and the clouds or a few trees and flowers, the street represents the everyday in our social life. It embodies it almost completely, like a digest which is interesting because it is so condensed. And this is despite being external to individual and social existence, or because of it. A place of passage, of interaction, of movement and communication, it becomes, via an astonishing volte-face, the reflection of the things it links together, something with more life in it than those things themselves. It becomes the microcosm of modern life. If anything is hidden, it tears it out from its darkness. It makes it public. It robs it of its privacy and drags it on to the stage of a spontaneous theatre, where the actors improvise a play which has no script. The street takes whatever is happening somewhere else, in secret, and makes it public. It changes its shape, and inserts it into the social text.

Like the everyday, the street is constantly changing and always repeats itself. In the unceasing shifts of times of day, people, objects and light, it repeats itself, tirelessly. The street is a spectacle, almost nothing but a spectacle, but not completely a spectacle, because we are in it, walking, stopping and participating. If you hurry you will not see the spectacle, even if you are part of it. Almost an absolute spectacle, but not completely, it is an open book, or rather a newspaper: it has news, banalities, surprises, advertisements. Analogous and homologous, the street and the newspaper join forces in our everyday life. Simultaneously, they make it and they represent it. Changing but always identical, the street only offers a limited number of surprises. If anything sensational (really sensational), extravagant, absurd, offensive or sublime happens, it only vaguely interrupts the diversified monotony of the absolute quasi-spectacle. Symbols stroll by unnoticed. In this day and age, who takes the symbolisms of cathedrals with their devils and divine figures seriously, or sees any drama in them? The street confronts us with a social text which is generally good, dense and legible. All kinds of people mingle in it, becoming almost interchangeable. In times gone by, when class differences were less clear-cut than nowadays, when there were 'estates' and 'castes' rather than classes, these differences were expressed loudly and clearly. The street was expressive. Nowadays, these ostentatious differences have disappeared; they would make the crowds which throng the Champs-Elysées or the Grands Boulevards unbearably gaudy. However, social differences are still visible, signified by a number of indexes and signs noticeable only to the trained eye. This is to say that the street encompasses a multitude of semeiologies. Do faces express anything? A little, but not much. Clothes and body language signify. So the spectacle of the street stimulates our desire to see things and forms our way of seeing them. How many women there are who have unknowingly become part of subtle systems of signs, entering them from within, and using them to classify other women with one simple glance at their shoes, their stockings, their hair, their hands and fingernails, their jewellery and their general appearance! A detailed analysis of the social text would reveal these partial systems of signs and significations which interweave or criss-cross like the items in a newspaper.[4]

The 'world of objects' as they appear in the street is like a large, front-page news item, and yet it constitutes one of the most subtle and least defined systems of signs. In the street, commodities are on offer, but their commercial essence is concealed. They want to be nothing but loveliness, enchantment, pleasure and serenity.[5] In the large modern city, the street postulates and confirms the harmony between needs, desires and goods. Paradise lost is rediscovered in the form of a parody; at every step original unity is restored in caricature. Goods, things and objects are on display; they are offered to our gaze in order to attract and stir up our desires, proclaiming their principle with no apparent irony: 'To each object its desire, to each of us our desires, to each desire its goods and its pleasures. There are goods and desires for everyone, democratically, even for children, even for people who are not very rich, but there are a lot more – all of them – for people who are.' Infinitely near, because they correspond to a desire which is both genuine and phoney, and yet frighteningly inaccessible, like superbly presented women up for sale, objects lead

their sovereign life behind the shop windows. The street is an intermediary between human lives, and its commodities are exchange
values elevated to sovereign heights. Raised to its zenith, fetishism
attains a kind of splendour; and, in an astonishing subterfuge, things,
goods and objects join forces with symbolism again to become the
symbols of wealth and pleasure without limits and without end.
Certain streets have the same beauty as museums, weary and lifeless.
It is a closed circuit in which products – commodities – are changed
into desirable and desired goods. Here, in this involuntary work, the
street, the specific beauty of our society is accomplished. Through the
interplay of objects offered and refused, the street becomes a place of
dreams and imagination, but also of reality at its most implacable. In
the street men and women – particularly women – pay fool's court to
things. Queen-things, fairy-things, holding court behind the transparent windows which parody the transparency of human relations, they
have the magic power to transform their male and female courtiers
into things. Window-shopping has its magic and its religion: the per-
fected, all-powerful commodity. Sanctified, goods coincide with the
spectacle which they and their advertisements offer. Consumption
gleams in all its hallowed splendour. Through all the possible and
impossible physical delights, all the dreams, all the frustrations,
money claims its kingdom, its empire, its pontificate.

Far away, in the factories (the ones which produce these wonderful
objects, or those which produce the means for their production),
everything is functional or is intended as such; everything is a signal –
the repetitive gestures of labour and its technical organization. Far
away, on the working-class estates, everything is functional, everything is a signal – the repetitive gestures by which the labour force
keeps on going in its everyday life . . .

11 Dialogue, discussion, conversation

We will understand the use and misuse of discourse by analogy with
the social text. Most semanticists, linguists and language theorists do
the opposite; they use discourse to understand other forms of communication and other texts and contexts.

First and foremost, the language of conversation uses banalities.

We talk about neutral things, i.e., really about things and about people seen as things: the weather, the neighbours, friends, the high cost of living and the vagaries of politics, pecking order and wages, who's sleeping with whom and who's cheating on whom. In this discourse bulging with redundancies and commonplaces, dreary word follows dreary word. It is clear, understandable, repetitive. However this apparently useless exchange of trivia signifies something. It bears witness to a generalized need. Shy, awkward, sometimes coarse and sometimes discreet, it is the need to communicate and to exchange something other than mere things. What is more, through the banality which ravages this level of discourse like an unchecked epidemic, stereotypes of everyday life are visible, with the result that trivial discussions and banal conversations, with the family, in the café or elsewhere, can undergo a sudden shift of perspective, to become highly interesting and full of meaning. (For example: conversations about cars, traffic and road accidents between upper-class or 'comfortably off' men; conversations about technical matters; discussions between women about fashion, etc.). *In triviality, it is the dominant representations which are signified, along with their stereotypes.*

Sometimes an unexpected impulse shifts the direction of the discussion. We find ourselves talking about our own lives in terms which go beyond banality (not too far, except in the case of those innocent fools who confide in people without suspecting that inevitably the day will come when these confidences will be used against them. Nevertheless we talk about ourselves up to a point, using keywords, such as love and hate, father and mother, childhood and old age, 'home' and away, family, the world). Then come the long words and the important theories, metaphors and values (usually brought in unawares, by implication) which play in discourse the role played by monuments in the city: proverbs rich in wisdom, usually of the resigned variety, proper nouns affording sudden revelations, dramatizations and absolute principles, truths about life, folklore – sometimes domestic, sometimes social – which often comes from the depths of times long past. At this point, the dialogue becomes overloaded; it grinds painfully to a halt. It becomes a dialogue of the deaf, just as dialogues do when they are extremely trivial, but in this case because it is too rich, and has trespassed beyond the zone of average communication. To go any farther it would have to cross over into poetry or spontaneous lyricism. And it is usually on the threshold of truth, at the instant when communication is at its deepest, that dialogue stops. Sooner or later dialogue will start using symbols in order to guarantee mutual comprehension, and what are symbols if not deteriorated, shattered or buried nucleuses of sensibility, emotion or affectivity? On the lowest level, opaqueness provides a fulcrum, and we are as happy as sandboys among our ambiguities and misunderstandings. On the highest level, it is the emptiness of luminous and transparent space, reminding us of earth and its charnel house of dead symbols, or of an even emptier heaven with its population of inaccessible representations. Only poetry has the wings to soar there. Communication shifts between the silence below and the silence above.

It sets all the levels into motion, and challenges them. It implies and supposes them all: the coherence of discourse and the banality of coherent discourse; words acting like signals which trigger predictable responses; emotivity which introduces images and transmits unexpected impulses into discourse; the emergence of symbols; the emptiness and inadequacy of intended meanings, the gaps, the absences.

5

The Theory of Accumulative and Non-accumulative Processes

1 Critique of the idea of progress

Philosophical and sociological critique of this idea has become rudimentary and banal, since it is dictated by the most obvious and the most easily provable facts. An entirely optimistic idea that progress could spread simultaneously through every area (an idea which was linked to a simplistic evolutionism) has quite literally collapsed during the course of the twentieth century. After Hegel and Marx, the general theory of dialectical movement had stipulated that the process of becoming in all sectors (nature, history, knowledge) would surely be more chequered – discontinuous, conflictual, riven by partial or general regressions – than time as the naive evolutionist pattern represents it. Events have fully vindicated the pattern presented by dialectical thought, and more than anyone could have imagined.

2 Uneven development

We have already stressed the extreme theoretical generality of this concept, which was introduced into Hegelian and Marxist dialectical thought by Lenin. The idea of *uneven development* makes the general critique of the continuist (evolutionist) pattern of the process of becoming more precise, specific and particularized. In our opinion, the implications and consequences of the idea of uneven development and the law derived from it have not yet been exhausted, particularly as regards everyday life. We have already suggested the hypothesis of a period not only where the hoe or the swing plough would coexist alongside interplanetary rockets, and where small farmers would continue to work the land by hand and go hungry while an 'elite' of technicians and managers would be exploring outer space, but also where a backward everyday life would coexist with a highly developed technology, in a way which would be difficult to bear. The situation of everyday life strikes us (unfortunately) as being a prime example of the law of uneven development. But the proposition can be reversed: the law of uneven development points to the possibility of an almost limitless range of human (social) situations at the very heart of economic and technological development, from the rearguard to the front line of action, to use a military metaphor.

We know that the underdeveloped sectors do not remain quietly held back like a troop of soldiers dragging their heels far from the front line. The sectors which are destined to suffer uneven development, be it temporary or long-lasting, soon realize that they are being occupied and brutally exploited. They must regain their freedom or win it back by combat. They remain subjected.

Critique of everyday life generalizes this experience of the 'backward' or 'underdeveloped' nations and extends it to the everyday in the highly developed industrial countries. It lays down the principle that the great upheaval which calls on the consciousness of those nations engaged in the drama of uneven development to emancipate themselves should reverberate through 'modernity' via an upheaval of everyday life and a general upheaval in the name of everyday life, given that it is a backward sector which is exploited and oppressed by so-called 'modern' society.

We insist that this is not simply a metaphor, an allegory, or a mere simile or superficial analogy, but that the problem is fundamentally the same. The link between the situation of the everyday and that of the proletariat goes to the heart of the problem: the transformation of the world, i.e., of the everyday life of today, in 'modern' society, given its history and its structures.

It is a deplorable situation, which we have barely begun to describe, and which we must try to explain. But how did it come about?

3 Non-accumulative societies

Among the many debts the sciences of society owe to Marx, one extremely important discovery stands out, although he himself did not develop its consequences fully – far from it. There is a distinction between two major types of society: one is based economically on simple reproduction, the other on reproduction on an extended scale. To put it even more precisely, the analysis of capitalist society reveals it to contain a double process, one called 'simple reproduction', and the other, 'reproduction on an extended scale'. The second supposes the first, and the first continues a process within capitalism which was inherent in precapitalist societies.

A society should not only produce and reproduce the quantity of goods which allows its population to survive (to reproduce itself biologically, to bring up children and to maintain – more or less adequately – its non-productive members). This strictly economic interpretation of the patterns presented in *Capital* (Volume 3, Part 7) does not go deep enough. *Society must also reproduce the social relations between its members.* Thus 'praxis' as Marx describes it cannot be content merely to reconstitute a basis for consumption. It maintains production relations and the social division of labour. Social relations retain a (relative) stability while the members of a society are constantly changing; they are born and they die, and pass from one group to another (through marriage, notably) while maintaining their relations. The 'praxis' described in this way on the economic level is therefore not repetition in the same sense as industrial activity is. It repeats itself in cycles. Marx describes and analyses the process of simple reproduction as a *cyclic* process. The patterns of simple reproduction express the distribution of human activities in a society based on a weak level of productive forces, but endowed with an inner cohesion (a 'structure'). Societies built on a (relatively) stable but stagnant base are destined to be balanced in a static way. In this very stagnation they demonstrate an extraordinary ability to resist and to persist. The cohesion of primitive communities removes them from the historicity which could shatter them from without, and from the 'incidental' history which would destroy them from within. They can be conquered and subjected, but as long as the conqueror does not annihilate them, they carry on. Structure persists by recreating itself indefinitely, in a circular way. This pattern seems valid for all pre-capitalist societies based on agriculture and handicrafts. Marx did little more than outline this kind of generalization, but it is based on the theoretical and methodological propositions intrinsic to *Capital* and to his *Contribution to the Critique of Political Economy*. According to Marx, the study of capitalism sheds light on what preceded it and not vice versa, which is what evolutionism and the simplified theory of progress believed.

It is self-evident that the members of a particular society are not aware of the circular process and the internal self-regulation which make them tend towards a static equilibrium. However, we should not think they are somehow unaware or falsely aware of their own 'praxis'. The study of agrarian systems and the distribution of tasks in peasant communities reveals great practical wisdom, although this wisdom was never able to express and transmit itself conceptually.

It is also self-evident that the stability of these societies was constantly being threatened by aberrant phenomena such as excesses, defects or 'disturbances' (the 'hubris' of Greek thought). Governed by their Wise Men, the assemblies and councils of elders, and by priests, warlords and political chiefs, these societies employed various means to eliminate such perturbations along with their causes. Similarly, they eliminated any threat of surplus population.

On this point, Marx was happy merely to present a pattern of simple reproduction and to make a few general observations which we will return to shortly. He made no attempt to determine in what way the structures of these societies were analogous or differing, nor to grasp the underlying reasons for their stability on the base as we have just described it. Here as elsewhere, this economic 'base' allows us to know the skeleton of this society, but not how it really functioned (its 'physiology'). It offers us conditions for possibilities, and general conditions for societies which differ greatly from each other to construct themselves. In any case, this was not the task Marx had set himself in *Capital*. He left the job of studying precapitalist societies to others, notably to ethnographers. Everyone knows that in *The Origin of the Family: Private Property and the State*, Engels tried to fill this gap using the work of the first modern ethnographers.

There is one important idea which enables us to understand the real structures of precapitalist societies and the reasons for the stability which has helped them to survive into our own era. We have met it before. *In archaic societies, the fundamental processes are cyclic, and these cycles remain very close to cosmic cycles and the rhythms which come from nature.* The economic process of simple reproduction, which, as Marx demonstrated, is cyclic in character, is an almost unnoticeable component of the cycles and rhythms which predominate as an organizing factor in these agrarian societies: hours and days, seasons and years, generations, youth and old age. We find these societies surprising. They organize themselves in time and according to time more than in space, while significantly they have no historical time or 'temporality' comparable to our own society but, instead, a time scale made up of intertwined cycles. We have linked these social rhythms to the most ancient of symbolisms, and we have had no problem in demonstrating their continuation (we deliberately do not say their 'survivals') in our present-day villages, as shattered, buried or deteriorated nucleuses.

Could it be that these archaic, peasant and craft-based societies (but with embryonic commercial activity) had no history? To believe so would be a naive mistake and an absurdity. These societies have a history, a double one, but in their own particular manner which is different from our own 'historicity'. On the one hand, and from the outside, conquerors established vast political entities – empires – on a multitude of peasant communities, and often by the use of embryonic commercial activities (such as barter, exchanges, or the possibility of exacting tributes and taxes). In this political framework, states and dominant classes which foreshadowed feudalism or the bourgeoisie began to take shape. Immobile and almost immovable on their static and stagnating 'base', these empires lasted until such time as a weak tremor might lead to their sudden collapse. Empires like this have lasted until the present day – The Turkish Empire, for example. Notable among this type of political formation are the pre-Columbian American empires, the Roman Empire, the Byzantine Empire and the great Asiatic empires, each with its own specific characteristics within the general context we have defined above.

On the other hand, the archaic societies in question also had a complex internal history, precisely in so far as there were differences between them. By his pattern of simple reproduction, Marx drew attention to an important fact. These archaic societies had a political economy, although the economic side of it was not predominant and determinant *stricto sensu*. Their political economy functioned blindly, spontaneously, almost automatically as the practice of economy in the precise sense of the term when we say that someone is *economical*: a distribution of tasks and products which is spontaneous to begin with, but which becomes increasingly conscious, in 'poor' societies controlled by governing groups which demand abstinence from the other groups, and sometimes from themselves. Marx criticized political economy and law as the knowledge and practice of non-abundance. Be that as it may, scarcity is a completely relative idea which cannot be taken to the absolute or be of any use as an explicative principle. A society without surplus product, in which labour allows for nothing more than the survival of its workers, will quickly disappear. In the archaic societies we are talking about, dominant groups, which were not yet classes in the exact, contemporary meaning of the term, were thus able to gain control of a certain surplus labour and surplus product. It is obvious that slavery and subsequently serfdom made it possible to increase surplus labour and to extort part of the surplus product all the more easily. These dominant groups seized the surplus social product and appropriated it to their needs and works. What is remarkable is that in most of these societies the 'masters' transformed the wealth they had levied into works, as if they felt they had to justify that levy to the people and account for it to the community, which had not yet been completely burst asunder. We use the term 'works' in its broadest sense: monuments, festivals, permanent or transitory works of art. As yet these masters justified their existence and their predominance not by using representations and ideologies, but by *symbols*, which they embodied physically in a multiplicity of works.

Only in this way can we understand how diverse these ancient societies were: violence and equilibrium, vitality and stability, poverty and splendour, shabbiness and beauty. In retrospect they offer us a diptych: on one panel, a realm of brutality and despotism, on the other, extraordinary creations in art, lifestyle, wisdom, culture and even philosophy (although the latter only emerges with conceptual thought and the awareness of discourse per se, which bring ancient wisdom to a close). Marxist thought contains the indications which enable us to approach the study of archaic or ancient societies in all their manifold aspects.[1] However, there is one particularly profound and well-known question raised by Marx, and which he himself did not resolve: how is it that the bourgeois and socialist cultures of today can be interested in works from distant periods, created in conditions which were very different from our own by groups (castes, embryonic classes) which established themselves using unbridled and limitless violence, and which used the meagre surplus social product to create all this sumptuousness? What can explain the lasting character of these works, these superstructures of defunct societies?

At this stage we will hazard a few conceptual elements for a theory. At the heart of archaic and ancient societies, everyday life was not separate from what was 'highest' and 'greatest' in culture and ideas. This is something we have already pointed out. 'Primitive' man, the archaic peasant and probably the citizen of ancient cities all knew full well how to distinguish between the sacred and the secular, the everyday and the sublime, while for us these two elements of their lives seem inextricably merged. This man may have believed that a given familiar object was possessed of an obscure power for good or for evil, but he still knew perfectly well how to put it to practical use; and he knew perfectly well when he was addressing that power and when he was not. Why? How? Because of the very nature of symbolism and of symbols, which enter the 'lived' and duplicate or reduplicate reality without becoming separate from it. Just as every object in these societies could easily become a work of art (all that was needed was a little effort and, far from being the exception, this effort was the rule. Absence of any art was the exception, and a sign of degeneracy), so everyday life could easily become a lifestyle. Every change in the men who commanded these societies and in the symbols which they used would have an influence on style in the everyday: it would be grandiose, sublime, sensual, sensuous, erotic or violent, according to the men and to the circumstances. From the very first peasant societies which saw the birth of meditation to the great empires and even to the Greek city states, almost every possible stylistic hypothesis was attempted.

Now if the analysis we are attempting here is at all correct, our own everyday life has a double character. On one hand, it has no style; in the context of a history which is moving ever farther away from the everyday, and of a globalized society which holds sway over it from the empyrean realms of the state, the utilitarian and the functional constitute not a style, but its opposite: the absence of style. On the other hand, there are some very ancient symbolisms which alone are able to restore some strength to gestures and actions which have been robbed of all meaning; although they have deteriorated and shattered, they still form effective nucleuses which, however destructive or in-adequate, are still active. How could we not grasp the works of the past? They interest us, they fascinate us, and we call upon them desperately to give us a sense and a style. In the name of the vast emptiness which is everyday life, our everyday life, we look towards everything which could point to or perpetuate a plenitude. Any age, it does not matter which. It is not aesthetic sensibility or ideology which acts as mediator, but everyday life.[2] However our interest in the objects and ideas of distant societies labours under one serious mis-conception. We perceive them as art objects, whereas in fact this art was not something external to the everyday or, as is supposed, high above it and trying in vain to enter it, but a *style of life*. What we per-ceive as theories and philosophies were in fact ways of everyday living. This is why the more we return to these objects and ideas, the more they disturb us. We are well aware that we do not understand them. We look for their historic context (when there was no history ana-logous to ours), their social context (when there was no society analogous to ours) or their ideological context (when abstract ideo-logical representations had not yet appeared, and concretely lived cosmic symbols and rhythms close to cosmic rhythms predominated).

4 The concept of the process of accumulation

Simple reproduction is and remains a necessary condition for all social life. From a certain date onwards (at the end of the Middle Ages in the European West) it gives way to another process, that of accu-mulation on an extended scale. Marx studied it schematically, restricting it to the economic point of view (and knowing full well that this level of reality does not encompass reality as a whole). In *Capital* he determines the reciprocal proportions of the different sectors of production which are essential for the effective development of repro-duction on an extended scale, i.e., the accumulation of capital.[3] Marx did not specify the historical conditions and diverse conjunctures which allow or allowed for the insertion of the process of accumulation into stable structures governed by the previous type of process.

The process of accumulation profoundly modifies and overturns the previous process. It does not abolish it. It encompasses it, and introduces the fundamental contradiction between the social character of productive labour and the private ownership of the means of production. Despite this fundamental contradiction (which will develop into the polarized and antagonistic 'bourgeoisie/proletariat' class contradiction) society must remain coherent and internally cohesive. Antagonisms can lead to breaks; contradictions do not stop society from constituting a whole (a totality). Self-regulating mechanisms change, but they do not disappear.[4] And so cyclic movements are not abolished. A process resembling a rising spiral segmented by numerous accidents encompasses the circular process, which from then on maintains a periodicity. Society as a whole continues to reproduce its relations and conditions of existence, but the socio-economic proportions inherent to simple reproduction are modified by the proportions necessary for accumulation on an extended scale. On analysis we find that they are still present, as conditions for a dynamic equilibrium (rather as we find ancient mechanistic physics present within modern physics). If the society of economic growth did not go on reproducing its social relations, it would crumble away. But this would only happen gradually, and on a limited level: the level of the fragmented division of labour and of the conscious relations between separate individuals, and of the separation between 'private' and 'public', and between 'the everyday' and 'the world as a whole'. On the level of society as a whole, on the level of property and production relations (of class relations), social cohesion continues to grow ever more strong. The economic mechanisms of self-regulation in themselves are not enough to guarantee it, and as they only come into play on a certain level, the cohesion of the whole is guaranteed in another way, on the level of a certain consciousness: by representations, ideologies, models, values, and also by new works, and finally, by the use and misuse of ancient symbolisms.

This process of accumulation involves society as a whole, and the men who compose it, in a historicity: in *history* in the accepted sense of the term, and which Marx characterizes as natural history or the prehistory of man as a true human being. As we understand it, this history differs quite profoundly from the history affecting archaic societies. It has its specific characteristics: the process of accumulation controls it and determines its conjunctures. Unlike in ancient societies (although it was certainly important), the economic sphere becomes predominant and determining. This history is made by individuals and groups, but blindly. Trapped as they are in a deep and many-sided alienation, it is something they must endure. And so the accumulative economic process comes in tandem with a political and ideological history which is particularly linked to uneven economic development. The historical (political and social) experience of recent times makes it necessary for us to continue to develop Marxist theory beyond the point Marx himself left it. To begin with, let us present several propositions:

a) Marx conceived of socialism both as the end to the process of accumulation, and as its aim. Once this process had reached a high degree of productive investments (of productivity and production) in the highly industrialized countries, the revolutionary proletariat would take over its administration. It would not bring accumulation to an end, but would immediately orientate it towards the conscious transformation of the world.

Our reinstatement of the Marxist project has already shown that Marx was concerned not so much with transforming the outside world as with metamorphosing everyday life. The alienation of the everyday as a residual deposit and a product of all the partial alienations would disappear. This prediction has not been borne out. However, from the historical moment when growth and accumulation (the level of the productive forces) made what Marx predicted *possible,* there was a qualitative change. This was the moment we entered into 'modernity' and into the permanent crisis of modernity which is now permeating every sphere.

b) The socialism achieved as the result of a proletarian revolution in a poorly industrialized country seems to differ somewhat from the Marxist programme (but let us be prudent and optimistic: it is different until further notice). Socialism appears to be a social and political means for accelerating the process of accumulation in backward and 'underdeveloped' countries; it corresponds to the 'globalization' of the process, and not to the end of it. It consists not of enjoyment of what has been accomplished, but of an intensification of the accomplishment itself. The destructive character of the process, which determined European history for centuries, is becoming modified; in certain aspects it is becoming weaker, and in others more accentuated. It is remarkably obvious that the process of accumulation is speeding up. The factors of saturation and rupture which threatened it for centuries in Europe have been eliminated, but the ideological, cultural, political and 'human' consequences of this activity entirely devoted to accumulation remain with us in a permanent state of challenge and extraordinary tension. It is to this world-wide situation, which Marx did not predict, that we owe the intensification of old forms of (ideological and political) alienation, and the invention of new forms of alienation (technological alienation, and total alienation of the everyday).

c) The process of accumulation appears as the central axis or backbone of modern history. It is in relation to this process that historical situations are characterized and become specific. Let us indicate several of its types: when the process develops spontaneously, antedating the formation of the state (e.g., England, the United States, and France, in part), when the state accompanies and stimulates the process (e.g., France, in part, Germany, Italy, and Tsarist Russia), when the state organizes and accelerates the process (e.g., the Socialist states), and when the state antedates the process of accumulation (e.g., the underdeveloped countries which have recently won their independence). As a consequence there are remarkable historical differences in the role these states play, in how they are structured and in the way they function. This does not take other considerations into account, such as legal modalities and property relations within the state.

5 Generalization of the concept

This is not the place to study the patterns (in *Capital*) of how reproduction on an extended scale functioned, or to give a close analysis of the historicity and diversity of the historical situations during this process, or to describe the changing historical conditions of accumulation. We know that Marx did not present these conditions in their totality and diversity. He restricted himself to England and English capitalism (as a type or an extreme case: a spontaneous process which antedated the formation of the state and subsequently minimized its role). This initial gap has never been adequately filled, and has led to some serious misunderstandings. Some people in the Marxist movement have been too exclusive in attributing the simple requirements of industrialization to the ferocity of the bourgeoisie. We now know that no nation and no country can escape these torments, although the modalities and the nature of the devastation may differ.

We will restrict ourselves to a few comments which will allow us to present the concept of accumulative process (or growth by accumulation) on its most extended scale. As soon as the economic historian examines the conditions of primitive accumulation in Western Europe, he will observe that there was an increase in discoveries and technical progress during the Middle Ages. This was pointed out by Marx, who did not share the opinion of evolutionist and liberal historians about the 'Dark Ages'. Subsequently the work of technologists and historians has extended our knowledge on this subject. When we examine this early 'capitalization' of techniques, we discover the complexity of the historical conditions: the renewal of urban life, the recovery in commercial exchanges, the rediscovery of Greek science. The recovery of commercial exchanges was the result of improvements in agricultural techniques attributable to the arrival from the East of peoples who had hitherto been nomadic (progress in the use of horses, harnesses, ploughs, crop rotation, etc.). Technical progress in the Middle Ages was due to the fusion of several contributions, as much as it was to any special inventive capability. What did these contributions have in common? How can we explain the renewal of this inventive capability? It was a moment when thought was rediscovering the ability to be conceptual and abstract. Now only logic can determine a 'level' of experience and of reflective thought which will enable concepts, abstract (mathematical, physical and biological) knowledge and techniques to be accumulated effectively and transmitted more skilfully than with using examples or day-to-day discourse. Only logic defines a coherence on a level which is above and beyond nature, empiricism and spontaneous sociability. Using the rediscovery of Greek culture, and on an analogous economic base (commodity production, urban life, increased communications and exchanges), but without an unmediated or mechanical link between this 'base' and the acquisitions it facilitated, the Middle Ages were able to redefine *the form* which the process of accumulation would take. Then, after having been interrupted and slowed down for many centuries, the process gained impetus, producing a veritable discontinuity in the sixteenth century (which is inaccurately called the Renaissance).

And so our idea of the process of accumulation is now much broader. Knowledge is an accumulative process, and so is technology. Taken together they presuppose the elaboration of a form and are part of the conditions of a specific process: the accumulation of capital, i.e., of the means of production, which begins deep within the capitalist mode of production. At first we saw the process of accumulation as something uniform, but now we are beginning to see that it is composed of several related processes. It is a sheaf, a fasces. Once we have distinguished between them, its components themselves appear to be accumulative processes. *Rationality, for example, has an accumulative character.* Among these activities, which are partial processes within a comprehensive process, we may include knowledge, technology, production and productivity, i.e., economics, culture in the accepted sense of the word (linked to rationality and knowledge) and maybe political action, in so far as it operates from established legal and bureaucratic superstructures, which also 'snowball'.

Every process of accumulation can be represented schematically by an exponential curve (a^x or e^x, at the fastest growth: here this is a temporal function, a^t or e^t). This exponential growth can only be a *tendency*, or rather it is generally only a tendency. When of necessity the process involves factors which slow it down (more or less deep and lasting saturation), the exponential curve takes on a much more complicated form, called a 'logistic' curve.[5] In point of fact, we know that historical events and conjunctures can interrupt or break any process of an accumulative kind.

We can use this observation to draw up a schematic of history over the last five centuries or so. It is doubly determined by the economic process of accumulation, which is its axis, and the conjunctures and events which propel, slow down or interrupt it. The process constitutes the determination of a historical necessity; the historical situations which appear around this central axis introduce chance, contingency and initiatives by individuals and groups.

We could even use it to extrapolate a general periodization of history which would redefine their place and their role in political economy, sociology and history, as follows:

First period: non-accumulative societies. Predominance of agricultural production, localized crafts. Barter or commerce 'in the pores' of this society. Complete or almost excess consumption of production in terms of immediate needs. Slow or zero demographic growth, interrupted by regressions (plagues, famines, wars). Transformations by the governing groups of living wealth (abstractly capable of being invested) into dead wealth: treasure, monuments, works of art. Knowledge of a frequently remarkable kind, but not accumulated (the preserve of groups of initiates, and disappearing almost completely whenever the groups themselves disappeared). High standard of art. Authentic lifestyles. Marked contrasts between splendour and brutality. Predominance of cyclic forms of social processes and time scales. Predominance of custom, which held the community together.

Second period: Accumulative societies (or to be more poetic: Promethean societies). Initially poorly defined appearance of the process of accumulation (its various conditions come into being independently). Transitions. Silent, bitter struggle between this process (and the men driving it forward) and the grandiose, venerable and vulnerable world of the past. Ideological delusions introduced by this struggle (the 'Renaissance'). Unleashing of the process in an increasingly violent way. Revolutionary surges. World-wide extension. Substitution of cyclic time with linear time. Industrial production taking over from agriculture. Predominance of law rather than custom. Socialization of society.

A third period which would begin with the transformation of everyday life (following a deliberate and conscious policy) after a long and difficult transition. Do we need to add that 'modernity' represents this transition precisely, and that we are part of it . . .?

The term we have just used, i.e., the '*socialization of society*', requires an explanation. In the pattern we have presented, the economic and the historical spheres match each other relatively easily. With the process of accumulation, history does not simply change direction. When it loses its cyclic character, it takes on a new sense, direction and meaning. This is not to say that it loses its violent and bloody character, but rather that something new appears. The economic sphere per se becomes the 'base' and the 'axis' of society and of its history. What is more, the constitutive links of the old society – links of consanguinity, links with the earth – become blurred or disappear within a vaster society. The process of accumulation shatters and subordinates whatever resists it: the limits of groupings, unmediated relations, pre-existing social structures. It does not entirely suppress them, since the family persists, and within the process nationhood comes into being. By submitting to the process of accumulation, groups originally formed by consanguinity and territory become its means, its implements and its context.

Society as a whole continues to consolidate and to form itself into a solid totality (or tries to). As a totality, its influence on its elements and members becomes increasingly profound: through the policies and effectiveness of state institutions, through culture, through ideology. In this way it submits them to the requirements of accumulation (acted out, of course, according to the aims, interests and perspectives of the dominant class). But *at the same time* we witness the appearance and consolidation of the individual and of private life, and of individualism as ideology. During the first historical period, the individual (in so far as we can talk of individuality) was always taken care of by a community. It protected him, but also it did not hesitate to sacrifice him ruthlessly. Then, during the period of accumulation, the individual acquires a certain practical and theoretical autonomy. He exists. But then society abandons him. Either he participates in accumulation, or he is on his own. He is on his own in so far as he exists as a 'private' person. Socially and legally, he has rights according to the law, and first and foremost the essential right to own property. This leads to a fundamental conflict between concrete reality and (legal and political) fictions, between theory and practice, between living and the law, between the hidden truth and the social appearance on display (represented). Officially, society respects the individual (a respect which 'representations' sanctify), but it is just as ready as it was in the past to turn against him. On the level of (national) society as a whole, the power of the state has all the necessary means at its disposal. In principle, in civilized society, the society of the process of accumulation, there is no more torture and there are no more massacres. Each individual can contribute to accumulation (of knowledge, of implements, of social capital, etc.). And yet 'needs must', and the requirements of accumulation outweigh all else.

This colossal and colossally contradictory process has a third aspect: it differentiates between groups and segregates them. From the seventeenth and eighteenth centuries onwards, across society as a whole, we see the emergence of sub-groups which hitherto had been ill defined and merged in what subsisted of the old community: children, young people, women, intellectuals, etc. Henceforth these large groups are seen as having their particularities, aspirations and claims. Differences such as these precede, announce and accompany the great polarization into classes: bourgeoisie, proletariat, middle classes. They make phenomena more complicated and are part of the 'socialization of society', with all its various aspects. The more effective accumulative society becomes as an integrating force, the more it loses control over its own elements. This society keeps its own inner contradictions alive and, surprisingly, it segregates as much as it unifies and individualizes. It emphasizes the particularities of these groups, and acts as mediator between the two aspects of singularity (the individual) and generality (unity and totality on the scale of society as a whole). Social segregation is based on the division of labour, but can be reduced to it, since it implies the intervention of analytic intelligence, which shatters, separates and dichotomizes. It is also not the same as reason, which is a function of accumulation, but reason makes use of it. Analytic intelligence probably reached its crisis with the advent of the bourgeoisie and of rationalist ideology, but it was not solely their preserve, since on the theoretical and ideological level it is an element of all accumulation and of the division of labour. Analytic intelligence applied itself actively and effectively, and the present-day social and human 'world' is to a large extent its handiwork. From then on analysis split up everything which could be split, until it almost ruined and (apparently) atomized the social totality. In our present-day society, everything which could be set apart, separated and 'autonomized' has been done so: aspects of labour, social functions, specialized activities, technology, the arts, the sciences, age groups, the sexes, classes, categories of urban inhabitants, and *of course, everyday life in relation to whatever is not everyday life*. So the 'socialization of society' conceals a dialectical movement: totality, or more exactly, totalization, individualization (or 'personalization' which had its abortive beginnings with individualism), and particularization, which becomes segregation at the hands of an extremely effective functional analysis of groupings and activities. This threefold movement encompasses a multitude of contradictions. It takes shape and emerges with the process of economic growth which 'conditions' it (which makes it possible). On one hand it depends upon accumulation, and on the other on representations, superstructures, and a socially and practically justified function: analytic intelligence.[6] What we have said so far only begins to explain and explore the consequences and implications of the concept of the process of accumulation. We will now draw a line under it, or otherwise it will deflect us from the task in hand. But we could take it further. For example we could ask ourselves whether the process of accumulation (with all its elements, which are themselves partial processes) bursts forth into the 'world' and nature like some sort of human miracle – a miracle laden with hopes and fears. Could it be born of a chance encounter between elements and factors which are mutually exclusive and with no connection other than this conjectural convergence, at a given moment in history? Or could it be the continuation of a deeper necessity?

We may suppose that, biologically and physiologically, life contains a *tendency* towards being accumulative which is immediately slowed and inhibited by opposing factors, such as saturations or obstacles. The growth of animal life is a prime example of this. Every species would flourish indefinitely if this expansion did not contain its own limits (its negation) within itself. In point of fact, every species is prey to other species. What is more, as it grows, every species modifies its own environment and destroys the species it in turn preys upon.[7]

As this process develops, the human brain (or rather the cortex) also seems to be an organ capable of 'capitalizing' experiences. It perpetuates and heightens the ability to which living 'substance' owes both its strength and its vulnerability: the ability to retain traces of the past while struggling to maintain itself within its environment at the heart of the present moment. The work of the Pavlovian school helps us to study the accumulative function of the brain and also to understand what hinders it. Men forget as much as they remember. The functioning of the cortex produces internal inhibitions and decelerations. The cortex is quickly 'saturated'; emotions disturb its accumulative but incomplete functioning. Self-regulations are never perfect and never allow for the complete 'capitalization' of what has been acquired. The same may be said of so-called psychological functions: memory per se, perception, intelligence.

And so it is as though a deeply rooted tendency within the process of accumulation, which in nature is frustrated by antagonistic 'factors', were emerging in man, in society, in history and in economy. Should we believe that in nature, cyclic rhythms originate in an embryonic accumulative process which returns to its point of departure? Should we go right back to the physical processes the growth of which is expressible by geometric progressions and logarithms? Such hypotheses go far beyond our aims and our competence.

6 Non-accumulative processes

The generalization we have just made of the concept of the accumulative process leads us to accept the existence of non-accumulative processes (not for the first time, but in a clearer light). They exist, as causes, effects, foundations or results.

Taken as a whole (the cortex, subcortical formations, the neurovegetative system), the human brain does not seem to function unilaterally, as one block. It comprises levels, differences in level, imbalances and conflicts. And much more than this, pathology seems inherent to human perfectibility, i.e., to its imperfections. Gaps, memory lapses and mistakes are part of how it functions. Men can make mistakes without going off track, and can then correct them. They can go astray, get lost, and then find themselves again. They can become alienated, and then disalienated. In the future there may be highly advanced machines which will duplicate logical, discursive and reflective thought. They may even surpass it in breadth and precision. Doubtless they will never have the power to forget. Forgetting is beneficial, in that it allows us to start again, but it is also harmful, in that it involves mechanical repetitions and gaps in accumulated experience. Will these machines duplicate affectivity and its disturbances, passion, laughter, boredom, fear of dying, alienation and disalienation? This is doubtful, unless we agree with the metaphysics of science fiction, which explores what is possible by using myths from the past.

Surely we must see *accumulative* functions in the activities of the brain (disjunctions which work on distinctions and differences, and 'capitalize' them), as well as *non-accumulative* ones. This idea could lead us to reconsider Pavlovian representations, which link a number of facts together, but then transform them into a system by a way of thinking which ignores dialectical method.[8] This hypothesis leads us to scrutinize nervous activity for levels, imbalances, differences and conflicts, while not breaking its incontestable unity.

Let us now move from the biological and physiological level to the psychological level in the total field we are hypothetically exploring. There is no justification for rejecting the thesis (which was robustly maintained by Marx and Engels) of a modification of human (sensory, perceptive, active) organs during the course of history and of the education of individuals. Surely it is impossible that labour should not have modified the eyes, the ears, the hands and the forms of sensory perception, all of which have their origins in nature. However, to what extent has it modified them? All we need is to look at the Lascaux and Altamira frescos to realize the naivety of the evolutionism which tries to assimilate the development of the body and its organs via labour with transformations of consciousness and reflective thought via abstraction and conceptualization. These age-old works of art reveal a sensory acuteness, a perceptive vivacity and a creative power of action and gesture which twentieth-century man finds astonishing; he is amazed, and wonders if Picasso's greatness is not due to his having rediscovered something of the freshness of our origins through the world of abstraction. Could we go so far as to maintain that the appropriation of external nature by the senses and the body is more active at the beginning of social and individual life, with primitive hunters, and with children? We certainly can. What does labour bring to this initial layer of perceptions? A great deal; first of all, abstractions and signs, and then signals. And yet, do not these great acquisitions come with partial regressions? When the abstraction of signs, and above all of signals, is superimposed on sensory perceptions, it constitutes a 'world' which is both external and abstract, the world of modernity which conditions individual gestures. Does this 'world' inhibit the freshness and vivacity of the senses? It certainly does, especially if it is true that in the modern world – with the perceptively efficient technology they represent – signals are characteristically accumulative. Hence, by contrast, the prestige of archaic objects, primitive arts, symbols, and the astonishment they provoke in men of the industrial era.

What we are suggesting about sensory perception can also apply to emotions and affectivity. They do not appear to be accumulative, which explains the way they crystallize around paradoxically durable symbols. As we already know, most of these symbols, if not all of them, come from the distant past of agrarian and craft-based societies. Their subsequent elaboration by philosophers, dramatists and poets helped to revive them, but without modifying them to any profound degree. With their origins deep within the direct and unmediated relations between men and nature, and between men themselves, they live on in islands of unmediated 'private' life which withstand the rising tide of relations mediated by commodities, money and technology. These symbols have become nucleuses of emotion and affectivity. When they are not used, exploited, consumed and devoured, they are attacked and concealed. When they crystallize (as the Father, the Mother, Woman, Virginity, Love, the Sun, the House, Water, Earth, Air, Fire, Hearth and Home) they degenerate, break up and scatter. They remain well outside the processes of accumulation.[9]

According to this criterion, we will classify human activities into two major types of process: *accumulative and non-accumulative*. Within this classification, we may discern genres or species: processes of accumulation which have been decelerated (saturated), liberated or accelerated, circular processes which have stabilized, and nucleuses which have degenerated or broken up, etc. This provides us with a starting point for an analysis of praxis and a representation of the process of human becoming. We have already drawn up a list of accumulative activities. Among non-accumulative activities we would include sensory perception, sensibility, sensuality, spontaneity, art in general, morality (subjective or deriving from custom, as distinct from objective morality which depends upon law and the state) and finally civilization in the broadest sense (as opposed to culture). The non-accumulative is also the non-rational. We use the term in its essentially relative sense, since there is no question of us positing an absolute (ontological) irrationality. We can also say that the accumulative would be related to space, while the non-accumulative would be related to time. However, there is no question of separating space from time.

Nor is there any question of separating the two types of process. They are permanently interactive, so that when we describe and analyse that interaction, we perceive various gaps, imbalances, differences and conflicts between levels. If our experience of 'modernity' is of a deep-rooted and ever-increasing malaise, our concepts will enable us to discover some of its causes and aspects, and perhaps to reveal the problem in its totality.

The problem in question is the problem of everyday life. Everyday life lies at the ill-defined, cutting edge where the accumulative and the non-accumulative intersect. On one hand, it must submit to the demands of accumulation, and suffer its effects and consequences. It exists on the level of the most pressing conditions and effects of the process of accumulation: cohesion, logic, language and, last but not least, signals. On the other hand it sees itself increasingly 'distanced' by the process, which becomes dissociated in the giddy heights of specializations and technology. In itself, it remains linked to rhythms, to cyclic time scales and to symbols.

This is merely putting what we have already said in another way. The everyday is situated at the boundary between the controlled sector (i.e., the sector controlled by knowledge) and the uncontrolled sector. This is ill-defined and dangerous border territory, particularly because its symbols give the illusory impression of controlling spontaneous nature, while the techniques which really do control it are increasingly hidden from view.

The malaise comes primarily from the extraordinary imbalance between the symbolic nucleuses and the acquisitions of abstract knowledge and technology, i.e., from the conflictual relation between the two processes. This imbalance itself has various aspects and various senses. The affective nucleuses are 'survivals' (in inverted commas; there can be no 'survivals' without a 'base' or 'foundation'). From a certain point of view, they seem more beautiful, more precious and more immediate than all the accumulations of experience and knowledge put together. From another rigorously equivalent and equally well-founded point of view, they are old-fashioned, ridiculous and backward. Similarly, from yet another point of view, the accumulative is the only 'truth' over and above 'the real'. It alone is important, great and creative, while the everyday knows itself to be negligible, superficial and non-essential. But another equally acceptable point of view would be that the everyday is the only thing which matters to mankind.

In themselves, symbols are only maintained by means of metaphorical language, words or the use of rather unusual words, literary or historical recollections, objects infused with meaning, and works of art. Their only 'bases' are their uncertain and 'private' social relations with nature, with the other and with the self. The vast tide of 'modernity' is sweeping these supports away. Economic backwardness and underdevelopment (villages, the mountains, the sea, picturesque tourist attractions, barren regions, etc.) feed these 'survivals' and maintain these nucleuses without breathing any new life into them. It is as though cyclic time scales have been ripped asunder by the linear time of the process of accumulation and have been left to hang in tatters within us and around us. And yet symbolisms, cyclic rhythms and the shattered or degenerate nucleuses continue to organize the everyday; they represent its stable centre and maintain the illusion of a pre-ordained harmony, if indeed we can still use that word.

The result is an incessant tension, and thus the possibility of sterile conflicts and pathological deviations, both in individual consciousness and in social consciousness. Reduced to silence amid all the verbiage and verbalisms, relegated to an obscurity which prompts us to speak of 'unconsciousness', private everyday life is built up around symbols which are constantly discredited by public life, economic and political praxis, signs, signals and significations. All that personal life has at its disposal to make itself into a conscious creative endeavour, and to give itself a conscious history, are these nucleuses buried within the deep secrecy of individual psychophysiological life: tastes and desires (amorous, erotic, affective, alimentary, etc.), or rather, the absence of tastes and desires. This is how public life, overtly subjected to accumulative processes, overwhelms private life, condemning it to powerlessness, unconsciousness and dissatisfaction. When it tries to become reconciled with private life, things are even worse: it invades it and absorbs it (cf. the mass media). In every case, everyday life is forsaken territory, an island of tears and tedium where man as the norm is normally cast away. The frontier between the controlled sector (controlled by knowledge and technology, and therefore by and in accumulation) and the uncontrolled sector is a no man's land where everyone lives more or less on the level of deteriorated and shattered spontaneity. The more people speak of adaptation, balance and harmony, the less real harmony, balance and adaptation there is. (And what do obsessions mean if not that even these conflicts are no longer creative?)

Within the individual, and at the heart of his consciousness and his ill-appropriated life, two processes are apparent: the rational and the irrational, the (relatively) conscious and the (relatively) unconscious. On one hand, if he cannot accumulate money, he accumulates experiences, and if he cannot accumulate capital, he accumulates knowledge. Even if they are fragmented, experience and knowledge join together to form a memory. On the other hand, there is something inside him which is ever more distant, ever more vulnerable, something he is consciously seeking, the childhood and the spontaneity which are as much a part of symbolisms as they are of memory. Is this not one of the secrets of the disturbed drama of modern life, this uneasy, private consciousness which is increasingly penetrated by the general process and is forced to conform to it, and yet which is becoming increasingly 'private' and trapped within the everyday? In fact, as soon as radical critique unmasks the situation in which consciousness and life are trapped, it seems intolerable, and we ask ourselves why the devastation is not even more destructive than it is.

7 The pedagogic and culturalist illusion

We must find a way out of this situation. How? By revolutionary praxis reconstructed in its totality. But what else? By following technology to its bitter end in order to reinvest it in an everyday life which has been metamorphosed, instead of merely observing the terrifying discrepancy between the two? By discovering new representations of time and imposing them (by persuasion) on time as we usually live it? By raising the everyday to the level of technology and by reinvesting technology in the everyday? By eradicating the old symbolisms and creating new ones, new images of life as a work of creativity?

But this is to jump the gun. Let us begin by closing off the false exits. In the modern world, pedagogic and cultural fictions have joined forces with the old legal, ideological and political fictions (the Citizen, everyone is equal before the law, etc.). The new fictions seize the baton when the old ones are too weak to stay in the race. What do they consist of? The attribution of the accumulative character to sensibility, emotivity and affectivity. Therefore it is considered possible to 'form' them in the same way as conceptual or technical knowledge through the accumulation of experiences, facts or representations, and despite all the failures of fiction both in the individual and on the scale of society as a whole.

It is obviously in the domain of art that this illusion and its consequences may be best observed. What is known about art grows in an accumulative way. The number of objects piled up in the universal museum and in the total library of books, records and films must increase exponentially. The viewer and the listener has increasingly easier and more frequent access to all works from all ages. It is assumed that when the various sources of knowledge are all bundled together in this way it will stimulate our powers of creativity, or even that technologies (and the last to be developed is always the best) will be a substitute for spontaneity. The two poles of activity – technological literacy and creative power – would merge. Not so. The welter of works, of knowledge and of technology comes in tandem with a gargantuan consumption which must surely be looting and devouring all the riches of ages which precisely did not accumulate, and which have left us their treasures in trust. The result is an astonishing sociological phenomenon: aestheticism (which is not caused and explained by its accumulative character alone) and its corollary, the permanent crisis of so-called modern art. In so far as there is such a thing as creativity, does it not come from a direct or indirect appeal to the symbolisms and the myths which supported it in times past, and from an effort to reinstate spontaneity in the face of the clutter of abstract culture and pedagogically cultivated consciousness? But nothing will spare symbolisms their inevitable dissolution. They too have already been relegated to the aberrant margins of culture: astrology and parascientific interpretations of science, science fiction, specific 'worlds' of women and of children, petty superstitions and ritualizations, and works of which it is impossible to say whether they are foretelling the future or falling into decrepitude at the very moment of their success.

The same is true of the moral sphere. Knowledge of morality, its history and its 'values' is expanding. Like discourse on aesthetics, discourse on morality and its 'values' is becoming increasingly facile. Ethics is the loser, and it will never be possible to extrapolate a practical lifestyle from moral knowledge.

And so the malaise of the everyday and of the 'privation' of private life is contaminating the higher spheres of art, ethics, creativity and the understanding between consciousnesses . . .

6

The Theory of Moments[1]

1 Typology of repetition

Previously we underlined the differences between several forms or types of repetition, which were mutually irreducible. Repetition of cycles and cyclic rhythms differs from repetition of mechanical gestures: the first of these types belongs to the non-accumulative processes, which have their own time scales, while the second belongs to the processes of accumulation, with their linear time scales, which are now continuous, now discontinuous. Repetition of behaviour patterns (conditionings) stimulated by signals cannot be assimilated to repetition of 'states', emotions or attitudes linked to symbols and emotional nucleuses. We must distinguish between repetition of situations (notably in pathological cases) and repetition postulated by certain systems (by Kierkegaard and Nietzsche, for example). If repetition, return or renewal of the same (or more or less the same) phenomenon should be understood according to each specific case and type, the same can be said of the relation between what is repeated and the newness which springs from repetition (for example, repetition of sounds and rhythms in music offers a perpetual movement which is perpetually reinvented).

Similarly, repetition of the *instant*, so frequently studied by philosophers (the *hic et nunc*, pure immediacy, the purely transitory in perception and the 'lived'), cannot be assimilated to repetition of the moment.

2 Moments and language

As regards the term 'moment', our first comment would be that it corresponds to the *sense* (expression + signification = direction) of a given word in general and common usage, or, if you prefer, to its lived *content*. Let us take the word 'love', which crops up so frequently in language. To what does it correspond? Is there a higher entity which is indicated by the word and which endows it with a general sense because it subordinates a set of situations and emotional or affective states? This classic Platonizing and rationalist theory is not tenable. And yet, if there is not a unified set of so-called 'love' situations and states, the word itself has no meaning. Could it be simply the abstract connotation of a range of states and situations with no concrete links between them? In this case, not only are there 'loves', as opposed to a few types of love, but an indefinite number of them, amorphous and multifarious. This equally classic, empiricist and sceptical theory is just as untenable. As we well know, it presents a challenge to language; it undermines and disintegrates it. Words are no more than arbitrary signs, and discourse is no more than a formal construction. But discourse is linked to praxis, a level of experience, and it has meaning because it has both a logical (disjunctive) form and an emotional and affective content, which it efficiently transmits. We understand it through its form and structure, but not only that. Communication presupposes all the levels, and all the tensions and conflicts between those levels; never complete, rarely real, it implies that the semantic field is neither opaque and solid like a stone, nor unstable like mist; it implies relative movements and relative stabilities. Why do the same words come back time and time again, with their images and symbols, and how do they make themselves understood? What is it that allows us to use the word 'love' in varying situations and conversations, and still be understood by the different people we are talking to? What is it that creates a certain alignment between the emotion expressed by one speaker and the emotion aroused in the other, just by the use of one word? When people are in love, or imagine they are, when they hate each other, or imagine they do, what is it that allows them to communicate what they are feeling or what they are not feeling, to recognize one another, to create misunderstandings and resolve them (up to a point), to rise above insinuation or silence, in short to avoid a dialogue of the deaf which would be no more than the sum total of two soliloquies (in which case language would be devoid of meaning, i.e., of effectiveness, and would inevitably waste away or would even have long since disappeared)? Through all the changes, 'something' remains. We would say that 'something' is the *moment*. Psychological terms (such as states, emotions, attitudes, behaviour patterns, etc.) do not adequately define it, since it implies a twofold recognition, of otherness – or rather, of the other – and of the self. This re-cognition, which joins forces in an original dramatic situation with what is known and what is unknown, explains and justifies the use of the word. It presupposes in turn the (confused or clear) perception of an analogy and a difference in lived time, i.e., a specific modality of repetition. 'Something' – which is certainly not a thing – is encountered once again. Both an illusion and a reality, lived time appears once more through all the veils and distances. It vanishes, and at the same time it makes itself known. No specifically sociological or historical determination can adequately define this temporality.

The theory of moments comes initially from an effort to give language significance and value, in the face of its critics (such as Bergson), and in spite of the undermining and disintegration of language which we are currently witnessing. It is the product of a violent protest against Bergsonism and the formless psychological continuum advocated by Bergsonian philosophy.[2] Its wish is to reinstate discontinuity, grasping it in the very fabric of the 'lived', and on the loom of continuity, which it presupposes (and consequently without making it abstract, and without merging it with the arbitrary and the purely formal – which is a reaction against exaggerated continuism, though not a supersession of it).

According to this process, we do not start from Logos (discourse and language), we come to it, time and time again. The theory does not postulate the value or the substantial reality of language. It does not take Logos as an axis of reference. On the contrary: it tries to reinstate language in all its power, by understanding (by knowing) certain conditions under which it can be fully exercised. Seeing it theoretically undermined by the attacks of some philosophers and poets, and practically (socially) undermined by signals, audio-visual imageries, jargons and by the isolation of minds incapable of communicating, it starts from an analysis of the conditions for communication. If it were too perfect, language would be of little use to communication, or rather, it would change it into a communion of angelic and disembodied minds (supposing that means anything). Everything would be instantly clear. Such magic transparency has not even the beauty of a dream. It implies a lack of depths, levels and planes, in life as it is lived. If it were too imperfect, language would fail to cope with differences; it would leave them to their own opaqueness. As it is, with its mobile complexity which is nevertheless 'structured' by constants, nucleuses and 'moments', language is of use to us. It is a good implement, and something more than just an implement . . .

More profoundly perhaps, the theory derives from a need to organize, programme and structure everyday life by transforming it according to its own tendencies and laws. It wishes to perceive the possibilities of everyday life and to give human beings a constitution by constituting their powers, if only as guidelines or suggestions.

This means that we are using the term 'moment' in a rather particular way, while still insisting on its day-to-day usage, and on the fact that certain words in common usage have a general, definable quality or property.

In day-to-day language, the word 'moment' and the word 'instant' are almost interchangeable. However, there is a distinction between them. When we say 'It was an enjoyable moment . . .', for example, it implies a certain length of time, a value, a nostalgia and the hope of reliving that moment or preserving it as a privileged lapse of time, embalmed in memory. It is not just any old instant, nor a simple ephemeral and transitory one.

In the Hegelian system, the term 'moment' receives special treatment.[3] It designates the major figures of consciousness; each of them (the consciousness of the master and that of the slave in their mutual relations, the stoicist or sceptical consciousness, the unhappy consciousness, etc.) is a *moment* in the dialectical ascent of self-consciousness. Even more essentially, *dialectical movement* marks the turning point of reality and of the concept: the fundamental intervention of the negative which leads to disalienation but also to renewed alienation, to supersession through negation of negation, but also to new stages in the process of becoming and to new figures of consciousness.

The Hegelian notion seems to have influenced day-to-day language. Did anyone talk about the 'historical moment' before Hegel? Definitely not.

Our use of the term will be more modest than Hegel's, but broader. We situate the 'moment' as a function of a history, the history of the individual. We consider that up to a certain point (very limited, and as yet, too limited) this history is his own creative undertaking, and that he recognizes himself within it, even if it is in a confused way. Moreover, the history of the individual in his everyday life cannot be separated from the social sphere. Narrow and limited though it is, it is part of other, broader works. However, the theory of moments parenthesizes these implications. Like all theories, it uses a justified abstraction to isolate its object. Moreover, it examines the 'moment' in general, and particular 'moments' in their relation with everyday life. Thus it does not presume to define them completely or exhaust them. There are other sciences and methods which could study these 'moments'.

The moment is a higher form of repetition, renewal and reappearance, and of the recognition of certain determinable relations with otherness (or the other) and with the self. Compared with this relatively privileged form of repetition, the others would be nothing more than raw materials, namely the succession of instants, gestures and behaviour, constant states which reappear after being interrupted or suspended, objects or works, and finally, symbols and affective stereotypes.

3 The constellation of moments

Among moments, we may include love, play, rest, knowledge, etc. We cannot draw up a complete list of them, because there is nothing to prevent the invention of new moments.

How and why should we classify any particular activity or 'state' as a moment? What should our indexes and criteria be?

a) *The moment is constituted by a choice which singles it out and separates it from a muddle or a confusion, i.e., from an initial ambiguity.* Natural and spontaneous (animal or human) life offers nothing but ambiguity. The same is true for the amorphous muddle we know as the everyday in all its triviality, where analysis discerns the detritus and the seeds of every possibility. Moments are there in embryonic form, but it is difficult to make them out with any clarity. And so it is in childhood and adolescence, in games and in work, in playing and in loving. If we are to particularize work, for example, be it of a material or intellectual nature, and if we are to specify the entire set of attitudes, behaviour patterns and gestures it groups together, we will need a very strict pedagogy and a great deal of effort. In a similar way, amorous playfulness – light-hearted chat, flirtation, teasing conversations, provocation – comes before love itself. Difficult to pick out in all this equivocal and muddled ambiguity, the one emerges very slowly from the other, and sometimes not at all. Until such time as we can distinguish between love and playfulness, there can be no love, or love can be no more. Love has its serious side. If it plays games, it dominates them. In this sense, love implies the project of love, of loving and of being loved. It chooses to constitute its moment. It begins with an attempt at a moment (and with the temptation of the moment, disturbing and frequently refused).

b) *The moment has a certain specific duration.* Relatively durable, it stands out from the continuum of transitories within the amorphous realm of the psyche. It wants to endure. It cannot endure (at least, not for very long). Yet this inner contradiction gives it its intensity, which reaches crisis point when the inevitability of its own demise becomes fully apparent. The manner of its duration means that it cannot be brought into harmony with continuous evolution, or with pure discontinuity (a sudden mutation or 'revolution'). It can only be defined as *involution*. Essentially *present* (an essential modality of *presence*), the moment has a beginning, a fulfilment and an end, a relatively well-defined start and finish. It has a history: its own . . .

And so 'love' is one particular love (the love of one man for one woman, or of one woman for one man). And it is also the succession of loves of one man or one woman, and a series of amorous passions in a broader history, the history of a family, of a group, of society (and finally, of the human being). The term 'moment' will be like a digest of all the analogies and differences involved.

c) *The moment has its memory.* For the individual and for groups, memory in love is not the same as memory in knowledge or in play. When we enter the moment we call upon a particularized memory (which does not exclude other memories completely, but relegates them to a background of 'misconsciousness' where they are disregarded). It is within this specific memory that the *re-cognition* of the moment and its implications are created.

d) *The moment has its content.* It draws it from conjunctures in more-or-less external circumstances, and incorporates it. All the content of moments comes from everyday life and yet every moment emerges from the everyday life in which it gathers its materials or the material it needs. The originality of the moment comes partly – and only partly – from its circumstantial content. Rather than tearing it, it weaves itself into the fabric of the everyday, and transforms it (partially and 'momentarily', like art, like the figure in a carpet). In this way it uses something it is not: something happening close by, something contingent and accidental. With its circumstantial contingencies, and while it lasts, the moment also has the *urgency of a command and a necessity.* So someone who makes up a game for children or for adults will use whatever he happens to have at hand (or on his lips: when there is nothing else available he will play with words).

e) *Equally, the moment has its form*: the rules of the game – the ceremonies of love, its figures and rituals, and its symbolism – the pace and principles of work for whoever is working, etc. This form imposes itself in time and in space. It creates a time and a space which are both objective (socially governed) and subjective (individual and interindividual). In this sense, the moment not only has a form; it 'is' this form and this order imposed on its 'content'.

f) *Every moment becomes an absolute.* It can establish itself as an absolute. It is even a duty for it to do so. Now we cannot conceive of the absolute, let alone live it. Therefore the moment proposes itself as the impossible. Here we are coming close to fundamental criteria. What love worthy of the name does not want to be unique and total, an impossible love? If someone has not wanted this, if he has not refused to compromise from the moment he fell in love, if he has not dreamed of the absolute, if he does not aspire to fulfil this dream (to be the first man to do so) and to achieve this fulfilment (to be the first man, the only one to do so) then he is not worthy to be called a lover. By analogy, play makes players and the player turns his game into an absolute: the aim, the meaning of life. He gambles everything which is not part of the game. It is a wager for random winnings – for the heady thrill of chance; his entire life becomes a stack of chips on the gambling table. Whoever wants knowledge sacrifices everything which is not knowledge in the pursuit of knowledge: everything becomes an object of knowledge and a means of knowing the object it is pursuing. The moment is passion and the inexorable destruction and self-destruction of that passion. The moment is an impossible possibility, aimed at, desired and chosen as such. Then what is impossible in the everyday becomes what is possible, even the rule of impossibility. And this is when the 'possible/impossible' dialectical movement begins, with all the consequences it entails.

g) Disalienating in relation to the triviality of everyday life – deep in which it is formed, but from which it emerges – and in relation to the fragmented activities it rises above, the moment becomes alienation. Precisely because it proclaims itself to be an absolute, it provokes and defines a determined alienation: the madness (not pathological, but often verging on delirium) of the lover, the gambler, the man of theory devoted to pure knowledge, the obsessive worker, etc. This specific alienation can be classified as one of a more general type, the alienation which threatens every activity within the very process of its accomplishment. In so far as it is alienating and alienated, the moment has its specific negativity. It is destined to fail, it runs headlong towards failure. Everything happens as if he – the man who has changed his passion into a 'world' – wanted to fail. Negativity operates at the heart of whatever tries to structure and constitute itself into a definitive whole, and to come to a halt. Inevitably, necessity and chance are destined to come together and to be superseded, and from that supersession the tragic is born. In our view, the link between the tragic and the everyday is profound; the tragic takes shape within the everyday, comes into being in the everyday, and always returns to the everyday: the tragic initial decision, which constitutes an absolute, and proclaims it, the tragedy of heartbreak, of alienation, of failure at the heart of fulfilment, of the return to the everyday to start the process all over again. This is how the contradiction between triviality and tragedy is determined, and we are bold enough to say that it can be overcome, and that the theory of moments gives a glimpse of its supersession . . .

We imagine so-called 'spiritual' life to be like a constellation, and this is a symbol we will deliberately use. In the light, or the half-light, of the everyday, the constellation of moments cannot be seen. But when something disturbing casts a shadow on the everyday, that constellation rises on the horizon. We each of us choose our star, freely, but with the impression of an irresistible inner necessity. No one is forced to choose. There is no astrological explanation for the constellation of moments: freedom has no horoscope. In this day and age, everyday life is lit by false suns: morality, the state, ideology. They bathe it in a phoney light, and even worse, they lower it to depths where possibilities cannot be perceived, and keep it there. Sadly, the stars of what is possible shine only at night. Sooner or later the everyday must dawn, and the suns must rise to their zenith (including the black sun of empty anguish). Until such time as mankind has transformed this light and this darkness, stars will shine only at night.

So-called 'spiritual' life offers several different absolutes: several paths towards totalization, several paths towards fulfilment, in other words, towards failure. This is how things are. And until things change, mankind can do nothing about it. If a man wants to be a man, this is how he will create himself, moving ahead as far as he can on one of these paths. Spiritually speaking, he is in a 'configurative space', with its given dimensions. However, this mathematical metaphor hides the truth: the freedom which dawns even in the inevitability of tragedy and the need for tragedy.

None of us can escape this drama, since absence of tragedy itself creates yet another dramatic situation: the desolation of everyday life, emptiness and ennui. And the moment? It is an individual and freely celebrated festival, a tragic festival, and therefore a genuine festival. The aim is not to let festivals die out or disappear beneath all that is prosaic in the world. It is to unite Festival with everyday life.

4 Definition of the moment

We will call 'Moment' *the attempt to achieve the total realization of a possibility.* Possibility offers itself; and it reveals itself. It is determined and consequently it is limited and partial. Therefore to wish to live it as a totality is to exhaust it as well as to fulfil it. The Moment wants to be freely total; it exhausts itself in the act of being lived. Every realization as a totality implies a constitutive action, an inaugural act.

Simultaneously, this act singles out a meaning, and creates that meaning. It sets up a structuring against the uncertain and transitory background of the everyday (and reveals it to be as such: uncertain and transitory, whereas before it appeared to be solidly and undoubtedly 'real').

Could this definition (which refuses to separate fact from value, with all the false problems that would create) be *philosophical*? Yes and no. Could it be an ontology? In one sense, yes, and yet the 'being' which is only revealed in what is possible does not correspond to the 'being' given behind the actual or within the actual as posited by classic ontology. The theory uses concepts and categories elaborated by philosophy, but outside of any system and any attempt at systematization. It uses them prudently, hypothetically, while consciously accepting a certain risk. It applies them to praxis: to everyday life, to individual man's relation with nature, society and self. The theory has no desire to be exclusive. In no respect does it rule out other theories or other perspectives. Ipso facto, it attempts to open an investigation which would no longer be strictly comparable with classic philosophy, but which would nevertheless continue it. It conceives of a kind of twofold critical and totalizing experience, and of a 'programmatic' which would not be reduced to a dogmatism or a pure problematic: the uniting of the Moment and the everyday, of poetry and all that is prosaic in the world, in short, of Festival and ordinary life, on a higher plane than anything which has hitherto been accomplished.

This theory does not fit into any philosophical category (and the same can be said of the theory of the semantic field). Could it be an *existentialism*? *Yes*, since it describes and analyses forms of existence, and *no*, since we could also say that it is 'essentialist'. It comprises a critique of existentialism and essentialism. We could say that moments are just as much 'essences' as they are attributes and modalities of 'being', or existential experiences. Furthermore we would be happier talking about 'powers' rather than 'essences', while making sure to remember that the theory has a practical goal: to transform these powers, these partial totalities which are destined to fail, into 'something' unforeseen and new, something genuinely total, which would overcome the 'triviality/tragedy' contradiction.

Similarly, the description of the 'lived' in the theory of moments could be baptized as 'phenomenological'. However, we have been very wary in our use of 'parenthesizing', so as to be sure to reinstate anything which we may have *momentarily* eliminated, and to avoid reducing the totality of the experience. Our descriptions and analysis were directed at praxis, and not at consciousness per se. We are dealing not with domains or regions, but with possibilities.

To conclude, let us say that we are determining a structure of possibilities and projects, while avoiding any structuralism by which actions could be predetermined.

In fact, in this day and age, there is a very widespread philosophism which sees philosophy everywhere and nowhere, and forces it into insignificance. We will have nothing to do with it, nor with the ontological presumption or the illusion of the most general (and the most 'nondescript') object.

If we must fit the theory of moments into some kind of classification, we will say that it has a contribution to make to an *anthropology*, but with two provisos: first that we do not confuse this anthropology with a culturalism (the cultural definition of man outside of nature and spontaneity), and second that we do not omit radical critique of all specializations, including anthropology. The latter obeys a general rule which we have already formulated axiomatically: in the domain of the social sciences, there can be no knowledge without a twofold critique, first of the reality which must be overcome, second of the knowledge already acquired, along with the conceptual implements necessary for the acquisition of further knowledge. And in the case of anthropology, surely the danger of making dogmatic statements (which would offer a limited and limiting definition of man) is greater than it is elsewhere, and surely its consequences would be much more serious.

In any event, all these considerations are only of marginal importance. What we need is a precise definition which will allow us to develop our analysis of moments.

5 An analytics of moments

So each moment can be characterized in the following ways: it is *perceived, situated and distanced*. And this just as much in relation to another moment as in relation to the everyday. However, the relation of the moment to the everyday cannot be determined by externality alone. The moment is born of the everyday and within the everyday. From here it draws its nourishment and its substance; and this is the only way it can deny the everyday. It is in the everyday that a possibility becomes apparent (be it play, work or love, etc.) in all its brute spontaneity and ambiguity. It is equally in the everyday that the inaugural decision is made by which the moment begins and opens out; this decision perceives a possibility, chooses it from among other possibilities, takes it in charge and becomes committed to it unreservedly. This choice is already a dramatic one: at the crucial point of decision, at the heart of the everyday, nothing is clear. How can we expect something which is blatantly relative and, even worse, ambiguous, to be absolute? What is possible and what is impossible are not yet part of the conflict; they are merged; there are no exact, predetermined limits which would enable a decision on what is possible and what is impossible. Once the choice has been made, we see that the 'subject' wishes something which is impossible in terms of the everyday; but the fact of making a decision changes what was a distant impossibility into an imminent possibility. For the passionate feeling which has now been aroused, what is impossible is precisely a criterion for possibility: it wants the impossible, it risks the possible to attain an impossible which at first seemed beyond the bounds of risk and chance. Effectively, when a decision is made it pushes back the boundaries of impossibility. In this sense, decision assumes the risk of failure completely, but it runs another risk for which it takes full and free responsibility (with the obscure but deep-rooted idea that by chance or by will-power it will avoid it), and that is the risk of terminal failure, when the moment's magnificent trajectory will be brought to an end. Decision refuses the initial failure, whereby the attempt is aborted and caricatured. So in the moment, the instant of greatest importance is the instant of failure. The drama is situated within that instant of failure: it is the emergence from the everyday or collapse on failing to emerge, it is a caricature or a tragedy, a successful festival or a dubious ceremony. In so far as it is inherent to the moment, to its goal, to its madness and its grandeur, failure must be considered as *terminus ad quem* and not as *terminus a quo*. If we are to understand and make a judgement, we must start not from the failure itself, but from the endeavour which leads to it. If there is a rise and a fall, a beginning and an end, the tragic is omnipresent in the genuine moment. Its fulfilment is its loss. Once again we are faced with the dialectical movement of 'totalization/negativity' or 'alienation/dis-alienation/realienation'.

The moment is not exactly the same as a 'situation'. The result of a decision and a choice – of an endeavour – the moment creates situations. Because it effectively links them together, in its capacity as a general term, it sums them up and condenses them. From then on they are no longer experienced in 'lived' banality, but are taken in charge at the heart of 'living'. We can attempt to define the relation between the moment and the 'situation' by starting with the difference between 'conjuncture' and 'structure'. The conjuncture is *almost* the situation, and the moment is *almost* the structure. However, in a conjuncture, there is less than the situation, and in the moment there is more than a structure. The conscious being 'in situation' is prey to an external conjuncture into which he must insert himself. As soon he attempts a moment, he is deliberately turning his situation into a risk: a series which from the start necessarily involves articulations in time and space, an order and a form imposed on the elements which have been taken from the conjuncture. And this is what properly and specifically constitutes the situation. Once more we are faced with the concept of the articulated, inner process of becoming, tending towards a specific end outside the general process of becoming, and constituted by a form which has been freely developed. It is a possibility which has been taken over and which will give a particularly intense and lived present moment. It will initially take a form which is as yet deprived of content (e.g., ceremony, ritual, rules of the game, principles of the activity, etc.). Decision gives this form its content, and this in turn creates a situation.

The moment commences and re-commences. It takes up the previous moment again (the *same* moment), reinvests its form and continues it after an interruption. This is the form in which it unfolds: ritual, ceremony and necessary succession. Thus moments lend themselves to formalisms (of love, of play, etc.), but if ever formalism triumphs, the moment will have disappeared. When the moment comes to an end, there is a break. In this sense, the theory of moments rejects both ambiguity and all philosophies of ambiguity, and formalisms and all ideologies of pure form (while reserving a place for them).

Like time, the moment reorganizes surrounding space: affective space – a space inhabited by symbols which have been retained and changed into adopted themes (by love, by play, by knowledge, etc.). The space of the moment, like time, is closed off by constitutive decisions. Anything which cannot be included is chased away.

Could *contemplation* be a moment? This can be argued for and against. There are a number of philosophical systems which imply that it is, or posit it as such. Perhaps all philosophy is an attempt to make contemplation a moment. If this is so, we could define philosophy as the deliberate structuring of the lived within contemplation, which it invests with value and factuality, spontaneity and culture. As we know only too well, a definition such as this renders philosophy unviable. Do moments die? Probably. If so, contemplation would be a dead moment.

As for the *look*, it is certainly not a moment. To constitute oneself as pure glance, to attempt the glance as a moment, to look with clear-sightedness (but at what? – at everyday life, and first and foremost the everyday life of other people), is obviously *tempting*. Since it is a practical and social fact, involving an important sensory organ and a form, looking seems capable of such an undertaking. Since the sex organ is capable of adventure, why not the eyes? Once the decision is taken, we become pure look, clear and clear-sighted: clairvoyant and voyeur. We draw strength and interest from the fact that we are outside what interests people in their everyday lives. This is doomed to fail from the outset, but this time the failure is not tragic, it is comic. The pure, disembodied glance which is so perceptive that it penetrates (or thinks it penetrates) the flesh of other people is one of the great comedies of our age. Penetrating and perceptive – subjectively – this glance is an objective feature of a world where everything becomes a spectacle for everyone, without any living participation. But the pure glance is unaware of this situation. Its own blindness condemns it. It seems that in contemporary philosophy there is a perpetual and ever-ambiguous seesawing between looking and knowing. Such an ambiguous mixture of effective knowledge and 'pure' glance seems unstable, untenable and unbearable. In the period when philosophy is withering away, could not philosophy be the Beautiful Soul of modern times?

With its various oscillations and compensations, this seesawing movement between looking and knowing caricatures ancient contemplation, which lived and died. Looking cannot hope to constitute or 'found' a moment. It destroys itself from the outset, and its possibility is sheer illusion.

We will not even ask whether fatherhood, motherhood, friendship, decency, etc., can constitute moments. These are virtues and qualities which can encourage endeavours and situations. As in the case of the pure glance, the endeavour collapses before it even starts, and sometimes even more ridiculously. And so there is not an unlimited or indefinite number of moments.

At the same time, we cannot wish the list of moments to be exhaustive. Were we able to complete it, we would be changing the theory into a system. Moments are mortal too, and as such, they are born, they live and they pass away. There is room not only for freedom, a limited freedom but a real one (which comes into being by structuring, destructuring or restructuring everyday life), but for inventiveness and discovery. In this day and age we are witnessing the formation of a moment: *rest*. With many ambiguities (non-work, leisure) and many ideologies and techniques (such as 'relaxation', or 'autogenic training'), modern man – because he needs to – is making an effort to live rest as a totality in itself, i.e., as a moment. Up until now, very little distinction used to be made between rest on the one hand and play and everyday life outside work on the other.

We can define *justice* both as a virtue and as an institution. We could see it as a moment if we were to restrict or broaden the concept to encompass what happens in the everyday and in individual consciousness (the consciousness of the social individual). The moment is constituted by the possibility of an act: in this case, the act of judgement. It is an action which never stops. We are always making judgements. And these judgements are always bad; we know they are, and we know that they are prejudiced and unsafe, and even that we have no right to make them in the first place. In practical terms, this act is thus both possible and impossible, and we try to live it as a totality. Since it takes its elements from everyday life, and since it tries to assess it, it does not accept it purely and simply for what it is.

And so a ritual is proclaimed, a ceremony, i.e., a form, and in extreme cases a formalism. Whoever judges, in other words, whoever wishes to judge, *summons* actions and events, from his own life and from the life of others (into which he enters to an unwarranted degree). His mind becomes ritualized, and it dons the regalia of the courtroom. The bill of indictment presents passions and past deeds to the court as proof in these criminal proceedings. Whoever is sitting in judgement has granted himself the power to do so. Self-appointed, he *summons* the witnesses. *He conducts the prosecution*, i.e., he investigates the circumstances and the motivation of actions (and usually loses track of them). He hears the evidence of the various witnesses. Finally, he *gives his verdict*; he passes judgement, but never does so without *appealing* to higher authorities (which do not exist, since he alone has decided to pass judgement).

It is easy to notice the similarity between the inner ceremony of the virtuous mind, and the highly externalized formalism of justice as an institution. And so the 'virtue or institution' dilemma is a false one, and the theory of moments resolves it.

The theory allows us to understand how and why justice becomes an *absolute* from the moment it is conceived. Whoever loves justice and wants justice – the Just Man – wants nothing but justice, and he judges everything according to justice. And yet he never manages to define it, let alone realize it. He determines justice according to what is just, and what is just according to justice. In this way he lapses into a specific alienation, the alienation of the moral consciousness which aspires to be absolute. To put it another way, justice as the goal of action (and philosophers fixed this goal for the worthiest actions of mankind) presupposes an action which goes far beyond that goal and which is inspired by other motives. Justice cannot be realized, or even begin to be realized, by its own powers alone. Its realization implies its suppression and its supersession.

Therefore the moment of justice has its alienation and its own negativity. It refers us to the Supreme Judge who would justify justice and realize it, who is always evoked and always absent. He maintains the powerful and beautiful image of the Last Judgement, which would also be the moment when the world is destroyed (*'pereat mundus, fiat justicia'*). Once we begin to judge, we never stop. How can we not judge? And yet: 'Judge not lest ye be judged.' Only the final, supreme judge, the ultimate authority, has the right to judge.

Like an ever-sought and ever-inaccessible absolute, the moment of justice obsesses our era. Hence the fixation with trials which is such a feature of contemporary art (in Kafka, Brecht, and quite a number of films, etc.).

We will return to the problem, but for the time being we will not include art or any activity which creates aesthetic works among moments. Provisionally, we will reserve the term for those activities which are undertaken in the lived and which do not produce an external object.

6 Moments and the everyday

We have still not isolated and defined this relation completely. Moments make a critique – by their actions – of everyday life, and the everyday makes a critique – by its factuality – of paroxysmal moments. We have not yet exhausted this reciprocity.

The moment cannot be defined by the everyday or within it, but nor can it be defined by what is exceptional and external to the everyday. It gives the everyday a certain shape, but taken per se and extrapolated from that context, this shape is empty. The moment imposes an order on the chaos of ambiguity, but taken per se this order is ineffectual and pointless. The moment does not appear simply anywhere, at just any time. It is a festival, it is a marvel, but it is not a miracle. It has its motives, and without those motives it will not intervene in the everyday. Festival only makes sense when its brilliance lights up the sad hinterland of everyday dullness, and when it uses up, in one single moment, all it has patiently and soberly accumulated.

And so the everyday cannot be reduced to 'empty moments', even though it is unable to grasp the exciting risks moments propose. Everyday life is a level within totality and for this reason it is denied totality, and it is unable to comprehend actions which unfold as totalities. They place themselves apart from everyday life; or rather, they try to live apart, and this is precisely how they miscarry, in all their splendour. Thus moments present themselves as duplicates of everyday life, magnified to tragic dimensions.[4] In this way – by critique – we can understand Lukács's well-known statements (about 'the anarchy and the chiaroscuro of everyday life') or Husserl's comments (on Heraclitian flux and the formlessness of the 'lived'), while

356

nevertheless avoiding privileging art or philosophy. There are men who are not artists and not philosophers, but who nevertheless emerge above the everyday, in their own everyday lives, because they experience moments: love, work, play, etc.

All that spontaneous life can offer is muddle and confusion: knowledge, action, play or love. The man of culture tends to single out the elements or 'formants' from what is given as a mixture of spontaneous vitality, and to use them to constitute moments. Furthermore he tends to unify what is given to spontaneous consciousness as discrete elements (life and death, vitality and the tragedy of failure). Thus, according to the theory of moments, culture does not detach itself from nature, nor does it superimpose itself upon it. Culture selects, it makes distinctions (sometimes in an exaggerated way, separating and isolating the elements it wishes to use to such a degree that any further development becomes impossible), and then it unifies. It is in everyday life that this painstaking labour of selection and unification unfolds. Everyday life is the native soil in which the moment germinates and takes root.

Nature appears to us like a gigantic wastage of beings and forms, like a frenzy of creation and destruction. Outrageously playful, immeasurably tragic, its failures, monstrosities, abortions and successes are incalculable. (And who knows, perhaps successes are merely monstrosities which chance has smiled upon.)

Everyday life already imposes a certain order in all this chaos, a certain economy in all this profligacy. Compared with so-called 'higher' and specialized activities, and compared to moments, the everyday appears as ambiguous as it does trivial. And yet it is the spontaneity nobody can do without. And yet, compared with nature, it is already more ordered and more beautiful, and more economical with its means and its ends.

Unmediated and endured by those who live it, the everyday acts as mediator between nature and culture. The false light which bathes it grows dim and is outshone by the true clarity of critique. At the same time, its apparent solidity bursts asunder to reveal it as the point where nature and culture come together. Culture, which perpetuates this situation, is dismantled theoretically, and nature regains its strength, but far away from man and the human, which now must be redefined.

The theory of moments will allow us to follow the birth and formation of moments in the substance of the everyday in their various psychic and sociological denominations: attitudes, aptitudes, conventions, affective or abstract stereotypes, formal intentions, etc. Perhaps it will even permit us to illuminate the slow stages by which need becomes desire, deep below everyday life, and on its surface. But most importantly, it must be capable of opening a window on supersession, and of demonstrating how we may resolve the age-old conflict between the everyday and tragedy, and between triviality and Festival.

The end of Volume II

Notes

1 Clearing the Ground

1. (*Trans.*) Specifically, the 'age such as ours' is the beginning of the 1960s, a time of particular political and cultural effervescence in France, with the Algerian troubles, the consolidation of Gaullism and the growing international prestige and influence of structuralism and the *nouvelle vague*. It was also a pivotal moment in Lefebvre's own career, since in 1961 he took up his post as lecturer in sociology at Strasbourg university, transferring to Nanterre in 1965. Many of the ideas in this book must have informed those lectures, which were so influential for what was to occur in 1968. In the quicksilver intellectual shifts and (sometimes bewildering) idiosyncrasies of his style, which is frequently nearer to speech than to conventional prose, the reader of this book may perhaps catch a glimpse of how exciting and charismatic these lectures must have been.

2. See *Critique of Everyday Life*, vol. I (Grasset, Paris 1947), trans. John Moore, Verso, London 1991.

3. See below, and Jean Lacroix, 'Le public et le privé', *Cahiers I.S.E.A.*, series M, no. 10, 1961.

4. For example, in 1961, *Les Petits Enfants du siècle* by Christiane Rochefort, and the film *Chronique d'un été*, directed by Jean Rouch and Edgar Morin. See also Lucien Goldmann's definition of the 'novel': 'It seems to us that the novel as a form is the transposition of everyday life in the individualistic society which was born of market production to the plane of literature . . .') *Médiations*, vol. 2, Editions Gonthier, Paris 1966, p. 149.

5. See Dionys Mascolo's *Le Communisme*, Gallimard, Paris 1953, which contains nearly all of them.

6. (*Trans.*) As the word for goods can be used in the singular in French –

un bien – it retains a sense of value and worth in the plural which it no longer has in modern English.

7. (*Trans.*) The word *jeu* has several meanings in French: play and games, gambling, and dramatic acting. Throughout the book Lefebvre plays on these ambiguities in a way which can only be paraphrased in translation.

8. *Internationale Situationniste*, no. 6, 1961, pp. 20–27. (*Trans.*) Debord's friendship with Lefebvre began in 1957 (he was thirty years his junior), and during the time they spent together, notably walking in the Pyrenees near Lefebvre's house in Navarrenx, their discussions about modernity, revolution and critique of everyday life were mutually influential. Debord edited the review from 1958 until its demise in 1969.

9. Let us remember the impassioned discussions on birth control and family planning, with all their practical and political consequences. The opposition to birth control by official Marxists and the Communist Party was very influential in the serious rifts which occurred during this period. This attitude is of great theoretical interest. In particular it shows that for the time being, in the Marxist movement and official communism, the idea of (technical) power of man over nature and the outside world has supplanted the Marxist idea of man's *appropriation* of nature and *of his own nature*.

10. Simone de Beauvoir must be congratulated for introducing this concept to philosophy and to the study of the situation of women. However, she did not clarify it. Before Simone de Beauvoir, women – and we mean women who read philosophers, and their entourage – refused to be 'things' or 'commodities'. Since her works have appeared, the same women call themselves 'subjects' who do not want to be treated as 'objects'. Sadly, the less charitable observer will note that many of them seem to want to have their cake and eat it too: they want to be objects (beautiful, well dressed, desirable, desired) and subjects (free, and recognized as such). Hence an additional ambiguity, which comes from the vocabulary of philosophy, and which has the advantage of being like a game. Furthermore, as one woman wittily put it: 'Of the two, the one most like an object is not always the one you think . . .'.

11. (*Trans.*) An attack on dogmatic communism. Lefebvre joined the PCF in 1928. However he became increasingly uneasy with its Stalinist policies, and his open criticisms, which came to a head with the Khrushchev report in 1956, led to his expulsion in 1957. Lefebvre's vehemence in this passage should be seen in this context.

12. Notably in the meetings of the Groupe d'études de sociologie de la vie quotidienne, (Centre d'Etudes sociologiques) and in various symposia.

13. Marx, 'Critique of Hegel's Doctrine of the State' in *Early Writings*, Penguin, Harmondsworth 1975, p. 90.

14. Maurice Merleau-Ponty, 'Philosophie et sociologie', *Signes*, Gallimard, Paris 1960, pp. 137–9.

15. See Henri Lefebvre, 'Psychologie des classes sociales', in Georges Gurvitch, ed., *Traité de sociologie*, vol. 2, PUF, Paris 1960, pp. 364–86.

16. (*Trans.*) A paraphrase of the controversial aphorism '*l'art est le plus haute joie que l'homme se donne à lui-même*', which Lefebvre attributed to Marx in *Contribution à l'esthétique* (1953), but which he later admitted was his own invention. This 'forgery' was one of the reasons given for his exclusion from the PFC in 1957. See above, note 11.

17. Cf. *Colloque de Royaumont*, 16–18 May 1961.

18. This is from a report sent by Christiane Peyre of the Centre national de la recherche scientifique (CNRS) to the Groupe d'études de sociologie de la vie quotidienne, Centre d'Etudes sociologiques, 1960–1. (*Trans.*) Lefebvre himself became a researcher at the CNRS in 1948, a post which he lost in 1953 because of his involvement in PCF activities. He was reinstated in 1954, and in 1960 he was appointed Director of Research.

19. Interviews such as these have been collected for the Groupe d'études by Nicole Haumont.

20. The term (*sociétés de loisirs*) was coined by Henri Raymond, who together with Nicole Haumont made a study of the Club Méditerranée.

21. See Michel Clouscard's studies of '*Les temps marginaux*' as reported to the Groupe d'études.

22. See the excellent film *Saturday Night and Sunday Morning*. (*Trans.*) Dir. Karel Reisz, GB 1960.

23. The expression (*le tragique du pauvre*) was coined by Georges Auclair in a report to the Groupe d'études.

24. These layers become apparent in genuinely 'undirected' interviews, especially when they are taped. The intervention of the tape recorder produces a greater 'distancing' than in the usual interview. The interviewee feels much less at ease and consequently, when the interview is well conducted, there are moments when, through the malaise, a deeper truth emerges.

25. On alienation and reification, see Lefebvre, *Dialectical Materialism*, trans. J. Sturrock, Jonathan Cape, London 1968.

26. Yugoslavia has retained the Marxist model, as we know, but not without difficulties and some bending of the rules.

27. We raised these problems in the Foreword to *Critique of Everyday Life*, vol. I, but without clarifying them.

28. Surveys of children living in several new housing developments where there are a large number of television sets have shown that boys and girls aged between 10 and 12 know an incredible number of technical details about things such as space rockets, but are ignoramuses about maths and

basic French grammar. The conclusion is that the 'civilization of the book' will disappear.

29. (*Trans.*) Lefebvre deals with this topic much more extensively in 'Notes on the New Town', the extraordinary Seventh Prelude of his *Introduction to Modernity* (trans. John Moore, Verso, London 1995, pp. 116–27), where he compares his own town of Navarrenx with the new town of Mourenx, built to house the workers at the oil refinery of Lacq, near Pau, and which he has in mind in this section.

30. This is what restricts the scope of a formal, structural and semeiological study of the romantic press and horoscopes, etc. Studies of this kind would look at themes, their combinations and their significations, but (here as elsewhere) would be unable to grasp their historicity, and therefore their *real meaning*. (*Trans.*) For the spelling of 'semeiological', see below chapter 2, note 1.

31. Summing up this point of view, Andrée Michel writes: 'Far from being a basic cell, to use an overworked phrase, or a natural grouping, to use a vulgarized definition which has been rife in France since Le Play, the family is nothing more than a resultant and a residual deposit; those functions which society has not yet shouldered are shouldered by the family . . .' (*Cahiers internationaux de sociologie*, no. 20). Therefore 'as an institution, the family does not antedate the group', which makes the consolidation of this 'residual deposit' even more surprising. We could quote various sociologists who would back up this interpretation: Gooda, *Die Struktur der Familie*, Cologne 1960; Pearsons, *Socialization and Interaction Process*, etc.

32. (*Trans.*) See above, footnote 13.

33. We borrow the expression from Abraham Moles. (*Trans.*) See *Information Theory and Esthetic Perception*, University of Illinois Press, Urbana and London 1966.

34. This is the gulf which Jean-Paul Sartre attempts to bridge in *Critique of Dialectical Reason*. (*Trans.*) Lefebvre had always been highly critical of Sartre. However, in his introduction to the *Critique*, Sartre tells us his method is based upon his reading of Lefebvre.

35. (*Trans.*) Lefebvre is quoting the title of Mallarmé's famous poem *Un coup de dés jamais n'abolira le hasard*.

36. J. Galbraith, *The Affluent Society*, Penguin, Harmondsworth 1958.

37. For a similar problem, see Alfred Sauvy, *Théorie générale de la population*, vol. 1, pp. 312–52, François Perroux in *L'Encyclopédie française*, vol. 20, and Abraham and Thédié in *Revue française de recherche opérationnelle*, no. 16, 1960. See also an interesting discussion in ibid., no. 19, 1961.

2 The Formal Implements

1. (*Trans.*) Throughout the book, Lefebvre chooses to employ *séméiologie* rather than the more conventional *sémiologie*, presumably to distance himself from that particular school of thought. I have observed this in my translation.

2. This is the theory of double maieutic which we developed elsewhere, but from a different perspective. (*Trans.*) The Socratic method of producing knowledge through questions and answers. See *Introduction to Modernity*, First Prelude, pp. 7–48.

3. The American sociologist Merton has made the distinction between the *working hypothesis* (which is empirical), and the *theoretical hypothesis* (which is developed conceptually). This distinction is valid in principle, but its view of 'the real' is limited. We will return to it when we examine that category.

4. See Mandelbrot, *Lecture de l'expérience*, PUF, Paris 1955, p. 43, on psychological transducers.

5. See Charbonnier, *Conversations with Claude Lévi-Strauss*, trans. J. and D. Weightman, Jonathan Cape, London 1969.

6. See A. Martinet, *Elements of General Linguistics*.

7. See Williams, *La Stratégie dans les actions humaines*, a remarkable popularization of the extremely technical work of von Neumann, de Luce and Raiffa, etc.

8. This is a reference to Bayes's theorem on strategies. See Claude Flament, 'Modèle stratégique d'influence sociale sur les jugements perceptifs', *Psychologie française*, April, 1959, a psychological rather than sociological study.

9. For a definition of the tragic, see Nietzsche, *The Birth of Tragedy* and Clément Rosset, *Le Philosophie tragique*, Paris, 1961.

10. (*Trans.*) A scotoma is a mental blind spot.

11. It would be impossible to deny the theoretical interest for the social sciences of these forms or structures which are initially apparent in material nature: circles and cycles, spirals, periodic phenomena, trees, networks. In the search for unity, this is a more useful direction than any systematized philosophy. In our view, however, they can only serve as *models*, which do not reduce the dualities of the representations (see below). A model is nothing more than a representation, and cannot exhaust the process of becoming.

12. Thus we will come across the *tree* figure in the theory of needs and the theory of social networks of communications, etc.

13. Alfred Sauvy, *Population*, no. 6, October 1961, p. 601, Marthelot, *Pays riches et pays de la faim*, 39e semaine sociale de France, 1952, and Henri Janne, *Colloque de 1956*, Institut Solvay, Brussels, etc.

14. The term is Galbraith's. It demonstrates how this production is only apparently directed towards needs. See Bernard Cazes, *Cahiers I.S.E.A*, series M, no. 10, p. 38.

15. The mathematical idea of *dimension* is not spatial. Thus the calculation of probabilities defines distributions in *one dimension* (the mathematical hope of a random variable) and in *two dimensions* (in the case of a random pair).

16. In Descartes, for example.

17. See 'Les dilemmes de la dialectique', *Médiations*, vol. 2.

18. 'Evènement et structures', *Cahiers I.S.E.A*, Series M, no. 6.

19. See Gestalt theory, or theory of forms, which had a great influence in all areas of the sciences of human reality. It is in the 'Gestaltist' tradition that we will find the best examples of this idea, whether the authors explained and admitted it or not.

20. See notably Claude Lévi-Strauss, *Structural Anthropology*, trans. C. Jacobson and B. Schoepf, Penguin Press, London 1968.

21. Georges Gurvitch, *Vocation actuelle de la sociologie*, 2nd edn, vol. 2, p. 441. See also *Cahiers internationaux de sociologie (CIS)*, no. 19, 1953, etc. (*Trans.*) Gurvitch was one of Lefebvre's staunchest friends, and it was through his interventions that he joined the CNRS in 1948. Between 1948 and 1965 Lefebvre published ten articles in the *CIS*, which Gurvitch edited.

22. (*Trans.*) Marx, *Early Writings*, pp. 424–8.

23. See the distinction between forms of family and systems of consanguinity in Engels, 'The Origin of the Family, Private Property and the State', in *Marx and Engels: Selected Works*, Lawrence and Wishart, London 1968, pp. 466–8. Quoting Marx, Engels demonstrates the *passivity of all systems* (political, juridical, philosophical) and how they lag behind the active forces and forms of development, and thus behind the theoretical and practical conflicts which ensue.

24. See G. G. Granger, *Pensée formelle et sciences de l'homme*. So it is not a question of 'latent structures' in the sense the term is used by American sociologists such as Lazarfeld and Guttmann.

25. See above, note 22.

26. (*Trans.*) When Lefebvre took up his post in the CNRS in 1948 (see chapter 1, note 18) his research topic was rural sociology. This had been one of his interests since the 1930s, but his active involvement in it dates from the war years, when his Resistance activities put him in contact with peasant communities in the valley of Campan in the French Pyrenees. This was to lead him in turn towards his theories on urbanism and the production of space which have since been so influential.

27. In our view the cleverly tempered idea of '*signifying structure*' does not avoid the shortcomings of structuralism in general. Who is 'signification'

for? How can one grasp a signification from inside? How can one grasp it from outside? Perhaps a god can, as a Mind, or simply the 'I' of the thinker. There can only be signifying structures in an imminent or transcendental way, and neither make very much sense.

3 The Specific Categories

1. See H. Lefebvre, 'Justice et vérité selon Nietzsche', *Arguments*, no. 15, 1959, pp. 13–19.

2. (*Trans.*) Lukács, *History and Class Consciousness*, trans. R. Livingstone, Merlin Press, London 1968, p. 27.

3. See Merton, *Elements of Sociological Method*, which is a study of political operations in the electoral 'machine' in the USA, with the 'boss', corruption, brutality and illegality, etc. According to Merton, moralistic criticism loses its validity when faced with what the 'functions' of the machine actually are. The 'boss' maintains the machine in good and effective working order by deliberately sharing power via a democratic constitution determined to uphold freedom. The 'boss' makes the law personal, and even humanizes it by adapting it to the real concerns of the population: inner-city areas, underprivileged groups which need assistance or advice. 'The Machine knits the links between men and women together with the complicated links of personal relationships.' Even backhanders have a function in the chaos of competition. 'Rackets' and 'gangs' facilitate social mobility, etc.

4. Merton, one of the few American sociologists before the 'New Wave' (Mills, Riesman) who penetrated the everyday life of American society, was introduced to Hegelianism via Marx and Engels, whom he quotes extensively in the book's footnotes.

5. (*Trans.*) Marx, 'Critique of Hegel's Doctrine of the State', *Early Writings*, p. 127.

6. See J. Huizinga, *Homo Ludens*, Routledge and Kegan Paul, London 1949, and the works of Roger Caillois.

7. Like the equalization of general rates of profit which Marx described and analysed as a self-regulating and stabilizing mechanism in a free-market capitalist society.

8. The existentialist thesis which defines the alienation of women as the treatment of a 'subject' as an 'object' adds very little to what Kant said, when he demanded respect for all 'subjects'. It goes back to before Hegelianism, for which objectivization is a necessity, i.e., the transformation of subjective intentions and tendencies into works, and goes so far as to condemn beauty, ornaments, fashion, and everything which makes 'woman'

beautiful and desirable, as alienating. (See A. Gorz, *La Morale de l'histoire*, Editions du Seuil, Paris 1959.) Intellectual activity is becoming misanthropic and ascetic again.

9. See, D. Riesman, *Lonely Crowd*, Doubleday Anchor Books (abridged edition) and Yale University Press, 1950; W. H. Whyte, Jr., *The Organization Man*, Penguin, Harmondsworth 1960; A. C. Spectorsky, *Exurbanites*, Berkeley Publications, 1955.

10. (*Trans.*) *Je est un autre.* Lefebvre is quoting from Rimbaud's *Une saison en enfer*. Conventionally, the translation would be 'I is another'.

11. This is implied in the work on the 'non-directive' by the American psycho-sociologist Rogers and his school in France, for example.

12. We have already published a series of articles (see notably *La Pensée*, 1956) in which we have taken this controversy up with several philosophers, in particular the late and much-missed Maurice Merleau-Ponty. We take them to task for applying the idea of ambiguity to the relations between being and consciousness, i.e., for generalizing it as an (ontological) philosophical category. In this context we consider it to be a specific (sociological) category.

13. See J. Galbraith, *The Affluent Society*.

14. (*Trans.*) A ceremonial activity among North American Indians involving the distribution of gifts.

15. According to the English historian Arnold Toynbee, every people responds victoriously to a challenge by *nature* (as long as it keeps its vitality: Egypt and the periodic Nile floods, England and sea defences, etc.), and this determines a perishable civilization. This theory is a useful and significant one. However, taken as an isolated hypothesis, and carried to the absolute, it becomes erroneous, and even dangerous. What we are considering here, sociologically, is challenge between groups.

16. See J. Duvignaud, *Pour entrer dans le XXe siècle*, Grasset, Paris 1960, where the author restricts the question (by limiting it to literature).

17. We borrow the expression (*rythmanalyse*) from Gaston Bachelard.

18. See G. Gurvitch, *Traité de sociologie*, and *La Multiplicité des temps sociaux*, Cours de la Sorbonne, 1957–8, CDU.

19. See Jean-Paul Sartre's old idea about 'to make and in making to make oneself', which is now very widely accepted as a formulation of *praxis*. (*Trans.*) In French, the verb *faire*, which means equally to make and to do.

20. The most recent example: information theory originated in telecommunications and in the transmission of telegraphic messages using a general conventional code. Zipf's Law was discovered by Estoup a long time before Zipf, in his studies of the work of shorthand typists. These important theories only developed thanks to radio and, above all, to television.

21. (*Trans.*) A reference to the 100 metre distance signs on French roads.

22. At the same time as theorems of existence were appearing, mathematicians introduced *dual* properties and demonstrated theorems of *duality*. This is connected with the influence concepts originating in physics have had on mathematics. (See Licherowicz, *Algèbre et analyse linéaires*, on the spectrum of a matrix, the inverse spectrum, etc.)

23. For Jean-Paul Sartre in *Critique of Dialectical Reason*, the stable (the 'practico-inert') is antidialectical. For Stéphane Lupasco's 'logic of contradiction', the logical level and the level of contradiction go beyond dialectical logic, and become merged. It is contradiction which produces stability.

24. This is more or less the attitude Jean-Paul Sartre adopts in *Critique*.

25. Obviously the gap between these two types of contradiction is not great. It is a distinction which already appears in the texts in which Hegel presents a kind of gradation, from distinction and difference to the alternative (antagonism), by way of contrariety, opposition, inner contradiction and antinomy. In the *Nürnberger Schriften* we are dealing with a progression which he observes empirically and turns into a general law. In Book 2 of *Greater Logic*, it is rather the result of reflection which develops the idea of dialectical movement. The Marxists have not added very much to Hegelian thought.

26. See W. H. Whyte, *The Organisation Man*.

27. (*Trans.*) Rastignac is the ambitious hero of Balzac's trilogy *Le Père Goriot: Illusions perdues* and *Splendeurs et misères des courtisanes*.

28. This essay on characterology was to appear in a projected trilogy we were to write in collaboration with Norbert Gutermann, *La Conscience mystifiée*, *La Conscience privée* and *La Conscience sociale*. Only the first of these appeared (*Les Essais*, Gallimard, Paris 1937). After the Liberation, we completed most of the project in Volume I of *Critique of Everyday Life*.

4 The Theory of the Semantic field

1. The system of telephone numbers, for example. Each one corresponds to a possible signal (a call or a reply). They make up a rigorous set which leaves little margin for error (for 'noise', to use the vocabulary of information theory). Moreover, the set of numbers reflects a network. Each one corresponds to a determined *place* in a determined space, and to a determined *time* (linear and discontinuous, for I cannot call A or answer him until I have finished answering B, and so on and so forth, through a series of disjunctions). Since each call and answer is a possible *event*, the set of numbers defines *a space of events*.

2. Notably in the work of André Martinet, which we have already mentioned.

3. In other words, there is a certain terminology which we are unable to accept. The mathematician does not use symbols, but signs, which are as stripped of content and as formal as possible, and almost like signals of operations which are stipulated in advance.

4. We will deal with the problems of semeiology, general semantics, 'semantemes' and partial systems of social signs when we look at 'communication models'.

5. (*Trans.*) A reference to Baudelaire's poem *L'Invitation au voyage*: '*Là tout n'est qu'ordre et beauté, luxe, calme et volupté.*'

5 The Theory of Accumulative and Non-accumulative Processes

1. In *Critique of Dialectical Reason*, Jean-Paul Sartre changes rareness into a fundamental and absolute category. He 'worldifies' rareness, creating a 'world' of rareness, violence and oppression. In doing so he fails to recognize the twofold aspect of these ancient societies (in which occasionally need almost became authentic desire . . .).

2. Here we are modifying somewhat a theory we sketched out elsewhere, which suggested that *form* might be the common measure between diverse cultures, notably between antiquity and 'modernity' (by analogy with formal logic and law which subsist across differing modes of production). This theory does not seem to be inaccurate, but can only be applied to a number of limited cases.

3. Marx also demonstrates how the cycle of economic crises in the context of free-competition capitalism re-establishes proportions by eliminating excess, and allows accumulation to resume. The crisis is part of the system's process of self-regulation. Marx reveals a dialectical movement: 'balance – crisis – resumption'. Thus our study does not agree with the often remarkable views of G. G. Granger, who emphasizes factors of structure and internal balance.

4. In free-market capitalism, adjustments (of values, prices and rates of profit) and the formation of an average rate of profit play this role of self-regulation and internal balance, across a cycle of crises.

5. Work on ecology and modern demography (in particular in France, with Alfred Sauvy and Jacques Fourastié) has used mathematics to explain such processes. According to a paper presented to the Groupe d'études by A. Moles, it could be possible to study the number of publications which

have appeared in different sectors of science in order to determine the tendency towards cumulative (exponential) growth and factors of slowing down and saturation more closely.

6. The ensuing situation is so confused that the representation of society on a world scale becomes obscured at the very moment it is taking shape as a totality. And so sociology (as an ideology) appears as a substitute for an inadequate consciousness, in tandem with the vague representation of a 'social whole' which exists but which cannot be grasped by the groups and the men who constitute it.

7. Volterra's equations express these processes mathematically.

8. The difference between *digital machines* (which operate upon unlimited discontinuity with increasing scope and precision) and *analogue machines* (which operate on continuous givens and models) brings a technical argument to our hypothesis. On the level of cortical activity, the cumulative process would be linked to the dichotomy and disjunction which appear in language, arithmetic and logic.

9. In the theory of the semantic field we could already have referred to the work of Gaston Bachelard. In several books which are so well known that it is pointless to name them, this eminent philosopher has demonstrated the role of symbolisms (and above all of symbols borrowed from the elements: Fire, Water, Earth, Air) in poetry, in dreams and in language. In another area of his work Gaston Bachelard dialecticizes the concepts of scientific knowledge (see notably *Le Nouvel Esprit scientifique*). We would like to stress one specific point. There is a break between these two parts of his work and thought. Why? Because philosophy refused to come full circle and form a system? Yes, maybe. But as we see it there is something else. One part of his work is concerned with the non-accumulative (symbols and symbolisms, cycles and cosmic rhythms, nucleuses of primary or protopathic affectivity in the individual, socialized emotivity in and through language . . .). The other part is concerned with the *cumulative* (modern techniques and scientific knowledge). From the point of view of our studies, this break does not disappear, but becomes a theme, sees itself as such, and takes on a sense.

The connection of symbolisms with the elementary everyday in the work of Gaston Bachelard has been highlighted very recently by Mucchielli: 'Starting from different directions, Piaget and Bachelard have shown that very general affectivo-motor schemes corresponding to very general and very archaic human situations (being lost, concealing oneself, getting up, falling down, being attacked, mating, taking shelter, etc.) constitute the essential part of what psycho-analytic literature calls unconscious symbolism, and may be considered to be the dynamic "forms" of series of behaviour patterns which are differentiated according to epochs and cultures, as well as the generating schematic of oneiric, mythic and legendary "images" which we call "symbolic"' (*Philosophie de la médicine psycho-somatique*, p. 134). In our view Mucchielli reduces the significance of symbolisms (notably their *poetic* sense).

6 The Theory of Moments

1. (*Trans.*) Lefebvre first proposed his theory of moments in his autobiography *La Somme et le reste*, 2 vols., La Nef, Paris 1959. It can be contrasted with the theory of situations developed by Debord in the *Internationale situationniste*. The difference of view led to the intellectual rift between the two men in the 1960s.

2. This protest is also expressed in Georges Politzer's brilliant philosophical pamphlet *Le Bergsonisme, fin d'une parade philosophique*. Philosophically, the 'theory of moments' is linked to an interpretation of Leibniz. The 'substantial' link (*vinculum substantiale*) between monads is itself a monad. In so far as knowledge and love, etc., are diverse attributes or powers of being, they have a reality which would equal that of reified consciousnesses (see Henri Lefebvre, *La Somme et le reste*).

3. Hegel draws his inspiration from classic mechanics (the 'moment of inertia', etc.), but he profoundly modifies the meaning of the term.

4. See Michel Butor, 'Le roman et la poésie', *Les Lettres nouvelles*, February 1961, where he clearly spells out that 'one of the tasks of the novel will be to re-establish a continuity between marvellous moments and empty ones'.

Index

Index

labour
   changing attitudes 68–70
   defining humans by 95
   distinction by humans 190
   housework 222–3
   and needs 190
   and new towns 79
   non-accumulative societies 320
   occupation and time cycles 49–55
   and praxis 233, 235
   and totality 189–90
language
   axiom of sociological method 101–2
   dialectical thought 256–9
   dialogue, discussion, conversation
      312–14
   levels of analysis 124, 125
   and moments 341–4
   philosophical discourse 25
   the semantic field 276–8
   and signs 283–4
   signs and significations in dialogue
      102–4
   structure/conjunction 166–70
   symbols, similes and analogies 285–6
   see also dialogue; signs and signifiers
Le Fort, Gertrud von
   La Femme éternalle 212
leisure
   divided from work life 68
   as escape 44
Lenin, Vladimir I. 3, 127
   antidialectic 250
   contradiction of democracy 137
   The Development of Capitalism in Russia
      144–5
   uneven development 315–16
levels
   concept of 118–20
   dialectical thought 152–3
   everyday life 124–5
   'micro' and 'macro' 139–42
   music 122–4
   physics and mathematics 120–22
   praxis 236–7

signs 281
   structural linguistics 124
   of thought 246
   thresholds 120, 122
Lévi-Strauss, Claude 119
Lie, Sophus 157
lived and living 216–18
logic 246
   characterology 263–4
   dialectical thought 152–3, 258
love
   and biological needs 8
   theory of moments 341–2, 345
Lukács, Georg 356
   History and Class Consciousness 186

magic and imagination 289–90
Maiakovsky, Vladimir 65
Marx, Karl
   alienation 207, 214
   Capital 243, 317–18, 322
   concept of accumulation 325–32
   concept of structure 157
   contradiction of democracy 137
   *A Contribution to the Critique of Political
      Economy* 159, 318
   Critique of Hegel's Philosophy of the State 21
   definition of socialism 223
   and Fourier 288
   historicity 21–2
   human problems 261
   non-accumulative societies 317–22
   and praxis 232, 235, 236–43
   on private life and state 89
   process of accumulation 322–5
   public and private 165
   and the real 194
   structure 159–60
   superstructure and base 237
   theory of needs 6
   totality 184–7
   transforming the world 23–4
Marxism
   defining human by labour 95
   dogmatism 17

Index